THE NEW BLACK HISTORY

THE CRITICAL BLACK STUDIES SERIES

INSTITUTE FOR RESEARCH IN AFRICAN AMERICAN STUDIES

Edited by Manning Marable
Columbia University

The Critical Black Studies Series features readers and anthologies examining challenging topics within the contemporary black experience—in the United States, the Caribbean, Africa, and across the African Diaspora. All readers include scholarly articles originally published in the acclaimed quarterly interdisciplinary journal *Souls*, published by the Institute for Research in African American Studies at Columbia University. Under the general editorial supervision of Manning Marable, the readers in the series are designed for university course adoption, as well as general readers and researchers. The Critical Black Studies Series seeks to provoke intellectual debate and exchange over the most critical issues confronting the political, socio-economic, and cultural reality of black life in the United States and beyond.

Titles in this series published by Palgrave Macmillan:

Racializing Justice, Disenfranchising Lives: The Racism, Criminal Justice, and Law Reader
Edited by Manning Marable, Keesha Middlemass, and Ian Steinberg

Seeking Higher Ground: The Hurricane Katrina Crisis, Race, and Public Policy Reader
Edited by Manning Marable and Kristen Clarke

Transnational Blackness: Navigating the Global Color Line
Edited by Manning Marable and Vanessa Agard-Jones

Black Routes to Islam
Edited by Manning Marable and Hishaam D. Aidi

Barack Obama and African American Empowerment: The Rise of Black America's New Leadership
Edited by Manning Marable and Kristin Clarke

New Social Movements in the African Diaspora: Challenging Global Apartheid
Edited by Leith Mullings

The New Black History: Revisiting the Second Reconstruction
Edited by Manning Marable and Elizabeth Kai Hinton

THE NEW BLACK HISTORY

REVISITING THE SECOND RECONSTRUCTION

EDITED BY

Manning Marable and Elizabeth Kai Hinton

palgrave
macmillan

THE NEW BLACK HISTORY

First published in 2011 by PALGRAVE MACMILLAN® in the United States—a
division of St. Martin's Press LLC, 175 Fifth Avenue, New York, NY 10010

Where this book is distributed in the UK, Europe and the rest of the world, this is
by Palgrave Macmillan, a division of Macmillan Publishers Limited, registered in
England, company number 785998, of Houndmills, Basingstoke, Hampshire RG21
6XS.

Palgrave Macmillan is the global academic imprint of the above companies and has
companies and representatives throughout the world.

Palgrave® and Macmillan® are registered trademarks in the United States, the United
Kingdom, Europe and other countries.

ISBN: 978-1-4039-8397-8 (hardcover)
ISBN: 978-1-4039-7777-9 (paperback)

Library of Congress Cataloging-in-Publication Data

  The new Black history : revisiting the second Reconstruction / edited by Manning
Marable and Elizabeth Kai Hinton.
    p. cm.– (Critical Black studies)
  ISBN 978-1-4039-8397-8 (hardback : alk. paper) -- ISBN 978-1-4039-
7777-9 (pbk. : alk. paper) 1. African Americans—History—1964– 2. African
Americans—History—1877–1964. 3. African Americans—Historiography. 4.
African Americans—Civil rights—History. 5. Black power—United States—
History. I. Hinton, Elizabeth Kai. II. Marable, Manning, 1950–2011.

E185.615.N37 2011
973'.0496073–dc23   2011026986

Design by Scribe Inc.

First edition: October 2011

10 9 8 7 6 5 4 3 2 1

CONTENTS

Foreword

Zaheer Ali

On April 1, 2011, the field of African American history and the broader academic community lost one of its sharpest, critical, most prolific voices. Manning Marable unexpectedly passed away after succumbing to complications arising from his long battle with sarcoidosis. Just three days before the release of his *Malcolm X: A Life of Reinvention*—the culmination of a decades-long study of the life and times of Malcolm X—Marable's death left a void in the critical discussions he had hoped to provoke about the human rights activist. The Malcolm that emerges from Marable's study is complex, worthy of both praise and criticism, and Marable obliges in providing both. Marable's *Malcolm X* is thus an act of iconoclasm, and like any act of iconoclasm it has generated strong reactions—it has been the subject of heated debates in print, on radio and television, and in community meetings around the country. At the same time, it has also garnered rave reviews, achieved bestseller status, and even placed its author's face on the front page of the *New York Times* for the first time ever. It would be tempting therefore to view *Malcolm X: A Life of Reinvention* as Marable's defining work, the final testament to his academic life and legacy.

Oftentimes death punctuates with a period, however, where the deceased had only intended, in life, to place a comma. Marable was not one to rest on his laurels. On the eve of the release of *Malcolm X*, he envisioned several new book projects for the coming years and had already completed work on this anthology. *The New Black History: Revisiting the Second Reconstruction* features one of the last pieces he would write for publication, and as such represents another comma turned into a period. Interestingly enough, the articles that Marable and his coeditor Elizabeth Kai Hinton gathered in this collection reflect the same intellectual commitment to reexamination Marable set out to do with *Malcolm X*. "A biography maps the social architecture of an individual's life," Marable writes in *Malcolm X*. And if his biography of Malcolm sought to challenge conventional notions about Malcolm's individual life, then *The New Black History* continues in that vein by challenging conventional notions about the social architecture of the Black freedom movement. The last decade has seen a wave of new scholarship challenging the regional, temporal, and ideological orthodoxies that centered histories of the Black freedom movement narrowly around narratives of the South, the 1950s and '60s, integration, and nonviolence. As part of this shift in historiography, the contributions featured here, by both more established as well as up-and-coming scholars, offer study after study that complicate those narratives and broaden our understanding of the Black freedom movement's spatial and chronological reach, as well as its ideological diversity.

But if this work is about new scholarship, it is also about new scholars. One of Marable's most enduring legacies will be his role as a mentor. Marable not only taught history, but he provided working models of knowledge production for generating and disseminating historical research, what he called "new knowledge" about the past. Once Marable seized upon an idea, it would become the organizing principle for a conference or seminar course, which would serve as a training ground for younger scholars, who were then recruited to work on research projects, which generated papers for publication in his journal *SOULS*, to be later anthologized in a book volume. As part of the Critical Black Studies Series, *The New Black History* is part of the chain of Marable's knowledge production process; many of its contributors were either former students of his and/or had their first published pieces featured in an earlier issue of *SOULS*. It is therefore fitting that in his introductory essay, he maps a genealogy of Black intellectual thought from the late nineteenth century to the present. For in many ways, *The New Black History* represents a passing of the torch from Manning Marable to the next generation of scholars to continue his critical examination of the past in order to envision a more just future.

BLACK INTELLECTUALS AND THE WORLD THEY MADE

MANNING MARABLE

This the American black man knows: his fight here is a fight to the finish. Either he dies or wins. If he wins it will be by no subterfuge or evasion of amalgamation. He will enter modern civilization here in America as a black man on terms of perfect equality with any white man, or he will enter not at all. Either extermination, root and branch, or absolute equality. There can be no compromise. This is the last great battle of the West.

—W. E. B. Du Bois, *Black Reconstruction in America 1860–1880*

I

THE US PRESIDENTIAL ELECTIONS OF 1876 AND 2008 are separated by 132 years and, at most, six generations of Americans. Yet in racial terms, the distance between these two events represents a historical epoch. In 1876, Democratic presidential candidate Samuel J. Tilden, then governor of New York, first appeared to defeat Republican Rutherford B. Hayes by roughly three hundred thousand popular votes. However, due to a handful of contested electoral votes, the election was thrown to the House of Representatives. A deal was brokered that elevated Hayes to the presidency. The so-called Compromise of 1877 removed federal troops that had been stationed throughout the South after the Civil War, and it gave tacit permission to Southern whites to restrict the political and civil rights of African Americans. Within two decades, most black males had been barred from the elective franchise; blacks were largely excluded from most public accommodations and barred from juries; and over one hundred blacks were lynched each year throughout the region. The terrible system of racial stigmatization and social exclusion that had emerged was called "Jim Crow."[1]

In November 2008, a Democratic senator from Illinois, Barack Hussein Obama, won the presidency over conservative Republican John McCain of

Arizona. Like other successful Democratic presidential candidates since Lyndon Johnson in 1964, Obama had constructed a broad support from blacks, Latinos, Jewish voters, voters under the age of thirty, and women. Obama polled 42 percent of all whites' votes, a figure better than Bill Clinton's vote in 1992 and comparable to John Kerry's vote in the presidential election of 2004. Of course, what made Obama's victory exceptional was the color of his skin—his ethnic identity as an African American. But what was most remarkable, however, was not Obama's race but the fact that a nation that had been constructed on slavery, and that had tolerated nearly a century of Jim Crow segregation, could elect as its chief executive and head of state a person of African descent.[2]

There were a number of factors that explain the transformation of America's racial culture. A profound change in white Americans' attitudes regarding the social integration and assimilation of racialized minorities certainly contributed to a more liberal political environment. The growth of a strong black and Latino middle class, and the desegregation of the labor force and even corporate elites, have also affected social relations. But the most important, single factor in the racial liberalization within US politics was the rise of the Black Freedom Movement, the social protest organizations, campaigns and thousands of demonstrations and strikes spanning the nineteenth, twentieth and twenty-first centuries by African Americans against US structural racism. These struggles, over time, produced generations of articulate, capable leaders, activists, and intellectuals who expressed the various demands and objectives of the African American masses. It is not an exaggeration to suggest that the black protest intelligentsia was largely responsible for theorizing and envisioning a new world, a world that ultimately would be without racial inequality, white supremacy and black oppression. They imagined and fought for the principles of social justice and human equality, the abolition of European colonialism, South African apartheid and US racial discrimination.

II

African American political culture prior to the Civil War (1861–1865) largely focused on the collective efforts to abolish slavery. The early groups of black leaders certainly disagreed over the effectiveness of different strategies to enhance black empowerment. Some, like Martin Delany, favored what would later become a black nationalist strategy, promoting the development of African American–owned businesses, racially exclusive social organizations and institutions, and the construction of all-black political movements. Others, such as Frederick Douglass, perceived Negro Americans as fundamental Americans who deserved full Constitutional recognition and civil rights.[3] They favored the achievement of racial reforms within America's democratic institutions, and the elimination of all barriers fostering racial stigmatization and exclusion. It was against this general theoretical and strategic background that the various political struggles by black leaders and intellectuals were waged.

The Compromise of 1877, which gave Republican Rutherford B. Hayes the presidency and removed federal troops from the South, ushered in a new historical conjuncture, which took nearly a quarter century to culminate into a new racial domain, or regime, called Jim Crow. Beginning in the 1880s and 1890s, southern towns and cities began adopting racial segregation codes and laws, leading to blacks' exclusion from juries, elections, and public accommodations. Thousands of blacks were lynched in racially motivated violence; thousands of black merchants, farmers and homeowners saw their properties burned or destroyed by racist whites. Starting with Mississippi in 1890, every former Confederate state held state constitutional conventions, eliminating blacks and many poor whites from their electorates.[4]

Faced with this extraordinary white backlash against the victories of the Reconstruction era, African Americans fought back, establishing new social organizations that inspired self help, group solidarity and in many cases, the growth of a black middle class. One of the first examples of black resistance were the "Exodusters," tens of thousands of African American farm families that fled the South, relocating to Oklahoma (then Indian Territory), Kansas and Colorado, in the late 1870s–early 1880s. Among middle class black women there was an impulse to establish gender-based organizations. In 1880 for example, former abolitionist and women's rights advocate Mary Ann Shadd Cary started the Colored Women's Progressive Franchise Association, which promoted the expansion of voting rights to black women. This group was a precursor to the National Association of Colored Women, founded by educator Mary Church Terrell in Washington, DC, in 1896.[5]

White racial vigilantism against blacks increased across the South: in 1883, blacks were murdered by rioting whites in Danville, Virginia; three years later, twenty African Americans were gunned down in a court room by whites in Carrollton, Mississippi. In rural areas, many black sharecroppers and small farmers responded to the violence by arming themselves. In Texas in 1888, black farmers established the Colored Farmers' National Alliance and Cooperative Union. Within four years, the Alliance won over hundreds of thousands of black farmers who joined across the South. Despite its demise because of political repression, the Alliance became an important conduit for thousands of blacks to join the insurgent Populist Party in the region.

Blacks were confronted with a new "political moment" in which the old rules regarding white domination and black oppression no longer held. African Americans needed to assert themselves politically, craft their own authentic voice, and also develop new tactics and strategies that went beyond those of the pre–Civil War era abolitionists. More importantly, what was required was the construction of a new racial consciousness and identity, a way of conceiving themselves as actors in the making of a new history.

The intellectual who best understood his times, and who created new methods for analyzing race and racism, was William Edward Burghardt Du Bois (1868–1963). Born in New England only three years after the end of the Civil War, Du Bois graduated from Fisk University in Tennessee in 1888; he subsequently matriculated as a junior at Harvard, graduating *cum laude* with a bachelor's degree in 1890. After studying for several years at the University of Berlin, Du Bois received his PhD in history from Harvard University in 1895. The first decade of Du Bois's professional career was largely devoted to social science research. He produced the first systematic, social survey of a black urban community with *The Philadelphia Negro* (1899). As a sociology professor at Atlanta University between 1898 and 1913, he held a series of annual research conferences that would form the foundations to Black Studies. In 1903 he published *The Souls of Black Folk*, the most influential collection of essays examining race in American life. *Souls* presented new theoretical constructs for interpreting African American identity, such as the concept of "double consciousness," the hybridic reality that blacks were both people of African descent as well as Americans.[6] But Du Bois also was actively involved in political and cultural organizing to empower African Americans. In 1900, he participated in a Pan-African Conference in London, organized by Trinidadian barrister Henry Sylvester Williams, that brought together for the first time black intellectuals and leaders across the African diaspora; it was at this conference that Du Bois issued his famous prediction that "the problem of the twentieth century is the problem of the color-line."[7] Five years later, Du Bois joined militant journalist William Monroe Trotter and others to establish the Niagara Movement, a civil rights formation that challenged the conservative politics and racial compromises of black educator Booker T. Washington.

It is difficult to appreciate the full measure of Du Bois's many contributions to black thought, especially in the fields of literature and literary criticism, sociology, political science, history, and cultural studies. But in regard to Du Bois's creative role in remaking black political culture, three interventions are noteworthy. First, in cofounding the National Association for the Advancement of Colored People (NAACP) in 1910, and as editor of the Association's magazine, the *Crisis* for a quarter century, Du Bois made the struggle to destroy legal segregation and structural racism central to black politics. Du Bois's rhetorical hammer-blows attacking racism were so memorable that generations of black Americans employed his arguments favoring civil rights as their own. Second, Du Bois linked international issues, especially the demand for the independence of Africa and the Caribbean from European domination, a major theme in African American politics and social thought. He led or inspired five significant Pan-African Congresses—respectively in 1919, 1921, 1923, 1927, and 1945—laying the basis for both revolutionary Pan-Africanism and the rise of independent African states after World War II. Third, from 1904 onward, Du Bois connected black progressive politics to the cause of socialism. In 1911, Du Bois formally joined the American Socialist Party, and although he resigned a year later, he continued to view himself as a "socialist-of-the-path." He had first been introduced to Karl Marx's writings when he was a doctoral student at the University of Berlin. But it was only after the Bolshevik Revolution of 1917 that Du Bois became fully aware of Marxian socialism. In 1926, he visited and traveled throughout the Soviet Union, and several years later at Atlanta University he taught a seminar called "Marxism and the Negro."[8]

The next decisive event that triggered a dramatic shift within the black intelligentsia was World War I and its aftermath (1917–1920s). A pivotal figure in this second cohort of black radicals was Hubert H. Harrison (1883–1927). Born in Concordia, St. Croix, Danish West Indies, Harrison immigrated to the United States in 1900. He continued his studies and in 1907 obtained employment as a clerk in the New York Post Office. His career as a literary critic began with an essay in the *New York Times*, in April 1907. Over the next decade, Harrison contributed hundreds of articles and reviews to *The Nation*, *New York World*, *New York Sun*, *Modern Quarterly* and the *New Republic*. He began promoting a political agenda that drew on both black nationalism and Marxian socialism. Joining the Socialist Club, Harrison built a popular following for his ideas with the publications *The Black Man's Burden* (1915), *The Negro and Nation* (1917), and especially *When Africa Awakens: The "Inside Story" of the Stirrings of the New Negro in the Western World* (1920).[9]

Harrison's development as a mass, popular leader, however, came about through his relationship with Marcus Garvey (1887–1940). Born in St. Ann's Bay, Jamaica, Garvey was trained as a journalist and printer, editing *La Nacionale* in Costa Rica in 1911, and working at the *African Times and Oriental Review* in London in 1912. In 1914, Garvey established the black nationalist–oriented Universal Negro Improvement Association and African Communities League, in Jamaica. Two years later Garvey relocated to New York, and the Jamaican leader and Harrison joined forces.

Further to the left than either Harrison or Garvey was Cyril V. Briggs (1888–1966). Born in Nevis, West Indies, Briggs immigrated to the United States and by 1912 secured employment as a journalist for the *Amsterdam News*. Attracted to revolutionary Marxism, Briggs cofounded the black socialist African Blood Brotherhood in 1917. In 1918, Briggs founded the *Crusader* magazine, and three years later joined the newly formed Communist Party. Briggs emerged as a sharp critic of both Garvey and the early civil rights leadership represented by Du Bois and the NAACP. Another influential West Indian who also gravitated toward Marxism-Leninism was Jamaican writer and poet Claude McKay (1889–1948). After immigrating to the United States, McKay briefly attended Tuskegee Institute and Kansas State University. Then he relocated to Harlem where he became involved in leftist politics. McKay joined with Briggs to establish the African Blood Brotherhood in 1917; he edited the radical periodical, the *Liberator*, in 1919 and was a contributing writer for the Marxist journal, *Workers' Dreams*. Like Harrison and Briggs, McKay challenged both the NAACP and the leadership of Du Bois. He charged that the Association "cannot function as a revolutionary working-class organization" because its focus was narrowly defined on the racial status of blacks. McKay argued that the main source of exploitation of African Americans was derived from the fact that the Negro "is of the lowest type of worker." Class oppression, not racism, was most decisive, McKay argued. Du Bois replied to McKay by praising the communists' racial egalitarianism, but he also questioned whether blacks should "[a]ssume on the part of unlettered and suppressed masses of white workers, a clearness of thought, a sense of human brotherhood, that is sadly lacking in the most educated classes." Du Bois warned McKay that he was "not prepared to dogmatize with Marx or Lenin" and that it would be "foolish to join a revolution which we do not at present understand."[10]

Du Bois's quarrels with McKay continued with the flowering of the Harlem Renaissance literary and cultural movement. With the 1928 publication of McKay's novel, *Home to Harlem*, Du Bois ruminated that the author had appealed to the "prurient demand on the part of white folk for a portrayal in Negroes of that utter licentiousness which conventional civilization holds white folk back from enjoying . . . As a picture of Harlem life or Negro life anywhere, it is, of course, nonsense." McKay was outraged by Du Bois's review, and he shot back, "Nowhere in your writings do you reveal any comprehension of esthetics and therefore you are not competent nor qualified to pass judgment upon any work of art . . . You mistake the art of life for nonsense and try to pass off propaganda as life in art!"[11] Curiously, the *Home to Harlem* literary controversy was one of the few instances when Marcus Garvey found full accord with Du Bois. McKay's novel was "a damnable libel against the Negro," Garvey fumed, attacking its author as a "literary prostitute."[12]

Although a good number of the prominent black radicals were from the Caribbean, some were recent migrants from the US South. The most prominent example of this group was Asa Philip Randolph. Born in Florida in 1889, Randolph, as a youth, moved to New York City, where he quickly became involved in trade union organizing, and Socialist Party politics. In 1916, Randolph and black activist Chandler Owen established the Independent Political Council in Harlem, which was dedicated to the promotion of socialism among blacks. Randolph and Owen also started the *Messenger*, a radical socialist magazine that vigorously opposed US entry into World War I. When Du Bois wrote an editorial "Close Ranks" in the *Crisis*, calling on African Americans to suspend their complaints about racial injustice for the duration of the conflict, Harrison was sharply critical.[13] Du Bois's statement was noteworthy, Harrison observed, "because of his former services to his race have been undoubtedly of a high and courageous sort." Despite his honorable record, his "statement" is a "'surrender' of the principles that brought him into prominence—and which alone kept him there." For Harrison, Du Bois "is regarded much the same way as a knight in the middle ages who had his armor stripped from him, his arms reversed and his spurs hacked off. This ruins him as an influential person among Negroes."[14] As Harrison's opposition to the NAACP and Du Bois deepened, he gravitated toward Garvey and his UNIA.

During these years, a significant progressive trend within African American thought was advanced by black women around issues of gender oppression. Two important advocates for women's equality were contemporaries of Du Bois: Ida B. Wells-Barnett (1862–1931) and Mary Church Terrell (1863–1954). Born in Holly Springs, Mississippi, Wells was educated at Fisk University and started her career as a journalist and newspaper publisher in Memphis. She became well-known throughout the country for her investigative journalism on lynchings and other racial atrocities. Relocating to Chicago, she became active in the women's suffrage movement and was a cofounder in 1910 of the NAACP.[15] Terrell was born in Memphis, Tennessee, and attended Oberlin College where she earned BA and MA degrees. In 1895, she was appointed to the Washington, DC Board of Education; and in 1896 she cofounded and served as the first president of the National Association of Colored Women. Throughout the first half of the twentieth century, Terrell participated in public demonstrations against Jim Crow segregation, and for many years she served as a vice president of the NAACP.[16] Both Wells-Barnett and Terrell expressed an antiracist feminism that was sharply at odds with white suffragist contemporaries like Susan B. Anthony and Carrie Chapman Catt. They were also central in introducing issues of gender inequality into the mainstream of black public discourse.

Two decades after the emergence of Wells-Barnett and Terrell as major black public intellectuals and activists, their advanced ideas about gender had spread significantly. Among black nationalists, the strongest advocate for women's rights and leadership was Garvey's articulate wife, Amy Jacques Garvey (1896–1973). Jacques Garvey was an important political interpreter of her husband's philosophy as well as a regular contributor to the *Negro World*. In her 1925 essay, "Women as Leaders," Jacques Garvey argued that a profound psychological and social transformation had taken place among modern women: "She agitates for equal opportunities and gets them; she makes good on the job and gains the respect of men who heretofore opposed her." Jacques Garvey viewed the feminist agenda advanced by white women in distinctly racial terms: "White women are rallying all their forces and uniting regardless of national boundaries to save their race from destruction, and preserve its ideals for posterity." Jacques Garvey insisted that black women were learning to imitate these white women, demanding their full share of rights: "Be not discouraged black women of the world, but push forward, regardless of the lack of appreciation shown you." Jacques Garvey warned her male colleagues that African American women "are tired of hearing Negro men say, 'There is a better day coming,' while they do nothing to usher in the day. We are becoming so impatient that we are getting in the front ranks, and serve notice on the world that we will brush aside the halting, cowardly Negro men . . . we will press on and on until victory is over."[17]

III

The next pivotal events that influenced black political consciousness were the Great Depression, and the rise of the Nazi menace. The US economic crisis left 50 percent of all African American workers unemployed. Black workers in urban ghettos responded with rent strikes and sparked economic boycotts against white-owned businesses that refused to hire blacks. Thousands of African Americans joined the US Communist Party; a smaller number became members of Social Democratic and independent Marxist parties.

Within this third cohort of black radicals, the greatest intellectual was Cyril Lionel Robert James. Born in Tunapuna, Trinidad in 1901, James's father was a schoolteacher, and his mother was "a reader," a great lover of literature. Acquiring his mother's passion, the young man became an excellent writer and budding novelist. From 1932 until 1938 he lived in England, where he was drawn into the left-wing politics of the British followers of Soviet dissident Leon Trotsky. James's three major works during this period were: *World Revolution: The Rise and Fall of the communist International* (1937), a Trotskyist analysis detailing the rise of Stalinism over the global communist movement; *Black Jacobins: Toussaint L'Overture and the San Domingo Revolution* (1938), a history of the eighteenth century Haitian revolution; and *A History of Negro Revolt* (1938), an examination of social protest movements and insurrections in colonial Africa and the

Caribbean. These three extraordinary works established James as arguably the most insightful social theorist writing on issues of race from a Marxist perspective. During his fifteen-year "exile" in the United States, James would build on this legacy, writing, "The Revolutionary Answer to the Negro Problem in the U.S.," a position paper of the Socialist Workers Party (July 1948); *Notes on Dialectics: Hegel, Marx, Lenin* (1948); *State Capitalism and World Revolution* (1950); *Notes on American Civilization* (1950); and the remarkable *Mariners, Renegades and Castaways: The Story of Herman Melville and the World We Live In* (written in 1952, privately published in 1953).[18]

The black intellectual most closely associated with James was Malcolm Nurse, better known by his pseudonym, George Padmore. Born in Trinidad, Padmore was a member of the black working class, which experienced the greatest discrimination among minorities. In the 1920s he immigrated to the United States, where he attended college at Fisk, Du Bois's alma mater, and Howard University. It was in the United States that Padmore was converted to the Communist Party. In less than a decade, he rose to the pinnacle of power inside the Communist International. "Up to 1945," James wrote subsequently, "there was hardly a single African leader . . . who had not passed through the school of thought and organization which George directed from Moscow. It gave information, advice, guidance, ideas about black struggles on every continent." After the rise of Hitler and international communism embraced a strategy of the "popular front" against fascism, black Marxists were told that the struggle to topple British and French colonialism in Africa had to be reduced. Padmore's response was to break with the communists, and he relocated to London and worked closely with James. When fascist Italy invaded Ethiopia, the two men formed the International African Friends of Ethiopia. Padmore soon became a political magnet, attracting West Indian and African activists living in Great Britain, such as Jomo Kenyatta and Kwame Nkrumah. It was around such idealists that Padmore organized the historic Fifth Pan-African Congress, in October 1945. It was Padmore who charted the strategy to topple British rule in Africa's Gold Coast, later Ghana. Like many Pan-Africanists and black revolutionaries, such as Frantz Fanon, Padmore turned against communism and made his peace with the capitalist West. His major theoretical work published in 1956, was titled *Pan-Africanism or Communism?*

A third Trinidadian whose writings profoundly shaped the black thought was Oliver Cromwell Cox. Born in 1901 in Port-of-Spain, Cox's father was the captain of a government schooner that sailed around the island enforcing colonial sea laws, a position that for a black family conveyed middle-class status. Like his older brothers, O. C. Cox was sent to the United States to study for a law degree. In 1929, Cox earned a BA degree from Northwestern University, but he soon came down with poliomyelitis. Cox never fully recovered and was forced to walk with crutches with great difficulty for the remainder of his life. Revising his plans, Cox decided to remain in the United States, and after an eighteen-month recovery, he entered the graduate program in economics at the University of Chicago. In 1932, Cox finished his MA degree with a brilliant thesis: "Workingmen's Compensation in the United States." Turning to sociology, in 1938 Cox earned his PhD at Chicago and began a career as a university professor, which would span over three decades. Cox's left-wing politics and identification with Marxism as a method of social analysis, however, denied him access to foundation and philanthropic support for his research. For a quarter century, he was denied faculty appointments at major research universities that refused to hire black scholars on the basis of race. He worked at a succession of historically black colleges, including Tuskegee Institute and Lincoln University in Missouri, where the pay was low. Despite his deprivations, Cox published a series of theoretically sophisticated works influenced by Marxism, including *Caste, Class and Race*, a study challenging Gunnar Myrdal's caste theories (1948); *The Foundation of Capitalism* (1959); and *Capitalism as a System* (1964).[19]

The British Caribbean was a remarkably fertile ground for the cultivation of radical thought, but it was not unique: other regions of the African diaspora, characterized by class struggles and racial oppression, produced intellectuals possessing similar ideas. One notable example from Martinique was Aimé Césaire. Born on June 26, 1913, in Basse-Pointe, Martinique, Césaire attended high school and college in France. During his studies in Paris, he cofounded a literary journal, the *Black Student*, that promoted the concept of negritude: pride and celebration in black identity. Césaire became well-known for his epic poems and essays, including "Negro I Am, Negro I Will Remain" and "Notes from a Return to My Native Land." Joining the French Communist Party, Césaire returned to Martinique during World War II and was elected mayor of Fort-de-France in 1945; except for a two-year hiatus in the mid-1980s, Césaire continued to serve in the post until 2001. He was instrumental in ending direct colonial rule in Martinique, with the island becoming an overseas department of France in 1946. In the 1950s, Césaire broke with the communists, establishing the Martinique Progressive Party in 1958 and subsequently affiliating himself with the French Socialist Party. Despite Césaire's more moderate economic views at the end of his life, he still maintained his unyielding commitment to anticolonial politics.

Within black America, the counterpart to radical intellectuals like C. L. R. James and George Padmore was Bayard Rustin (1910–1987). Born in West Chester, Pennsylvania, Ruskin attended college at Wilberforce University, Cheney State College, and the City College of New York. Recruited into the Young Communist League in the 1930s, Rustin soon broke with the communists and became a democratic socialist. With the outbreak of the Second World War Rustin became a conscientious objector and was imprisoned by the US government for several years. Becoming involved in the Congress of Racial Equality, Rustin was jailed in North Carolina in 1947 when he demonstrated against racial segregation on public buses. In 1956, he traveled to the Jim Crow South to become a chief lieutenant to Dr. Martin Luther King, Jr., during the historic Montgomery Bus Boycott. Along with activist Ella Baker, Rustin helped to organize King's Southern Christian Leadership Conference. In 1963, he served as the chief organizer of the March on Washington, DC, attracting 250,000 civil rights protestors to the capital. Through his longtime friendship with fellow socialist and trade union leader A. Philip Randolph, Rustin came to exercise great influence within the labor movement. As Rustin approached sixty years old, however, he grew more conservative politically, criticizing King's opposition to the US war in Vietnam, and defending Israel's interests against the Palestinians.[20]

Each of these intellectuals, throughout most of their respective careers, identified themselves with some version of socialism or Marxism. Padmore, Césaire and Rustin were all members of the Communist Party for a time. Cox was not directly involved in leftist politics, but his studies, especially *Caste, Class and Race*, were perceived by many critics as orthodox Marxism. Both James and Césaire were artists and cultural workers who understood that plays, poetry, and prose were an effective means to transform the imaginations of the oppressed. This element in their work directly relates to Du Bois, who was not only an influential social scientist but also one of the greatest artists of his generation whose creativity challenged racism.

IV

In May 1954, in the Brown v. Board of Education decision, the US Supreme Court, by a unanimous ruling, outlawed racial segregation of public schools.[21] This was the culmination of a series of legal victories won by the NAACP Legal Defense Fund and its brilliant litigators, Charles Hamilton Houston and Thurgood Marshall, over Jim Crow. The white South responded by organizing political and legal efforts to block the implementation of desegration. This campaign was called "Massive Resistance," and it inspired the birth of a middle class segregationist movement, the White Citizens' Councils. Blacks who belonged to the NAACP in the South could have their home mortgages called in by white-owned banks; frequently they were fired from their jobs, and in the cases of civil rights, leaders like Mississippi's NAACP secretary Medgar Evers, they were murdered.[22]

A new "political moment" had begun for the Black Freedom Movement, a new phase of struggle in which the collapse of legal segregation was now possible. What was required were new kinds of tactics: massive, civil disobedience campaigns in the streets, economic boycotts, the construction of "freedom schools." Black churches became bulwarks for community organizing and collective motivation; historically black colleges like Howard University, Fisk University and Spellman College trained young black women and men to lead campaigns and strikes to challenge the system, but their leadership was more than political intervention. It was crafting a language of resistance and racial pride that could sustain the masses through difficult times.

From the vantage point of the entire postwar era, from 1945 to 2010, there were three distinct generations of African American activists and intellectuals: first, the cohort of post–World War II, coming to political maturity during the civil rights and Black Power movements, such as James Baldwin, Amiri Baraka, Pauli Murray, and Walter Rodney; second, the "Baby Boomers," intellectuals born between 1946 and the early 1960s, whose formative political experiences included the Gary, Indiana, Black Political Convention of 1972, the antiapartheid mobilization to topple South Africa, the Jesse Jackson presidential campaigns of 1984 and 1988, and the controversial Anita Hill-Clarence Thomas Supreme Court hearing of 1991; and third, the hip-hop generation of intellectuals born roughly between 1964 and 1985, whose consciousness was defined by the terrorist attacks of 9/11, the Katrina Hurricane crisis of 2005, and Barack Obama's stunning election of 2008. In the second group (1946–1964), one finds Cornel West, bell hooks, Clayborne Carson, Gerald Horne, Michael Eric Dyson, Patricia Williams, Lani Guinier, Charles Ogletree, Joy James, Robin D. G. Kelley, and Barbara Ransby. Within the younger group, prominent intellectuals include Peniel Joseph, Premilla Nadasen, Grant Farred, Julia Sudbury, Mark Q. Sawyer, Geoff Ward, Melissa Harris-Lacewell, Cathy Cohen, and Jeffrey Ogbar. What separates the vast majority of these scholars born after World War II from the earlier intellectuals is that the post-1945 group were generally not members of socialist or Marxist parties or organizations. As a consequence, they frequently did not emphasize the important connections between theory and practice that were central to the work of Du Bois and James. This often led to a rupture from the problems and concerns of the black working class, and a style of analysis that was excessively abstract.

The black intellectuals who emerged after World War II, however, were deeply immersed in politics challenging racism for several reasons. In the former Gold Coast ruled by the British in 1957, Kwame Nkrumah—a protégé of both C. L. R. James and George Padmore—led Ghana into independence. Within a decade, over three dozen newly independent black countries in sub-Saharan Africa and the Caribbean also emerged. With the outbreak of the Montgomery, Alabama, bus boycott in December 1955, led by Dr. Martin Luther King, Jr. and Rosa Parks, the US Black Freedom Movement entered twenty years of intense social protest—first to achieve desegregation, and subsequently to win Black Power.

Many in this post–World War II group who were influenced by Marxism were organic intellectuals, women and men who were not traditionally trained by scholars but who had developed a sophisticated concept of society and a richly, theoretically grounded approach to the construction of social protest movements. One such intellectual was Robert F. Williams. Born in 1925, Williams came to prominence in the late 1950s when, as a local leader of the NAACP, he advocated the use of armed self-defense to combat white racist violence. In 1961, Williams was wrongly accused of kidnapping a white couple and for holding them hostage for several hours during the eruption of racial violence in his town. Fearing that he would be convicted Williams fled to Cuba, where he broadcasted militant programs on a half-hour program aimed from African Americans, called "Radio Free Dixie." Several years later, Williams relocated to communist China, where he became acquainted with Mao Zedong. In 1969, he returned to the United States and engaged in a seven-year battle to avoid extradition to North Carolina. Legal charges were eventually dropped against Williams in January 1976.[23] Another key black activist influenced by the left was James Forman. Born in 1929, Forman, in his early thirties, became the executive director of the Student Nonviolent Coordinating Committee (SNCC), the most radical desegregation group of the early to mid-1960s. Forman's major tasks for SNCC included fundraising, developing strategy, and ideological development of the group's mostly college-aged members. An independent leftist, Forman encouraged SNCC organizers to study Mao

Zedong and Frantz Fanon, and deliberately urged arrests and nonviolent confron-
tations sixties, Forman and SNCC chairman Stokely Carmichael pushed SNCC
into a hasty and later unsuccessful merger with the Black Panther Party. In 1969,
Forman drafted the "Black Manifesto," demanding that religious denominations
pay into a reparations fund five hundred million dollars to compensate African
Americans for crimes committed during slavery. He later became president of the
Washington, DC–based Unemployment and Poverty Committee, and was active
in Democratic Party politics. He died at the age of seventy-six in 2005.[24]

An important turning point in the scholarship of African American socialist
and Marxist thought occurred in the early 1980s, with the nearly simultaneous appearance of three distinctive theoretical works. The first was produced by
then-communist philosopher and radical feminist Angela Y. Davis. Born in Birmingham, Alabama in 1944, Davis studied with Herbert Marcuse and in the late
1960s became the object of a political firestorm, as California Governor Ronald
Reagan sought to remove her from a faculty appointment at the University of
California at Los Angeles. Her involvement with the Black Panther Party led
to her unjust arrest and two-year incarceration as one of the Federal Bureau of
Investigation's (FBI's) "Ten Most Wanted List." While incarcerated, Davis produced a brilliant essay on the complex status of African American women during
slavery. After her vindication in court, she examined the oppression of government victims of surveillance and harassment.[25] Her 1981 study, *Women, Race
and Class*, was an impressive intervention in several respects. First, it vigorously
argued that class, gender, and race were interdependent structures of domination and exploitation, reinforcing one another. Davis argued that the history of
black women was uniquely constructed on these hierarchies, and that their acts
of resistance were fashioned from their experiences as women, as workers, and as
black people.[26] In later years, Davis has developed sharp analysis of the US prison
industrial complex and the social and human consequences of mass incarceration.
Two of Davis's great strengths are her depth of knowledge in social history and
her awareness into issues of gender. For example, her critique of the racism within
the American suffragist movement starkly illustrated how "whiteness" blinded
many white women from making common cause with African American women.

The second critical work of black Marxism to emerge in the early 1980s was
produced by political scientist Cedric Robinson. Born in Oakland, California in
1940, Robinson received his BA degree in social anthropology from the University of California at Santa Barbara. Since 1979, Robinson has cited C. L. R. James
as being among those key intellectuals who influenced his world view. Robinson's
initial work, published in 1980, was an examination of the concept of "leadership" within the discipline of political science.[27] That same year, he cofounded
Third World News Review, aired on the Santa Barbara campus. The program
featured Robinson's sharp commentaries against the conservative administration.
In 1985, Third World News Review expanded to a television program format,
and it continued its media activities for more than two decades.[28]

In 1983, Robinson published *Black Marxism: The Making of the Black Radical
Tradition*. The central thesis was that a series of black intellectuals, such as Du
Bois and James, were instrumental in developing a critical of white supremacy

and black oppression that could be termed "Black Marxism." Robinson argued that the black radical tradition, unlike European Marxism, placed the emancipation of Africa and the Caribbean from colonialism and the abolition of Jim Crow segregation inside the United States as fundamental tasks. He emphasized the struggle against racism as essential for the development of successful working-class movements. Black Marxism had a profound and enduring impact on the hip-hop generation of black and Latino intellectuals who came to maturity in the early twenty-first century.[29]

The third radical, theoretical work that reshaped black left discourse was my sociological 1983 study, *How Capitalism Underdeveloped Black America*. Inspired by Guyanese Marxist Walter Rodney's *How Europe Underdeveloped Africa*, I argued that American racism and capitalism were intertwined systems of economic and social oppression. Under these exploitive conditions, what had developed among African Americans were two different societies: a black elite of professionals, managers, and members of the upper class who exercised relative privilege, and the black majority of workers, the unemployed, and prisoners, whose lives were destroyed by oppression. *How Capitalism* predicted the rise of the US prison industrial complex, which increased the black incarceration rate from 650,000 prisoners in 1983 to 2.1 million prisoners twenty years later. Following the lead of Angela Davis, *How Capitalism* also made a strong case for a robust black feminism as a central aspect of African American radical thought.[30]

Finally, over the past twenty years, black radical thought has been deeply influenced by what has been termed "black feminist thought"—scholarship based on the theoretical intersectionality of gender, sexuality, race, and class. Two distinctly different types of black feminist scholarship are provided by the works of anthropologist Leith Mullings, and cultural critic bell hooks. Receiving her PhD in cultural anthropology at the University of Chicago, Mullings has been a Professor at the City University of New York since 1981. In 2009, she was elected president-elect of the American Anthropological Association. Mullings has produced a series of scholarly works that integrated gender, race, and class themes in the United States and transnationally. Her first study, *Therapy, Ideology and Social Change* (1984), was a study of traditional healing among ethnic Ghanaians. Turning to the United States, she subsequently examined new developments in urban anthropology, in the edited volume, *Cities of the United States* (1987), and *Stress and Resilience* (2001, with Alaka Wali), a detailed ethnographic survey of reproductive health among women in central Harlem. With coeditor Amy Schulz, Mullings applied the scholarship of intersectionality to women's health issues in *Gender, Race, Class and Health* (2006). She then returned to Third World politics and protest in her edited volume, New *Social Movements in the African Diaspora: Challenging Global Apartheid* (2009). No armchair scholar, Mullings has been directly involved in black left politics for decades. In 1996, for example, she cofounded the Black Radical Congress, an African American activist organization that challenged the reactionary politics of Rudolph Giuliani in New York City in the 1990s and the repressive national policies of the George W. Bush administration.[31]

One of the most prolific African American feminist writers of the past three decades has been bell hooks (Gloria Watkins). Born in Hopkinsville, Kentucky in

1952, hooks received her undergraduate degree at Stanford University in 1973. She subsequently earned her MA at the University of Wisconsin in 1976, and her doctorate at the University of California at Santa Cruz in 1983. Her first book manuscript, which eventually became *Ain't I A Woman*, was originally written in draft form during her years at Stanford. The book was perceived as a black feminist manifest that to a degree paralleled Michele Wallace's controversial *Black Macho and the Myth of the Superwoman*. But unlike Wallace, hooks was a socialist, a radical who employed a class analysis to critique racism and patriarchy. hooks's 1984 study, *Feminist Theory: From Margin to Center*, was a strongly engaged, theoretical work that challenged many of the tenets of mainstream feminism. Central themes in hooks's work include: a critical examination of pedagogy and how education and culture can form the basis for constructing an alternative consciousness; her commitment to the politics of resistance as a means of self-discovery and cultural affirmation; and the effort to define a black feminism drawing cultural memories, stories, and social interactions. After the publication of hooks's and Cornel West's *Breaking Bread* in 1991, hooks's writing moved away from both class analysis and politics and emphasized aesthetics and modes of cultural representation, such as black images in film. Works on such themes include *Art on my Mind: Visual Politics* (1995), and *Reel to Real: Race, Sex, and Class at the Movies* (1996).[32]

The political evolution of the radical black intelligentsia over the past 150 years, in summary, has been toward the effort to remake America's flawed democratic institutions, by dismantling institutional racism and other forms of systemic oppression. The arguments for racial reform and social change have evolved over time but have drawn from Marxism periodically as an effective method of social analysis to explain the interactions between race, class, and power. What remains unresolved is whether or not black American political culture will retain its progressive and activist leanings in a period of globalized capitalism and the current triumph of neoliberalism in politics. Barack Obama is without question the most progressive politician ever elected to the American presidency but as a black man, will Obama's identification with American power transform African Americans into uncritical defenders of the US state, so long as it is racially integrated?

NOTES

1. See Manning Marable, *Race, Reform, and Rebellion: The Second Reconstruction in Black American and Beyond, 1945–206*, 3rd ed. (Jackson: University Press of Mississippi, 2007), pp. 3–11.
2. See Manning Marable and Kristen Clarke, eds., *Barack Obama and African American Empowerment: The Rise of Black America's New Leadership* (New York: Palgrave Macmillan, 2009).
3. This is one of the clearest expressions of Frederick Douglass's liberal integrationist address of 1865, "What the Black Man Wants," in *Let Nobody Turn Us Around: An African-American Anthology* ed. Manning Marable and Leith Mullings, 2nd ed. (Lanham, MD: Rowman and Littlefield, 2009), pp. 122–128.
4. The best, and essential, source on Reconstruction and its aftermath remains W. E. B. Du Bois, *Black Reconstruction in America, 1860–1880*.

5. "Mrs. Terrell, 90, Women's Leader," *New York Times*, July 29, 1954.

6. See David Levering Lewis, *W. E. B. Du Bois: Biography of a Race, 1868–1919* (New York: Holt, 1993); August Meier, *Negro Thought in America, 1880–1915* (Ann Arbor: University of Michigan Press, 1969); and Manning Marable, *W. E. B. Du Bois: Black Radical Democrat*, rev. ed. (Boulder, CO: Paradigm Press, 2005).

7. See Manning Marable, "The Pan-Africanism of W. E. B. Du Bois," in *W. E. B. Du Bois on Race and Culture: Philosophy, Politics and Poetics*, ed. Bernard Bell, Emily Grosholz, and James Stewart (New York: Routledge, 1996), pp. 193–218; and W. E. B. Du Bois, *The World and Africa: An Inquiry into the Part which Africa Has Played in World History* (New York: International Publishers, 1965).

8. Marable, *W. E. B. Du Bois*, pp. 99–120.

9. See John G. Jackson, *Hubert Henry Harrison* (Austin, TX: American Atheist Press, 1987); and Winston James, *Holding Aloft the Banner of Ethiopia: Caribbean Radicalism in Early Twentieth Century America* (London: Verso, 1998).

10. W. E. B. Du Bois, "The Negro and Radical Thought," *Crisis* 22 (July 1921): pp. 102–104.

11. W. E. B. Du Bois, "The Browsing Reader," *Crisis* 35 (June 1928): pp. 202, 211; and Claude McKay to W. E. B. Du Bois, in *The Correspondence of W. E. B. Du Bois*, ed. Herbert Aptheker (Amherst: University of Massachusetts Press, 1973), pp. 1:374–375.

12. Marcus Garvey, "Home to Harlem: An Insult to the Race," *Negro World*, September 29, 1928.

13. W. E. B. Du Bois, "Close Ranks," *Crisis* 16 (July 1918).

14. Hubert H. Harrison, "The Descent of Du Bois," in *When Africa Awakens* (New York: Porro Press, 1920).

15. See Mildred I. Thompson, *Ida B. Wells-Barnett: An Exploratory Study of an American Black Woman* (Brooklyn, NY: Carlson Publishing, 1990); "Mrs. Ida Barnett, Colored Leader, Dies Suddenly," *Chicago Tribune*, March 25, 1931; and "Ida B. Wells-Barnett, Noted Club Woman, Dies Suddenly," *Chicago Defender*, March 28, 1931.

16. See Mary Church Terrell, *A Colored Woman in a White World* (Washington, DC: Ransdell, 1940); Sharon Harley, "Mary Church Terrell: Genteel Militant," in *Black Leaders in the Nineteenth Century*, ed. Leon Litwack and August Meier (Urbana: University of Illinois Press, 1988), pp. 291–307.

17. A. Jacques Garvey, "Women as Leaders," *Negro World*, October 25, 1925. Also see Ula Yvette Taylor, "The Veiled Garvey: The Life and Times of Amy Jacques Garvey," PhD diss., University of California at Santa Barbara, 1992.

18. The best introductions to C. L. R. James's philosophical thought are James, *The Future in the Present* (London: Allison and Busby, 1977); and James, *Notes on Dialectics: Hegel-Marx-Lenin* (London: Allison and Busby, 1980).

19. A bibliography of Oliver C. Cox's major works includes *Caste, Class and Race* (New York: Doubleday, 1948); *The Foundations of Capitalism* (New York: Philosophical Library, 1959); *Capitalism and American Leadership* (New York: Philosophical Library, 1962); *Capitalism as a System* (New York: Monthly Review Press, 1964); and *Race Relations: Elements and Social Dynamics* (Detroit: Wayne State University, 1976).

20. An excellent introduction to Rustin is Devon W. Carbado and Donald Weise, eds., *Time on Two Crosses: The Collected Writings of Bayard Rustin* (San Francisco: Cleis Press, 2003).

21. Marable, *Race, Reform, and Rebellion*, pp. 38–39.

22. Ibid., p. 70.

23. David Stout, "Robert F. Williams, 71, Civil Rights Leader and Revolutionary," *New York Times*, October 19, 1996.

24. Douglas Martin, "James Forman Dies at 76; Was Pioneer in Civil Rights," *New York Times*, January 12, 2005.

25. Angela Y. Davis, ed., *If They Came in the Morning* (New York: Third Press, 1971).

26. Angela Y. Davis, *Woman, Race and Class* (New York: Random House, 1981).

27. Cedric Robinson, *Terms of Order: Political Science and the Myth of Leadership* (Albany: State University of New York Press, 1980).

28. Elizabeth Robinson, "Twenty-Five Years of the Third World News Review," *Race and Class* 47, no. 2 (October 2005).

29. Cedric Robinson, *Black Marxism: The Making of the Black Radical Tradition* (London: Zed Press, 1983).

30. Manning Marable, *How Capitalism Underdeveloped Black America*, 2nd rev. ed. (Boston: South End Press, 2001).

31. Author's note: Mullings and I have also coedited two works: *Let Nobody Turn Us Around: An African American Anthology*, 2nd rev. ed. (Lanham, MD: Rowman and Littlefield, 2009); and coauthored *Freedom: A Photographic History of African American Struggle* (London: Phaidon, 2002).

32. A short list of bell hooks's works includes *Ain't I a Woman? Black Women and Feminism* (Boston: South End Press, 1981); *Feminist Theory: From Margin to Center* (Boston: South End Press, 1984); *Yearning: Race, Gender and Cultural Politics* (Boston: South End Press, 1990); bell hooks and Cornel West, *Breaking Bread: Insurgent Black Intellectual Life* (Boston; South End Press, 1991); *Teaching to Transgress: Education as the Practice of Freedom* (New York: Routledge, 1994); *Art on my Mind: Visual Politics* (New York: New Press, 1995); *Reel to Real: Race, Sex, and Class at the Movies* (New York: Routledge, 1996); and *Remembering Rapture: The Writer At Work* (New York: Henry Holt, 1992).

PART I

DISRUPTING REGIONAL BOUNDARIES

HOUSING, URBAN DEVELOPMENT, AND THE PERSISTENCE OF RACIAL INEQUALITY IN THE POST–CIVIL RIGHTS ERA SOUTH

JOHN A. KIRK

THE HISTORIOGRAPHY OF THE CIVIL RIGHTS STRUGGLE has changed dramatically over the past quarter of a century. Early histories that appeared prior to the 1980s concentrated primarily on Martin Luther King, Jr. and the familiar *Montgomery to Memphis* narrative of his life.[1] Since the 1980s, a number of studies examining the civil rights movement at local and state levels have questioned the usefulness and accuracy of the King-centric *Montgomery to Memphis* narrative as the sole way of understanding the civil rights movement. These studies have made it clear that civil rights struggles already existed in many of the communities that King and the organization of which he was the president, the Southern Christian Leadership Conference (SCLC), ran civil rights campaigns in during the 1960s. Moreover, those struggles continued long after King and the SCLC had left those communities. Civil rights activism also thrived in many places that King and the SCLC never visited.[2]

As a result of these local and state studies, historians have increasingly framed the civil rights movement within the context of a much longer, ongoing struggle for black freedom and equality, unfolding throughout the twentieth century at local, state, and national levels. This in turn has helped to broaden the range of issues that historians have explored in relation to the civil rights struggle, which have, for example, variously included the role of women's activism, the role of violence and armed self-defense, and the international dimensions of the struggle.[3]

In recent years, the work of urban historians in particular has offered an important challenge to the way that we conceptualize the civil rights movement. Studies by Thomas Sugrue, Arnold Hirsch, and others have explored the role of race and urban development in cities across the United States.[4] In doing so, they have shifted the focus of historians from more traditional areas of study, such as desegregation and voting rights (which the civil rights struggle successfully addressed through the 1964 Civil Rights Act and the 1965 Voting Rights Act), to the structural issues of urban planning and neighborhood development. This shift in emphasis has forced attention on the areas in which the civil rights movement failed to decisively impact and to the relatively neglected episodes within the civil rights canon. This includes, for example, Martin Luther King and the SCLC's 1965–66 Chicago campaign, where they failed in their bid to win "open housing" for blacks in that northern city, and the failure of the 1966 civil rights bill that contained fair housing proposals.[5]

A case study of Little Rock, Arkansas, demonstrates how this different conceptual framework challenges existing assumptions about the locus of civil rights struggles. The defining event of Little Rock's civil rights history at national, state, and local levels, has undoubtedly been seen as the 1957 school crisis. As a seemingly progressive city in an upper South state, Little Rock had at first appeared to blaze a trial for compliance with the 1954 *Brown v. Board of Education* school desegregation decision when the city school board almost immediately announced integration plans. In September 1957, when this plan was due to be implemented, however, Governor Orval E. Faubus surrounded the downtown Central High School with National Guard troops to prevent the entry of nine black students. Eventually, President Dwight D. Eisenhower was forced to federalize National Guard troops and send in federal soldiers to ensure the safe passage of the nine students into the school.[6]

From an urban history perspective, this essay argues that the city's most decisive response to *Brown v. Board of Education* was in fact the pre-emptive strategy of slum clearance and urban redevelopment in the early 1950s rather than the massive resistance of the later 1950s. Without doubt, this policy shaped race relations in the city more fundamentally over the long term, even up to the present day, than the short-term effects of the school crisis.

From its earliest days, Arkansas's state capital of Little Rock, located at the center of a predominantly rural state, had developed a reputation for having a far more progressive racial climate than surrounding areas. The scarcity of labor in the city during the pre–Civil War period meant that skilled black slaves were in demand and that they had some leeway in bargaining better terms of employment and more social freedom. After the Civil War, many of these skilled blacks, along with a new influx of blacks from rural Arkansas and other states, enjoyed prominent positions as educators, businessmen, and politicians in the Republican Reconstruction government. Even when segregation and disfranchisement curtailed black social and political freedom in the post-Reconstruction era, black businesses and institutions continued to flourish well into the twentieth century.[7]

A reflection of the city's more progressive racial outlook was the fact that in Little Rock there were no laws to prohibit blacks and whites living in the same area and racially mixed neighborhoods did exist. Due largely to economic constraints, the location of black institutions, and the practicalities of finding security in numbers, there were however discernible black districts just off the downtown black business district of West Ninth Street and toward the east of the city. Nevertheless, a 1941 study sponsored by the Greater Little Rock Urban League noted, "While Negroes predominate in certain sections . . . in Little Rock, there are . . . no widespread . . . 'Negro sections' [of residence]."[8]

Postwar housing and urban development in Little Rock, as in many other communities, was profoundly shaped by a landmark piece of federal legislation passed by the United States Congress in the Housing Act of 1949. It was this piece of legislation that prompted city officials in Little Rock to embark upon an aggressive racial redistricting to create a more geographically segregated city—a policy more often viewed as a response to rather than a pre-emptive strike at undermining the gains of the modern civil rights movement. Embodying lofty socially progressive ideals, the Housing Act declared that every American deserved a "decent home and a suitable living environment." Three principle policies were advanced to achieve that goal: a program of federally funded slum clearance and urban redevelopment; a boosting of Federal Housing Administration (FHA) mortgage insurance; and a commitment by the federal government to build 810,000 new public housing units within six years.

Although it shaped federal policy for much of the rest of the twentieth century the act had a mixed legacy. The most controversial aspect was the rapid racialization of urban redevelopment programs. "Slum clearance" quickly translated into "Negro clearance" just as its successor "urban renewal" later became known as "Negro removal." As historian Arnold R. Hirsch explains, northern cities used the federal legislation to consolidate and extend their long-established tradition of segregated housing. In southern towns and cities it was often used to actually establish a pattern of segregated housing to replace what had in the past been the close proximity of black and white areas of residence and even racially mixed neighborhoods. The hard figures demonstrate just how racialized housing policy became. By January 1952, the 53 earmarked slum clearance projects nationwide involved the removal of 41,630 families, 85 percent of them black. The 266 slum sites proposed for redevelopment as public housing projects involved the displacement of 55,778 families, 74 percent of them black. Ultimately, more public housing units were torn down than built under the act. The ambitious target of 810,000 new public housing units, which constituted only an estimated 10 percent of the required stock, took not six but twenty years to build.[9]

On the surface at least, the city's slum clearance and urban redevelopment plans held out the promise of better conditions for Little Rock's black population by eradicating poor housing and replacing it with new public housing units. Certainly, black community leaders enthusiastically supported the plans, believing that it would deliver significantly better conditions for the black population.[10] Yet white city planners had very different ideas about how slum clearance and urban redevelopment money would be spent. Their focus was less on improving the conditions of the black community and more on using funds to perpetuate and even extend segregation in the city. B. Finley Vinson, head of the Little Rock Housing

Authority (LRHA) and its slum clearance and urban redevelopment director, has freely admitted that "the city of Little Rock through its various agencies including the housing authority systematically worked to continue segregation" through its slum clearance and public housing projects.[11] At a public meeting in 1964, Little Rock housing director Dowell Naylor was asked outright "Is development in housing in Little Rock drawing racial groups together or silently drawing them apart?" Naylor answered, "Drawing them apart."[12]

The intent of city planners to use federal housing policy as an instrument for achieving residential segregation was first evident when black areas of residence were targeted for redevelopment apparently as much for their proximity to white neighborhoods as their slum status. The first part of the city designated as a "blighted area" for demolition and clearance was a ten-block area of homes at the heart of the downtown Little Rock black community.[13] Blacks viewed the area, as one resident, Lola S. Doutherd put it, as "the choicest area of the Negro residential section . . . It contains many churches, schools, completely modern homes, paved paid out streets, and it is within easy walking distance to the business section of the city." Doutherd further alleged that "coercion and intimidation" was used by the LRHA to force black residents to sell their properties in the area. The LRAH "threatened the owners by telling them if they did not sell at the appraised price, they would be ordered in court and given less, or evicted from their homes," she claimed. When residents did sell under duress they often found themselves with no alternative accommodation to move into and too little money to buy elsewhere in the city. A group of local residents led by R. O. Burgess, a locomotive machinist, launched an unsuccessful lawsuit to save their homes.[14] The Dunbar School Project, as it became known, was just one example of many similar stories of urban redevelopment in Little Rock.[15]

While the LRHA evicted black residents downtown it proceeded to build black public housing units on the edge of the city limits as far away from white neighborhoods as possible. The first public housing projects built under the redevelopment plans were the four hundred units of Joseph A. Booker Homes, named after a former president of Little Rock's Black Arkansas Baptist College, built in the far southeast city limits.[16] Subsequent housing projects would follow a similar pattern. By 1990, the major public housing projects of the 1950s had 99 percent black occupancy and 41 percent of all public housing units were located in predominantly black areas of east Little Rock. By contrast predominantly white areas had only 5 percent of the city's public housing units and there were none at all in the far west of the city.[17]

The location of Joseph A. Booker Homes demonstrated not only the intent of the LRHA to construct a more residentially segregated city but also the underlying rationale for doing so. Clearly defining certain parts of the city as "black" and "white" areas paved the way for the *de facto* segregation of numerous other associated facilities and particularly, given the looming prospect of a desegregation ruling by the US Supreme Court in the early 1950s, schools. An example of this was the construction in 1952 of Booker High School next to Joseph A. Booker Homes. By a stroke of convenient racial gerrymandering it emerged that although Booker Homes and Booker High School fell within the city limits and thus could qualify for federal funds for slum clearance and urban redevelopment purposes, at the same time the Little Rock School District ended just short of the school so that it fell instead within the jurisdiction and funding of the Pulaski County Special (Rural) School District. When the school opened in September 1952 under chronically crowded conditions, there was still not enough room to accommodate all the children of the black families resident at Booker Homes. Over a hundred black students were left stranded without provisions for their education. The city refused to take responsibility for them, with acting superintendent of Little Rock schools Dr. Ed McCuiston suggesting that they pay a private tuition fee of $12.50 a year to attend city schools. This was a sum beyond those black families whose low income qualified them for public housing in the first place.[18] Such was the outrage among black and some white sections of the population in Little Rock that the Arkansas General Assembly was forced to rush through a "Booker Bill" that required Booker High School to be incorporated into the Little Rock School District. At a meeting of the Little Rock School Board, which remained bitterly opposed to incorporating Booker High School and lambasted the actions of state legislators for compelling them to do so, a new superintendent of schools, Virgil T. Blossom, was appointed.[19]

Blossom pursued a new schools building strategy that initiated a program of construction that worked hand in hand with city planners to ensure segregated schools followed the pattern of segregated housing, even as the US Supreme Court handed down its ruling in the 1954 *Brown v. Board of Education* case that segregated schools were unconstitutional.[20] In the wake of *Brown*, the Little Rock branch of the National Association for the Advancement of Colored People (NAACP) pressed Blossom for a statement about the city's school desegregation plans. He informed them that before any desegregation took place the school board intended to build two new schools. Horace Mann High School would be built in the predominantly black eastern part of the city and Hall High School would be built in the affluent white suburbs of the west. Nevertheless, Blossom insisted that the two new schools, although clearly based in black and white residential areas, would not have a set racial designation. Rather, Blossom assured local NAACP members, the school board planned to desegregate all three of the city's high schools, Horace Mann High, Hall High, and the downtown Central High, along color-blind attendance zones in 1957. Elementary schools, he told them, would follow sometime around 1960.[21] Most NAACP members accepted the plan on the basis that it promised to actually enact a program for desegregation, in contrast to the declarations of other cities and states that they would attempt to defy the court's decision altogether through "massive resistance."[22]

Much of the local NAACP's optimism vanished a year later when the Supreme Court handed down its school desegregation implementation decision that became known as *Brown II*. In handing down its original ruling, the court delayed details of how school desegregation would be carried out. It had hoped that school boards would take the initiative to draw up the most appropriate plans for their own communities. However, greeted with howls of opposition from some white southerners, the court appeared to backtrack. It ambiguously told school boards that they must only make a "prompt and reasonable start" to desegregate "with all deliberate speed." No definite deadline was set for when integration had to begin and there was no indication of what exactly constituted compliance with the *Brown* decision in terms of how many students were to be integrated and at what grades. Indeed, the court even listed the "local problems" that might be given as reasonable excuses for delay. The court decentralized the task of administrating school desegregation by handing this responsibility to federal district judges and to local school boards. The overall message to the South seemed to be that it could take as long as it wanted to desegregate schools.[23]

Brown II had a profound impact on school desegregation plans in Little Rock. Soon after, Virgil Blossom announced that he was to modify his original school desegregation proposals. The most important development was the introduction of a transfer system that would allow students to move out of their assigned school attendance zone. Under the original Blossom Plan, it was clear that new schools were being strategically placed in conjunction with city planning policy to provide attendance areas that would ensure a majority black attendance at Horace Mann High and a majority white attendance at Hall High. The assignment of black students to Horace Mann High, although they lived closer to Central High, had confirmed the intentions of the school board to limit the impact of desegregation as much as possible.[24]

Even so, the original plan had allowed for integration that involved several hundred pupils. The modified plan, however, reflected Blossom's belief that *Brown II* allowed his original plans for limiting the impact of desegregation to be taken even further. The modified Blossom Plan allowed whites to opt out of attendance at Horace Mann High without giving blacks the right to choose to attend Hall High. Furthermore, it allowed only token integration at Central High. To encourage the shift of white pupils from Horace Mann High the school board clearly designated it as a black institution by assigning an all-black teaching staff there. The school board then declared that it intended to open Horace Mann High as a segregated black school in February 1956, a move that would establish a clear precedent for black attendance the year before the school was supposed to desegregate.[25] Blossom's actions clearly had the tacit support of the city's business and professional elite, the group of people that also drove city planning policy. In 1955, for his efforts Blossom was named Little Rock's "Man of the Year."[26]

In December 1955, outraged by developments that had taken place without any consultation with them, Little Rock's NAACP executive board members voted to file a lawsuit against the Little Rock school board. They contacted the NAACP's Legal Defense Fund southwest regional attorney, Ulysses Simpson Tate, for advice on how to proceed. The Little Rock NAACP was especially concerned at plans to open Horace Mann High as a segregated school in February 1956. However, Tate cautioned against seeking an injunction to prevent the opening of Horace Mann High. Instead, he urged the branch to take the positive step of petitioning for the admission of black students to white schools when Horace Mann High opened.[27]

On January 23, 1956, thirty-three black students applied for admission to four different white schools in Little Rock. All principals of the schools refused entry to the students and referred them to Blossom. Daisy Bates, president of the Arkansas State Conference of the National Association for the Advancement of Colored People branches (ASC), accompanied nine of the black students to Blossom's office. There, Blossom explained that he had to "deny their request . . . in line with the policy outlined [by the school board]." Blossom was adamant that school desegregation would take place, as planned, in 1957. Daisy Bates told reporters after the meeting that "I think the next step is obvious. We've tried everything short of a court suit."[28] On February 8, 1956, the ASC's attorney Wiley A. Branton filed suit in the US District Court against the Little Rock school board for desegregation on behalf of thirty-three students under the title of *Aaron v. Cooper*.[29]

At the trial in August 1956, the US District Court backed the modified Blossom Plan. However, this had more to do with confusion within the ranks of the NAACP rather than the strength of the Blossom plan. The Little Rock NAACP built its case on very specific terms that asked simply for the enforcement of the original Blossom Plan. In order to reinforce the strength of its argument, branch members went to great pains to select individual examples of black students who faced particular hardship under the modified Blossom Plan. Tate had different ideas about the case. He did not confer with local branch officials before the trial. When he flew into Little Rock the day before the scheduled hearings in the case, he claimed that he was too tired to take instructions and immediately retired to his room to rest. The next morning, he ignored the case built by the Little Rock NAACP and proceeded to argue the national NAACP line for the immediate and complete integration of all schools. This was the same line taken by the national NAACP in all its other sixty-five integration suits against school boards in the upper South at that time.[30]

Tate's line of argument lost the lawsuit by playing straight into the hands of the school board. Tate did not demand that the school board should live up to the promises that it had already made. Rather, by demanding wholesale immediate integration, he allowed school board attorneys to contend that their clients were acting in accordance with the "with all deliberate speed" guidelines laid down by *Brown II*. Judge John E. Miller upheld their argument. Offering a shred of consolation for the local NAACP, Miller retained federal jurisdiction in the case to make sure that the school board now carried out the Blossom Plan along the lines that it had indicated in court.[31] The Little Rock NAACP branch was naturally disappointed at the outcome of the lawsuit. In consultation with their attorney Wiley A. Branton, director-counsel of the NAACP Legal Defense Fund, Thurgood Marshall, and special counsel to the NAACP, Robert L. Carter, they decided to appeal.[32] The Appeals Court at St. Louis heard arguments in *Aaron v. Cooper* on March 11, 1957. Again, the court upheld the modified Blossom Plan, stating that the school board was indeed operating within a timetable that was reasonable given the local problems of desegregation in the South. However, the Appeals Court reaffirmed Judge Miller's ruling that the school board was now obliged to carry out its modified plan, beginning with the desegregation of high schools in September 1957.[33]

The issue of school desegregation swiftly reached its denouement in Little Rock in the latter half of 1957. Over the summer of 1957, Blossom drew up attendance zones for admission to Central High that included two hundred black students. He then asked L. M. Christophe and Edwin L. Hawkins, the principals of the Black Horace Mann High and Dunbar Junior High School, to determine how many of their students wanted to apply for transfer. Thirty-two pupils from Horace Mann High and thirty-eight from Dunbar Junior High indicated an interest in attending Central. Blossom asked the principals to screen each student individually and to make a judgment as to their suitability for selection. This was based on a range of factors including intelligence (Blossom insisted that all those selected must possess an IQ of over one hundred), personality traits, and social skills. When this process was completed, the principals forwarded the names of suitable candidates to Blossom for further screening.[34]

Blossom forged ahead with the plans for attendance zones and screening, again without bothering to consult the Little Rock NAACP. The NAACP only learned of the new plans through the black community grapevine. Upon hearing the news, Daisy Bates contacted the principals of the two black high schools, who confirmed that the selection process was already under way. The principals suggested that Bates contact Blossom for an explanation of his actions. When Bates contacted Blossom, he agreed to meet with local NAACP officials.[35]

At the meeting, Blossom explained his actions by comparing the situation in the schools to the desegregation of baseball, where Jackie Robinson had been selected as the first black player because of his high personal standing, conduct, and morals. Similarly, Blossom stated, "I feel that for this transition from segregation to integration in the Little Rock school system, we should select and encourage only the best Negro students to attend Central High School—so that no criticism of the integration process could be attributed to inefficiency, poor scholarship, low morals, or poor citizenship."[36]

Questioned by local NAACP officials, Blossom admitted that he could not legally turn down an application from a student simply because he or she did not meet his own personal criteria. However, Blossom made it clear that he would do everything to discourage such a candidate. With regard to the new attendance zone, which further limited the pool of potential black applicants to Central High, Blossom told the Little Rock NAACP that he was prepared to invoke the state's Pupil Assignment law if any complaints were raised. Furthermore, Blossom asserted that he would make any final decision on transfers to Central High. "I know it is undemocratic, and I know it is wrong," Blossom told them, "but I am doing it."[37]

Since it was now too late to challenge the new measures in court the Little Rock NAACP was forced to accept the further changes to the Blossom Plan.[38] After a grueling round of interviews conducted personally by Blossom, the number of students permitted to integrate Central High School stood at seventeen. After further black students withdrew, the number went down to just nine students. They were Minnijean Brown, Elizabeth Eckford, Ernest Green, Thelma Mothershed, Melba Pattillo, Gloria Ray, Terrance Roberts, Jefferson Thomas, and Carlotta Walls.[39]

The inherent weaknesses of the Blossom Plan and its efforts to tailor school desegregation to the trend of geographical exclusion in city planning became apparent as the September date for desegregation moved closer. In choosing to desegregate Central High School alone, Blossom introduced pointed class issues into the already contentious issue of school desegregation. Central High was located in what was still a racially mixed neighborhood of blacks and working-class whites who could not afford to or did not want to leave their close-to-downtown homes. Whites in that neighborhood were keenly aware that white city leaders were effectively pushing them to the forefront of the city's desegregation plans by targeting Central High for integration while building a new segregated white school in the predominantly affluent upper- and middle-class western suburbs. As one resident complained to Little Rock Chamber of Commerce president E. Grainger Williams, "You of the Chamber of Commerce are financially able to send your children to private schools, you are able to live in a secluded housing project. You have no worries about integration, because you can evade every iota of it."[40]

The focus on Central also had significant tactical ramifications. Segregationist activism in the city was concentrated in the hands of a relatively small but vocal number of people in Little Rock's Capital Citizens' Council (CCC). Concentrating school desegregation in September 1957 on just one site, in a neighborhood from which the CCC drew a significant amount of its support, made the practicalities of mobilizing opposition to it far easier. As the date approached, the CCC looked to turn up the heat by inviting two high-profile segregationists, Georgia Governor Marvin Griffin, and former speaker of the Georgia House of Representatives, Roy V. Harris, to speak in Little Rock. At the meeting Griffin lauded the 350 present as "a courageous bunch of patriots." Harris told them that Griffin would use the highway patrol to resist school desegregation if necessary, and if that failed, he would enlist "every white man in Georgia."[41]

On August 27, a newly formed segregationist group with close links to the CCC, the Mother's League of Central High, filed suit in the Pulaski County Chancery Court.[42] Acting as spokesperson for the group, Mrs. Clyde Thomason claimed that recent events caused "uncertainty of the law, conflicting court decisions and a general state of confusion and unrest." This would lead to "civil commotion" if the school board implemented its desegregation plan. Dramatically, the Mother's League called Governor Faubus as its star witness. Faubus had been equivocal about school desegregation since his election in 1954. In his first two-year term he had refused to be drawn into the issue and had left desegregation plans to local school boards without any interference. When Jim Johnson, head of the state organization of Arkansas's Citizens' Council, stood for governor in 1956, Faubus had adopted segregationist rhetoric to outflank his opponent. After winning reelection, he once again appeared to backtrack, telling reporters, "Everyone knows no state law supersedes a federal law" and "[i]f anyone expects me to use them to supersede federal laws they are wrong."[43] On the stand in August 1957, Faubus testified that he believed violence would occur if plans for school desegregation went ahead, citing unsubstantiated reports of increased weapons sales in the city and the recent confiscation of revolvers from both white and black students.[44] In doing so, he made a political calculation that he could win more votes as a segregationist than as a moderate. He was right: Faubus subsequently won an unprecedented six consecutive terms in office while those perceived as being "soft" on integration were removed from office by the voters.[45] Although the local court issued an injunction against school desegregation, this was easily overturned under NAACP challenge in the US District Court.[46]

In September 1957, with the Blossom Plan about to be implemented and nine black students set to attend Central High School, Governor Orval E. Faubus acted on his political instincts. He surrounded the school with National Guard troops to prevent it from desegregating. After pressure was applied from President Dwight D. Eisenhower and the courts, Faubus withdrew the guardsmen. However, when the nine black students attempted to enter the school they were mobbed by whites determined to prevent desegregation. Although they made it into the school, they were later removed for their own safety. Events forced Eisenhower to act. He federalized National Guard soldiers and sent in federal troops to protect the nine black students. Soldiers remained on guard at the school throughout the academic year. When they were removed over the summer of 1958, Faubus set about ensuring the closure of all the city's schools to prevent desegregation. This led a group of local white women to form the Women's Emergency Committee to Open Our Schools (WEC). Putting pressure on local white city businessmen to intervene in light of the social and economic costs that Faubus's actions were causing, the WEC successfully persuaded a slate of business-backed candidates to stand for election to the school board. When they won control, they opened the schools in a token desegregated basis in August 1959.[47]

The business and professional elite's plans for slum clearance and urban redevelopment shaped city school policy through the late 1950s and 1960s. Prominent Little Rock white liberal Adolphine Fletcher Terry, a cofounder of the Women's Emergency Committee that had helped to resolve the impasse in public education created by the 1957 school crisis, was particularly critical of the role played by William F. Rector, a leading city insurance and real estate man. In 1970 she wrote, "Our school board has become more and more his [Rector's] creation; he is proud of the fact and he boasts of it. When new people come to town, and are looking for homes, his agents take them to additions in the far west and assure them 'there will never be a nigger in the schools your children will attend.'"[48] New resident Albert Porter had firsthand experience of this practice from a black perspective when he moved to Little Rock in 1966 to take up a post as a business manager at Philander Smith College. When he looked to purchase a new home, Porter was directed to Granite Heights, a new private housing development located near Booker Homes. When Porter asked to see housing in another part of the city he was told simply "this is where blacks live."[49]

Terry also accused city real estate agents of engaging in the practice of "block-busting" in downtown areas that were increasingly becoming absorbed into the growing and advancing black east end of the city as Little Rock's white population moved relentlessly westward. Block-busting involved purposefully moving a black person or family into a remaining area of white residence to encourage whites to move out. As white residents deserted the area, often selling their homes cheaply to do so, those houses were then sold to blacks at inflated prices that many black buyers had to accept given the ongoing shortages of adequate private housing stock available to them. Meanwhile, new homes were built in the expanding white affluent suburbs of west Little Rock that were sold to those whites who wanted to escape interracial downtown neighborhoods and who could afford to do so.[50] In 1971, when busing threatened to circumvent the purpose of residential segregation by forcing cross city transportation of students to ensure integrated schools, Rector announced the construction of the private Pulaski Academy for those who "don't like busing."[51] Between the public plans of the LRHA and the private practices of Little Rock businesses and real estate agents, Little Rock became an increasingly racially separate city, with the black population concentrated in the eastern and downtown areas and the white population concentrated in the west.

A study conducted by Little Rock's Racial and Cultural Diversity Task Force in 1992 indicated just how profoundly the city's race-driven urban redevelopment plans had impacted since the 1950s. Taking the city's census tracts as its benchmark, the 1992 study found that ten tracts in the east of the city were now 90 percent black and housed 46 percent of the city's entire black population. Only 2 percent of Little Rock's white population lived in those neighborhoods. Nineteen tracts to the west of the city housed 76 percent of the city's white population. A buffer zone between the two areas, containing fourteen census tracts, was notionally "integrated" with 54 percent white and 46 percent black residency. Citywide, however, the study concluded that 70 percent of Little Rock residents lived "in either an area of white or black isolation." The movement of people across the city to create these racially separate neighborhoods was evident. In the 1960s and 1970s, forty-one thousand whites moved from east to west Little Rock, while seventeen thousand blacks moved—or were moved—in the opposite direction. black neighborhoods in the east were worse off in every way. Black families were poorer, with 64 percent earning less than twenty-five thousand dollars a year, while 60 percent of white families in the city earned over that amount. Overall there was a 60 percent per capita income difference between blacks and whites. Of those families in the city below the poverty level, 68 percent were black. The unemployment rate for blacks was 153 percent higher than for whites. Crime was a far greater problem in black than white neighborhoods. Although blacks made up approximately one-third of the city population, black people accounted for over 50 percent of those arrested by the Little Rock Police Department and 97 percent of suspects for violent crime. Meanwhile, 80 percent of violent crime victims were black. The most conspicuous development in the schools was the amount of white students in the racially isolated census tracts of west Little Rock whose parents chose to opt them out of the public schools system altogether. Four out of every ten students in those areas attended private schools.[52]

Little Rock's slum clearance and urban redevelopment plans suggest that even as local civil rights activists successfully battled to end segregation in the 1960s their efforts were already being comprehensively undermined. The whole rationale for segregation laws from the 1890s onward was the amount of interracial mixing that was actually taking place in rapidly expanding towns and cities. Segregation looked to counteract this interracial mixing by instituting laws that imposed a clear distinction between the races that might otherwise have been blurred by the extent of day-to-day contact.[53] By embarking upon a policy of geographical residential racial separation from the 1950s onward the need for segregation laws was gradually eroded. If blacks and whites were separated in different parts of the city, and interracial contact radically lessened as a consequence, then there was no longer any need for laws to formally provide for a distinction between the races. Geographical separation replaced segregation as an instrument of racial discrimination, which ensured that many city facilities would remain segregated by virtue of their location close to black and white areas of residence.

Changes in Little Rock's city government in the 1950s also conveniently coincided with shifting urban demographics. In 1957, a mayor-alderman ward-based form of city government was replaced by a new manager-commissioner citywide form of government.[54] This meant that the potential for translating the growing concentration of the city's black population in certain areas into corresponding black political strength and representation was diluted by new "at-large" city elections that instead reflected the political strength of a white majority electorate. Urban redevelopment in Little Rock effectively set in process structural changes in the 1950s that were already in the process of nullifying the racial changes that would take place in the following decades. Recent events have opened up a new chapter in the story. As with many other cities, urban development in Little Rock has begun to shift toward a redevelopment of previously abandoned downtown areas, potentially reversing the westward expansion of previous decades. In 1996, the River Market District development turned "a string of decaying warehouses into a viable neighborhood of trendy loft apartments, art galleries, bars and restaurants" in the downtown area. The charity foundation Heifer International's headquarters are nearby as is the new William Jefferson Clinton Presidential Library. Developers are eyeing downtown riverfront land encroaching into the traditionally black east end of the city to turn into a multimillion-dollar marina and condos. Exactly what this means for the city's race relations is as yet unclear. Potentially, it holds out the prospect of reunifying white and black areas of residence and bringing them back together again. Equally, it may represent the forward advance of the white western suburbs that threatens to steamroll what remains of the most integrated parts of the city and push blacks once again further out into the most marginalized fringes of the east. Already, this is the concern. As black east end resident Estella Watson points out, "If you are going to build condos along the river front, who can afford to live there? They're pushing blacks out. They're not giving us anything." Meanwhile, a change back to a ward-based system of city government in the 1990s may well give blacks a greater political voice in unfolding city affairs. Whichever way the new struggle over Little Rock's downtown goes, it promises to shape the future of the city and its race relations well into the twenty-first century just as fundamentally as the last surge of urban redevelopment did in the mid-twentieth century.[55]

NOTES

1. See, for example, Lawrence D. Reddick, *Crusader Without Violence: A Biography of Martin Luther King, Jr.* (New York: Harper & Brothers, 1959); Lerone Bennett, Jr., *What Manner of Man: A Biography of Martin Luther King, Jr.* (Chicago: Johnson Publishing, 1964); William Robert Miller, *Martin Luther King, Jr.: His Life, Martyrdom and Meaning for the World* (New York: Weybright and Talley, 1968); David L. Lewis, *King: A Critical Biography* (Urbana: University of Illinois Press, 1970); Jim Bishop, *The Days of Martin Luther King* (New York: G. P. Putnam's Sons, 1971).

2. William H. Chafe, *Civilities and Civil Rights: Greensboro, North Carolina and the Black Struggle For Freedom* (New York: Oxford University Press, 1980); Robert J. Norrell, *Reaping the Whirlwind: The Civil Rights Movement in Tuskegee* (New York: Alfred A. Knopf, 1985); David R. Colburn, *Racial Change and Community Crisis: St. Augustine, Florida, 1877–1980* (New York: Columbia University Press, 1985); John Dittmer, *Local People: The Struggle For Civil Rights in Mississippi* (Urbana: University of Illinois Press, 1994); Charles M. Payne, *I've Got the Light of Freedom: The Organizing Tradition and the Mississippi Freedom Struggle* (Berkeley: University of California Press, 1995); Glenn T. Eskew, *But For Birmingham: The Local and National Movements in the Civil Rights Struggle* (Chapel Hill: University of North Carolina Press, 1997); Adam Fairclough, *Race and Democracy: The Civil Rights Struggle in Louisiana, 1915–1972* (Athens: University of Georgia Press, 1995); Stephen G. N. Tuck, *Beyond Atlanta: The Struggle for Racial Equality in Georgia, 1940–1980* (Athens: University of Georgia Press, 2001); John A. Kirk, *Redefining the Color Line: Black Activism in Little Rock, Arkansas, 1940–1970* (Gainesville: University Press of Florida, 2002).

3. On women's activism in the movement see Vicki Crawford, Jacqueline Rouse, and Barbara Woods, eds., *Women in the Civil Rights Movement: Trailblazers and Torchbearers, 1941–1965* (Brooklyn: Carlson Publishing, 1990); Belinda Robnett, *How Long? How Long? African American Women in the Struggle for Civil Rights* (New York: Oxford University Press, 1997); Peter J. Ling and Sharon Monteith, eds., *Gender in the Civil Rights Movement* (New York: Garland Publishing, 1999) reprinted (New Brunswick, NJ: Rutgers University Press, 2004); Bettye Collier-Thomas and V. P. Franklin, eds., *Sisters in the Struggle: African American Women in the Civil Rights-Black Power Movement* (New York: New York University Press, 2001). On the role of violence and armed self-defense, see Timothy B. Tyson, *Radio Free Dixie: Robert F. Williams and the Roots of Black Power* (Chapel Hill: University of North Carolina Press, 1999) and Lance Hill, *The Deacons for Defense: Armed Resistance and the Civil Rights Movement* (Chapel Hill: University of North Carolina Press, 2004); on international dimensions see Michael L. Krenn, ed., *Race and US Foreign Policy During the Cold War* (New York: Garland Publishing, 1998); Michael L. Krenn, *Black Diplomacy: African Americans and the State Department, 1945–1969* (Armoruk, NY: M. E. Sharpe, Inc., 1999); Mary L. Dudziak, *Cold War Civil Rights: Race and the Image of Democracy* (Princeton, NJ: Princeton University Press, 2000); Thomas Borstelmann, *The Cold War and the Color Line: American Race Relations in the Global Arena* (Cambridge, MA: Harvard University Press, 2002); Carol Anderson, *Eyes Off the Prize: The United Nations and the African American Struggle for Human Rights, 1944–1955* (New York: Cambridge University Press, 2003).

4. Thomas J. Sugrue, *The Origins of the Urban Crisis: Race and Inequality in Postwar Detroit* (Princeton, NJ: Princeton University Press, 1996) and "Crabgrass-Roots Politics: Race, Rights and Reaction Against Liberalism in the Urban North, 1940–1964," *Journal of American History* 82 (Sept. 1995): pp. 551–78; Arnold R. Hirsch, *Making the Second Ghetto: Race and Housing in Chicago, 1940–1960* (Illinois: University of Chicago Press,

1983) and "Massive Resistance in the Urban North: Trumbull Park, Chicago, 1953–1966," *Journal of American History* 82 (Sept. 1995), 522–50. A number of other works have explored similar themes, notably and most recently, Robert O. Self, *American Babylon: Race and the Struggle for Postwar Oakland* (Princeton, NJ: Princeton University Press, 2003).

5. On King and the SCLC's Chicago campaign, see Alan B. Anderson and George W. Pickering, *Confronting the Color Line: The Broken Promise of the Civil Rights Movement in Chicago* (Athens: University of Georgia Press, 1986) and James R. Ralph, Jr., *Northern Protest: Martin Luther King, Jr., Chicago, and the Civil Rights Movement* (Cambridge, MA: Harvard University Press, 1993). On the 1966 civil rights bill see Stephen Grant Meyer, *As Long As They Don't Move Next Door: Segregation and Racial Conflict in American Neighborhoods* (Lanham, MD: Rowman and Littlefield, 2000).

6. See Kirk, *Redefining the Color Line*, chapter 5.

7. On black life in early Little Rock, see Paul D. Lack, "An Urban Slave Community: Little Rock, 1831–1862." *Arkansas Historical Quarterly* 41 (Spring 1982), pp. 258–87; Willard B. Gatewood, *Aristocrats of Color: the Black Elite, 1880–1920* (Bloomington: Indiana University Press, 1990), pp. 92–95; John William Graves, *Town and Country: Race Relations in an Urban/Rural Context, Arkansas, 1865–1905* (Fayetteville: University of Arkansas Press, 1990), chapter 6; Tom Dillard, "Perseverance: Black History in Pulaski County, Arkansas—An Excerpt." *Pulaski County Historical Review* 31 (Winter 1983), pp. 62–73.

8. *Writers' Program of the Work Projects Administration, Survey of Negroes in Little Rock and North Little Rock*, Compiled by the Writers' Program of the Work Projects Administration in the State of Arkansas, Little Rock, 1941, Special Collections Division, University of Arkansas Libraries, Little Rock, pp. 61–64.

9. On the Housing Act of 1949 see the special issue of *Housing Policy Debate* 11 (Issue 2, 2000), pp. 291–520 (published by the Fannie Mae Foundation and available online at http://www.fanniemaefoundation.org/programs/hpd/v11i2-index.shtml), particularly Robert E. Lang and Rebecca R. Sohmer, "Editors Introduction," Alexander von Hoffman, "A Study in Contradictions: The Origins and Legacy of the Housing Act of 1949," Arnold R. Hirsch, "Searching for 'Sound Negro Policy': A Racial Agenda for the Housing Acts of 1949 and 1954," Jon C. Teaford, "Urban Renewal and Its Aftermath," and Charles J. Orlebeke, "The Evolution of Low-Income Housing Policy, 1949 to 1999."

10. *Arkansas Gazette* (Little Rock) and *Arkansas Democrat* (Little Rock), May 10, 1950.

11. B. Finley Vinson, February 25, 1993 (Little Rock), interview with author.

12. Greater Little Rock Conference on Religion and Race, "Confronting the Little Rock Housing Problem," box 7, folder 76, Arkansas Council on Human Relations Papers, Special Collections, University of Arkansas Libraries, Fayetteville.

13. *Arkansas Gazette*, January 29, June 8, 1952.

14. *Arkansas Gazette*, August 29 and October 2, 1952. See also the materials on *R. O. Burgess et. al v. Little Rock Housing Authority et. al.* in Leffel and U. A. Gentry papers, box 1, folder 9, Special Collections, University of Arkansas Libraries, Little Rock.

15. See Nat Griswold, "The Second Reconstruction in Little Rock," 1968, unpublished manuscript in author's possession; Ben F. Johnson III, *Arkansas in Modern America, 1930–1999* (Fayetteville: University of Arkansas Press, 2000), pp. 148–61; Martha Walters, "Little Rock Urban Renewal," *Pulaski County Historical Review* 24 (March 1976), pp. 12–16; Margaret Arnold, "Little Rock's Vanishing Black Communities," *Arkansas Times*, June 1978, pp. 36–43; and Stuart Eurman, "Consolidating Cities: An Urban Fiction," *Pulaski County Historical Review* 42 (Spring 1994), pp. 19–22.

16. *Arkansas Gazette*, July 13, 1950; February 11, 1951.

17. "A Report of the Racial and Cultural Diversity Task Force," submitted to *The Steering Committee of Future—Little Rock*, December 31, 1992. Copy in author's possession.

18. *Arkansas Gazette*, February 15, 20, 21, 1953.

19. *Arkansas Gazette*, February 27, March 3, 4, 6, 1953.

20. *Arkansas Gazette*, March 6, 1953. For further discussion on Blossom's school policy and the 1957 Little Rock school crisis see John A. Kirk, "Massive Resistance and Minimum Compliance: The Origins of the 1957 Little Rock School Crisis," in Clive Webb, ed., *Massive Resistance: Southern Opposition to the Second Reconstruction* (New York: Oxford University Press, 2005).

21. Georg C. Iggers, "Arkansas Professor: The NAACP and the Grass Roots," p. 286, in Wilson Record and Jane Cassels Record, eds., *Little Rock, U.S.A.* (San Francisco: Chandler Publishing Co., 1960); Little Rock Board of Education to Legal Redress Committee NAACP, Arkansas, September 9, 1954, Virgil T. Blossom Papers, Special Collections Division, University of Arkansas Libraries, Fayetteville.

22. Iggers, "Arkansas Professor," pp. 286–87.

23. On Brown II and its aftermath, see J. Harvie Wilkinson III, *From Brown to Bakke: The Supreme Court and School Integration: 1954–1978* (New York: Oxford University Press, 1979), pp. 61–95.

24. *Southern School News* (Atlanta), July 1955, p. 3; Iggers, "Arkansas Professor," p. 287.

25. Iggers, "Arkansas Professor," p. 287.

26. Numan V. Bartley, *The Rise of Massive Resistance: Race and Politics in the South during the 1950s* (Baton Rouge: Louisiana State University Press, 1969), chapter 14.

27. Iggers, "Arkansas Professor," pp. 288–89.

28. *Southern School News*, February 1956, p. 11.

29. Ibid., March 1956, p. 4; Wiley A. Branton, "Little Rock Revisited: Desegregation to Resegregation," *Journal of Negro Education* 52 (Summer 1983), p. 253.

30. Iggers, "Arkansas Professor," p. 290.

31. Branton, "Little Rock Revisited," p. 254; Tony Freyer, *The Little Rock Crisis: A Constitutional Interpretation* (Westport, Conn.: Greenwood Press, 1984), pp. 56–58.

32. "Our Reason for Appeal," Rev. J. C. Crenchaw, n.d., box 4, folder 10, in Daisy Bates Papers, State Historical Society of Wisconsin, Madison; Branton, "Little Rock Revisited," pp. 255–56.

33. *Southern School News*, May 1957, p. 2; Branton, "Little Rock Revisited," pp. 255–56.

34. "Report of Conference Between Little Rock School Superintendent and NAACP Representatives, May 29, 1957," group II, series A, container 98, folder "Desegregation of Schools, Arkansas, Little Rock, Central High, 1956–1957," National Association for the Advancement of Colored People Papers, Manuscript Division, Library of Congress, Washington, DC.

35. Ibid.

36. Ibid.

37. Ibid.; *Arkansas State Press* (Little Rock), June 7, 1957.

38. Mrs. L. C. Bates to Mr. Robert L. Carter, August 2, 1957, group II, series A, container 98, folder "Desegregation of Schools, Arkansas, Little Rock, Central High, 1956–1957," NAACP Papers (Washington, DC); Virgil T. Blossom, *It Has Happened Here* (New York: Harper and Row, 1959), pp. 19–21.

39. Daisy Bates, *The Long Shadow of Little Rock: A Memoir* (New York: David McKay Company, Inc., 1962), p. 59.

40. Unsigned letter to E. Grainger Williams, March 25, 1959, box 1, folder 1, E. Grainger Williams Papers, Special Collections, University of Arkansas Libraries, Little Rock. On race and class issues in Little Rock see also C. Fred Williams, "Class: The Central Issue

in the 1957 Little Rock School Crisis," *Arkansas Historical Quarterly* 56 (Autumn 1997), pp. 341–44; Karen Anderson, "The Little Rock School Desegregation Crisis: Moderation and Social Conflict," *Journal of Southern History* 70 (August 2004), pp. 603–36; Pete Daniel, *Lost Revolutions: The South in the 1950s* (Chapel Hill: University of North Carolina Press, 2000), chapter 12.

41. *Southern School News*, September 1957, p. 6; Roy Reed, *Faubus: The Life and Times of an American Prodigal* (Fayetteville: University of Arkansas Press, 1997), pp. 196–97; Robert Sherrill, *Gothic Politics in the Deep South* (New York: Ballantine Books, 1969), pp. 105–6.

42. On the Mother's League, see Graeme Cope, "'A Thorn in the Side'?: The Mothers' League of Central High School and the Little Rock Desegregation Crisis of 1957," *Arkansas Historical Quarterly* 57 (Summer 1998), pp. 160–90.

43. Neil R. McMillen, "The White Citizens Council and Resistance to School Desegregation in Arkansas," *Arkansas Historical Quarterly* 30 (Summer 1971), p. 104; Reed, *Faubus*, p. 188.

44. Warren Olney III, Assistant US Attorney General, to Arthur B. Caldwell, US Attorney General, September 13, 1957, box 5, folder 2, Arthur Brann Caldwell Papers, Special Collections Division, University of Arkansas Libraries, Fayetteville; Reed, *Faubus*, p. 199; Corrine Silverman, *The Little Rock Story* (Tuscaloosa: University of Alabama Press, 1958), pp. 6–7.

45. See Reed, *Faubus*.

46. Branton, "Little Rock Revisited," pp. 259–60; Reed, *Faubus*, pp. 199–200; Silverman, *The Little Rock Story*, p. 7.

47. See Kirk, *Redefining the Color Line*, chapter 5.

48. Mrs. Adolphine Fletcher Terry to Mr. William H. McClean, Commercial National Bank, Little Rock, Arkansas, March 9, 1970, Fletcher-Terry Papers, series I, box 3, folder 3, Special Collections, University of Arkansas Libraries, Little Rock.

49. Albert Porter, May 7, 1993 (Little Rock), interview with author.

50. Terry to McClean, March 9, 1970, Fletcher-Terry Papers.

51. *Arkansas Democrat-Gazette* (Little Rock), October 26, 2003.

52. "Report of the Racial and Cultural Diversity Task Force."

53. Howard Rabinowitz, *Race Relations in the Urban South*, 1865–1890 (New York: Oxford University Press, 1978) argues that segregation emerged as an alternative to separation and exclusion during that period. Graves, *Town and Country* and "Jim Crow in Arkansas: A Reconsideration of Urban Race Relations in the Post Reconstruction South," *Journal of Southern History* 55 (August 1989), pp. 421–48, argues for a relatively more fluid and complex set of race relations emerging across Arkansas at the time.

54. Elizabeth Jacoway, "Taken By Surprise: Little Rock Business Leaders and Desegregation," p. 21, in Elizabeth Jacoway and David R. Colburn, eds., *Southern Businessmen and Desegregation* (Baton Rouge: Louisiana State University Press, 1982).

55. *Arkansas Democrat-Gazette*, May 31, 2001 and October 6, 2002.

CHAPTER 2

THE PRESSURES
OF THE PEOPLE

MILTON A. GALAMISON, THE PARENTS' WORKSHOP, AND RESISTANCE TO SCHOOL INTEGRATION IN NEW YORK CITY, 1960–63

LISA YVETTE WALLER

THIS ESSAY EXPLORES THE EARLY EFFORTS OF the Reverend Milton A. Galamison and the Parents' Workshop for Equality in New York City Schools to organize for public school integration in the 1960s. In order to appreciate fully the historical significance of the endeavors of Galamison and the workshop, it is necessary to consider trends in the literature of the civil rights movement. Among most scholars of the civil rights movement and Americans in general, the African American liberation struggle and the resistance that it generated are understood to have been Southern phenomena. Too often, civil rights historiography focuses on the Southern movement, excluding activism in the North. This Southern orientation dominates in the production of local studies and general histories.[1] Following this pattern, John Ditmer, Charles Payne, and Stewart Burns have produced acclaimed works since 1994; each of these is a local investigation focusing on the civil rights struggle in the Deep South.[2] Glen Eskew's recent work explores the intersection of local activism in Birmingham with the national movement. Although his description of the national movement includes a Northern base of organizational power (quintessentially embodied in the National Association for the Advancement of Colored People [NAACP]), the work fails to consider Northern grassroots civil rights activism. The action of Eskew's national movement is in the South.[3] The failure to pay attention to the Northern struggle results from a narrow perspective concerning the sensibility of Northern African Americans that is shared by many scholars. They argue that nonviolent direct action did not appeal to people who lived in Northern ghettos. The notion that inner-city African Americans rejected the tactics that proved so effective in the South goes unquestioned in large part because of historians' tendency to take up the thread of Northern protest with the advent of the rebellions in 1964.

John Salmond begins his recent work on the movement with the New Deal and *Brown*; however, he does not give great consideration to protest in the Northern arena until his discussion of the mid-1960s.[4] In their volumes, Robert Weisbrot and Thomas Brooks follow similar trajectories, turning to Northern protest late in the movement's history.[5] Whereas Weisbrot's belated references to the Northern struggle give the impression that the civil rights movement was a Southern phenomenon until the 1960s, Brooks explicitly accepts this chronology, stating that the civil rights struggle moved from the South to the North during this period.[6] This progression is rearticulated by Jack Bloom in his discussion of the movement.[7]

In their recent work, Armstead Robinson and Patricia Sullivan engage in a reevaluation of the movement's history; however, they fail to reconsider the accepted locus of the civil rights struggle. They also assume the movement to have been centered in the South. They begin: "A quarter century ago, the civil rights movement stirred the conscience of the nation while contributing to the demise of Jim Crow. In the decade following the 1954 *Brown* decision, the movement for racial equality in America gained critical momentum, *fueled by the courage, determination, and hope of countless individuals in communities through the* South . . . Despite the far-reaching gains of the *southern struggle*, riots in northern urban centers made clear the extent to which racial injustice and inequality permeated the fabric of American life."[8]

Adhering to the trend in chronology, Robinson and Sullivan's work does not address the urban North until 1965. Turning their attention to the conditions of African Americans in the ghettos, in their work of 1991, they say:

"School desegregation and the right to vote had little relevance to the lives of increasing numbers of poor blacks trapped in the nation's decaying inner cities. The widely hailed victories of the southern movement only increased the levels of frustration and despair in urban centers, and this despair helped to spark rioting, particularly in cities."[9]

In a discussion of 1978, preceding the one just cited above, Dorothy Newman, Nancy Amidel, and Barbara Carter address the people of Harlem and Bedford-Stuyvesant. Arguing against systematic Northern resistance to racial oppression, they say, "Theirs was not the carefully organized and skillfully articulated protest of the nonviolent movement in the South. This was spontaneous."[10] These analyses posit a passive, disorganized, inarticulate African American population in the urban North. They presume the Northern African Americans waited for the struggles of their Southern counterparts to bring them liberation. They suggest that African Americans in the urban centers of the North exploded into chaos because the Southern initiative had not changed their lives. The idea that Northern African Americans began to challenge their oppression in the mid-1960s, more than a decade after the winds of change began to transform the South, obscures significant local organizing efforts that were sustained in Northern inner-city communities over long periods of time, not only during the twentieth century, but also earlier, in the 1800s.[11]

As the Parents' Workshop activities demonstrate, the New York school integration campaign (the epitome of the civil rights movement in the city) was highly organized. It was neither chaotic nor impulsive. Well before the advent of the urban rebellions, activists employed research, rallies, and boycotts to forward integration. Counter to the expectations created by the literature, the movement grew more organized in the mid-1960s as activists in Galamison's Parents' Workshop and other grassroots groups organized mass meetings, and school boycotts that captured the attention of large numbers of African American integrationists, their allies, and their adversaries in New York. In 1964, the year said to have ushered in a time of disorganized rioting in New York City, the first citywide school boycott was called by the Parents' Workshop and the Citywide Committee for Integrated Schools. This "sit-out" was the culmination of more than a decade of organizing and protest that was conceived and carried out by the workshop and other local groups in the city. As the New York City example shows, Northern African Americans themselves organized and demonstrated for change in their communities during the 1950s and 1960s. Their expectations were elevated by the ideology, rhetoric, and actions that surrounded these local efforts, not by the victories of the Southern struggle alone.[12]

The promise of organized African American activism in New York City was embodied by the Parents' Workshop. Founded by Galamison in 1959, the workshop was deeply influenced by the minister, who served as the group's president and provided much of its ideological direction throughout its existence. Echoing themes that Galamison had articulated publicly for a decade, the workshop set the following objectives for itself: "to work for the integration of the schools of New York; [to work] for full and equal opportunity for learning for all the children of our city; to end all school discrimination against Negro and Puerto Rican children; and to preserve, improve and expand our free and democratic public school system."[13] Members of the organization argued that those with children in the schools needed to take the initiative in order to overcome the resistance of school officials to integration. Workshop leaders encouraged parent members to recruit additional people with children in the schools to the organization.[14] In order to do this, parents quickly became versed in the school integration issue. They gained confidence and ability as they participated in the workshop's efforts.[15] Accepting Galamison's belief that activism was central to the task ahead, members understood that they would have to organize and force change upon the system.

The Parents' Workshop was a grassroots enterprise, initially housed at Siloam Presbyterian Church. The group was poorly funded, offering memberships at the rate of one dollar for individual "boosters" and ten dollars for organizations like Parent-Teacher Associations (PTAs), which comprised a significant proportion of workshop membership.[16] Regular meetings were held in Brooklyn and Manhattan.[17] The Parents' Workshop also had outlets in Queens and the Bronx.[18] Workshop offices were open during the summer and the school year to offer information and coordinate activities concerned with bringing integration to the city's public schools.[19]

Most of the Parents' Workshop leaders and members were African American women who had children in the public schools. Of ten area chairmen in Brooklyn, nine were women.[20] Significant PTA and Parent Association (PA) participation insured that rank-and-file membership was primarily female as well. The workshop acknowledged its female dominance when, in an attempt to attract more attention to segregated conditions in Brooklyn, it sent form letters to ministers declaring, "We mothers, grandmothers, [and] aunts must round up our families, friends and neighbors and start *now* to rectify the ills in our community!"[21] These women radicalized their child-rearing and other familial roles, conflating them with political protest.

The female initiative in the Parents' Workshop is not surprising; women have often taken the lead in matters related to child rearing and education. Female empowerment in the Parents' Workshop also conformed to the vitality of women's leadership that was evident within the organizations and institutions over which Galamison presided. During the 1960s, thirteen of eighteen deacons and nine of twenty-six ruling elders at Siloam Presbyterian church were women.[22] The proportion of female deacons and ruling elders had risen significantly following Galamison's installation as head minister of the church.[23] Women's participation on the elder board was particularly significant because the elders managed the church rather than engaging in the committee and auxiliary work that church-women traditionally performed.[24] Women within the Siloam congregation must have been gratified to hear the minister declare from the pulpit, "We have no idea of what women can be because they have never been permitted to be all they can be. Man has had every opportunity to show what he really is; and he has shown what he is by the very fact that he has deprived women of the same possibility."[25] Although leadership among Parents' Workshop women resulted primarily from their drive and initiative, Galamison's rejection of male domination and his receptivity to women's power provided a positive environment within which women's leadership could grow.

The Composition of the Parents' Workshop reflected an important tradition of African American women's school activism in New York. This activity was widespread in the city during the 1950s. In May 1952, parents, the overwhelming majority of whom were women, organized the Committee for the Improvement of Textbooks. The committee was organized to evaluate texts used by children in the public schools. Its goal was to eliminate books that presented negative stereotypes of African Americans and other ethnic groups.[26] Members also hoped to exclude from the system texts that completely ignored minority groups.[27] PA-affiliated women who were interviewed by reporters for the *New York Amsterdam News* in the 1950s criticized parents who were not active in their PAs and PTAs.[28] They argued that this negligence had a negative impact on the children living in low-income areas.[29] In March 1959, mothers at PS 83 in Brooklyn success-fully concluded a three-year struggle to end the double session at their children's school.[30] This female activist tradition was pushed even further once the work-shop was operative in the city.

In 1960, Milton Galamison, Annie Stein, Thelma Hamilton, and the other members of the Parents' Workshop for Equality in New York City Schools set out to force the Board of Education to take specific action aimed at achieving citywide integration in the schools.[31] Following up on parents demands, workshop leaders requested a meeting with Superintendent Theobald for April 25 at school headquarters.[32] Well aware that school officials required coercion if they were to move, Galamison's group orchestrated a rally to be held at Siloam a few days before the meeting.[33] Intensifying the pressure on Theobald, the workshop arranged for people attending the rally to be given postcards demanding integration that were addressed to the superintendent. Workshop members also urged participants at the rally to attend the coming meeting with Theobald.[34] This gathering demonstrated the workshop's ability to mobilize a significant number of New Yorkers around the schools issue. The rally also showed that the Parents' Workshop had allies in other organizations concerned with New York's public schools. Representing the workshop, Galamison was joined on the rally's program by officers from the Intergroup Committee on New York's Public Schools and the Urban League of Greater New York.[35]

The April rally successfully attracted support for the workshop and attendance at the meeting with Theobald. Two hundred parents descended on 110 Livingston Street to speak with the superintendent. Galamison began with an introduction in which he cast workshop members as Americans exercising their democratic right to protest.[36] He shared parents' chief complaint: They were upset that school policies were reducing the possibility of African American children obtaining access to a more integrated educational environment. Galamison spoke specifically to the fact that, by the spring of 1960, only children on part-time instruction could qualify for busing to a less-crowded school.[37] Further, rather than being allowed to bypass closer schools in order to attend a more distant facility where their enrollment would contribute to creating an integrated environment, children were being sent to the nearest institutions that could accommodate them.[38] Following Galamison, several women who represented PAs and PTAs in Bedford-Stuyvesant, Williamsburg, and Brownsville spoke.[39] These activists chastised Theobald, arguing that his timid gradualism proved that he was more concerned with placating racists than with ensuring the rights of African American children.[40] Before leaving the meeting, workshop members demanded voluntary transfers aimed at integration without regard to utilization issues or multiple sessions, teacher equalization, and a program and timetable for desegregating the city's schools.[41] These were not forthcoming.

Having seen the effectiveness of the school boycott during the 1958 Brooklyn Seven struggle, Galamison and the Parents' Workshop resolved to produce a massive Brooklyn protest in order to force the board to act.[42] At rallies, the Parents' Workshop threatened to initiate its most dramatic demonstration to date—a mass "sit-out" in which at least two thousand boycotting children and their parents would gather outside of school buildings and local superintendents' offices until their concerns were addressed concretely.[43] Toward this end, the workshop organized for six months in the spring and summer of 1960. The structure of the workshop allowed them to gain a significant amount of support within the communities; although the organization was citywide, the workshop was broken down into smaller units that served individual boroughs and neighborhoods.[44] Local organization and leadership allowed grassroots activists to attract neighborhood parents and groups with great efficacy. During the 1960 campaign, area captains obtained the mailing lists of churches and other organizations from individuals in their local membership. They created distribution committees to stuff envelopes and otherwise spread the word about integration actions.[45] The church committee garnered the support of ministers and congregations that offered their churches to accommodate children who would sit out in September.[46] The rallies that were held during the summer of 1960 demonstrated the importance that the issue of educational equity held for African Americans in New York and made the threat of a boycott more palpable to school officials.[47] This activity sprang directly from the workshops' insistence on a program of dramatic action for integration.[48]

The Parents' Workshop tactics succeeded; the boycott threat led Theobald to call a meeting with the workshop and other civil rights leaders on the day before school was scheduled to open in September. As a direct result of the political pressure applied by the Parents' Workshop, Theobald agreed to implement the Open Enrollment program, a permissive zoning initiative that was the first desegregation plan to be attempted in New York City's public schools.[49] The workshop continued with preparations for the boycott until the superintendent agreed to include elementary schools in the program.[50] With this concession won, the group called off the demonstration, but their work over the summer reaffirmed the effectiveness of organized, direct action at the grassroots level.[51] Justified, Galamison later reflected in the Parents' Workshop newsletter that "New York responded only to the threats and pressures of the people . . . There is a lesson to be learned from this. It means that the only course for the people is social action."[52] The importance of the role of the Parents' Workshop in producing Open Enrollment cannot be overstated. Their effort belies the notion that the board voluntarily implemented the program in the absence of sustained effort on the part of African American activists and parents.[53]

Open Enrollment began as a pilot project in September 1960 and expanded into a full program of the public school system in September 1961.[54] The board of education's Central Zoning Unit selected Open Enrollment schools based on the ethnic composition of the institutions and the rate of space utilization. At the elementary and junior high school levels, "receiving" schools had 75 percent or more "other" students and were utilized below 90 percent.[55] "Sending" schools were 90 percent or more African American or Puerto Rican.[56] Participation in the program was completely optional; pupils received an application that their parents completed if they were interested in having their children transferred to one of the receiving schools on the Open Enrollment roster.[57]

Ironically, though the Open Enrollment Program was the New York City school system's first major concession to school integrationists, it also embodied a major component of official resistance: the voluntarism that the board and the superintendent promoted during the school integration struggle. Although many observers thought it laughable that Southern white officials, parents, and teachers would take it upon themselves to create multiracial school environments, officials in New York adhered to voluntarism throughout the 1950s and 1960s as a visible method of producing school integration. The belief that this approach would effectively bring racial balance to the New York City public schools further indicates that New York's school officials viewed the Northern school predicament as fundamentally different from the Southern situation. Additionally, they behaved as though Southern white people were fundamentally different from those in the North. Whereas it would take federal troops and national attention to compel Southern whites to relinquish enclaves of white privilege, school policymakers in New York relied on whites to surrender willingly to integration. New York school officials took the lead neither in developing a strong integration policy nor in compelling public school children and their parents to participate in the initiatives that were attempted.

The Parents' Workshop advanced where school officials retreated; members put a tremendous amount of time and effort into making Open Enrollment a success. They published the reading scores and locations of the receiving schools that were in the program.[58] The workshop informed the parents of potential Open Enrollment participants about transportation routes and led them on tours of receiving schools.[59] Area chairpersons served as facilitators for parents who wanted information or needed assistance in applying to the program.[60] Additionally, the workshop announced that the Jefferson Avenue Educational Center, housed in Galamison's Bedford-Stuyvesant church, would provide remediation in reading and math in order to facilitate the successful adjustment of Open Enrollment students to their new schools. The strength of the Parents' Workshop in Brooklyn led to the highest percentage of transfers occurring in that borough.[61]

In order to keep Open Enrollment and integration at the center of the city's concerns, Galamison repeatedly introduced the workshop's agenda to politicians and school officials in the city. Mayor Robert Wagner's attempt to maintain the fiction that the schools fell outside of the political arena[62] was challenged by Galamison's demands that he demonstrate leadership on school integration. Angry that the mayor had neglected to appoint an African American to a committee that he organized to study the schools, Galamison arranged meetings with the Republican candidate for mayor, Wagner himself, and the candidates for city comptroller.[63] Later, when a new board of education was seated, Galamison wrote every member in order to acquaint them with the workshop and present them with the threat that boycotts and other actions would continue until the board extended Open Enrollment and produced a plan and a timetable for desegregation of the city's schools.[64]

The aggressive activism of workshop members caused New Yorkers to view the organization as a central source of information and advocacy regarding the board of education's Open Enrollment program and the school system's integration policy. The organization's status as the primary organization to help communities grapple with Open Enrollment is reflected in the numerous requests for speakers and information that local people directed to the organization. Leaders in PAs repeatedly contacted the workshop, requesting individuals who could inform local parents about the program.[65] Once the board of education approved the fourth and fifth grades at PS 289 for participation in Open Enrollment, the chairman of the school's education committee asked that the Parents' Workshop supply a member who could discuss implementation of the program at this grade level.[66] The chairman of the Community School Action Committee for Districts 43 and 44 in Brooklyn expressed a desire to meet with Galamison and the workshop to discuss the schools issue.[67] Presidents of the PAs of many city schools requested that workshop representatives attend meetings designed to stimulate parents and assist them in helping their children with schoolwork.[68] When members of the Fort Greene Houses Tenants' Association decided to fight for better education in their neighborhood schools, they asked that the workshop provide them with information on zoning, comparative class size, racial demographics, and teacher experience.[69] Association member Clara Krell said, "We know from observation and experience that things should be different, [but] we do not have the figures to back us up, and we are sure that in any discussion we would present our arguments more strongly if we had statistics."[70] This was exactly the type of function that the workshop was intended to perform; statistician Annie Stein and others could supply data to support the empirical knowledge of neighborhood residents, information that school officials rarely respected. More than a year after her initial request, Krell had become secretary of the Tenants' Association and continued to rely on the workshop for speakers and information regarding the schools.[71]

Despite the efforts of the Parents' Workshop, there was only limited participation in the Open Enrollment program. During the pilot year, fewer than 3 percent of the pupils who received applications actually transferred to receiving schools.[72] The rate of involvement did not improve significantly for the duration of the program.[73] Ultimately, Open Enrollment failed appreciably to improve racial balance in the city's schools because school officials undermined the plan and because African Americans were ambivalent about the program.

The lack of enthusiasm with which many school officials approached Open Enrollment as a remedy for segregation was initially evident in their hesitancy to have the public view desegregation as the program's primary emphasis. Frequently, school officials stressed that Open Enrollment was meant to manage more effectively discrepancies in school utilization.[74] Evidence indicates that the sentiment of school personnel ultimately led them to sabotage the program. Many parents reported that they did not receive detailed information on eligibility and participation in the program.[75] One reason for this was the fear, held by several principals in the ghetto, that a "brain drain" would occur in their institutions if the brightest students with the most capable parents availed themselves of the transfer program and moved to schools outside of the area.[76] Some understood this response as a reasonable desire to retain model students in the ghetto, where they could inspire other children.[77] Others believed that this reaction reflected a cynical fear that children from the ghetto might leave their neighborhood schools and perform better at receiving schools in white areas. This improvement would reflect badly on ghetto school personnel, demonstrating that the educational problems in the inner city were not due to deficiencies among the pupils but to neglect by teachers and principals.[78] Further, skeptics felt that the brain drain argument proved that employees in ghetto schools believed that there were only a few bright children among their students.[79] Responding to various concerns, principals often circulated Open Enrollment transfer information at times calculated to produce a low response. At other times, school personnel failed to distribute material at all.[80] Even when school employees issued transfer request forms in a timely fashion, the turnaround time for receipt by school principals could be quite short.[81] Sabotage was not alone in undercutting participation; the relatively low number of receiving schools at the junior high school level meant that many families wanting to transfer under the Open Enrollment program were denied their requests.[82]

The Parents' Workshop attempted to remedy many of the problems that families experienced as they tried to participate in the program. When significant numbers of parents attended a workshop meeting and reported that their applications for admittance to Open Enrollment junior high schools were denied, the Parents' Workshop investigated the amount of space available in participating junior high schools.[83] The workshop eventually suggested that the designated racial percentages of receiving schools be altered, allowing more institutions to participate; however, members could not fully develop a plan because the board of education refused to provide the workshop with space utilization and racial composition data.[84] In the face of official opposition, the Parents' Workshop held an overnight sit-in at 110 Livingston Street and won placement in integrated schools for those children who participated in the demonstration.[85]

The Parents' Workshop engaged in a hard sell in order to overcome not only the resistance of school officials but also the ambivalence of African American and Puerto Rican parents. Members organized rallies at which Galamison discussed reasons that African Americans and Puerto Ricans should transfer out of their neighborhood schools.[86] In public gatherings and literature, the workshop unfailingly presented the minister's views on the benefits of integration. The group argued that children who transferred would develop improved self-esteem.[87] They would be better prepared for job training and college, and they would be less fearful of competition with individuals from different backgrounds.[88] Fact sheets on Open Enrollment in the primary grades warned, "THIS IS IMPORTANT! Most of the damage suffered by our children because of separate and unequal schools occurs in the elementary grades . . . compare the reading levels of the sending and receiving schools, and you will see the advantage of transferring your child."[89] Workshop literature also appealed to social justice and race pride, equating participation in the transfer program with action aimed at dismantling the edifice of segregation and discrimination in the South.[90] Finally, the group argued that Open Enrollment would teach children of all races to work together without any false sense of inferiority or superiority.[91]

While the workshop pressured the board to include more schools on the Open Enrollment roster, many African American parents demonstrated their impatience with the program. Parents complained that Open Enrollment put the burden for integrating the schools on children of color, and they insisted that whites ought to share in the effort to create a more just society.[92] Both Puerto Rican and African American parents were hesitant to send their children far from home to attend school. Parents also worried that their children would be the victims of mistreatment in hostile receiving schools.[93] Their concern was not misplaced. The Parents' Workshop received several complaints of children being segregated by classroom in integrated Open Enrollment schools.[94] One observer in the Bronx described how Open Enrollment worked in a neighborhood elementary school. Approximately thirty children arrived at the school by bus. School employees did not allow the Open Enrollment students to enter the school yard with the other students. Instead, they entered the school through a side door and remained in their classroom all day. These Open Enrollment students even had lunch and recess in their classroom.[95] White parents whose children attended a receiving school in Flatbush complained to Galamison that Open Enrollment transfer students were being segregated in the cafeteria.[96] Unconvincingly, the principal explained that the children were contained in their section of the lunchroom because they were served hot soup that they might spill on other students if they had access to the entire space.[97]

Ironically, the fact that poor educational conditions in the ghetto were so widespread informed the decisions of some parents to keep their children in inner-city schools, forgoing participation in the Open Enrollment program. These parents saw educational neglect in the ghetto as a community problem. From the perspective of many parents, Open Enrollment provided individual children with the possibility of breaking free from the constraints of the ghetto and having an improved chance at success, but the benefits of participation in the program were not to be shared by those who remained in the community. According to this understanding, neighborhood schools were not improved through the Open Enrollment initiative. Indeed, voluntary transfer plans were not designed to integrate or otherwise benefit ghetto schools.[98] Community-focused parents believed that reliance on the program failed to serve the collective. Instead, Open Enrollment drew attention away from the poor-quality schools that continued to miseducate children who remained in the ghettos.[99] Writing in the Parents' Workshop newsletter, African American parent Barbara Bonhomme stated this position definitively. She began with a discussion of the positive educational experiences that her son and daughter had after they transferred to an integrated school. She continued:

"Individual triumphs are not enough, however. We must remember that the Negro people can only truly rise (and our own children with them), when *all* children are taught equally. Open enrollment is a tiny wedge of freedom, pushed into a school system which degrades and oppresses nonwhite people."[100]

Bonhomme was cognizant of Open Enrollment's limitations; nevertheless, she and the Parents' Workshop saw the program as an important step toward integration. They hoped that mixed schooling would ultimately ensure that all children were taught equally. Skeptical parents rejected the idea that the solution to inequality in education was to be found in leaving the neighborhood to pursue integrated instruction. One parent complained that transfer programs improperly suggested to children "that to receive anything good, they must leave the Negro neighborhoods."[101] Activist Olivia Taylor rejected integrated public education because she did not feel that it provide a proper context for the development of a positive African American image for her daughter.[102] Reflecting on the Open Enrollment initiative, parent, teacher, and activist Gwen Timmons argued that she and other African Americans were "brainwashed" into believing that white people had the best of everything and that children from the ghetto would improve simply by gaining access to white schools. She evoked Washingtonian ideology when considering the program's shortcomings, declaring, "I believe in working on putting down your bucket where you are and making the people accountable for teaching your children teach them where they are."[103]

During the early 1960s, professor of social work and school activist Preston Wilcox prepared a report on an East Harlem-Yorkville transfer program in which he, too, argued that initiatives that drew African American children from local classrooms stigmatized African American schools and damaged the community by siphoning off the strongest students and their parents.[104] For Wilcox and the parents whose ideas he shared, the solution to the schools problem involved improving local schools, even if they remained segregated.[105] Those who declared their preference to stay in the neighborhood schools and to demand remedial programs and extra services reflected concern not only for their children but also for the schools in their communities.[106] Galamison persisted in his antagonism toward parents who subordinated integration to equalization. Believing that they had been hoodwinked into accepting continued segregation, he argued adamantly against their position.[107] Galamison certainly had to justify integration to white racists and African American nationalists;[108] however, the Open Enrollment debate illustrates the extent to which the minister and the workshop also had to defend their integrationist program to ordinary African Americans who did not promote a nationalist agenda.

Galamison's hostility notwithstanding, many community-focused African Americans continued to forward alternative visions of equal education for ghetto children. Their rejection of the transfer program indicates that locally based remedies for unequal education did not result simply from frustration with persistent segregation. Rather, they sprang in large part from a community-centered oppositional thought that informed African American demands for power well in advance of the 1966 Intermediate School 201 incident, the harbinger of Black Power politics in the New York City public schools crisis.

By 1963, when Open Enrollment was replaced by the Free Choice Transfer Plan, many parents and civil rights leaders had turned away from voluntary transfer initiatives as solutions to the problem of segregation in the schools.[109] Increasingly, they began to demand school reorganization, pairings, and other nonvoluntary plans that would compel white students and their families to take on the burden of integrating the system.[110] The rejection of voluntary transfers also resulted from the board's unwillingness to fortify Open Enrollment with more far-reaching initiatives. When the Parents' Workshop won Open Enrollment as a concession from the board of education, they viewed it as the beginning of what should have become an effective, citywide drive in the direction of integration.[111] Toward this end, Galamison and the Parents' Workshop consistently demanded a plan on citywide integration that included a schedule for its completion.[112] They were repeatedly denied. In the face of Open Enrollment's failure to engender further initiatives toward integration and given the minimal numbers of children, relative to those enrolled in the system, who actually transferred, the program was ultimately considered a failure.[113] Following the pattern of permissive transfer schemes in general,[114] Open Enrollment in New York City caused no significant long-term desegregation.[115] Aware of this failure, Galamison and the Parents' Workshop were left to organize a citywide coalition and a series of major school boycotts designed to intensify the pressure toward achieving integration throughout New York City.

NOTES

1. Notable exceptions include Alan Anderson and George Pickering's work on the Chicago public school integration struggle of the 1950s and 1960s; James Farmer's discussion of integrationist nonviolent direct action campaigns in Chicago, New York, and other northern cities in the 1940s; and Clayborne Carson's exploration of the challenges that confronted Northern SNCC chapters in the 1960s. See Alan B. Anderson and George W. Pickering, *Confronting the Color Line: The Broken Promise of the Civil Rights Movement in Chicago* (Athens: University of Georgia Press, 1986); James Farmer, *Lay Bare the Heart: An Autobiography of the Civil Rights Movement* (New York: Arbor House, 1985); Clayborne Carson, *In Struggle: SNCC and the Black Awakening of the 1960s* (Cambridge: Harvard University Press, 1981). Just as I prepared "Holding Back the Dawn" for submission in its final form, Clarence Taylor's work *Knocking at Our Own Door* was released. Earlier, Taylor produced a study of African American churches in Brooklyn and, during the research phase, became interested in Galamison. It is gratifying to know that I am not alone in my assessment that Galamison is an important figure in the civil rights struggle. Although the sources led us in similar directions, we have pursued different avenues of inquiry. I am particularly interested in exploring the legacy of African American school protest and placing the New York City school integration movement into the context of African Americans' debates over separate and integrated education. This forces the historian to reckon with Galamison's failure to address adequately and responsibly the best means of bringing the benefits of equal education to the masses of children in the ghetto. I also find that the emergence of the movement is illuminated by an in-depth exploration of school conditions and the politics surrounding the "discovery" of inequality in the system. See Clarence Taylor, *Knocking at Our Own Door: Milton A. Galamison and the Struggle to Integrate New York City Schools* (New York: Columbia University Press, 1997).
2. Stewart Burns, ed., *Daybreak of Freedom: The Montgomery Bus Boycott* (Chapel Hill: University of North Carolina Press, 1997); John Dittmer, *Local People: The Struggle for Civil Rights in Mississippi* (Urbana: University of Illinois Press, 1994); Charles M. Payne, *I've Got the Light of Freedom: The Organizing Tradition and the Mississippi Freedom Struggle* (Berkeley: University of California Press, 1995).
3. Glenn T. Eskew, *But for Birmingham: The Local and National Movements in the Civil Rights Struggle* (Chapel Hill: University of North Carolina Press, 1997), pp. 14–52.
4. Salmond does not turn to the North until his final chapter, which is tellingly entitled "The End of the Movement." See John A. Salmond, *"My Mind Set on Freedom": A History of the Civil Rights Movement, 1954–1968* (Chicago: Ivan R. Dee, 1997).
5. Robert Weisbrot, *Freedom Bound: A History of America's Civil Rights Movement* (New York: W. W. Norton, 1990), pp. 238–242, and Thomas R. Brooks, *Walls Come Tumbling Down: A History of the Civil Rights Movement, 1940–1970* (Englewood Cliffs, NJ: Prentice-Hall, 1974), pp. 232–233. Weisbrot and Brooks look at school activism in New

York City, but in the isolated context of the 1960s. Weisbrot considers the Ocean Hill-Brownsville affair of 1967–68 and the subsequent United Federation of Teachers strike. Brooks discusses the school boycott of 1964.

6. Brooks, *Walls Come Tumbling Down*, p. 192.
7. Jack M. Bloom, *Class, Race, and the Civil Rights Movement* (Bloomington: Indiana University Press, 1987), pp. 1, 186.
8. Armstead L. Robinson and Patricia Sullivan, "Reassessing the History of the Civil Rights Movement," in Armstead L. Robinson and Patricia Sullivan, eds., *New Directions in Civil Rights Studies* (Charlottesville: University Press of Virginia, 1991), p. 1; emphasis added.
9. Ibid., p. 5.
10. Dorothy K. Newman et al., *Protest, Politics, and Prosperity: Black Americans and White Institutions, 1940–1975* (New York: Pantheon, 1978), p. 21.
11. August Meier and Elliot Rudwick point to a tradition of nonviolent direct action protest aimed at segregated schools in the North during these periods. See August Meier and Elliot Rudwick, "The Origins of Nonviolent Direct Action in Afro-American Protest: A Note on Historical Discontinuities," in August Meier and Elliot Rudwick, eds., *Along the Color Line: Explorations in the Black Experience* (Urbana: University of Illinois Press, 1976), pp. 359–362, 378–379.
12. The resistance that suffused the ranks of high level school officials, local school personnel, and various communities constricted and ultimately suffocated the school integration movement in New York City. The disappointment of this initiative provided a direct rationale for the level of African American frustration and despair that was manifest in the urban rebellions of the 1960s.
13. Parents' Workshop for Equality in New York City Schools, "Constitution of the Parents' Workshop for Equality in N.Y.C. Schools," November 1960, Galamison Papers, SHSW. Members of the Parents' Workshop were agitated by the persistent retardation, low standardized test scores, undertrained teachers, and decaying physical plants that plagued the children of New York's ghettos.
14. Parents' Workshop for Equality in New York City Schools, "Fact Sheet on the Open Enrollment Schools—1961," Galamison Papers, SHSW.
15. *News from the Parents' Workshop for Equality in New York City Schools*, February 1961, Galamison Papers, SHSW; Dorothy Lane to Area Captains, August 25, 1960, Galamison Papers, SHSW.
16. *News from the Parents' Workshop for Equality in New York City Schools*, September 1962, Annie Stein Papers, PEA; *News from the Parents' Workshop for Equality in New York City Schools*, March 1961, Galamison Papers, SHSW. Fiscal troubles were constant for the workshop; however, Galamison insisted that members not become overly concerned with funding and membership, issues that came to dominate his time at the helm of the Brooklyn NAACP.
17. *News from the Parents' Workshop for Equality in New York City Schools*, November 1962, Annie Stein Papers, PEA; *News from the Parents' Workshop for Equality in New York City Schools*, December 1961, Annie Stein Papers, PEA.
18. Milton A. Galamison, "An Analysis of the Board of Education Open Enrollment Policy," September [1960], Galamison Papers, SC.
19. *News from the Parents' Workshop for Equality in New York City Schools*, October 1962; *News from the Parents' Workshop for Equality in New York City Schools*, June 1963. In addition to addressing integration, the Parents' Workshop also provided parents with information on other educational matters, such as the differences between the types of diplomas offered by the high schools.

20. Parents' Workshop for Equality in New York City Schools, "Questions and Answers on the Junior High Open Enrollment," Galamison Papers, SHSW, p. 2.

21. Parents' Workshop for Equality in New York City Schools, form letter, May 11, 1963, Galamison Papers, SHSW.

22. Siloam Presbyterian Church Bulletin, January 19, 1966, Galamison Papers, SC.

23. Siloam Presbyterian Church Bulletin, January 19, 1966, Galamison Papers, SC; Siloam Presbyterian Church Bulletin, June 19, 1949. Galamison Papers, SC.

24. Mrs. Gwendolyn Timmons, interview by the author, Brooklyn, NY, November 3, 1997.

25. Milton A. Galamison, "Are You Fit to Be Tied?" sermon delivered at Siloam Presbyterian Church in Brooklyn, NY, January 29, 1956, Galamison Papers, SC; Milton A. Galamison, "Doing What Becomes You," sermon delivered at Siloam Presbyterian Church in Brooklyn, NY, October 22, 1950, Galamison Papers, SC; Milton A. Galamison, "This Also Is a Son," sermon delivered at Siloam Presbyterian Church in Brooklyn, NY, April 24, 1955, Galamison Papers, SC. Galamison was not a fully realized feminist; he articulated the suspect ideas that women were sharp tongued and that they were "adomers" rather than "producers." This notwithstanding, his public statements in favor of women's empowerment predominated. Galamison's apprehension of the politics of women's oppression was exceptional in its day.

26. "Textbooks Purging—To Exclude Insults—Backed by Parents," *New York Amsterdam News*, March 14, 1953, p. 15.

27. Ibid.

28. C. Gerald Frazer, "Many Feel Dissatisfied with Schools," *New York Amsterdam News*, October 31,1953, p. 34.

29. Ibid.

30. "Double Sessions Battle Won by Moms at PS 83," *New York Amsterdam News*, March 28, 1959, p. 20.

31. Galamison, "Promises, Promises." Chap. 3 of unpublished manuscript entitled "Period of the Pendulum," 1970, Galamison Papers, SC, NYPL, p. 12. Stein and Cumberbatch had advised Galamison to continue his leadership role at the NAACP; however, in the wake of continued subversion at the Brooklyn branch, they shortly joined him at the Parents' Workshop.

32. Milton A. Galamison to PTA presidents, April 16, 1960, Galamison Papers, SHSW.

33. Galamison to PTA presidents, April 16, 1960.

34. Parents' Workshop for Equality in New York City Schools, "Rally for Equality," Galamison Papers, SHSW, pp. 1–2; Parents' Workshop for Equality in New York City Schools, "Rally for Equality in New York City Schools," Galamison Papers, SHSW.

35. Parents' Workshop for Equality in New York City Schools, "Rally for Equality in New York City Schools."

36. Milton A. Galamison, "Introductory Remarks: Conference with the Superintendent of Schools, Dr. J. J. Theobald," April 25, 1960, Galamison Papers, SHSW.

37. Ibid.

38. Ibid.

39. Parents' Workshop for Equality in New York City Schools, press release, April 25, 1960, Galamison Papers, SHSW.

40. Ibid.

41. Galamison, "Introductory Remarks."

42. Clarence Taylor speculates that in proposing a boycott, Galamison and the Parents' Workshop were influenced by the Harlem Nine demonstration. Certainly, the workshop was aware of the Harlem protest; however, attention must be given to the Brooklyn Seven boycott. Galamison's direct involvement in this demonstration and its culmination

in relatively immediate concessions established the central precedent for the workshop's activities at this time. On the precedent for the 1960 boycott threat, see Clarence Taylor, *Knocking at Our Own Door*, p. 102.

43. Galamison, "Promises, Promises," pp. 12–13; Parents' Workshop for Equality in New York City Schools, press release, June 8, 1960, Galamison Papers, SHSW. The protesters signed a pledge that they would participate in the sit-out.

44. Parents' Workshop for Equality in New York City Schools, "Constitution of the Parents' Workshop for Equality in N.Y.C. Schools," pp. 1–2. Carolyn Eisenberg underestimates the local, working-class component of the workshop because she groups it with other citywide organizations, which she argues tended to be made up of middle-class individuals. The workshop was actually a confederation of local, grassroots organizing units. See Carolyn Woods Eisenberg, "The Parents' Movement at I.S. 201: From Integration to Black Power, 1958–1966: A Case Study of Developing Ideology," PhD diss., Columbia University, 1971, pp. 38–39.

45. Lane to Area Captains, August 25, 1960.

46. Milton A. Galamison to Samuel R. Johnson Jr., August 29, 1960, Galamison Papers, SHSW.

47. Parents' Workshop for Equality in New York City Schools, press release, June 8, 1960; Dorothy Lane to Area Captains, August 25, 1960; Parents' Workshop for Equality in New York City Schools, "Spot Announcement," Galamison Papers, SHSW.

48. Parents' Workshop for Equality in New York City Schools, press release, June 8, 1960.

49. Bert E. Swanson, *The Struggle for Equality:School Integration Controversy in New York City* (New York: Hobbs, Dorman and Company, 1966), p. 18; David Rogers, *770 Livingston Street: Politics and Bureaucracy in the New York City School System* (New York: Random House, 1968), pp. 17, 243, 397; Eleanor Bernert Sheldon and Raymond A. Glazier, *Pupils and Schools in New York City: A Fact Book* (New York: Russell Sage Foundation, 1965), p. 76; Galamison, "Promises, Promises," p. 13.

50. Irving Goldaber, "The Treatment by the New York City Board of Education of Problems Affecting the Negro," PhD diss., New York University, 1964, p. 190.

51. Activists became increasingly convinced that studies and presentations alone would never produce integration.

52. Milton A. Galamison, "Has the Supreme Court Decision Failed?" *News from the Parents' Workshop For Equality in New York City Schools*, September 1962, Annie Stein Papers, PEA.

53. Arguing "New York is after all not Little Rock," Midge Decter completely eclipses the protest that produced Open Enrollment, erroneously attributing the program's genesis to the board's own commitment to integration. See Midge Decter, "The Negro and the New York Schools," *Commentary* 38, no. 3 (1964): 26.

54. Sheldon and Glazier, *Pupils and Schools in New York City*, pp. 77–78. In 1963, school officials ended Open Enrollment and replaced it with a program called the Free Choice Transfer Plan. Some observers view the Free Choice Transfer Plan as an extension of its predecessor. Thus they date the end of Open Enrollment in 1967. For this discussion, Open Enrollment and Free Choice Transfer are distinct.

55. Sheldon and Glazier, *Pupils and Schools in New York City*, p. 77. "Other" was the designation given to white students. In part, utilization figures were used to avoid overcrowding receiving schools. Over time, the utilization figure for some receiving schools was raised to 95 percent.

56. Sheldon and Glazier, *Pupils and Schools in New York City*, p. 77. Technically, schools with 90 percent or more "other" students were eligible to be both receiving and sending

schools. In fact, nonwhite children were those who made up the overwhelming bulk of the transfer pool.

57. Sheldon and Glazier, *Pupils and Schools in New York City*, p. 78.
58. Parents' Workshop for Equality in New York City Schools, "Fact Sheet on the Brooklyn Junior High Schools—Open Enrollment Program," February 1961, Galamison Papers, SHSW; Parents' Workshop for Equality in New York City Schools, "Fact Sheet on the Open Enrollment Schools—1961," Galamison Papers, SHSW; Parents' Workshop for Equality in New York City Schools, "Fact Sheet #5: The Open Enrollment Policy— December 1961," December 4, 1961, Galamison Papers, SHSW; Galamison, "Promises, Promises," p. 14.
59. Parents' Workshop for Equality in New York City Schools, "Questions and Answers on the Junior High Open Enrollment," Galamison Papers, SHSW; Rogers, *110 Livingston Street*, p. 24.
60. *News from the Parents' Workshop for Equality in New York City Schools*, December 1963.
61. *News from the Parents' Workshop for Equality in New York City Schools*, February 1961, Galamison Papers, SHSW; Rogers, *110 Livingston Street*, p. 24.
62. Rosemary Clemens, "New York City Mayors as Policy Makers in Education," PhD diss., New York University, 1973, pp. 3, 89, 204–207. Clemens argues that Wagner's political savvy, reflected in his refusal to engage school policy overtly, allowed him to acquire "tremendous, unharnessed political influence" and provide educational "leadership." Clemens can come to this conclusion because she fails to consider the school integration issue. Regarding this matter, Wagner's silence was disturbing to African American and Puerto Rican activists. The mayor offered no leadership at all, and if he did possess unharnessed political influence, he refrained from employing it overtly or covertly in the interest of integration.
63. Parents' Workshop for Equality in New York City Schools, press release, August 11, 1961, Galamison Papers, SHSW.
64. *News from the Parents' Workshop for Equality in New York City Schools*, October 1961, Galamison Papers, SHSW.
65. Elizabeth Hill to [Thelma] Hamilton, December 5, 1962, Galamison Papers, SHSW.
66. Esther Linder to Thelma Hamilton, December 30, 1962, Galamison Papers, SHSW.
67. Evelyn Millman to Milton Galamison, October 4, 1961, Galamison Papers, SHSW.
68. Shirley Cohen to the Parents' Workshop, February 18, 1962, Galamison Papers, SHSW; Percy Jenkins to Milton Galamison, March 20, 1963, Galamison Papers, SHSW.
69. Krell to Graves, December 7, 1961.
70. Ibid.
71. Krell to the Parents' Workshop, January 7, 1963, Galamison Papers, SHSW.
72. Sheldon and Glazier, *Pupils and Schools in New York City*, p. 78.
73. Galamison, "Promises, Promises," p. 15; Rogers, *110 Livingston Street*, p. 305; Stein, "Strategies for Failure," Harvard Educational Review 41 (2): 164. By 1962, approximately nine thousand children had transferred. This was less than 3 percent of eligible children.
74. Swanson, *The Struggle for Equality*, p. 19; Galamison, "Promises, Promises," p. 13.
75. Galamison, "Promises, Promises," p. 14; Rogers, *110 Livingston Street*, pp. 24, 306–307.
76. Rogers, *110 Livingston Street*, p. 309.
77. Galamison, "Promises, Promises," p. 14.
78. Ibid., p. 13.
79. Rogers, *110 Livingston Street*, p. 309.
80. Galamison, "Promises, Promises," p. 14; Rogers, *110 Livingston Street*, pp. 307, 310.

81. Parents' Workshop for Equality in New York City Schools, "Questions and Answers on the Junior High Open Enrollment." During the pilot stage, parents had only fourteen calendar days to receive the form, decide to participate, choose a school, and return the application.

82. Sheldon and Glazier, *Pupils and Schools in New York City*, p. 78.

83. *News from the Parents' Workshop for Equality in New York City Schools*, April 1961, Annie Stein Papers, PEA.

84. *News from the Parents' Workshop for Equality in New York City Schools*, May 1962, Annie Stein Papers, PEA.

85. *News from the Parents' Workshop for Equality in New York City Schools*, October 1962, Annie Stein Papers, PEA.

86. Parents' Workshop for Equality in New York City Schools, "Rally on Open Enrollment," Galamison Papers, SHSW.

87. Parents' Workshop for Equality in New York City Schools, "Fact Sheet #5"; Parents' Workshop for Equality in New York City Schools, "Rally on Open Enrollment"; Parents' Workshop for Equality in New York City Schools, "Questions and Answers on the Junior High Open Enrollment"; Parents' Workshop for Equality in New York City Schools, "Fact Sheet #3: Open Enrollment in Queens County—January 1961," Galamison Papers, SHSW.

88. Parents' Workshop for Equality in New York City Schools, "Fact Sheet #5"; Parents' Workshop for Equality in New York City Schools, "Fact Sheet #3."

89. Parents' Workshop for Equality in New York City Schools, "Fact Sheet #3."

90. Parents' Workshop for Equality in New York City Schools, "Questions and Answers on the Junior High Open Enrollment"; Parents' Workshop for Equality in New York City Schools, "Rally on Open Enrollment."

91. Parents' Workshop for Equality in New York City Schools, "Rally on Open Enrollment"; Parents' Workshop for Equality in New York City Schools, "Fact Sheet #5."

92. Galamison, "Promises, Promises," p. 15; Sheldon and Glazier, *Pupils and Schools in New York City*, p. 82; Rogers, *110 Livingston Street*, p. 307. Galamison complained regularly that the board insisted on its exclusive right to make educational policy, while when it came to integration, the board left the initiative to parents.

93. Mrs. Gwendolyn Timmons, interview; *News from the Parents' Workshop for Equality in New York City Schools*, February 1961.

94. *News from the Parents' Workshop for Equality in New York City Schools*, n.d., Annie Stein Papers, PEA.

95. Louis Kushnik, "Race, Class and Power: The New York Decentralization Controversy," *Journal of American Studies* (Great Britain) 3, no. 2 (1969): 204–205.

96. Galamison, "Promises, Promises," p. 16.

97. Ibid.

98. The shortcomings of Open Enrollment were not lost on Galamison and the workshop. In the October 1961 newsletter, complaints about the one-sidedness of the program and its inability to integrate ghetto schools were shared. Nevertheless, Galamison was convinced that Open Enrollment was the appropriate beginning for the New York City school system. See *News from the Parents' Workshop for Equality in New York City Schools*, October 1961.

99. Fred Powledge, "Nonwhite Pupils Shun School Plan," *New York Times*, January 29, 1964, p. 19.

100. Barbara Bonhomme, "Experience in an Integrated School," *News from the Parents' Workshop for Equality in New York City Schools*, n.d., Annie Stein Papers, PEA

101. Powledge, "Nonwhite Pupils Shun School Plan," p. 19.

102. Daniel Hiram Perlstein, "The 1968 New York City School Crisis: Teacher Politics, Racial Politics and the Decline of Liberalism," PhD diss., Stanford University, 1994, p. 283.

103. Mrs. Gwendolyn Timmons, interview.

104. Eisenberg, "The Parents' Movement at I.S. 201," p. 119. Wilcox prepared the report for the New York City Commission on Human Rights in 1961.

105. Bonhomme, "Experience in an Integrated School"; Galamison, "Promises, Promises," p. 17; Rogers, *110 Livingston Street*, p. 99; Powledge, "Nonwhite Pupils Shun School Plan," p. 19. Earlier in the decade, the *New York Amsterdam News* interviewed African American mothers about conditions in Harlem's schools. Mrs. Wilhelmina Lewis argued, "It's better to build up the community than to run out of it." See Frazer, "Many Feel Dissatisfied with Schools," p. 15.

106. Rogers, *110 Livingston Street*, p. 99; Galamison, "Promises, Promises," p. 17. Rogers maintains that the board deliberately reinforced the neighborhood school preference among African Americans and Puerto Ricans by providing more special services in sending schools than receiving schools. For more on the discrepancies between sending and receiving schools, see Sheldon and Glazier, *Pupils and Schools in New York City*, pp. 92–94.

107. It was as though Galamison realized that African American ambivalence toward Open Enrollment foreshadowed the decline of the school integration movement and his vision. With the coming of the community control movement, Galamison had great difficulty adjusting to the shifting demands of African American activists.

108. Taylor, *Knocking at Our Own Door*, p. 119.

109. Rogers, *110 Livingston Street*, p. 25.

110. Sheldon and Glazier, *Pupils and Schools in New York City*, p. 82; Milton A. Galamison, "Pulling Out the Rug," *News from the Parents' Workshop for Equality in New York City Schools*, n.d., Annie Stein Papers, PEA; Galamison, "Promises, Promises," p. 15; Rogers, *110 Livingston Street*, p. 307.

111. *News from the Parents' Workshop for Equality in New York City Schools*, October 1961, Galamison Papers, SHSW; Rogers, *110 Livingston Street*, p. 24.

112. Parents' Workshop for Equality to Bernard E. Donovan, *News from the Parents' Workshop for Equality in New York City Schools*, n.d., Annie Stein Papers, PEA; Rogers, *770 Livingston Street*, p. 24.

113. Perlstein, "The 1968 New York City School Crisis," p. 272. Perlstein finds that fewer than twenty thousand students participated in Open Enrollment and Free Choice Transfer combined. These programs spanned seven years.

114. George Richard Meadows, "Open Enrollment and Fiscal Incentives," in Florence Hamlish Levinsohn and Benjamin Drake Wright, eds., *School Desegregation: Shadow and Substance* (Chicago: University of Chicago Press, 1976), p. 143.

115. A study by the Center for Urban Education found that the Open Enrollment program had done little to change the educational achievement of participating pupils. The work stated, "In terms of the objectively measurable criteria, the open enrollment children gained nothing that those who remained in the sending schools did not." The most telling measure, reading achievement, was roughly equal for students in the program and those who remained in segregated schools. See Center for Urban Education, "Evaluations by Center for Urban Education of Special Board of Education Programs," 1966, Rose Shapiro Papers, MML.

CHAPTER 3

THE CAMPUS AND THE STREET

RACE, MIGRATION, AND THE ORIGINS OF THE BLACK PANTHER PARTY IN OAKLAND, CALIFORNIA

DONNA MURCH

The great exodus of poor people out of the South during World War II sprang from the hope for a better life in the big cities of the North and West. In search of freedom, they left behind centuries of southern cruelty and repression. The futility of that search is now history. The Black communities of Bedford-Stuyvesant, Newark, Brownsville, Watts, Detroit, and many others stand as testament that racism is as oppressive in the North as in the South. Oakland is no different.

—Huey Newton[1]

INTRODUCTION

IN 1948 HARRY HAYWOOD WROTE, "THE NEGRO Question is agrarian in origin . . . It presents the curious anomaly of a virtual serfdom in the very heart of the most highly industrialized country in the world."[2] World War II and the advent of the mechanical cotton picker resolved this contradiction by spurring the single largest black population movement in US history. In an ever-expanding tide, migrants poured out of the South in pursuit of rising wages and living standards promised by major metropolitan areas. In 1940, 77 percent of the total black population lived in the South with over 49 percent in rural areas; two out of five worked as farmers, sharecroppers, or farm laborers. In the next ten years, over 1.6 million black people migrated North and westward, to be followed by another 1.5 million in the subsequent decade.[3]

The repercussions of this internal migration were felt throughout the United States leaving their deepest imprint on West Coast cities that historically possessed small black populations. California's lucrative defense industries made the state a prime destination for southern migrants. By 1943, the San Francisco Chamber of Commerce declared the Bay Area "the largest shipbuilding center in the world."[4] Sociologist Charles Johnson explained, "To the romantic appeal of the west, has been added the real and actual opportunity for gainful employment, setting in motion a war-time migration of huge proportions."[5] Oakland's black population mushroomed from 8,462 residents in 1940 (3 percent) to an impressive 47,562 in 1950 (12 percent).[6] A pattern of chain migration continued until 1980, when Oakland reached the racial tipping point with 157,484 black residents, 51 percent of the city's total.[7] The resulting shift in demography secured Oakland's position as the largest black metropolis in Northern California.

In two decades after World War II, Oakland's recently settled African American community produced one of the most influential local Black Power movements in the country.[8] First- and second-generation migrants who came of age In the late 1950s and early 1960s composed not only the leadership but also the rank-and-file of large segments of the Black Panther Party (BPP) and other Black Power organizations.[9] In contrast to their parents who entered the San Francisco Bay in Area in a time of economic boom, postwar youth faced a rapidly disappearing industrial base along with increased school, neighborhood, and job segregation. However, socioeconomic factors alone cannot explain the development of Bay Area radicalism. In response to the rapidly growing, and disproportionately young, migrant population, city and state government developed a program to combat "juvenile delinquency" that resulted in high rates of police harassment, arrest, and incarceration.[10] With its founding in October of 1966, the Black Panther Party for Self Defense (BPPSD) mobilized against this new scale of repression by organizing young people throughout the Bay Area. Within a few short years, the Oakland-based group dropped the words "Self Defense" from its name and expanded into an international force with chapters in over sixty-one US cities and twenty-six states.[11]

Although the BPPSD is best known for its armed police patrols and embrace of "brothers off the block" as revolutionary vanguard, this essay argues that its origins lay in black student and campus struggles at Merritt College and the University of California, Berkeley. While we often think of Black Studies as the product rather than the catalyst of postwar social movements, in the Bay Area fights over curriculum and hiring in the early 1960s were integral to the emergence of Black Power after Watts. Radical groups like the Panthers reflected not only the problems but the ambitions of California's migrant communities, who saw schooling as "the primary vehicle for their children's upward mobility."[12] Oral testimony reveals that for many black families, greater educational access helped inspire western migration itself. Melvyn Newton, brother of the Panther cofounder Huey Newton, expressed this sentiment most clearly: "We were children of migrants that came here for social opportunity . . . families . . . came with the dream of sending their kids to school. I don't know if they necessarily knew what schools were like out here, but they knew what the conditions were like out there."[13] Given the postindustrial restructuring of Oakland's economy and penal system, the need for quality education took on a particular urgency.

BLACK MIGRATION AND WORLD WAR II

Prior to World War II, the black community of the San Francisco Bay Area was tiny. In the first quarter of the century, black residents actively discouraged migration, because of limited economic opportunity. World War II ushered in a new era; national defense brought an unprecedented policy and capital investment in the state. The federal government invested over forty billion dollars in West Coast factories, military bases, and other capital improvements. The resulting economic and demographic changes to the region were immense.[14] In 1943, the San Francisco Chronicle summed up this process by announcing that "the Second Gold Rush" had begun.[15] While people fled from regions throughout the South, and brought with them a diversity of experiences and backgrounds, Bay Area war migrants shared some particular characteristics. The majority came from Texas, Louisiana, and Oklahoma with Arkansas and Mississippi contributing lesser numbers.[16] With an average age between twenty-two and twenty-three, they were younger than the resident population and disproportionately female.[17]

In addition to the obvious economic incentives, the San Francisco Bay Area held a special allure for these young migrants. Racial segregation functioned like a palimpsest whose layers grew denser with the passage of time. The recent migration of the East Bay's black community meant that prior to the population influx spurred by World War II, formal systems of racial control had not yet been consolidated. Black rates of property ownership in California ranked among the highest in the nation, and in contrast to their places of origin, black migrants suffered less physical repression, worked largely outside agriculture, and had greater access to public services.[18] Most importantly, the state's promise of higher quality public education at all levels tapped a persistent, if understudied, motive for black migration throughout the twentieth century.[19]

By 1945, national defense industries had produced more than six hundred thousand jobs for African Americans and drawn a million black southerners to northern and western industrial centers. Although Bay Area shipyards resisted hiring black workers at the outset of the War, systematic organizing efforts by C. L. Dellums, the local business agent for the Brotherhood of Sleeping Car Porters (BSCP), and other civil rights leaders, forced both unions and local employers to hire African Americans.[20] Their campaign provided this newly settled population with unprecedented economic opportunity. In the Bay Area over 70 percent of black migrants found work in the shipyards, and black female employment tripled.[21] Southern migration combined with a changing job structure inaugurated the formation of a strong black working-class movement. C. L. Dellums, a close friend of A. Philip Randolph and uncle to future Congressman Ronald Dellums, remained a touchstone of local black politics in subsequent decades, and his union became one of the most powerful black institutions in the East Bay. However, this era of abundance proved fleeting as postwar demobilization led to large scale unemployment and economic uncertainty.[22]

DEINDUSTRIALIZATION

As migrants sought to realize their newfound opportunity, a new and more repressive racial order emerged. African Americans who had fled the poverty and brutality of the South soon found new barriers erected in their wake. In 1946, the Final Report of the Fair Employment Practice Committee argued, "The entire West Coast Area is characterized by problems which in newness and intensity distinguish it from the rest of the country."[23] Black labor's remarkable gains quickly receded. The workforce employed by shipbuilders shrank from two hundred fifty thousand at the war's height to twelve thousand people in 1946.[24] In Oakland and South Berkeley, five short years of boom were followed by long decades of bust. Immediately after the War ended, Oakland entered a period of industrial decline and structural unemployment became a permanent feature of the local economy. By 1960, the federal government officially classified Oakland as a depressed area.[25] Despite California's thriving Cold War economy, Oakland limped along. Deindustrialization had a devastating social impact on African American residents. In 1959, one quarter of the total population in Oakland lived under the poverty line and roughly 10 percent earned less than two thousand dollars per year.[26] Union discrimination, concentration in temporary wartime industry like shipyards, and entrenched patterns of employer discrimination, relegated much of the growing black population to secondary labor markets. Black youth remained most vulnerable to economic retrenchment, facing high rates of unemployment and repression from local law enforcement.[27]

POLICE REPRESSION AND "JUVENILE DELINQUENCY"

Among historians, it is well recognized that white residential and capital flight from cities was a direct reaction to black migration. In Oakland and other metropolitan areas in California, however, city and state government's postwar preoccupation with "juvenile delinquency" was an equally important development. Racial anxieties about the city's rapidly changing demographics led to an increasing integration of school and recreational programs with police and penal authorities. In this context, the discourse of "juvenile delinquency" took on a clear racial caste, leading to wide-scale policing and criminalization of black youth. While extensive police harassment and arrest of black migrants started during the population influx of World War II, it vastly intensified in the period of economic decline that ensued.[28]

In the 1950s, public service agencies fielded the cascade of disputes that followed from black settlement in white enclaves. School grounds and recreation areas became volatile flashpoints of racial conflict. White neighborhoods undergoing swift racial transition sought to obtain funds from the city council to reorganize social service agencies. When city government refused to allocate money for specific areas, groups of residents banded together to form the Associated Agencies (AA) and District Community Councils (DCA).[29] In its final form, the AA of Oakland encompassed three tiers of government responsible for youth and family services. At the local level, the AA integrated Oakland's public school system, recreation, and police departments with the county's probation, welfare, and health agencies. In turn, these local groups were linked up with the California Youth Authority, the state's largest penal authority for juvenile offenders.[30] Meetings with multiple family service and juvenile agencies allowed them to work together to identify and monitor "troublemakers."[31] The most disturbing aspects of this integration of recreational and police agencies, was the tracking of youths identified as delinquent. Police monitored, and even arrested, individuals that had been identified by school and recreational staff, despite the fact that they had no prior record. Increasingly, the category of black youth itself became defined as a social problem at best, and as a criminal presence at worst.

Local politicians used Cold War metaphors of contagion and containment to describe black residents with the greatest threat emanating from the youth. Oakland city manager Wayne Thompson, a self-professed liberal, explained the preventative logic behind introducing police and penal presence into the local school system to stem the tide of "delinquency." "If you didn't stop it, it would spread into the business sections and even infect the industrial community," Thompson warned. "We had eyes and ears in those areas to alert us in advance . . . Before the Associated Agencies program, it was an admission of weakness on the part of the school official, or . . . failure if he even let a policeman in the door . . . What a change now! The first man they call is the police."[32]

In the mid-1950s, a restructuring of the Oakland Police Department (OPD) exacerbated this situation. Changes in East Bay law enforcement reflected a national trend toward "legalistic policing," characterized by modern equipment, formalized systems, and greater emphasis on juvenile detention. Oakland's new police chief dissolved local precincts, concentrated the OPD into a single headquarters, and overhauled hiring practices in favor of better educated, more affluent candidates.[33] In practice, these policies created an almost exclusively white middle-class force that resided outside the city and had little understanding or connection to the neighborhoods they served.[34] Oakland's reinvigorated police force became a constant and intrusive presence in people's lives. Systematic arrests of young offenders linked them into the web of professional services, including probation officers, judges, and child guidance clinics, further blurring the line between "authoritative" police functions and family services.[35] Given the pervasive hostility toward black migrants, this framework laid the basis for the simultaneous criminalization of black youth and long-term neglect of black families.

BLACK STUDENTS AND THE ROOTS OF BLACK POWER

While Black Power has often been treated as a post-Watts phenomenon, its roots in the East Bay stretch far back into the decade preceding the urban rebellions.[36] Public education became the most immediate arena in which migrant youth confronted a hostile white establishment and mobilized against it.[37] Black students entered secondary schools and universities in large numbers at a time when the California system of higher education was undergoing a major restructuring. Faced with a mushrooming population and a conservative fiscal structure, state policy makers sought to contain costs while expanding capacity. Projections warned that student populations would increase nearly fivefold in fifteen years. In 1960, 227,000 students were enrolled in higher education; by 1975 the total reached one million.[38] California's university system, with its integrated tiers of community colleges, state, and public universities, led the nation in superior levels of funding, infrastructure, and quality of instruction. In 1960, the statewide Master Plan for Higher Education vastly increased the number and capacity of junior colleges and mandated that they admit all applicants with high school diplomas. Urban campuses greatly expanded black working class college enrollment, and provided an institutional base for political organizing. By 1969, the San Francisco Bay Area boasted one of the highest rates of minority college completion in the nation.[39] Full access to community colleges became particularly important given racial segregation and inequalities in the city's primary and secondary schools.

The Oakland Unified School District consistently allocated resources to segregated white schools in wealthy areas of the city, while neglecting overcrowded schools in the "flatlands." In the early sixties, this issue came to a head with the building of Skyline High School in the Oakland hills. Black parents and civil rights leaders charged the school board with "gerrymandering" the district and draining resources from the rapidly integrating schools in the low lying areas of the city. Discrimination extended beyond issues of unfair financing to the racialized culture of the schools themselves. Starting in 1957, black students and their families protested low standards and achievements in West Oakland's all-black McClymonds High School. They cited the low rate of college attendance among "Mack" graduates, and a recurring pattern of counselors and school officials discouraging students from continuing their education.[40] An FEPC report published several years later identified differential standards as a pervasive problem throughout the district. Principals and teachers in majority black schools repeatedly emphasized the importance of discipline, comportment, and hygiene over academic achievement.[41] In the spring of 1966, the Ad Hoc Committee for Quality Education (AHCQUE) formed to protest the school board's unfair use of resources and the school's miseducation of their children.[42] Over the next decade, flatland parents and their supporters vigorously contested the increased police presence in the schools, the failure to hire black faculty and staff, and the self-fulfilling prophecy of lowered expectations producing poor academic results.

DONALD WARDEN AND THE AFRO-AMERICAN ASSOCIATION

In the San Francisco Bay Area, some of the most important battles over curriculum and social access took place at the university level. Within less than a decade, unprecedented numbers of black students entered college for the first time, and urban campuses became major sites for political organizing. In the spring of 1961, Berkeley graduate students from a variety of disciplines and a sprinkling of undergraduates from UC Berkeley and San Francisco State began to meet regularly. Donald Warden, a second year student at UC Berkeley's Bolt School of Law, emerged as the "leader" of the study group. In early March, he wrote a series of editorials to the Daily California, denouncing Roy Wilkins, the National Association for the Advancement of Colored People (NAACP), and the civil rights strategy of integration.[43] Students debated books of immediate political relevance and hosted weekly forums throughout the Bay Area. Charter members included Henry Ramsey, Donald Hopkins, Ann Cooke, Mary Lewis, and Maurice Dawson.[44] As the group cohered, they chose the name Afro-American Association (AAA) and limited membership exclusively to people of African descent.[45] Ernest Allen, a Merritt student who later joined, described the choice as containing a "revolutionary . . . sense of rebirth" paralleling the Nation's repudiation of "slave names."[46] W. E. B. Du Bois's *Souls of Black Folk*, Carter G. Woodson's *Miseducation of the Negro*, and Ralph Ellison's *Invisible Man* numbered among their selections, however, E. Franklin Frazier's *Black Bourgeoisie* and Melville J. Herskovits' *The Myth of the Negro Past* elicited the most debate.[47] The discussion and the controversy these two volumes engendered had the greatest impact on the Association's evolving ideology. Ultimately, the AAA successfully fused Herskovits and Frazier's opposing views on African survivals to fashion its own antiassimilationist ideology.[48]

Many of the ideas generated in the Association, including their debates about the nature of identity, African retention, and the integrationist sins of the black middle class, anticipated cultural nationalist thought of subsequent years.[49] In May of 1961, Association members worked together with the UC Berkeley campus chapter of the NAACP to bring Malcolm X to speak. Soon after, a group of students began regularly attending the Nation's mosque, Temple 26B, in West Oakland. Although the Association remained secular, their rhetoric revealed the NOI's clear influence.[50] Opposition to integration, understood as forced assimilation, served as unifying theme; their public speeches, often reserved their greatest rancor not for the dominant white society, as for the compliant "Black Bourgeoisie." Warden and others in the Association argued that while civil rights leaders spoke of desegregation and compliance with Brown, what they truly advocated was assimilation. They encouraged their members to learn Arabic and Swahili, and in the midsixties began manufacturing an African inspired garment called the "Simba."[51] Ronald Everett, later known as Karenga, joined the Association in 1963, and helped establish a Los Angeles chapter. Historian Scot Brown notes that "Warden, though not specifically defining the group as cultural nationalist, set in motion many of the cultural concepts and organizing principles that Karenga utilized in US."[52]

The AAA was not content to simply remain a study group, Warden and others moved to become integral to the East Bay's larger African American community. Association members experimented with different forms of activism, including sponsoring the "Mind of the Ghetto" youth conference at McClymonds High in West Oakland. However, Harlem style street rallies remained the AAA's most consistent form of outreach.[53] Although street speaking had long been a staple of black nationalist political culture, the AAA adapted it to the particularities of the Bay Area. A pattern developed in which the Association held rallies in San Francisco until early afternoon, before moving on to Oakland and to Richmond. The exile of Robert F. Williams prompted one of the first street speaking sessions. Association members traveled down to Seventh Street, the central black business district in West Oakland, and held up the newspaper headlines, loudly proclaiming their support.[54] Looking back, Maurice Dawson remembered the uproar over Williams' exile as a turning point. The name Robert F. Williams was poised on everyone's lips. "[He] ain't scared of nothing or nobody," Dawson explained. "This was the talk of the Bay Area . . . It was the genesis of the growth and evolution, frankly, of racial pride in the East Bay."[55]

In early 1963, the AAA reached the height of its powers and influence. The Association offered an effective mix of black cultural nationalism and colorful display that helped mobilize a whole generation that passed through Bay Area schools. The support the Association received from different segments of the black community reflected its profound appeal. Many participants in the Association later became prominent across a broad spectrum of black politics. On the electoral front, Ronald Dellums briefly attended meetings along with future Oakland Mayor Elihu Harris, and local powerbrokers Ortho Green, Henry Ramsey, and Donald Hopkins. Charter member Ann Cooke went on to publish in the groundbreaking feminist anthology The Black Woman; while political radicals Ernest Allen, Cedric Robinson, Huey Newton, and Bobby Seale socialized with nationalists Ronald Karenga, Fritz Pointer, and David Patterson.[56] In sum, the Association represented a foundational stage in the evolution of black politics in California. While an older school of historiography has emphasized the divisions between civil rights and electoral politics on the one hand, and black nationalist and Black Power thought on the other, the history of the AAA clearly demonstrates how the two were nurtured together in this early student movement.

Despite the Association's many accomplishments, this period of unity was short-lived. The AAA soon underwent a series of splits that alienated a core portion of its more radical membership. Students interested in socialism and direct community action became frustrated by Warden's recalcitrant anticommunism and his resistance to more concrete forms of political organizing. Others questioned his political integrity and personal motivation.[57] Nevertheless, the AAA helped launch a new era of black activism and institution building that culminated in the founding of the BPPSD.

MERRITT COLLEGE, BLACK STUDIES, AND
THE BLACK PANTHER PARTY

While the AAA recruited throughout the East Bay, its largest following emerged at Merritt College, affectionately known to black residents as "Grove Street." Ernest Allen explained, "The fact that it [Merritt College] was located right in the middle of a community was a historical accident, but what people made of it was something else."[58] The boundary between Merritt and North Oakland was completely porous. People passed on and off the campus, and many residents from the surrounding area hung out in the cafeteria, a major hub for debate.[59] By locating their headquarters adjacent to the school and regularly staging street rallies on campus grounds, the Association helped ignite a militant black student movement.

Until the late fifties, African American presence on California campuses was too small and diffuse to be called a community. Although the University of California did not collect statistics on the racial breakdown of the Berkeley student population until 1966, anecdotal evidence reveals that there were less than one hundred black students out of nearly twenty thousand. As the civil rights movement progressed these figures began to slowly increase, until by 1966, black students, including both native born and African, breached the 1 percent barrier with 226 undergraduate and graduate students enrolled in Berkeley.[60] Although these gains were significant, the expansion of the black student body at community colleges dwarfed that of the comparatively elite University of California system. By 1965 black students made up nearly 10 percent of Merritt College's total enrollment, and within two short years, they formed over 30 percent of the student body. A mutually reinforcing dynamic took hold in which the increase in black students fed political organizing and political organizing, in turn, attracted people who would never have considered attending college.[61]

Many of these students were not only the first members of their family to attend college, but they were also recent arrivals from the South who still retained strong cultural ties to their families' places of origin. Their intermediary status as migrants led them to look "backwards as much as forwards" and helped to provide additional motivation for seizing opportunities unimaginable to them and their families a decade before.[62] While Huey Newton was exceptional in many ways, his background typified that of the growing black student body at Merritt College. He was the child of Louisiana migrants, raised in poverty in Oakland by parents who had come to California in search of better jobs and more educational opportunity. Similarly, Bobby Seale was a first-generation migrant from Dallas, Texas.[63] In the late 1950s, Seale began taking night classes at Merritt with hopes of earning a degree in engineering. As his interest in "American Black History" grew, he shifted his emphasis from technical training toward the humanities.[64] Attending community college was the single biggest influence on their radicalization, Newton later explained: "It was my studying and reading in college that led me to become a socialist . . . The transformation from a nationalist to a socialist was a slow one, although I was around a lot of Marxists."[65]

In the mid-1960s, Merritt students began organizing to have Black Studies classes included in the regular curriculum. Between 1964 and 1966, Virtual Murrell, Alex Papillion, Isaac Moore, Kenny Freeman, Ernest Allen, and Douglas Allen formed the Soul Students Advisory Council (SSAC).[66] Leo Bazille, who became president of Soul Students in 1966, described the organization as a place where "youth met and devised political involvements." The same year they changed their name to "Black Student Union," a new term at the time. One of the Council's first accomplishments was a large rally at Merritt protesting the draft of blacks into the military. However, their fight to implement black history classes at Merritt and to increase the hiring of black faculty and staff became their most sustained campaign.[67]

After a confrontation with white faculty member Rodney Carlisle over the content of his "Negro History" class, Huey Newton became involved in this protracted struggle.[68] He saw it as an important chance to implement a new type of organizing. Newton proposed sponsoring a rally in support of the Afro-American History Program in which SSAC members would invite the press, strap on guns, and march outside Merritt College on Malcolm X's birthday. This type of action would enable

Soul Students to mobilize not only students but the populations surrounding the school, including the "lumpen proletariat," the key constituency for social revolution.[69] A display of armed self defense would impress the community, call attention to police brutality, and intimidate Merritt's administrators into taking the students' demands more seriously.[70] Soul Students refused, and Newton refocused his attention on the world beyond the "the sandbox politics" of the community college.

While the BPP had its origins firmly in early student activism at Berkeley and Merritt College, Seale and Newton quickly distanced themselves from their campus roots and cultivated their image as "brothers off the block." Newton viewed the gun as a powerful "recruiting device" that would attract youth from the broader community; thereby, bridging the gap between students and the grassroots. This duality, merging different strata from "college and community," remained a hallmark of the BPP throughout its history. Given the sharp spike in local college attendance, this dynamic was strongest in Oakland, but it was true for other chapters as well. In describing the Chicago chapter, David Hilliard likened their strategy to Bunchy Carter's efforts in Los Angeles: "They [tried] to forge an alliance between the two largest concentrations of black youth—the campus and the streets."[71]

While many black nationalist and New Left groups hoped to do this, the Panthers set about achieving this broad coalition through spectacular displays challenging state violence. As Newton searched for a medium to "capture the imagination" of Oakland's black community, he turned to the law library at the North Oakland Service Center, a poverty program that employed Bobby Seale. Drawing on his training from law school, Newton pored over the California penal code and resurrected an old statute that legalized carrying unconcealed weapons. After much discussion with peers over the right to bear arms, Newton and Seale decided that they needed a concrete political program before initiating police patrols. In October 1966, in less than twenty minutes, Seale and Newton drafted the "Black Panther Party Platform and Program" in the North Oakland Poverty Center.[72] One of the Panthers' first community actions took place on Fifty-Fifth and Market near the antipoverty program where Newton and Seale were working. Several pedestrians had been killed at the intersection, which had no stoplight. They attempted to get the city to put up a stop sign and made little progress with local bureaucracy. So they went out and started directing traffic; within weeks, the city installed a signal. This strategy of forcing the hand of local government through assuming some of its powers was repeated a number of times throughout the Party's history.[73] Policing the police, food giveaways, and public service actions like the one on Market, highlighted the simultaneously negligent and repressive role of government in Oakland's black neighborhoods. The implicit message was clear—either improve state services or face an armed movement of local youth.

CONCLUSION

Ultimately, Oakland's Black Power movement is best understood through the historical circumstances that produced it. Large-scale migration to California, impelled first by defense industry and the inertia of chain migration—and later by the death throes of agricultural tenancy—created a displaced population that remained shut out of the major avenues of decision making. For first generation migrants, shipyard and defense related employment promised a vast increase in living standards that quickly dissolved in the War's aftermath. As jobs and money flowed to the suburbs in coming decades, the core of the migrant population found itself trapped in the familiar cycles of poverty and debt. For the young, the situation was most difficult of all—they faced not only economic uncertainty but the constant threat of police harassment and incarceration.

As they approached college age, federal funding and an expansive network of community colleges provided newfound access to integrated higher education. Black students seized this opportunity, and used it as an arena for addressing the most immediate circumstances of their lives. College campuses became major sites for political organizing, and first-generation attendees articulated the grievances of the larger community. Black Studies and student union struggles created strong networks of activists that would later venture beyond the campus into grassroots and community organizing after 1965. The AAA, US Organization, and the BPP all had origins in these campus based struggles. Huey Newton said it best: "Everyone—from Warden and the AAA to Malcolm X and the Muslims to all the other groups active in the Bay Area at that time—believed strongly that the failure to include black history in the college curriculum was a scandal. We all set out to do something about it."[74]

NOTES

1. Huey Newton, *Revolutionary Suicide* (New York: Writers and Readers Publishing, Inc., 1973), p. 14.
2. Harry Haywood, *Negro Liberation* (Chicago: Liberator Press, 1976), p. 11.
3. Manning Marable, "Foreword" in Rod Bush's *The New Black Vote: Politics and Power in Four American Cities* (San Francisco: Synthesis Publications, 1984), p. 3; Nicolas Lemann, *The Promised Land: The Great Black Migration and How It Changed America* (New York: A. A. Knopf, 1991), p. 6
4. Quoted by Albert S. Broussard, "In Search of the Promised Land: African American Migration to San Francisco, 1900–1945," in *Seeking El Dorado: African Americans in California*, ed. Lawrence de Graafe et al. (Los Angeles: Autry Museum of Western Heritage, 2001), p. 190.
5. Charles Johnson, *The Negro War Worker in San Francisco: A Local Self-Survey* (San Francisco, 1944), p. 1.
6. US Bureau of the Census, *Population by Age, Race, and Sex in Oakland, Calif. by Census Tracts: 1940*.
7. US Department of Labor, "Data from Census Bureau Estimates for Oakland, California," 1980 Census, Run No. 831120, p. 4.
8. For a sustained discussion of the complex relation of the Black Panther Party to the concept of Black Power, see Donna Murch, "When the Panther Travels: Race and the Southern Diaspora in the History of the BPP, 1964–1972," Conference Paper, Diaspora and the Difference Race Makes Symposium, Black Atlantic Seminar, Rutgers University, February 16, 2007.
9. Donna Murch, "The Urban Promise of Black Power: African American Political Mobilization in Oakland and the East Bay, 1961–1977," PhD diss, UC Berkeley, 2004.

10. After conducting extensive oral history interviews with activists in the Bay Area Black Power movement for my dissertation, I was struck by how many had served time in the California Youth Authority and other penal institutions. For a representative sample, see Donna Murch, "Interview with Emory Douglas," March 7, 2002, "Leon White," August 9, 2002, "Fritz Pointer," March 12, 2002; Judith May, "Struggle for Authority: A Comparison of Four Social Change Programs in Oakland, California," PhD diss., UC Berkeley, 1973.

11. Newton, *Revolutionary Suicide*, pp. 110–127; Murch, "Interview with Ernest Allen," February 3, 2002; Murch, "The Urban Promise," p. 147; Paul Alkebulan, "The Role of Ideology in the Growth, Establishment, and Decline of the Black Panther Party: 1966 to 1982," PhD diss., UC Berkeley, 2003, p. 104.

12. Quote taken from Jeanne Theoharis, "'Alabama on the Avalon': Rethinking the Watts Uprising and the Character of Black Protest in Los Angeles" in *The Black Power Movement: Rethinking the Civil Tights-Black Power Era*, ed. Peniel E. Joseph (New York: Routledge, 2006), p. 33.

13. Murch, "Interview with Melvyn Newton," March 15, 2002.

14. Albert Broussard, *Black San Francisco: The Struggle for Racial Equality in the West, 1900–1945* (Lawrence: University of Kansas, 1993); Gerald D. Nash, *The American West Transformed: The Impact of the Second World War* (Lincoln, NE.: University of Nebraska Press, 1985), p. 17.

15. Marilynn S. Johnson, *The Second Gold Rush* (Berkeley: University of California Press, 1993), p. 30.

16. Broussard, *Black San Francisco*, p. 192; Gretchen Lemke-Santangelo, *Abiding Courage: African American Women and the East Bay Community* (Chapel Hill: University of North Carolina Press, 1996); Johnson, *Negro War Worker*.

17. According to Charles Johnson, in the nineteen-to-twenty-four age group, women outnumbered men by two to one; Charles Johnson, *Negro War Worker*, p. 6.

18. Lawrence B. De Graaf and Quintard Taylor, "Introduction" to *Seeking El Dorado*, p. 24; Murch, "Interview with Walter Bachemin," June 28, 1998, p. 1; William Henry Brown, "Class Aspects of Residential Development and Choice in Oakland Black Community," PhD diss. UC Berkeley, 1970, p. 86; This dynamic was reenacted inside the state itself. Large numbers of southern migrants who first settled in Los Angeles, which had a much older and larger African American community, later chose to move north in search of a less hostile environment. Also see Floyd Hunter, *Housing Discrimination in Oakland, California; A Study Prepared for the Oakland Mayor's Committee on Full Opportunity and the Council of Social Planning, Alameda County* (Berkeley, CA: 1964), p. 14.

19. In my oral history interviews with migrants, this theme frequently emerged. See for example, Murch, "Newton," "Bachemin."

20. Donna Murch, "The Problem of the Occupational Color Line," unpublished paper, p. 15.

21. Charles Wollenberg, *Marinship at War: Shipbuilding and Social Change in Wartime Sausalito* (Berkeley: Western Heritage Press, 1990), p. 71.

22. C. L. Dellums, *International President of the Brotherhood of Sleeping Car Porters and Civil Rights Leaders*, Northern California Negro Political Series, Regional Oral History Office, Bancroft Library, UC Berkeley; Robert Self, *American Babylon: Race and the Struggle for Postwar Oakland* (Princeton, NJ: Princeton University Press, 2003).

23. Committee of Fair Employment Practice, Final Report, June 28, 1946, Institute for Governmental Studies, University of California Berkeley, p. 77.

24. Oakland Police Department Report (6), p. 23, Oakland Public Library; Marilyn Johnson, *Second Gold Rush*; Murch, "The Problem of the Occupational Color Line."

25. Edward, C., Hayes, *Power Structure and Urban Policy: Who Rules in Oakland?* (San Francisco: McGraw-Hill Book Company, 1972), p. 48.
26. Ibid., p. 44.
27. Hayes, *Power Structure and Urban Policy*; Marilynn Johnson, *Second Gold Rush*, p. 167; Gretchen Lemke-Santangelo, "Deindustrialization, Urban Poverty and African American Community Mobilization in Oakland, 1945 through 1990s," *Seeking El Dorado*, pp. 343–376.
28. Johnson, *Second Gold Rush*, p. 167; OPD Report (6).
29. May, "Struggle for Authority," pp. 115–117.
30. Ibid.; Evelio Grillo, *Black Cuban, Black American: A Memoir* (Houston: Arte Publico Press, 2000), p. 131; Laura Mihailoff, "Protecting Our Children: A History of the California Youth Authority and Juvenile Justice, 1938–1968" (UC Berkeley, 2005).
31. May, "Struggle for Authority," p. 24.
32. Ibid., p. 128.
33. May, "Struggle for Authority," p. 130; Oakland Police Department History 1941–1955, Part 6, 36–40.
34. May, "Struggle for Authority," pp. 130–135; Oakland Police Department History 1941–1955, Part 6, pp. 36–40.
35. May, "Struggle for Authority," p. 130.
36. Komozi Woodard, *A Nation within a Nation: Amiri Baraka (LeRoi Jones) and Black Power Politics* (Chapel Hill: University of North Carolina Press, 1999); Self, *American Babylon*; Peniel E. Joseph, *Waiting 'Til the Midnight Hour: A Narrative History of Black Power in America* (New York: Henry Holt, 2006). For new literature on the history of Black Studies see also Peniel E. Joseph, "Black Studies, Student Activism, and the Black Power Movement," in *The Black Movement*, pp. 251–277 and Noliwe Rooks, *White Money, Black Power: The Surprising History of African American Studies and the Crisis of Race in Higher Education* (Boston: Beacon Press, 2006).
37. For a sustained discussion of the roots of the Bay Area Black Power movement in postwar struggles over California higher education see Murch, "Urban Promise of Black Power."
38. John Aubrey Douglas, "Brokering the 1960 Master Plan: Pat Brown and the Promise of California Higher Education," in *Responsible Liberalism: Edmund G. "Pat" Brown and Reform Government in California 1958–1967*, ed. Martin Schiesl (Los Angeles: Edmund G. "Pat" Brown Institute of Public Affairs, 2003), p. 86; John Aubrey Douglas, *The California Idea and American Education*; Sidney W. Brossman and Myron Roberts, *The California Community Colleges* (Palo Alto, CA: Field Educational Publications, 1973).
39. "Completion Levels: Percentage of High School and College 'Completers' (Aged 25 and Over) in Selected Cities, 1969," in *Historical Statistics of Black America*, ed. Jessie Carney Smith and Carrell Peterson Horton (Detroit: Gale Research, 1995), p. 530.
40. Jonathan Spencer, "Caught in Crossfire: Marcus Foster and America's Urban Education Crisis, 1941–1973," PhD diss, New York University, 2002, pp. 361–363.
41. Jonathan Spencer quotes an article from 1952 in which the planners of the new McClymonds building described how their choice of design suited "the modified curriculum" meant to "fit the needs of the pupils in the area." Although biology was still required, McClymonds possessed a different "set of contents and set of objectives . . . [with] a good deal of attention . . . to the care of the hair, skin and feet." Spencer, "Caught in Crossfire," p. 361.
42. Ibid., p. 363.
43. Warden, Letters to the Ice Box, *Daily California*, 1 March (1961), 22 March (1961).
44. Murch, "The Urban Promise," p. 99.

45. Lisa Rubens, "Interview with Donald Hopkins," unpublished transcript, Regional Oral History Office, UC Berkeley, September 29, 2000.

46. Murch, "Interview with Ernest Allen," July 3, 2001.

47. Murch, "Interview with Dawson," July 26, 2002; "Interview with Khalid Al Mansour," July 22, 2002.

48. Ibid.

49. Scot Brown, *Fighting for US: Maulana Karenga, The US Organization, and Black Cultural Nationalism* (New York: New York University Press, 2003), pp. 25–29.

50. Murch, "Dawson."

51. Murch, "Mansour"; Khalid Al Mansour, *Black Americans at the Crossroads—Where Do We Go From Here?* (New York: First African Arabian Press, 1990).

52. Brown, *Fighting for US*, p. 28.

53. James Edward Smethurst, *The Black Arts Movement: Literary Nationalism in the 1960s and 1970s* (Chapel Hill: University of North Carolina Press, 2005), pp. 260–262.

54. Murch, "Dawson"; Timothy Tyson, "Introduction: Robert F. Williams, 'Black Power,' and the Roots of the African American Freedom Struggle," in Robert F. Williams, *Negroes With Guns* (Detroit: Wayne State University Press, 1998), p. xxvii.

55. Murch, "Dawson."

56. Murch, "Mansour."

57. Newton, *Revolutionary Suicide*, pp. 60–66; Bobby Seale, *Seize the Time* (New York: Random House, 1970), p. 21; Murch, "Interview with Mary Lewis," March 18, 2002.

58. Murch, "Allen."

59. Murch, "Melvyn Newton."

60. Gabrielle Morris, *Head of the Class: An Oral History of African-American Achievement in Higher Education and Beyond* (New York: Twayne Publishers, 1995), pp. xvii–xviii.

61. "Special Report on Minority Group Relations Presented to the Trustees," *Peralta Colleges Bulletin* 5, no. 8 (January 12, 1968): p. 2.

62. Eric Hobsbawm, *Primitive Rebels: Studies in Archaic Forms of Social Movement in the 19th and 20th Centuries* (New York: W. W. Norton & Company, 1959), p. 108.

63. Seale, *Seize the Time*, pp. 3–6.

64. Ibid., pp. 3–12.

65. Newton, *Revolutionary Suicide*, p. 69.

66. Seale, *Seize the Time*, pp. 26, 30.

67. Murch, "Interview with Leo Bazile," February 19, 2001.

68. Seale, *Seize the Time*, p. 20.

69. Ibid., pp. 30–31.

70. Newton, *Revolutionary Suicide*, pp. 108–109.

71. David Hilliard and Lewis Cole, *This Side of Glory: The Autobiography of David Hilliard and the Story of the Black Panther Party* (New York: Little, Brown and Company, 1993), p. 228; Robyn Ceanne Spencer, "Repression Breeds Resistance: The Rise and Fall of the Black Panther Party in Oakland, CA, 1966–1982," PhD diss., Columbia University, 2001, p. 44.

72. Newton, *Revolutionary Suicide*, pp. 115–116.

73. Murch, "Newton."

74. Interestingly, Warden distanced himself from the successes at Merritt rather than claiming credit. He described the Merritt student movement with the following words: "[T]hat leadership tended to be what the press would call more militant, more radical, and out of that grew the Black Panther movement." Newton, *Revolutionary Suicide*, p. 72; Murch, "Mansour."

PART II

TRANSNATIONAL DIMENSIONS

CHAPTER 4

SPOKESMAN OF
THE OPPRESSED?

LORRAINE HANSBERRY AT WORK:
THE CHALLENGE OF RADICAL
POLITICS IN THE POSTWAR ERA

REBECCAH WELCH

ON MAY 24, 1963, PLAYWRIGHT LORRAINE HANSBERRY attended a civil rights meeting with Attorney General Robert F. Kennedy in New York City. There, at the behest of fellow author James Baldwin, she joined a number of friends and colleagues—including sociologist Kenneth Clark, and singers Harry Belafonte and Lena Horne—to speak with Kennedy regarding race relations in America. Many of these participants, according to the *New York Times*, did not hold official positions in any civil rights organization. They were, nevertheless, "prominent Negroes," "intellectuals," and "professionals" who had served as "unofficial spokesmen for their race."[1]

Robert F. Kennedy's parley with black intellectuals was not particularly unusual for the time. As a number of scholars have shown, the importance of US race relations to Cold War diplomacy placed a premium on individuals who would speak to racial issues in concert with dominant narratives of racial progress and equality.[2] This imperative was especially acute in 1963, when the civil rights movement met with increased resistance and hostility on the ground, scattering

I am grateful for the generosity of Matthew Lyons, Jewel Gresham Nemiroff, Margaret Wilkerson and the Estate of Lorraine Hansberry for providing access to papers in the Lorraine Hansberry Collection. I also want to thank Mia Bay, Thomas Bender, Wallace Best, Dayo Gore, Robin D. G. Kelley, Robert Korstad, Rob Mickey, Mary Nolan, Peniel Joseph, and Cynthia Young for reading this article in various incarnations, as well as the generous support of the Institute on Race and Social Division at Boston University, the W. E. B. Du Bois Center for African and African American Culture and the Rare Book and Manuscript staff of the Schomburg Center for Research in Black Culture.

headlines of racial violence across the front lines of the Cold War. 1963 is well known for the March on Washington. But 1963 also marked the year policemen turned dogs and horses on peaceful marchers in Birmingham; the year National Association for the Advancement of Colored People (NAACP) leader Medgar Evers was murdered near his home in Jackson, Mississippi, and the Birmingham bombing killed four young girls at the Sixteenth Street Baptist Church. Lorraine Hansberry, for her part, made it clear to reporters that she was not meeting with Kennedy to serve as a soothing Cold War photo op. Indeed, as if to underscore the resolute nature of her stance, the *Times* hastened to add that a few of the spokesmen, including "Miss Hansberry," had earned reputations as "angry young Negroes."[3]

Cognizant of the major shifts taking place in the postwar world and their relationship to political culture, Hansberry wrestled the image of an "angry young Negro" to her advantage. She was well matched for the kind of diplomacy that a meeting with Kennedy required. Challenging the sleek promotional photograph of her that smiled out from the pages of the *Times*, the thirty-three-year-old playwright assured reporters that she had not come, in her words, to have a polite "tea" at the White House.[4]

Lorraine Hansberry's attempt to influence the publicity around this meeting captures a watershed moment in the early 1960s when the force of the Cold War and anticolonial movements raised the issue of racial democracy to a globally ascendant public debate. Although Hansberry's sophisticated awareness of international politics and the powerful role she accorded artists in the struggle for social justice may have found a public platform during the 1960s, her politicization had strong antecedents in the 1950s. Apprenticed by a group of veteran black internationalists who believed in the transformative power of art in revolutionary change, Hansberry was well equipped to intervene in the emerging political culture of the 1960s. At a time when McCarthyism had seriously weakened the authority of Paul Robeson and pushed him out of the spotlight, young thinkers like Hansberry, previously under the tutelage of Robeson and other black leftists, gained an unprecedented measure of public influence. Although trenchant economic and sociopolitical analyses were not new to her and her postwar peers, the opportunities for public discussion of racism and imperialism had dramatically increased since their political coming of age during the height of the McCarthyism.

This was especially true for the young playwright. In 1959, on the heels of her success with *A Raisin in the Sun*, Hansberry was actively culled as a "media expert" and "a leader in the mass media field."[5] Embracing the chance to address a popular audience, Hansberry never lost sight of the militant black diaspora that gave her a voice in public affairs, and used her privileged status to broadcast the freedom struggles of an era. Having been trained as a journalist and playwright, a cultural worker and political organizer, she carefully blended these skills to deliver well-crafted political messages in the public sphere. Under Hansberry's pen, historical oppression became the front rather than the back story in racial debates. And her editorials and short essays cast marginal figures—workers, women, African Americans and anticolonial militants—in full dimension, moving them to center stage. Her expansive political vision, linking race and class struggle with an analysis of sex and gender discrimination, interlocked the histories of women, black Americans and colonial peoples abroad, and marked Hansberry as a crucial progenitor of both the Black Power and Feminist movements.

Nevertheless, a close examination of her experience with mass culture underscores some voices were drawn into the high-stakes media skirmishes that surrounded her tenure in the spotlight—from whites who did not particularly want to hear what Hansberry had to say to blacks who questioned her ability and qualifications to represent the race. Over time these seemingly competing pressures worked in tandem to largely obscure the political and cultural agency of the artist, whose postwar critique of racism and imperialism was far more radical and enduring than history's repetition of dominant narratives of celebrity concession allow.

Among the earliest of those critical voices was Harold Cruse, who considered the rise in celebrity proof of the "utter impoverishment" of the black left's intellectual and political mission.[6] "Hansberry, talking to the television rostrum on art and culture *a la Negre*," wrote Cruse in *The Crisis of the Negro Intellectual*, "was like a solitary defender, armed with a dull sword, rushing out on a charger to meet a regiment."[7] Contrary to Cruse's comments, however, a middle ground between unfettered expression and co-optation to manipulate the publicity machinery as best they could. Indebted to an earlier era of cultural front politics, Hansberry and her peers were determined to negotiate the challenges of celebrity and promote a meaningful role for public intellectual work in the postwar era.

A careful examination of Lorraine Hansberry's response to the media challenges of the 1950s and 1960s builds on her established reputation as a dramatist to underscore her equally compelling but less celebrated contribution as a nonfiction writer to postwar political culture. In the end, her ability to mobilize the politics of an older black left to respond to the radical transformations of the 1960s foreshadowed the high level of artistic experimentation associated with the Black Arts Movement (BAM) and renders Hansberry a critical and provocative bridge between the civil rights and Black Power eras.

"I want to reach a little closer to the world," Hansberry once shared with James Baldwin.[8] It was an expansive sentiment that Baldwin would memorialize in the preface to her autobiography, as he would the contradictory image of her walking home from the meeting with Robert F. Kennedy with her face "twisted, her hands clasped before her belly, eyes darker than any eyes I have ever seen before."[9] Unlike Cruse's cartoonish image of Hansberry with a dull sword charging, Baldwin chose to seal his memory of the author with the image of her solitary walk home, an impression that plays on Cruse's tone of isolation with far greater accord. Using poetic form, a genre somewhat uncharacteristic of him, Baldwin wrote of that day in 1963:

> I knew I could not call her.
> Our car drove on; we passed her.
> And then, we heard the thunder.[10]

James Baldwin's slide into poetry with its abbreviated composition suggests, at the very least, that he sought to convey a nearly wordless sympathy for the playwright. With its paradoxical allusion to speechlessness ("I knew I could not call her") and sound ("and then, we heard the thunder")—there is something of the spokesman's simultaneous importance and irrelevance; history's passage and power, shaking beneath the individual historical actor. "Do we not all feel that, at the very least," Hansberry once pleaded, as if she were speaking to this contradiction directly, "that the spokesmen of the oppressed, are entitled . . . to scream for help as they please?"[11]

Hansberry's question was not a capitulation. It was a demand. Contemporary scholarship has rightly understood *A Raisin in the Sun* as a model text of revolutionary Pan-Africanism and radical feminism, as a work that inspired a range of Black Power activists in the 1960s. But the innovative form of address Hansberry used in her nonfiction writing served as an equally bold harbinger of the experimental spirit of the Black Arts and Black Power movements. Like the young playwrights and radicals who would follow in her wake, Hansberry brought her art and politics to the masses. In this context, Hansberry's internationalism and her public efforts to address racial injustice on the local, national, and global level—however imperfect or partial—reflect the hopes and struggles of a postwar generation that historiography has only just begun to unravel.

Lorraine Vivian Hansberry was born on May 19, 1930, in Chicago, Illinois, to Carl and Nannie Hansberry. Her young life, by most standards, was unique. The Hansberry household entertained a salonlike atmosphere of notable black politicians and intellectuals, including Paul Robeson, Duke Ellington, and Walter White, to name a few. In addition to these social networks, her uncle, William Leo Hansberry, a pioneering professor of African history at Howard University, passed through the Chicago area often and brought young, bright students from the African continent with him. The rich cultural and political education she garnered from these experiences left her with an intellectual curiosity that could not be satisfied with college study alone. After two years of course work at the University of Wisconsin she left to seek "an education of a different kind."[12] Hansberry moved to New York City in 1950 where she immediately joined the staff of Paul Robeson's monthly, *Freedom*, and continued her education, studying African history under the tutelage of W. E. B. Du Bois at the Jefferson School of Social Science.[13] Hansberry would work with the Harlem-based *Freedom* and a number of other black radical organizations in the city during the first half of the 1950s, participating in a variety of social justice causes that galvanized the interracial left.

"I remember Lorraine Hansberry when she first came to New York," recalled friend and writer John Oliver Killens. "We engaged in many dialogues and shared many concerns about the world, about its movement in the direction of fundamental change . . . The question that would always come up was—what role should the artist play in bringing this change about?"[14] Killens' memory captures the tumult that lay beneath the repressive atmosphere of McCarthyism. Throughout the post–World War II period, anticolonial movements shook the world and radically altered individual lives and imaginations. In the United States, this explosive shift, combined with the surge of urban migration and a burgeoning civil rights movement, created an almost unimaginable confluence of political possibility. Postwar Harlem, a Mecca of vibrant and internationally attuned communities, reflected and participated in many of these transformations. There, intellectuals like William L. Patterson, Robeson and Du Bois built progressive associations and forged contact with a new generation of black artists—a group that included Hansberry and John Killens, along with Julian Mayfield, Ruby Dee, Ossie Davis, Loften Mitchell, Alice Childress, John H. Clarke, and Sidney Poitier. These young artists, coming out of urban institutions that explicitly advanced the role of culture in political struggle, stood poised at the center of these postwar changes.

Paul Robeson, in particular, helped politicize many in this milieu. During this period, Robeson championed a number of social justice causes and Hansberry and her peers were drawn into a loose network of black radical institutions in New York City including the Council on African Affairs, the National Negro Labor Council, the Committee for the Negro in the Arts, and the Civil Rights Congress (CRC).

Organizations like the CRC provided Hansberry with a comprehensible frame to relate to the progressive movement. The CRC not only fostered an antiracist and internationalist framework but promoted political and intellectual experimentation.[15] Many CRC campaigns utilized artists' labor around high profile trials. Its national executive secretary, William Patterson, believed that most people were "visually minded," and he considered it generally difficult to present a full and clear appreciation of the issues to a wider public "through lecture and discussions alone." As a result, he actively encouraged cultural performances of CRC initiatives.[16] Experienced in theater, many young writers were asked specifically to contribute dramatic work to the campaigns. Writer and theater historian Loften Mitchell remembered attending rallies "first as an usher, then as a script-writer," a pattern of apprenticeship that matched Lorraine Hansberry's experience.[17] In numerous meetings to agitate or raise money, Hansberry was asked to compose or direct a short piece, or was called upon to give a reading.[18] More commonly, however, she produced texts readily translatable into staged performances. She wrote two scripts in the early 1950s, one to raise money to restore Robeson's passport (which had been revoked by the State Department in 1950), the other to benefit *Freedom* magazine.[19]

The dramatic form appealed to Hansberry because it allowed the artist to fashion debate and communication in sharp relief. As she explained more fully, "I'm particularly attracted to a medium where not only do you get to do what we do in life every day—you know, talk to people—but to be very selective about the nature of the conversation."[20] In this way, a dramatic piece could be carefully designed to impassion; to encourage an audience to question its assumptions, and ultimately "[to] have them do what you want them to do."[21]

But attention to form was not limited to drama. Hansberry and her peers were well versed in the play of genres, particularly in the relationship between journalism and theater, politics and publicity work. Hansberry strongly believed that mass culture provided an attractive venue for the transformative power of art. Unlike those who feared the totalizing logic of the mass culture industry during the postwar period, Hansberry saw a ready audience for political courting. In a letter to Hoyt Fuller, the editor of *Negro Digest*, for instance, she outlined her inclinations toward popular venues: "As far as I am concerned there is no audience worth writing for (or otherwise producing for) other than the popular one." Hansberry continued, "I regard myself, and ever will do so, as a 'popular' writer. I am aware that the artists in the world hold that as an epithet; to me it is the supreme tribute, as I know of no achievement or development in the history of world literature, drama, painting, film that was not evolved out of the process of communication with the broadest base of 'the people.'"[22]

If the militant edge of art depended on its well-crafted form, then its breadth was an added boon.[23] As Mary Dudziak has shown, the intersection of global social justice movements with Cold War imperatives amplified racial politics in the public sphere; and television, radio and popular magazines increasingly began to provide intellectuals like Hansberry with the expanded access they so eagerly sought.[24]

The intricate debts and innovations that marked her response to public intellectual work in the early 1960s suggest that Hansberry focused on the liberating possibilities behind new media.[25] Although she was eager to discard the "paper curtains" of the McCarthy era, Hansberry's skills (honed in the radical black left) as a writer and organizer, journalist and playwright, helped her to create an entry point into this new narrative landscape. The role demanded a considerable amount of her time, thought, and strategy. But Hansberry wore it with a sober optimism and desire for collective liberation that marked her political education. In the end, she used the flexibility of her media training to sustain a black radical vision in the public sphere and affirmed an image of public intellectual activity that included the active participation of women of color in postwar political thought.

THE ESSAYIST AS PLAYWRIGHT: WORKPLACE POLITICS AND THE STAGING OF HISTORY

In 1958, *Ebony* editor Dale Wright wrote Hansberry a letter and suggested that they "throw a little light on" the unknown author: "I don't recall having seen your photo anywhere or read anything about you anywhere." He explained, "We like to look for stories that others may have missed and I am therefore proposing that we write a profile on you in one of our magazines." This note was one of the first of many like it to come along; letters curious about this unfamiliar, young writer who had somehow gotten her play on Broadway.[26] Lorraine Hansberry was, of course, not new to the city's writing scene. She began working at *Freedom* magazine in 1950 and became an associate editor in 1952. Although she continued to freelance for the magazine, toward the end of 1953 Hansberry resigned from her editorial post to begin writing full time. Although she is best known for *Raisin*, Hansberry's dramatic interests were wide ranging. At the time of her death she had a number of dramas and screenplays in draft form, with settings that ranged from the American South, Africa and Haiti, to dramas that explored eighteenth-century England, ancient Egypt, and early American Navajo culture.[27] Between 1954 and 1958, she worked odd jobs around the city of New York and continued to write. But after 1959 and *A Raisin in the Sun*, Hansberry was catapulted from relative obscurity to celebrity within less than a year.

A prolific playwright, Hansberry was also a formidable essayist and provocative interview subject. Her negotiation of media openly borrowed from her background as an activist and playwright. Interviews, in particular, adapted to the paradigm of effective politicized drama because they engaged in a form of abbreviated debate or conversation around a conflicting set of viewpoints.[28] Editorials and dissenting quips openly borrowed from this model of a highly controlled conversation. Through "living arguments," Hansberry was able to create the image of a shared discursive space in order to help transform and contest dominant narratives from below.

Take, for instance, a *Village Voice* piece critical of author Norman Mailer. Here Hansberry carefully reframed her analysis of Mailer's personal race prejudice to decry American foreign diplomacy. "There is certainly nothing fresh in the spectacle of white people insisting on telling all sorts of colored peoples how they should behave to satisfy them," she wrote of Mailer. "It is, to say the least, the most characteristic aspect of the nation's foreign policy."[29] And in a *New Yorker* interview in 1959, Hansberry slipped a small reference to anticolonialism into an article that had nothing to do with foreign news or diplomacy. Responding to a question of how she was enjoying the afterglow of *Raisin*'s success, she located her personal achievement in the context of the African Diaspora. With a single sentence, she shifted the question away from the rise in her personal fortunes to the wave of liberation movements that were changing the fortunes of people throughout the world: "One of the reasons I feel so free," she responded, "is that I feel I belong to a world majority, and a very assertive one."[30] Whether through an extended analysis or a dry and incisive aside, Hansberry offered an alternative perspective, resting her public commentary in a global and historical frame.[31]

THE PLAYWRIGHT AS A CELEBRITY: GENDER POLITICS AND STAGING OF INTELLECTUAL WORK

Although Hansberry's struggle in the context of mass media was informed by an earlier era of radical cultural politics, her emergence in the public sphere of the early 1960s was marked by new challenges. Foremost among these was the role of celebrity. "Every Negro celebrity is, according to white America, an authority on race relations," wrote contemporary Loften Mitchell.[32] Mitchell's observation engaged the excessive and untenable components of black celebrity in this era. Public recognition may have developed out of an appreciation of professional achievement, yet celebrity itself embodied a tenuous thread to the labor that lay beneath. Fame may have allowed intellectuals to showcase their skills and have a voice in public affairs.[33] But occupying the space was riddled with contradiction. "Certainly prudence dictated to nearly all the celebrities who did not have political organizations to back them up," friend and writer Julian Mayfield wrote sympathetically, "but now depend for their bread on the commercial market place, controlled by whites. It is a tightrope," he added, "[that] no [artist] ought to be forced to walk."[34]

Although the relationship with dominant culture offered a slippery and unequal exchange, Hansberry and her generation of black leftists did not engage the medium with naiveté. The obvious dangers of alienation had always been a professional risk. In a speech given to the Committee for the Negro in the Arts in 1952, Robeson explained the importance of artists' responsiveness to community needs and initiatives. "We must continue to help break down all barriers in the concert field, in the opera houses, in the theaters, in the films, in television, radio, in the salons of painting and photography," he urged. "But in doing this, we must not lose respect for or fail to deepen and help to develop the great tradition bequeathed to us, we must not extract ourselves from our communities."[35] The nature of Robeson's concern had not significantly changed a decade later, but the potential breadth of that gap had arguably grown.

After the Broadway production of *A Raisin in the Sun*, Hansberry moved from laboring as an unknown to writing for a rapidly expanded audience. Solicitations arrived from a range of periodicals from *Ebony* to *Mademoiselle*.[36] Judging from the range of periodicals that Hansberry wrote for in the early 1960s, "the broadest base of 'the people'" signified a wide demographic public—one that included blacks and whites, working and middle-class readers alike. As she told the *New Yorker* in 1959, "I now get twenty to thirty pieces of mail a day." Some of these letters were invitations to teas, lunches, and dinners. Others were requests to write books and adapt mystery stories for the movies.[37] Many came from progressive causes, civil rights organizations, and women's groups, all hoping to coax the young author to speak at a particular event. According to the *New Yorker* interview, Hansberry openly disliked "the concomitants of being a celebrity," and sometimes associated the media's glare with being "besieged."[38] Although Hansberry entertained doubts as to whether celebrity status could work as a tool of liberation, her optimism regarding the benefits of intellectual work marked her actions and she fought to promote critical public debate on the social justice issues that were shaking her world.[39]

With Robeson's photograph decorating her work desk, it is likely that she was mindful of his struggles as she made her way as an artist and spokeswoman in the early 1960s. Indeed, Paul Robeson's experience in the 1950s provided her with a deeply cautionary sense of how to use celebrity for political ends. Although the singer's reputation worked to build a following, even during the height of persecution against him, his experience with censorship underscored the fact that media negotiation was a labor not a luxury, a fair-weather medium to be handled with care.[40]

The costs were as real in the 1960s as they were a decade earlier. Critics questioned this generation's political commitment and centered that criticism on their relationship with white power brokers. The emergent spectacle of celebrity only added new teeth to the familiar charge. "How can anyone maintain that a writer who took part in . . . debate with white liberals, and the celebrated summit meeting with Attorney-General Robert Kennedy was not trying to pose as a spokesman?" Harold Cruse asked rhetorically, shifting attention from Hansberry's political message to her political persona.[41]

As evidenced by Cruse's barb, celebrity status not only failed to shield artists from racial discrimination, but a new set of labels beset many of those in public life. On the one hand, as historian Ben Keppel shares, there was the polished image represented by the "poised and dignified" reputation of Sidney Poitier who, in Keppel's words, stood for the ideal or "quintessential American."[42] On the other hand, race leaders were overdrawn as crazy, arrogant blacks at odds with racial and national progress. Loften Mitchell catalogued the litany well:

> It should be noted that the white press has not allowed another Negro hero to escape unscathed. Paul Robeson was too far left of center. Jackie Robinson too explosive and loud-mouthed. Floyd Patterson too frightened and neurotic, Sonny Liston too shady a character, Bill Russell too black-conscious . . . And Adam Clayton Powell is too flamboyant, James Baldwin and LeRoi Jones and John Killens too angry, William Branch and Alice Childress too arrogant and so on and so forth.[43]

Lorraine Hansberry was not immune to the kind of representational crisis that worked to undermine her political message. Foremost among her challenges was the play of her own subjectivity. As a black woman intellectual, she evoked a series of representative tensions "when and where" she entered the public sphere, to borrow Paula Gidding's phrase.[44] This challenge was not lost on many of her contemporaries. "You've made history and quite creatively. It's all the more significant and brilliant because you're so young and a Negro woman, having to overcome a few more extra hurdles than the male of the species," wrote former New York City Councilman Benjamin Davis in a letter to Hansberry, "so all of us should feel even more proud, and the men a little less smug in their 'supremacist' airs."[45] Davis' thoughtful and personal response to Hansberry's achievement, tough repeated among some of her colleagues, was often overshadowed by the open misogyny of critics. Harold Cruse's language regarding *A Raisin in the Sun* stands as a good case in point. He branded the play a feminized and "glorified soap opera," likened Hansberry's commentary to "bleating" and "snapping," and characterized her analysis in general as "oversimplified" and "over-emotionalized."[46]

Similarly, a great deal of speculation surrounded Hansberry's private life. Marked alternatively as a diminutive and determined, media coverage of her often struck an ambiguous note. A *New York Times* article, for instance, described her as "voluble, energetic, pretty and small."[47] The dissonance of these images is echoed in comments made by some of her contemporaries. To friend Julian Mayfield, the fact that Hansberry "looked like a coed" but could be "so serious and to the point," rendered her intellectualism somewhat troubling—the unexpected presence of a bold and incisive power of reason in a starkly female frame. The fact that Hansberry "was always trying to think things through," to his memory, struck some of her contemporaries as a "distinctly unsweet and unfemale" virtue.[48]

But the imprint of class and elite status also framed the tenor of many of the images. As Baldwin would write, "[Hansberry's] fame was to cause her to be criticized very harshly, very loudly, and very often by both black and white people who were unable to believe, apparently, that a really serious intention could be contained in so glamorous a frame."[49]

Hansberry's own middle-class origins, her devotion to interracial exchange, and the fact that her plays fashioned white characters with complexity, may have all served as fodder for these critiques. But although she may have carved out an image of herself as a middle-class bohemian, a number of critics represented her background and politics in a profoundly unbalanced and caustic light.[50] To them, her "middle-class" outlook degraded her cultural contributions and limited her political role in black liberation struggle. Not womanly or black enough to represent the race, they argued, Hansberry stood precipitously on the edge of betrayal from the black community.

Hansberry, for her part, interpreted the representative tension that surrounded her role differently and used the pressures of mass media to shape the public dimension of her art.[51] After 1959 and *A Raisin in the Sun*, Hansberry's opinions increasingly secured a published forum but the content of her editorials steadfastly resisted simplification. In an article written in *Ebony*, for example, Hansberry provoked her largely black audience along global, racial, and gender lines. A fairly open-ended assignment from the start, the series' subject, "Black Womanhood," drew a variety of responses from writers. Unlike many of the others commissioned for the installment, however, Hansberry's expansive racial geography of the imagination situated her black women on the plantations of Brazil and the United States.

For three centuries, Hansberry declared, black women endured and wrestled against the "fiercest oppression of modern history." "It is the complex of womanhood," she continued, "which now awakens with varying degrees of consciousness thus far to find itself inextricably and joyously bound to the world's most insurgent elements: the people of Africa and Asia."

Hansberry's engaged black internationalism, often associated with masculine feats, offered a vision of a gendered dispute that located women as vanguards of revolutionary change. Moreover, given the salience of a Pan-African perspective in the narrative, it is interesting to observe her vision of global solidarity open to the possibility for interracial alliances. Foregrounding an "ailing world which sorely needs *our* defiance" (emphasis mine), she stretched the parameters of "our" to include nonblacks. "May we," she urged "as Negroes, or women, never accept the notion—'our place.'"

Although a small detail, her use of the phrase "Negroes or women," instead of "Negro women," may not necessarily suggest a wider constituency to participate in antiracist and antisexist protest. But the language does legitimize gender oppression in a way that invites belonging, and that even might allow women of color to see themselves in common cause with other women.

Ultimately, Hansberry's espousal of a Pan-Africanist interracialism nettled critics who viewed her flexible, pragmatic politics as muddled thinking or opportunistic posing. To these detractors, Hansberry's stress on commonalities seemed to embody a leftwing bent on consensus theory or, alternatively, a variant of "left-liberal internationalism" recently evinced by Christina Klein and her work on Cold War culture.[52] But these same postwar influences, I would argue, sound an alternate register with the playwright. The simple fact that Hansberry offered militant black women across the globe as the vanguards for social change should be enough to place her vision in uneasy relation to those narratives that softly, but unequivocally, championed US expansionism.

In the end, Hansberry would publicly defend and continue the project of cross racial work alongside her push for racial self-determination at a time when that sort of balancing act became increasingly unpopular. Moreover, she would explore gender and sexual oppression with equal interest to friend and contemporary James Baldwin although many of these thoughts would find their fullest public expression anonymously.[53] But unlike Baldwin, who was largely resistant to the allures of Pan-Africanism, Hansberry connected the interlocking histories of sex and gender oppression to race and class struggles—linking what she called, "anti-homosexual sentiment" to the oppression of women, black Americans, and colonial peoples abroad.[54]

Atypically trenchant in her analysis of heterosexual discrimination, her stance is all the more remarkable given the increasingly polarized political landscape that had begun to valorize "authentic" forms of black masculinity and femininity. If the nonnormative thinking of figures like Baldwin and Hansberry troubled their willingness to confirm to traditional sex and gender roles that were gaining legitimacy in the black freedom struggle, these transgressions in subjectivity would heighten their vulnerability to charges of sycophancy and betrayal at certain turns in the movement's future. National Urban League's Whitney Young, for example, touched on this perspective directly. "While Lorraine Hansberry is a gifted playwright and while Baldwin is a gifted writer," he said, "these are not people who either by their experiences or by their training or by their whole emotional orientation, are by any means leaders of the Negro Revolution."[55] Is it possible that Hansberry played on this same tenor of instability to sustain a dramatic presence in public life? The content of Young's aspersion casts Hansberry outside the circle of race leaders. But interestingly, she remains very much in the frame, a topic of discussion despite his unease.

James Baldwin once wrote, "The general reaction to famous people who hold difficult opinions, is that they can't really mean it. It's considered . . . to be merely an astute way of attracting public attention, a way of making oneself interesting . . . sell[ing] one's books."[56] Perhaps the truth of Hansberry's postwar intellectual life lies somewhere in between political sincerity and professional expediency. Indeed, if we return, as we began, to Hansberry's meeting with Kennedy, her actions not only provide an ideal context to challenge Whitney Young's concerns regarding her viability as a race leader—but they suggest, simultaneously, that "making oneself interesting" may not have been a liability.

By 1963, her tenure in the spotlight had familiarized her with the political promise, and fragility, that such a diplomatic encounter held. Staged words had the power to unsettle as much as connect, revealing the work intellectual labor required of its practitioners. If her celebrity had gotten her into the room with Kennedy, her media skills set her words in motion; Hansberry demonstrated her sophisticated understanding of the representative layers of media work and her own relationship to it.

Consistent with her highly choreographed interventions, Hansberry put her own body on the same stage as her narrative landscape. In one well documented moment, she highlighted the image of "white copy standing on [a] Negro wom-an's neck" to dramatize the unchecked violence of the nation, an image that she knew would play poorly in the context of the Cold War. However, this same image also resonated with her own position vis-á-vis Kennedy. Though not a seamless connection, the symmetry placed Hansberry in common cause with these marchers. While at the same time, the *differences* between her and these mil-itants allowed the playwright to create an explosive political message of violence without severing the basis of dialogue with the Attorney General.[57] It was a very savvy use of her privileged voice as spokeswoman of the oppressed. Interestingly, Hansberry chose to end the meeting with this image of state repression, a kind of dramatic flair that worked to her advantage. "[And] then," recalled Baldwin of the meeting's end, Hansberry "smiled [at Kennedy]," extended her hand to him, and left the room, followed soon after by the others.[58]

Whether moving from side, center, to off stage—or imbuing a formal, ratio-nal meeting with sensory and brutal content—Hansberry layered the tensions of gender, race, and class to deliberately provoke debate without sundering it. Drawing on an admixture of sympathy and command, she exposed the impos-sible seductions and contradictions of her role. "We all know," she once said sympathetically, of the difficulty that "colors all efforts" to try to really "talk to one another" across racial borders.[59] Hansberry used those tensions without nec-essarily resisting the seductions of celebrity culture, but she may have embraced its imaginary value, rechanneling the drama surrounding the image of a black woman intellectual at work in close sympathy with her own political desires.

THE LIMITS OF STAGING: BLACK AND RED

John Oliver Killens would celebrate Hansberry's heated precision in staged events like these, calling her literary acumen "one of the fastest guns in the east."[60] I figure the best way to approach all these talk shows is to act as if you don't expect to be invited back again, and to say what's on your mind," Hansberry once told Julian Mayfield directly.[61] To Mayfield's memory, Hansberry pushed the enve-lope: "[S]he accepted radio and television engagements which bored her, and speaking engagements which challenged her, for the sole purpose of getting across her racial view from the black perspective." In short, "[Hansberry] intended to use what leverage she had while she could."[62] These bold choices mark her as an underacknowledged political strategist. But some also reveal the bounds of public political candor in this era.

There were, of course, obvious limits to her ability to manage a stage. It should also not come as a surprise, for example, that Hansberry steadfastly rejected oppor-tunities that would have openly compromised her.[63] She was repeatedly asked by the United States Information Agency (USIA) to submit "one or two scenes" of *A Raisin in the Sun* for overseas readership. Like the meeting with Kennedy, this request was not extraordinary. As Frances Stonor Saunders has documented, the CIA attempted—and, in a number of cases, succeeded—to enlist prominent art-ists and cultural organizations in their Cold War battles.[64] Her response, however (unlike many of her fellow New York intellectuals at the *Partisan Review*), reveals a heightened sensitivity to the underlying motives of government solicitations in the context of the Cold War.[65] Although Hansberry eagerly sought diasporic connections in the black world, she balked at transatlantic offerings that aimed to selectively exploit her status in order to further its own agenda with audiences of color worldwide—not naming her expertise explicitly but counting on its cultural capital abroad. The letter of permission from the USIA was neither signed nor returned by the author. Jotted atop a similar 1964 request by the United States Information Agency, sits a note written in Hansberry's hand. "This is for propaganda purposes which intends to give a false notion of 'Negro achievement' in USA," it reads. "Ignore."[66]

Although Hansberry was unwilling to have her celebrity persona serve as mitigating fodder in the battle of hearts and minds any more than her cultural work, as public appearances by prominent black Americans became more frequent, mass media failed the hopes many had in its cultural and democratic promise. One of her letters to the *New York Times* marked the parameters of his postwar stage.[67] It is worth looking at this essay briefly.

On January 17, 1961, Patrice Lumumba, the Prime Minister of the Congo, was brutally murdered, and his death inspired demonstrations across the globe. In a letter written on the heels of the assassination, Hansberry quickly condemned the assassination in print and allied herself with the demonstrators who organized outside the United Nations. Although the UN demonstration featured a number of globally minded nationalists, journalists spun the event as Soviet inspired a common anticommunist tactic of tainting black militancy with Party provocation.[68] Hansberry joined other dissenting voices and countered the inflammatory charges of anticommunism of the mainstream press in her letter. But she did so without erasing the presence of communists, a move that set her apart from a number of sympathetic accounts.

In a subtle shift, Hansberry supplanted the popular image of Ralph Bunch (who had spoken out against the demonstration) with that of Benjamin Davis or, in her words, "any other Negro who had the passion and understanding to be there."[69] Davis later thanked Hansberry personally for noting his presence at the UN rally. "My participation in the picket line was very humble and small in the total picture," he wrote her, "but there are times when the unity of the Negroes can have dramatic impact, and the murder of Lumumba was one of those times."[70] Hansberry seemed to agree. She too demanded "high and steadfast unity among Negroes" in the face of the atrocity. And in widening the representative community and pulling other viable race leaders into the mix—particularly communists and former communists—she raised the powerful image of a black nationalist and Marxist coalition. The explicit connection she drew between older black leftists and young nationalists was bold indeed.

Just as she had carefully positioned herself in the same trajectory with militant women in the black diaspora, Hansberry allowed the images of black nationalists to comingle with her own and that of Davis. This forthright radicalism may have cost her. Julian Mayfield thought it did. When editors of major periodicals understood that Hansberry was not going to, in Mayfield's words, "retire into . . .'idle and luxurious simplicity,'" they stopped printing many of her letters.[71] Hansberry's passionate and uncompromising stance with the media drew an accessible yet distinctly radical blueprint for change. But blurring her middle class glamour with militant women was a very different project than juxtaposing her popularity with the distinctly unpopular communists. As a result, Hansberry ability to both soothe and foreground the rupture in the national narrative found its limit in the specter of black and red.

THE CELEBRITY AS ACTIVIST: CULTURAL
WORK AND THE STAGING OF POLITICS

Julian Mayfield contacted Lorraine Hansberry on the eve of *A Raisin in the Sun*. "I take selfish pleasure in all this, and I'm sure the other writers of our group feel the same way," he wrote to her. "With 'Raisin' you have blasted a hole that will make things better for the rest of us."[72] Hansberry approached media with a sober optimism and desire for collective liberation that marked her early political education. But although she struggled to capture the capricious benefits of the spotlight and promote a meaningful role for public intellectual work in the postwar era—she did not do so perfectly, or even to her own satisfaction. Hansberry openly mused on what sometimes seemed like the yawning gap between the politics of the pen and that of the streets. On July 17, 1964, roughly six months before her death, Hansberry took these concerns to heart. "Have the feeling I should throw myself back into the movement. Become a human being again," she wrote, "but that very impulse is immediately flashed with a thousand vacillations and forbidding images." She continued, "*Comfort* has come to be its own corruption . . . I rather *looked forward* to going to jail once. Now I can hardly imagine surviving it at all. Comfort. Apparently I have sold my soul for it. I think when I get my health back I shall go into the south to find out what kind of revolutionary I am" (italics Hansberry's).[73] Hansberry's confession suggests that there were serious risks to public intellectual activity. Years afterward, the cost of commanding a public platform was not forgotten on Baldwin. Her brisk walk out the door of her meeting with Kennedy, he would write, was the last time he would see Hansberry on her feet. The playwright died in 1965 at the age of thirty-four, a little over a year after the fateful summit in New York City.

Baldwin would not be alone in equating her death with the cost of entertaining a political platform. His posthumous musings on the author's life tapped a dramatic and sharp vein. "The pressure of being a writer is one thing, but the pressure of being a public figure is another," he wrote, "the strain can kill you . . . it is certainly one of the things that killed Lorraine, who was very vivid, very young, [and] very curious."[74] The combined specter of fame and death reveal the mindset of those that witnessed the slow but inexorable attrition of race men and women. But the association between violence and celebrity is striking. Like Baldwin, Mayfield linked the terrible fate of leaders like Patrice Lumumba to Hansberry's premature death. Ending his memorial tribute to the playwright on a somber note, his allusion to possible intrigue suggests that, in Mayfield's imagination, these skirmishes of the pen and platform were not simply the stretches of armchair intellectuals but a political offense that engendered an equally militant response. "I can't avoid a final observation," wrote Mayfield. "I have never been resigned, personally or politically, to the death of Lorraine Hansberry." He concluded, "This might be a sort of paranoia, and one must run the risk of the accusation . . . They [US intelligence] plotted murder of foreign leaders, and character assassination at home . . . There was no depth to which US intelligence would not sink . . . Now that much of the shabby mess is out, we must ask, "Why not murder radical blacks?" Especially those with a platform. I think of three young black people who died during the period, Franz Fanon, Frank Lloyd Brown and Lorraine Hansberry . . . We have a right to wonder."[75]

During the BAM, the notion that words were weapons achieved a level of cultural cachet hardly worth questioning. Yet it was an idea that Hansberry had struggled to set the stage for during which much of her tenure in the postwar period. Her deep interest in black aesthetics and power inspired her theatrical reworkings from the start.

Lorraine Hansberry's innovative form of address met the demands of public intellectual work in the context of celebrity culture. With one eye on a burgeoning mass media and another on the explosive potential of liberation struggles across the globe, the artist struggled to deliberately engage the pressing exigencies of her time. While some criticized her celebrity, others affirmed the symbolic importance attendant to her rise. Editor Lerone Bennett Jr., for instance, suggested that Hansberry and her play marked the hopeful tenor of the times. She was, according to Bennett, "a person announcing the coming of something," the rise of a people on the heels of the Montgomery boycott and on the eve of the Greensboro sit-ins.[76]

Hansberry's effort to raise the struggles of the oppressed to the world stage marks an important and underexamined chapter in the history of black politics and culture. Until recently, the history of postwar black radicalism argued that governmental prosecution of leftwing activists and organizations dramatically circumscribed radical initiatives at the onset of the Cold War and relegated the 1950s to the margins, either as the decline of the radicalism of the 1930s and 1940s or as the calm before the storm of the black nationalist and Black Power movements.[77] A number of scholars, however, have begun to reassess the role and periodization of Black radical politics in the postwar period.[78] As a result, the image of the oppressive 1950s has begun to give way to a revised portrait, where the quiet seething of global decolonization lay beneath the pitch of anticommunist repression.

Indeed, if one weighs the experience of Lorraine Hansberry and her peers, it is clear that the 1950s was a *constitutive* moment for the radical education of Black leftists. She used the lessons of the McCarthy era to address a revolutionary shift in the political climate. Her labors as a spokeswoman suggest that her savvy negotiation of media, her trenchant analysis of foreign policy, and her interlocking vision of oppression were heavily indebted to the eclectic political culture she experienced during the 1950s.[79] She fought for clemency for the Rosenbergs; assailed the assassination of Lumumba. Hansberry, Davis, Dee, and Mayfield worked in common cause with Malcolm X; their paths crossing in the Harlem campaigns for Robert F. Williams and h is battles in Monroe,

North Carolina; and again, in the riotous demonstration in midtown following the murder of the young Congolese leader, Patrice Lumumba. Indeed, Malcolm X was only eight years older than Lorraine Hansberry. She shared, in the words of Ossie Davis, Malcolm X's belief in the "power words have over the minds of men"; shared the "bristling agitation" on behalf of their people with an eye to unity and global struggle, reaching, "stretch[ing] out [their] hands towards truth."[80] As a result, Hansberry's story reveals the longstanding struggles of a generation to register a lasting impact on black art and antiracist politics at the middle of the century.

NOTES

1. *New York Times.* "Robert Kennedy Confers Today with Theater Men on Race Issue." May 27, 1963; *New York Times.* "Robert Kennedy Consults Negroes Here About North." May 25, 1963; *New York Times.* "Robert Kennedy Fails to Persuade Negroes at Secret Talks Here." May 26, 1963.

2. See Ben Keppel, *The Work of Democracy: Ralph Bunche, Kenneth B. Clark, Lorraine Hansberry, and the Cultural Politics of Race* (Cambridge, MA: Harvard University Press, 1995), and Mary L. Dudziak, "Josephine Baker, Racial Protest, and the Cold War," *Journal of American History* 81 (September 1994): 543–570.

3. "Robert Kennedy Consults Negroes Here About North," *New York Times*, May 25, 1963.

4. Lorraine Hansberry, *To Be Young, Gifted and Black: Lorraine Hansberry in Her Own Words* (New York: Vintage, 1995), p. 220.

5. Esther Peterson, Executive Vice Chairman of The President's Commission on the Status of Women, to Lorraine Hansberry, February 15, 1963. Lorraine Hansberry Papers, Estate of Lorraine Hansberry, Croton-on-the-Hudson, New York (hereafter referred to as LHE). I was able to review a box of Hansberry's papers while at the Estate in Croton-on-the-Hudson. The collection has been since transferred to the Schomburg Center for Research in Black Culture.

6. Originally published in 1967, *The Crisis of the Intellectual* tackled over forty years of the history of Black politics and thought. Nearly six hundred pages long, broken into twenty-eight chapters, fifteen of which were devoted to a group of post World War II Black artists in New York City that included Hansberry and her peers. With the keen eye of an insider, Cruse asked hard and important questions in a bold and iconoclastic style but he painted his postwar generation with wildly polemical strokes. In his view, they were a bourgeois clique, the darlings of the "leftwing interracial set." Their "middle-class" outlook and "integrationist" frame degraded their cultural contributions and delimited their political role in Black liberation struggles in the United States. See Harold Cruse, *The Crisis of the Negro Intellectual: A Historical Analysis of the Failure of Black Leadership* (New York: Quill, 1984), pp. 220, 267, 498. For a critique of Cruse that contextualizes the struggles of the Black postwar left see Peniel E. Joseph, *Waiting 'Til the Midnight Hour: A Narrative History of Black Power in America* (New York: Henry Holt, 2006).

7. Cruse, *The Crisis of the Negro Intellectual*, p. 102.

8. Lorraine Hansberry cited by James Baldwin in *To Be Young, Gifted and Black*, p. xiv.

9. James Baldwin, "Lorraine Hansberry at the Summit," *Freedomways* (4th Quarter, 1979): p. 272.

10. Ibid.

11. Lorraine Hansberry, "Miss Hansberry on Blacklash," *Village Voice* (July 23, 1964): pp. 10, 16.

12. Seven R. Carter, "Lorraine Hansberry," in *Dictionary of Literary Biography: Afro-American Writers After 1955* (Detroit: The Gale Group, 1985), p. 122. Also see Steven R. Carter, *Hansberry's Drama: Commitment Amid Complexity* (Urbana: University of Illinois Press, 1991).

13. Gerald Horne, *Black and Red: W.E.B. Du Bois and the Afro-American Response to the Cold War, 1944–1963* (Albany: State University of New York Press, 1986), pp. 262–263.

14. John Oliver Killens, "Lorraine Hansberry: On Time!" *Freedomways* (4th Quarter 1979): pp. 273–274.

15. The Civil Rights Congress (CRC) fought several well-known civil rights and civil liberty cases during the 1940s and 1950s. The organization also authored a petition to the UN in 1951, charging the US government with genocide against African Americans under the 1948 UN Convention on the Prevention and Punishment of the Crime of Genocide. Also see William Patterson, *The Man Who Cried Genocide: An Autobiography* (New York: International Publishers, 1991), pp. 157–158.

16. In 1951, for example, Lorraine Hansberry traveled to Mississippi as part of the CRC women's auxiliary, Sojourners for Truth and Justice, in order to boost the campaign of accused rapist and political prisoner, Willie McGee. As part of her activism she wrote a poem about McGee's wife, Rosalee, for distribution in leftwing periodicals. The Sojourners for Truth and Justice was initiated by Charlotta Bass, Shirley Graham, Louise Thompson Patterson, Alice Childress, Rosalie McGee. See Horne, *Communist Front? The Civil Rights Congress, 1946–1956* (Rutherford, NJ: Fairleigh Dickinson University Press, 1988), 87, 98, 208.

17. Loften Mitchell, *Black Drama: The Story of the American Negro Theater* (New York: Hawthorne Books, Inc., 1967), p. 177.

18. Author's interview with William B. Branch, December 1, 1999 (changes made in transcript during second interview on December 14, 1999), New Rochelle, NY.

19. Julian Mayfield, "Lorraine Hansberry: A Woman for All Seasons," *Freedomways* (4th Quarter 1979): p. 266.

20. Lorraine Hansberry, *To Be Young, Gifted and Black: Lorraine Hansberry in Her Own Words* (New York: Random House, 1995), p. 138.

21. Ibid., p. 139.

22. Lorraine Hansberry to Mr. Fuller, July 12, 1962, Lorraine Hansberry Papers, LHE.

23. For work on the politics and aesthetics of the Popular Front see Michael Denning, *The Cultural Front: The Laboring of American Culture in the Twentieth Century* (London; New York: Verso, 1996); James Edward Smethurst, *The New Red Negro: The Literary Left and African-American Poetry, 1930–1946* (New York: Oxford University Press, 1999).

24. Keppel, *The Work of Democracy*, p. 3.

25. Esther Peterson, Executive Vice Chairman of The President's Commission on the Status of Women, to Lorraine Hansberry, February 15, 1963, LHE. Barbara Savage has shown that radio elicited the same kind of hope in new technology. Barbara Savage, *Broadcasting Freedom, Radio, War, and the Politics of Race, 1938–1948* (Chapel Hill: University of North Carolina Press, 1999).

26. Wright (sic) to Lorraine Hansberry, September 19, 1958, Lorraine Hansberry Papers, LHE.

27. Carter, *Hansberry's Drama*, p. xii.

28. Hansberry, *To Be Young, Gifted and Black*, p. 119.

29. Lorraine Hansberry, "Thoughts on Genet, Mailer, and the New Paternalism," *Village Voice* (June 1, 1961): pp. 10–15.

30. Hansberry as cited in White, "The Talk of the Town," pp. 33–35.
31. Hansberry, letter to the editor re: Porgy and Bess debate, Lorraine Hansberry Papers, LHE.
32. Loften Mitchell, *Black Drama: The Story of the American Negro Theater* (New York: Hawthorne Books, Inc., 1967), p. 138.
33. Hansberry, "Miss Hansberry on 'Backlash,'" p. 10.
34. Mayfield, box 1, folder 12, Julian Mayfield Papers, SCH.
35. Paul Robeson, "Speech to the CNA Convention January 26, 1952," Reel 2, Paul Robeson Collection, SCH. Also see James Baldwin, *No Name in the Street* (New York: A Laurel Book, Dell Publishing, 1972), p. 12.
36. Wright [sic] to Lorraine Hansberry, September 19, 1958, Lorraine Hansberry Papers, LHE.
37. Lorraine Hansberry as cited in E.B. White, "The Talk of the Town," *The New Yorker* (May 9, 1959): pp. 33–35.
38. Hansberry as cited in Fisher, "Birthweight Low, Jobs Few, Death Comes Early," pp. 3, 9.
39. Lorraine Hansberry, "Miss Hansberry on 'Blacklash,'" *Village Voice* (July 23, 1964): pp. 10, 16.
40. For an analysis of the iconic status of later black feminists see Joy James, *Shadowboxing: Representations of Black Feminist Politics* (New York: St. Martin's Press, 1999). Future research might find it extraordinarily fruitful to consider Paul Robeson as a cultural symbol in his own right, much as scholars have done with Malcolm X.
41. Cruse, *The Crisis of the Negro Intellectual*, p. 411.
42. Keppel, *The Work of Democracy*, p. 1.
43. Mitchell, *Black Drama*, p. 127.
44. Paula Giddings, *When and Where I Enter: The Impact of Black Women on Race and Sex in America* (New York: William Morrow, 1984).
45. Benjamin Davis to Lorraine Hansberry, May 4, 1959, Lorraine Hansberry Papers, LHE.
46. Cruse, *The Crisis of the Negro Intellectual*, pp. 278, 284.
47. *New York Times*, April 9, 1959.
48. Mayfield, box 15, folder 9, Julian Mayfield Papers, SCH.
49. Baldwin, *To Be Young, Gifted and Black*, p. xix.
50. A personal letter written to Hansberry in 1961 by (then) LeRoi Jones explicitly drew on this likeness, for example, when he told her that she represented and "[spoke] for the American middleclass." A Raisin in the Sun, as a number of scholars have argued, was hardly a sentimental view of middle-class assimilationist politics. The play popularized the relationship between the continent of Africa and African Americans in the diaspora and tackled segregation, poverty, and the struggle for intraracial solidarity in a family crisscrossed by ideological, gender, class tensions. And although LeRoi Jones would later revise his conservative assessment of the author, lauding Raisin as antecedent of the Black Arts movement and Hansberry as someone on the cutting edge of the struggles of the Black freedom, the point had been made. His early impression—along with others— helped shape an image of the playwright that would last nearly two decades. LeRoi Jones to Lorraine Hansberry, June 13, 1961, Lorraine Hansberry Papers, LHE.
51. She balked at the notion of writing in white face, arguing that images of the Black middle class challenged whites and deprived many of them of the sensational, minstrelsy-fed images of African-American life they sought. Nevertheless, this jab at her class status was ironic, particularly coming from LeRoi Jones. Jones had his own middle class subjectivity to consider—not to mention the fact that he had achieved celebrity himself with Dutchman and Blues People. More to the point, Jones would measure the subject of fame with frank sympathy, only to leave Hansberry out. "I write now, full of trepidation

because I know the death this society intends for me," Jones wrote. "I see Jimmy Baldwin almost unable to write about himself anymore. I've seen Du Bois, Wright, Chester Himes, driven away—Ellison silenced and fidgeting in some college. I think I almost feel the same forces massing against me, almost before I've begun." It is worth noting that Jones' compassion circle extends exclusively to men. See Amiri Baraka, "LeRoi Jones Talking," in *Home: Social Essays* (Hopewell, NJ: Ecco Press, 1998), pp. 179–188.

52. For more on middlebrow sentimentalism in the context of postwar international affairs See Christina Klein, *Cold War Orientalism: Asia in the Middlebrow Imagination, 1945– 1961* (Berkeley: University of California Press, 2003).

53. James Baldwin's growing affinity with Hansberry in the late 1950s begs for an extended analysis, one that I do not provide here. A careful analysis of her appropriation of sexual roles within the context of the postwar period awaits forthcoming biographical work as well as full and public access to her papers. Nonetheless, the circumstances of their initial meeting and their continued literary and political collaboration centered on a shared interest in sexual politics and cross-racial communication. The power Hansberry afforded women was not lost on Baldwin. As he recalled of their meeting with Robert F. Kennedy, Hansberry actively shifted the discussion away from the perils of Black manhood to the candid oppression of African-American women, a move Baldwin acknowledged if not sympathized with. Kenneth Clarke, "A Conversation with James Baldwin," in John H. Clarke, ed., *Harlem: A Community in Transition* (New York: Citadel Press, 1964), p. 125. Audre Lorde and Baldwin would debate the importance of exploring gender discrimination in the Black community decades later; suggesting that Hansberry's impact on this score was partial. Lorraine Hansberry to the editor *Commentary* (March 5, 1963) written in response to Podhoretz's article "My Negro Problem and Yours" in *Commentary* (February 1963).

54. In the late 1950s and early 1960s Hansberry wrote several letters to two homophile publications, *One* and *The Ladder*, under the initials "LN" or "LHN" Judging from the letter she wrote to *The Ladder*, Hansberry's sexuality worked to expand her understanding of the interrelated nature of oppression. Early on, she explicitly framed "homosexuality" as a "question of human rights." Lorraine Hansberry, letter to the editor, April 18, 1961, Lorraine Hansberry Papers, LHE. Lorraine Hansberry, unpublished (unmailed) letter to the editor of *One*, April 18, 1961, and unpublished transcript entitled, "Simone de Beauvior and The Second Sex: An American Commentary," 1957 as cited in Carter, *Hansberry's Drama*, p. 6. Robert Nemiroff has argued that Hansberry's sexuality was not "a peripheral or casual part of her life but contributed significantly on many levels to the sensitivity and complexity of her view of human beings and of the world." Robert Nemiroff as cited in Carter, *Hansberry's Drama*, p. 6.

55. Carol Polsgrove, *Divided Minds: Intellectuals and the Civil Rights Movement* (New York: W. W. Norton and Company, 2001), p. 183.

56. James Baldwin, *No Name in the Street,* p. 20.

57. Hansberry, *To be Young, Gifted and Black*, p. 220.

58. "And I am glad," Baldwin hastened to add, "she was not smiling at me." See Baldwin, "Lorraine Hansberry at the Summit," p. 272.

59. Hansberry, *To Be Young, Gifted and Black*, p. 201.

60. Killens, "Lorraine Hansberry: On Time!" pp. 275, 276.

61. Mayfield, "Lorraine Hansberry: A Woman for All Seasons," p. 265.

62. Mayfield, box 21, folder 12, Julian Mayfield Papers, SCH.

63. Similar solicitations are on record for James Baldwin. It should come as no surprise that Baldwin's critique of Wright's Native Son, "Everybody's Protest Novel," was popular propaganda fodder for anti-Communist publications at home and abroad.

64. Frances Stonor Saunders, *The Cultural Cold War: The CIA and the World of Arts and Letters* (New York: The New Press, 1999).

65. For an interesting view of the subject of gender and cultural imperialism in the Black diaspora see Jacqueline Nassy Brown, "Black Liverpool, Black America, and the Gendering of Diasporic Space," *Cultural Anthropology* 13 (1998): pp. 291–325.

66. Evelyn Eisenstadt to Lorraine Hansberry, January 8, 1962, Lorraine Hansberry Papers, LHE. The letter refers to a previous letter dated December 14, 1961. Also note attachment in Bob Nemiroff's handwriting, which reads: "Significantly, never signed or mailed."

67. Patrice Lumumba was born in the village of Onalua in Kasi province, Belgian Congo on July 2, 1925. Thirty-five years later, this former postal clerk, intellectual, activist, and trade union leader became the first prime minister of the Democratic Republic of the Congo. Lumumba's arrest, imprisonment, and execution sullied many hands and research has only just begun to reveal the shared responsibility in his death. See Ludo De Witte, *The Assassination of Lumumba* (London: Verso, 2001); Brenda Gayle Plummer, *Rising Wind: Black Americans and U.S. Foreign Affairs, 1935–1960* (Chapel Hill: University of North Carolina Press, 1996). Also see movie *Lumumba*, directed by Raoul Peck (Zeitgeist Films, 2001).

68. Historian Brenda Plummer, in fact, has shown that a number of nationalist groups were in attendance that night, including members of the Universal African Legion, International Muslim Society, and the Brooklyn-based United Sons and Daughters of Africa. Plummer, *Rising Wind*, p. 302.

69. Hansberry, "Congolese Patriot," letter to the editor, *New York Times*, March 26, 1961, p. 4.

70. Benjamin Davis to Lorraine Hansberry, n.d., Lorraine Hansberry Papers, LHE.

71. Mayfield, box 21, folder 12, Julian Mayfield Papers, SCH.

72. Julian Mayfield to Lorraine Hansberry, April 7, 1959, Lorraine Hansberry Papers, LHE.

73. Hansberry, *To Be Young Gifted, and Black*, pp. 249–250.

74. James Baldwin, interview, *Black Scholar* (December 1973–January 1974): p. 41.

75. Mayfield, box 21, folder 12, Julian Mayfield Papers, SCH.

76. Lerone Bennett and Margaret Burroughs, "A Lorraine Hansberry Rap," *Freedomways* (4th Quarter, 1979): p. 229.

77. For instance, see Manning Marable, *Race, Reform, and Rebellion: The Second Reconstruction in Black America, 1945–1990* (Jackson: University Press of Mississippi, 1991); Penny Von Eschen, *Race Against Empire: Black Americans and Anticolonialism, 1937–1957* (Ithaca: Cornell University Press, 1997); Plummer, *Rising Wind*.

78. Gerald Horne and Manning Marable's scholarship on Black leftwing activity in the postwar period is longstanding and prolific. Other notable works that re-examine the postwar period include but are not limited to: Martha Biondi, *To Stand and Fight: The Struggle for Civil Rights in Postwar New York City* (Cambridge: Harvard University Press, 2003); Rod Bush, *We Are Not What We Seem: Black Nationalism and the American Century* (New York: New York University Press, 1999); Kevin Gaines, "African-American Expatriates in Ghana and the Black Radical Tradition," *Souls* (Fall 1999): pp. 64–72; Peniel E. Joseph, ed., *The Black Power Movement: Rethinking the Civil Rights-Black Power Era* (New York: Routledge, 2006) and *Waiting 'Til the Midnight Hour*; Suzanne Smith, *Dancing in the Streets, Motown and the Cultural Politics of Detroit* (Cambridge: Harvard University Press, 1999); Timothy Tyson, *Radio Free Dixie: Robert F. Williams and the Roots of Black Power* (Chapel Hill: University of North Carolina Press, 1999); Komozi Woodard, *A Nation Within a Nation: Amiri Baraka and Black Power Politics* (Chapel Hill: University of North Carolina Press, 1998); Penny Von Eschen, "Who's the Real Ambassador? Exposing Cold War Radical

Ideology," in Christian G. Appy, ed., *Cold War Constructions: The Political Culture of United States Imperialism* (Amherst: University of Massachusetts Press, 2000); Cynthia Young, "Havana Up In Harlem: LeRoi Jones, Harold Cruse and the Making of a Cultural Revolution," *Science and Society* 65 (Spring 2001). For a good review of the history of Black Power scholarship see Peniel E. Joseph, "Black Liberation Without Apology: Reconceptualizing the Black Power Movement," *The Black Scholar* (Fall 2001): pp. 2–19.
79. Mitchell, *Black Drama*, p. 182.
80. Ossie Davis, *Eulogy*, Faith Temple Church of God, February 27, 1965.

CHAPTER 5

BLACK CRUSADERS

THE TRANSNATIONAL CIRCUIT OF ROBERT AND MABEL WILLIAMS

ROBESON TAJ FRAZIER

IN FEBRUARY 1970, ROBERT FRANKLIN WILLIAMS STOOD in a government deposition room before the United States Subcommittee to Investigate the Administration of the Internal Security Act and Other Internal Security Laws. There, he was pressured to defend his experiences as an American exile and resident of Cuba and China. For the last nine years, he and his family had been living abroad as political refugees, and during this period, Robert and his wife Mabel's political activity and the transnational media apparatus they created to disseminate their radical positions provided them with access to a network of government officials, activists, intellectuals, and guerilla soldiers in the Third World anticolonial movement. Moreover, while these relationships and Robert and Mabel Williams's open criticism of US racism and imperialism had made them icons among the US civil rights and Black Power movements, they also had made them enemies of the US state.

Perceived by some black radicals and revolutionary nationalists as the diplomatic equivalents to Malcolm X, Robert and Mabel Williams established an innovative and international self-run communication and propaganda network from 1961 to 1969 that used various media to connect African Americans to Cuba, Tanzania, and China. The couple drew blacks' attention to these nations as revolutionary sites for alternative conceptions and projections of development, communal investment, and historical transformation. They distinguished African Americans, Cubans, Chinese, and Tanzanians as constitutive members of a transnational community of oppressed populations that were challenging global white supremacy and reshaping world affairs.[1]

HAVANA

In the fall of 1961, the Monroe, North Carolina, police department falsely accused Robert of kidnapping a white couple. Robert, Mabel, and their two sons, Bobby and John, eluded the Monroe authorities and the Federal Bureau of Investigation (FBI), and the Cuban government granted the refugees asylum. Just two years earlier, Robert had gained national attention when, as an organizer and chapter president for the National Association for the Advancement of Colored People, he strayed from the national headquarters' ideological policy of nonviolence. He and Mabel advocated armed self-defense and violent retribution against white supremacist attacks and racial violence, calling for blacks to "meet violence with violence, lynching with lynching."[2] Unwilling to be silenced by wings of the civil rights establishment that denounced practices of self-defense, Robert and Mabel expanded on the utility of such practices through a self-produced and -circulated newsletter, *The Crusader*. In the newsletter, they highlighted the racial injustice experienced by blacks in the South, emphasizing the increasing waves of radicalism that were emerging from Southern blacks, and connected these struggles to international movements against imperialism, colonialism, and racial oppression.

An international struggle that garnered wide attention in the pages of *The Crusader* was the Cuban Revolution of 1959. According to Robert and Mabel, the overthrow of Fulgencio Batista's government by a band of leftist revolutionaries and nationalist guerillas and the toppling of US imperialism in a nation that the United States had controlled for more than half a century made the Cuban Revolution the "source of hope for all oppressed people throughout the world."[3] Robert would travel to Cuba twice in 1960 to see firsthand the reorganization of Cuban society and advancements made by the Cuban government and its leading figures, Prime Minister Fidel Castro and diplomat and guerilla-warfare strategist Ernesto "Che" Guevara. These experiences prompted the Williams family to seek political refuge in Cuba.

In Cuba, they became members of an international community of government officials, national liberation activists, guerrilla soldiers, intellectuals, artists, workers, students, and expatriates. Their arrival coincided with the influx of several contingents of African diplomats, liberation groups, and students into Havana, and within this political and social culture, Robert and Mabel were exposed to a wider circulation of ideas and arguments.[4] Mabel explained that being in Cuba "enhance[d] our ability to get the word out . . . Going to Cuba enhanced our platform, expanded greatly our contacts, our mailing lists, the people we could reach and the people who could hear our story . . . [We were] building a grassroots underground media network that became worldwide."[5] *The Crusader* found a new home in Cuba, where its publication was advanced as a result of donations, volunteers, and the print shop of the National Institute for Agrarian Reform. With Castro's permission, Robert and Mabel were also allowed to host a radio show, *Radio Free Dixie*, at Cuban radio station Radio Progreso and, later, at Radio Havana. By means of these media technologies, Robert and Mabel criticized US racial practices and US globalism and worked to solidify Third-World support for the black liberation struggle.

In addition to Cuba, one of the first nations to immediately respond to Robert and Mabel's entreaties for international support was the People's Republic of China (PRC). PRC leader and Chinese Communist Party Chairman Mao Zedong, after receiving a letter from Robert in 1962, responded by issuing his "Statement Supporting the Afro-American in Their Just Struggle Against Racial Discrimination by US Imperialism" just days before the August 1963 March on Washington for Jobs and Freedom. In the statement, Mao expressed China's support for the civil rights movement, stating that US imperialism was not an exception to US democracy but rather its enabler and coercive counterpart.[6] In the following days, mass rallies were held in China, where more than ten thousand Chinese people, alongside members of the US expatriate community, reaffirmed Mao's statement and communicated their solidarity with their black brothers. The PRC government also invited Robert and Mabel to visit China and participate formally in China's fourteenth-anniversary National Day celebrations in Beijing. On this trip to China and a subsequent journey a year later, they were made privy to a society, government, and political culture to which few US citizens had access.

Robert and Mabel's trip to China and their subsequent reports on their experiences in the nation were particularly important and exceptional for that time. US journalists were then unable to report from mainland China as a result of the State Department's decree making US citizens' travel to China illegal (US journalists responsible for China coverage thus had to operate mainly out of Hong Kong). Since the early 1950s, the Korean War, rampant anticommunism in the United States, and declining US-China relations had led the US government to isolate and contain China in international affairs, and this drastically affected the information the US public received about China. Not only did Robert and Mabel's encounters in China provide a snapshot of a formerly semicolonized nation in its early stages of development, modernization, and social transformation, but their perspective also countered the negative depictions of China found in much of US mainstream media.

In China, Robert and Mabel found a people "hopeful about changing the world and changing their status within the world" and a nation that was "fast becoming a great world power."[7] In factories, schools, medical facilities, communes, political meetings, and communities, they were able to witness some of the strides China was making toward becoming self-determinate and self-sufficient. China's rapid development and modernization, Robert and Mabel surmised, made it a future force to be reckoned with, one that might radically reshape the bipolarity of the Cold War US-Soviet division. "The mighty Chinese people have lifted themselves from the dark ages of feudalism to age of Atoms in fifteen short years. Their growth potential is infinite," Robert and Mabel explained.[8] China's capacity for economic expansion and social advancement and its solidarity with the black freedom struggle meant the African American public was gaining a very important and powerful transnational ally. "The East *is* Red," Mabel and Robert announced. "650 Million [of our] soul brothers [have relayed their] . . . support!"[9]

Deteriorating personal relations with the Cuban government led the Williams family to leave Cuba. Robert had bumped heads with several representatives

of the Cuban Communist Party because of his criticism of antiblack racism in
Cuba and his endorsement of black nationalism. Over time, Robert and Mabel
had come to feel that despite the achievements of the Cuban Revolution, Afro-
Cubans remained relegated to the worst living conditions and the worst jobs.
Robert concluded, "There is yet some hangover from the old system of tradition . . . Many Cuban officials were educated in the United States . . . and they
have gone back to Cuba and the government, and though now they claim to be
socialist, they still have some of the same attitudes, and that is that Blacks are to
be discriminated against, and power should be in the hands of whites. So it is a
different form of discrimination. It is more subtle." Mabel agreed, arguing that
among government officials and Cuban Communist Party members, "people did
not want to identify with anything African, or Afrocentric . . . The more African,
the more kinkier your hair the farther you were away from government."[10] Cuban
communists responded by labeling the Williamses as "black racists" whose deep
color consciousness and rigid support of black nationalism blinded them from
the possibility of a worldwide communist revolution composed of workers of all
shades, not just oppressed groups of color.

   Systematically isolated and neutralized by the Cuban establishment, Robert
and Mabel determined that their time in Cuba was near its end. After learning
from China's ambassador to Cuba that they could continue their radical work on
Chinese soil, they secretly packed their things. On July 15, 1966, they traveled
to China under the pretense that they were headed on a short diplomatic mission
to North Vietnam to broadcast antiwar messages to black American troops stationed in South Vietnam and fighting in the Vietnam War. Weeks passed before
the Cuban government learned that Robert and Mabel were gone for good.

BEIJING

As residents of China, Robert and Mabel Williams were treated like unofficial
cultural diplomats and guests of state who were connecting the US public to China's struggles to become independent, self-determinate, and modern. Housed in a
compound that had once served as the Italian embassy, Robert and Mabel found
that, as with their initial experiences in Cuba, the Chinese government encouraged them to expand their media apparatus. In Beijing, *The Crusader* printings
increased from fifteen thousand to sixteen thousand copies per issue in Havana to
thirty thousand to forty thousand, the only difference being that now the newsletter was produced at Robert and Mabel's convenience rather than monthly.[11]
In addition, while a Chinese transmitter allowed their radio shows to be broadcast periodically to African nations, Robert convinced the Chinese government
to increase its production of shortwave broadcasts aimed at black Americans.[12]
These strategic changes increased *The Crusader* and *Radio Free Dixie*'s audiences
and provided Robert and Mabel with access to new networks of political actors,
most especially in Asia and Africa.

   Robert also coproduced a documentary film, *Robert Williams in China*, based
on his and Mabel's extended tour of the PRC in November 1964. A master-
piece of propaganda, the film documented how fast the PRC government and

Chinese population were modernizing and industrializing Chinese society. The film was intended primarily for Third-World governments and liberation movements seeking fiscal and technical aid and for governments and groups skeptical of China's rapid growth, most especially in the West.[13]

The libraries of Howard University and the University of North Carolina, Chapel Hill (UNC), were the first US-based institutions to obtain copies of *Robert Williams in China* in 1967; UNC previewed the film on the Tuesday after they received it.[14] Copies were later sent to the International Center of George Peabody College for Teachers in Nashville, Tennessee; the Bentley Library at the University of Michigan, Ann Arbor, also now houses a copy of the film.

Robert and Mabel relocated to China shortly after the start of the Cultural Revolution, a three-year period of mass social upheaval. Established as a campaign to generate a new revolutionary culture for Chinese political and social life, the Cultural Revolution ultimately transmuted into waves of economic and political turmoil that took the lives of millions of Chinese. However, while Robert and Mabel did not agree with the extreme violence and political censure that occurred during the Cultural Revolution, they believed that it was making profound changes in China's class relations and in particular institutions. Robert argued that class distinctions had been eliminated from the Chinese educational system and military and that the leadership of the two institutions was controlled more and more by groups representing the working class rather than middle-class bureaucracies. Schools and the military, he added, were increasingly using dialectical models of decision making that prized community involvement and cross class exchanges.[15] Cognizant that these types of changes still did not mean a vast reorganization or confrontation with the PRC government and the Chinese Communist Party's centralization of political power, Robert and Mabel still championed these examples of the Chinese working class's sharing power in schools and the military. They believed that such practices could play a central role in the efforts of the black working class and working poor people to mobilize and galvanize their communities in resisting racial tyranny and socioeconomic inequality.

From abroad, Robert also served as president-in-exile of two black American revolutionary nationalist organizations: the Revolutionary Action Movement and the Republic of New Afrika (RNA). In this position, he brought greater awareness to the imaginary community between blacks and Chinese. For many US-based black radicals and nationalists inside and outside these organizations, Robert and Mabel's exile in China added to China's mystique. The couple received many letters in which US supporters indicated their growing curiosity about Chinese life, politics, and culture. One proclaimed, "Mao Zedong's thought has no color and is indispensable to any revolutionary fighter," while Afro-Cuban dissenter Carlos Moore remarked to Robert, "It is a wonderful thing that there exists a place like China where true and dedicated men, such as yourself, can find refuge . . . Never before have we had such sanctuaries for revolutionary thinkers and militants. There must be more places like China where our people can find support and be able to count on as a sure base."[16] Nowhere was this imaginary community more present than in Mao's publicized condemnation of Martin Luther King Jr.'s murder in April 1968. Another declaration engineered upon

Robert's recommendation, Mao's "Statement in Support of the Afro-American Struggle Against Violence" asserted that King's assassination was a product of the dangerous climate of hate and oppression in the United States. Nevertheless, Mao insisted that an emergent base of US revolutionaries, primarily composed of blacks, was repelling these conditions by destabilizing racial discrimination and US imperialism.[17]

DAR ES SALAAM

While in China, Robert and Mabel learned a great deal about Tanzania, an ally of the PRC and an emerging sovereign nation that the Williamses soon found to be almost as captivating as China. Having declared independence from Britain in 1961, Tanzania by the late 1960s was deemed by many people as a future success story of African self-government. For instance, a number of black Americans extolled the principles of African-based socialism and cooperative economics articulated by Tanzania's first president, Julius Nyerere. Tanzania consequently became a destination for black American tourism and saw the establishment of a vibrant black American expatriate community. Moreover, as one of the most Chinese-oriented of all the African nations during the 1960s and 1970s, Tanzania gained a great deal economically and politically from its alliance with the PRC.[18]

Robert and Mabel traveled to Dar es Salaam, Tanzania, in May 1968. There they met with representatives from African liberation organizations such as the Pan African Congress of Azania, the Liberation Front of Mozambique, the Popular Movement for the Liberation of Angola, the Southwest African People's Organization, the Zimbabwe African People's Union, the Zimbabwe African National Union, and the African National Congress. These liberation movements had established bases of operations in Tanzania to strategize and train for anticolonial wars against white settler regimes in South Africa and Rhodesia (Zimbabwe), as well as in Portugal's African colonies.

While in Tanzania, Robert embarked on a 1,470-mile motorcycle journey from Dar es Salaam to Zambia. Traversing rugged roads and the rocky terrain of Zambia's mountains, Robert modeled his trip after "the cross country treks of China's youth" during the Cultural Revolution. In the village of Bulongwa, located in Tanzania's Iringa region, he conversed with Tanzanians who expressed their excitement about Tanzania's independence and referred favorably to the role China was playing in helping facilitate Tanzanian development. The group, Robert explained, spoke happily about China and was "proudly wearing the badges of Chairman Mao Tse-tung."[19] China's large investment in Tanzania was made abundantly clear to Robert as he rode along the construction of the Chinese-financed Tanzam railway, watching as pieces of it were laid down. Robert deemed the 1,060-mile railway, which would ultimately connect Zambia's copper belt to Tanzanian ports, as proof of China's investment in Third-World affairs and commitment to plant seeds of development in other parts of the world.[20]

DETROIT

In Dar es Salaam, Robert and Mabel arranged with US embassy officials a "one-way" US passport, "good for a single journey to the US to face the charges" against Robert.[21] They returned to China and spent a year finalizing the details of their return to the United States, working with their attorneys to ensure that Robert would not be immediately imprisoned in Monroe or a federal jail cell. Mabel, John, and Bobby traveled ahead of Robert and arrived in Detroit in August 1969. One month later, Robert and his attorney, RNA member and cofounder Milton Henry, deplaned from a Boeing 707 at Detroit Metropolitan Airport. A crowd of RNA members and a cluster of Wayne County police officers and FBI agents awaited the two men. Wearing a blue Chinese suit similar to that worn by Mao, Robert walked down the tarmac, clenched fist raised high in the Black Power salute. He was immediately taken into custody by the FBI and released on a personal recognizance bond of ten thousand dollars.

Over the following year, Robert served as a research associate at the University of Michigan, Ann Arbor, where he wrote a still-unpublished manuscript about his experiences abroad. At the university, Allen Whiting, a professor at Ann Arbor and one of Secretary of State Henry Kissinger's key China affairs advisors, hounded Robert to provide details about China's modernization process and Chinese diplomacy. Ever reluctant to share any information with the US government, Robert was later forced to appear in front of a congressional subcommittee, where he artfully evaded the majority of its members' questions.

Robert and Mabel Williams's transnational and international work must be understood as an endeavor to propagate an expanded and new narrative of African Americans' relationship to world revolutions, one that drew from traditions of struggle waged both inside and outside the United States. Their propaganda from abroad signaled their understanding that the words, sounds, images, news, and arguments of radical and revolutionary international media had to operate in a dialogic fashion with the actual day-to-day activism and work of black political struggle and resistance. Mabel explained it best: "To continue the fight from without it must be constantly attacked by our people from within."[22]

NOTES

1. For scholarly works and biographies on Robert and Mabel Williams, see Robert F. Williams, *Negroes with Guns* (New York: Marzani & Munsell, 1962); Robert Carl Cohen, *Black Crusader: Robert Franklin Williams* (New York: Lyle Stuart, 1972); Tim Tyson, *Radio Free Dixie: Robert F. Williams and the Roots of Black Power* (Chapel Hill: University of North Carolina Press, 1999); Ronald J. Stephens, "Narrating Acts of Resistance: Explorations of Untold Heroic and Horrific Battle Stories Surrounding Robert Franklin Williams' Residence in Lake County, Michigan," *Journal of Black Studies* 33, no. 5 (2003): 675–703; Bill Mullen, *Afro Orientalism* (Minneapolis: University of Minnesota Press, 2004); *Robert and Mabel Williams Resource Guide* (San Francisco: Freedom Archives, 2005); Besenia Rodriguez, "'De la esclavitud yanqui a la libertad cubana': US Black Radicals, the Cuban Revolution, and the Formation of a Tricontinental Ideology," *Radical History Review* 92 (Spring 2005): 62–87; Walter Rucker, "Crusader in Exile:

Robert F. Williams and the International Struggle for Black Freedom in America," *The Black Scholar* 36, nos. 2–3 (Summer 2006): 19; Ronald J. Stephen, "'Praise the Lord and Pass the Ammunition': Robert F. Williams' Crusade for Justice on Behalf of Twenty-two Million African Americans as a Cuban Exile," *Black Diaspora Review* 2, no. 1 (Fall 2010): 15–28.

2. Williams, *Negroes with Guns*, 63.

3. Vicente Cubillas, "Robert Williams: De la esclavitud yanqui a la libertad cubana" (Robert Williams: From Yanqui Slavery to Cuban Liberty), *Bohemia* (1961): 74–77.

4. Carlos Moore, *Castro, the Blacks, and Africa* (Los Angeles: University of California, Los Angeles Latin American Studies, 1991).

5. Mabel Williams, interview with the author, October 4, 2010.

6. Mao Zedong, "Statement Supporting the Afro-American in Their Just Struggle Against Racial Discrimination by US Imperialism," August 8, 1963.

7. Williams, interview; "China: New Hope of Oppressed Humanity," *The Crusader* 5, no. 2 (February 1964): 16.

8. "China: America's Shades of Waterloo," *The Crusader* 6, no. 3 (March 1965): 5–7.

9. "The East is Red: 650 Million Soul Brothers Cable Support," *The Crusader* 6, no. 1 (July–August 1964), 5.

10. "Testimony of Robert F. Williams," *Hearings Before the Subcommittee to Investigate the Administration of the Internal Security Act and Other Internal Security Laws, Second Session, Part 1: February 16, 1970* (Washington, DC: US Government Printing Office, 1970), 92.

11. Ibid., 49.

12. Robert Franklin Williams Collection (hereafter, WC), Box 1, Correspondence, September 1966, Bentley Historical Library, University of Michigan.

13. WC Box 14, Videocassettes: Robert Williams in China 1964, Reels 1, 2, and 3.

14. "Testimony," 42; WC Box 1, Correspondence, May–June 1967: Letter from William S. Powell, June 19, 1967.

15. WC Box 2, Correspondence, January 1969: Robert Williams, "An Afro-American in China," 1–11.

16. WC Box 1, Correspondence, July–September 1967: Letter from Richard Gibson, July 27, 1967; WC Box 7, Correspondence, 1966–1969: Letter from Carlos Moore, February 4, 1967.

17. Mao Zedong, "Statement in Support of the Afro-American Struggle Against Violent Repression," April 16, 1968.

18. George T. Yu, "China's Role in Africa," *Annals of the American Academy of Political and Social Science* 432 (July 1977): 108.

19. Robert Williams, "In Africa," *The Call: Journal of the Afro-Asian Writers Bureau* 1 (1969): 20–22.

20. Robert Williams's focus on the developing relationship between China and Tanzania is especially interesting when considering contemporary debates about China's role in African infrastructure projects.

21. WC Box 9, FBI Files, Section 9: 1968–1969. Months later, in a letter to William Kuntsler, Williams confirmed obtaining this "limited passport" and announced his future return to the United States. See WC Box 2, Correspondence, September–December 1968: Letter to William Kuntsler, November 7, 1968.

22. "Letter to the Readers," *The Crusader* 1, no. 4 (December 23, 1961), 5

CHAPTER 6

PEACE WAS THE GLUE

EUROPE AND AFRICAN
AMERICAN FREEDOM

BRENDA GAYLE PLUMMER

EUROPEANS LEARNED FROM THE FREEDOM STRUGGLES WAGED by African Americans in the second half of the twentieth century in political as well as cultural ways. What they absorbed from their knowledge of African American insurgencies and their exposure to specific individuals, organizations, and movements was often indirect, filtered through discourses about politics and ethics, support for decolonization, and especially through local traditions of peace and antinuclear organizing. At the same time, Europeans expressed considerable ambivalence about race, especially in the context of increased immigration of people of color after World War II, and specifically about African Americans, often seen simultaneously as victims of oppression and as examples of a debased American popular culture. A combination of doubt and expectation attends the contours and limits of African American and European shared perspectives. Most discussions of these connections emphasize the therapeutic effects that freedom from racial constraints had on black Americans fortunate enough to cross the Atlantic and live life in countries where race was not all-consuming.

This essay seeks to augment that extensively documented aspect of diaspora history in arguing that the civil rights and Black Power movements also provoked political debate and action that European activists used to interpret and affect conditions in their own countries.

Emphasis on culture has all too often suggested a one-way exchange, with blacks the net beneficiaries of European benevolence. As Yohuru Williams has observed, one common conception of black movements renders them "the product of foreign influences that extended from Marcus Garvey and Frantz Fanon to Che Guevara and Mao Tse Tung. Such images create the impression that African–Americans were greatly influenced by foreign contacts with little impact or contribution of their own."[1] A closer look at the link between African

American insurgencies and Europe reveals a richer and more nuanced set of relationships.

Certain scholars express skepticism about the significance of such links, as well as doubts about the extent of African American politicization more generally. "Black radicals . . . tried to make the international connection by linking their fight to the worldwide struggle being waged by the poor and oppressed against imperialism," Manfred Berg claims. "Beyond the exchange of solidarity addresses and the granting of exile," Berg found little to indicate that black insurgency was "influenced by international developments."[2] Berg and other writers have looked in the wrong places for evidence of the link. Peace would serve as the connection between social movements at home and abroad.

AFRICAN AMERICANS IN EUROPE

The possibility of deliverance from American racism formed a key component of how African Americans before 1960 conceptualized diaspora life in Europe. Individual Europeans, many believed, were innocent of the sins of racism. While the imperialist histories of European states clearly implicate these countries in the crimes of slavery and racial oppression, they did not often bring slavery—or many people of color—home. Black visitors in the nineteenth century remarked on how novel they appeared to their white hosts. Nancy Prince, who had made her living as a domestic servant in New England, was presented, along with her husband, to the tsar and tsarina of Russia in 1824, possibly as exotic curiosities from the West. Prince described a prerevolutionary Russian society based on class, but not racial, distinctions. "There was no prejudice against color," she recalled in her memoir. "There were there all casts, [sic] and the people of all nations, each in their place."[3] Prince's narrative suggests that she was comfortable with class hierarchy in her host society but objected to racial slavery and discrimination based on color. As late as 1955, James Baldwin would write about the sensation his appearance in a snow-covered Swiss hamlet would cause: "From all available evidence no Black man had ever set foot in this tiny Swiss village before I came. I was told before arriving that I would probably be a 'sight' for the village; I took this to mean that people of my complexion were rarely seen in Switzerland, and also that city people are always something of a 'sight' outside of the city." Baldwin described a pre-Lenten ritual in the village where children in blackface went door to door soliciting alms to redeem the souls of African slaves. He attributed the shock that this practice created in him to his socialization as a black American and pardoned village children's naive and fascinated use of the word *neger*.[4]

African Americans traveling in Europe described how exhilarating they found the absence of the color bar in public accommodations. They often attributed bigotry, when encountered, to US influence. Future civil rights activist Mary Church Terrell as a young woman studied in Germany between 1888 and 1890, staying in Berlin and avoiding Dresden, which she saw as a white American and British enclave rife with Anglo-Saxon prejudice.[5] W. E. B. Du Bois described in his autobiography the attempts of a white American woman to disrupt a budding romance between him and the daughter of the German family he lived with while a university student abroad.[6] In these constructions, pernicious influence from the United States limits black access to European society. Du Bois's own decision not to pursue a relationship with the German woman because of the handicaps a white wife would present for him in America owes much to the constraints imposed by the racism of his native land.

The degree to which expatriation disrupted the life plan laid out for blacks by American society proved a source of satisfaction for emigrants. Cartoonist Ollie Harrington remembered the consternation that such black freedom seemed to cause among white Americans. "Hemingway, F. Scott Fitzgerald, all the great American writers were all in Paris at one time or another," he noted. "But when Black expatriates sort of joined the 'fraternity,' it wasn't a very popular thing with the authorities in the United States and you can easily see why." Crossing a geographic border also meant crossing a political and psychological one: "These were really disrupting ideas which existed. Blacks had to be held in check. They had to fear white law, and that sort of thing. Living in Paris and having experiences that Blacks shouldn't have was not conducive to a smooth course towards whatever American history would finally produce."[7]

The African American–European nexus is thus conventionally conceived of as a set of circumstances that permitted blacks living away from the control of US laws and mores to enjoy social freedoms in the midst of a compliant and largely innocent host population, untainted by racism. The reality was somewhat more complicated. Released from the strictures of segregation and bias, the expatriate could now pursue her aptitudes and inclinations. In the nineteenth century, when the most literate Americans had not discovered the cultural richness of their own country and retained a colonial's admiration of European civilization, black painter Henry O. Tanner's and black sculptor Edmonia Lewis's respective exoduses were not unusual moves. In succeeding generations, many others followed them. Josephine Baker, Claude McKay, Richard Wright, Ollie Harrington, and Chester Himes number among the best known, but other talents also figure in the European segment of the African American diaspora.[8]

Accounts of black life in Europe most often see these individuals as revitalized by the chance to escape Jim Crow. Europe is the net benefactor. Less attention is paid to African American influence on European thought and political practice, especially as most writing on the subject of black expatriates in Europe focuses on the cultural realm. I am exploring here that facet of the African American and European connection that speaks more directly to power relations and the challenges mounted to them. In so doing, I am making a somewhat artificial distinction between the influences on Europe of African Americans per se and other peoples of the African diaspora, as well as that of Asian immigrants and others. While focusing on African Americans truncates a very complex set of interactions, it also affords an opportunity to turn a lens on a rarely examined feature of transatlantic history.

Global attention turned to the civil rights movement in the United States at a time when western European males had long ago won citizenship rights through class-driven politics. Workers' rights were at the core of mass pressures for social and political change. After World War II, liberal democracies upheld by US firepower muted worker insurgency in some countries. Labor politics nevertheless continued, more vigorously in some places than others, and served as a check on efforts to restore the laissez-faire capitalism of the past. On the surface, it would seem that Western Europeans would be little concerned about racial matters in the United States and even less in linking them to events in their home countries. As it turned out, however, they expressed substantial interest in African American movements. They interpreted the knowledge they derived from observing America through the filter of their Cold War experience. European states have been more important in shaping the post–World War II order than a focus on Soviet–American bipolarity suggests.[9] An examination of the ways in which smaller states challenged the ideological and political hegemony of the United States and the Soviet Union allows fresh thinking, not only about the role of Europe in world affairs, but also about how nongovernmental actors influenced viewpoints and actions.

European interest in the political agenda created by African American activists derived in part from an ongoing conversation among social movements across a spectrum from center to left, and across oceans. As Doug McAdam has noted, "[E]stablished organizations/networks are themselves embedded in longstanding activist subcultures" that "function as repositories of cultural materials." "Succeeding generations of activists" thus learn from past struggles and choose, discard, or revise what history has to offer. Movements created out of specific conditions in particular countries can also resonate with the national experience of people in other places. "If it was once sufficient to interpret or predict social movements around the shape of the nation state, it is less and less possible to do so today," Sidney Tarrow observes.[10]

After the Allied victory in World War II, the United States installed a Pax Americana in Western Europe and entered into an uneasy truce with the Soviets in which both powers grudgingly tolerated the existence of their respective spheres of influence but never acknowledged the legitimacy of each other's claims to domination. Neither was above searching for opportunities to undermine the troubled modus vivendi that prevailed for the next forty-four years. Nations under US protection thus recovered from the war under the shadow of juggernauts and faced the real possibility that war could resume. The existence of nuclear arms enhanced feelings of insecurity among states caught in the middle. Secrecy accompanying the development of atomic weaponry and the exclusion of mass publics from debate about security issues also raised questions about the extent and strength of democracy. The exigencies of postwar reconstruction and sentiments of gratitude toward the United States for such programs as the Marshall Plan initially muted some of the misgivings.

The restoration of prosperity, beginning in the 1950s, revived the desires of many Europeans for a more coherent and independent sense of national identity. Some questioned whether the interminable Cold War standoff was having a deleterious impact on the future of their countries and began to suggest that security did not always mean compliance with US and Soviet agendas. Roosevelt and Stalin had carved up Europe at the Yalta Conference in 1945, some reasoned, and neither had European interests at heart. The remedy, then, was to create a foreign policy for the continent that restrained its American and Soviet overlords and reaffirmed the identity and integrity of each country. A European "third way" would evaluate Cold War policies on the merits of their overall impact, not solely in terms of their benefit to the superpowers.

African Americans had also come to take a nuanced view of Cold War conflict. After World War II, accusations of communist subversion had retarded the progress of the civil rights movement as racists and their allies used the Red smear to discredit those fighting for the ballot and against segregation. National security, they argued, required the repression of dissent. Many African Americans consequently dismissed the communist issue. This included some conservative figures, such as Elk leader and black Republican W. C. "Billy" Hueston, who wrote a letter to President Eisenhower requesting clemency for convicted spies Julius and Ethel Rosenberg. Musician Dizzy Gillespie numbered among those making a distinction between self-affirmation and toeing an ideological line. "We refused to accept racism, poverty, or economic exploitation, nor would we live out uncreative humdrum lives merely for the sake of survival," he recalled. "But there was nothing unpatriotic about it. If America wouldn't honor its Constitution and respect us as men, we couldn't give a shit about the American way."[11] Black New Yorkers showed little hesitancy in responding to the radical singer Paul Robeson's troubles with the government, according to his biographer, Martin Duberman: "The red menace did not strike most Harlemites as notably more invidious than the white one."[12] Conventional civil rights organizations, however, made a point of distancing themselves from leftist politics and associations in order to please liberal sympathizers and putative supporters in government. Unlike the more established groups, the Student Nonviolent Coordinating Committee (SNCC) opposed making an issue of radical participation in the movement, viewing it as a distraction from the real business of securing civil rights.[13]

MID-CENTURY CHANGE

In Europe, France provided the most flamboyant demonstration of the break with bipolarity, especially when Charles de Gaulle returned to power in 1958 with a mission to revive the prestige that France once enjoyed as premier nation on the continent. De Gaulle's vision did not embrace a collaborative Europe with France as one of many partners but, rather, a Europe in which an incontestable France played a dominant role. The French had wanted to retain their largest colony, Algeria, home to a sizeable French settler community, as the centerpiece of a revived nationalism. The Algerians wanted independence, however, and in the ensuing revolutionary war, De Gaulle came to acknowledge the impossibility of returning to the past. The French discovered, as they had at Dienbienphu, that military might alone cannot create lasting political solutions. French policy, in spite of its idiosyncrasies, including the determination to join the nuclear club and the subsequent withdrawal from NATO, reflected a growing general dissatisfaction in Europe with the obligation to subordinate national ambitions to Cold War exigencies.[14]

The Algerian National Liberation Front (FLN) launched a late summer offensive against the French homeland in 1958. They attacked gas stations, police precincts, and a munitions plant, with fatalities on both sides. Insurgents tried, but failed, to assassinate the former governor-general of Algeria. Official revenge was swift and savage. Police targeted swarthy people for beatings, mistakenly including Portuguese and Spaniards in the mix. In Paris, a violent police force led by a former Nazi collaborator tortured Algerian prisoners. There were disappearances. The Parisian public remained indifferent as Arab bodies floated in the Seine. Newspapers that protested the abuses had their issues seized, and the authorities foiled other legal efforts to address human rights claims. Even after the French government began serious talks with the FLN in 1961, Algerians living in France continued to be victims of racist ire. "In the course of the month of September 1961, people began to hear talk of North African cadavers being pulled out of the Seine," Jean-Luc Einaudi writes. Some survived these drownings by the police and lived to tell about it.[15]

This ugliness disrupted the Parisian idyll of the black expatriates, as people of color came under increasing suspicion. James Baldwin wrote eloquently of his trumped-up arrest in Paris for the alleged theft of a bed sheet. Future African American feminist Frances Beal, arrived in Paris without prior knowledge of the conflict. She was impassively witnessing a street protest when a French police officer hit her on the head with a cape weighted with metal balls.[16] Physical escape from the United States, black travelers of this era discovered, did not always shield them from racism.

France was not alone in animosity toward nonwhites. In the United Kingdom, Caribbean immigrants began arriving after World War II to satisfy a labor shortage. As their numbers grew, so did conflicts with white Britons, which culminated in the Notting Hill riots of 1958. These disturbances embarrassed Britain and shocked the world, and their occurrence on the eve of African independence sensitized Her Majesty's government to the issue of how new Commonwealth members would perceive British society.[17] From that point on, the United States was not the only one walking the tightrope between domestic race relations and foreign policy.

Clearly, at the turn of the sixties decade, Britain and France, facing the dismantling of their empires and the ingress of formerly subjugated people, could not be categorized as wholly receptive to the strivings of blacks, nor could they as easily take the moral high ground in comparison to the United States. The riots in England "far surpassed, in violence," segregationist North Carolina governor Luther Hodges told an English churchman, "anything that has ever occurred in North Carolina."[18] Martin Luther King, invited to the University of Newcastle upon Tyne to receive an honorary degree, identified "the problem of racism, the problem of poverty and the problem of war" as critical worldwide concerns. King drew parallels between the ghettoization of Caribbean and Asian peoples and the discrimination against them in the United Kingdom, and the plight of black Americans in the United States. The Nobel laureate's remarks became the focus of local debate both in the press and among the public.[19]

West Germany, unlike Britain and France, found itself in a somewhat different, although still ticklish, position vis-á-vis the United States and the question of race. The Federal Republic lay at the center of a divided Europe and depended heavily on the US army to underwrite its own security. Germans winked at separate entertainment facilities for black and white GIs in their country even though racial segregation was against their own law. The ironies of defeat in a war fought largely in defense of a white supremacy that subsequently flourished among the victors were not lost on German sensibilities. Americans in West Germany tried to avoid the subject. This even extended to Supreme Court Justice Earl Warren, who visited in 1959 but apparently at the State Department's request, refrained from talking about integration or anything else controversial during his stay.[20]

German diplomats in the United States were nervous about racial conflicts in their host country. The consul in Atlanta sent home a pamphlet published by a Georgia segregationist that reminded him of Nazi arguments. Envoys tried to dodge the American racists who wanted to frequent German consulates. When the American Nazi Party demonstrated against black entertainer Sammy Davis Jr.'s marriage to Swedish actress May Britt, the German consul in Los Angeles felt compelled to make a public statement distancing the Federal Republic from American storm troopers.[21] To Germans, the term "racism" recalled the errors of the Third Reich, although more than a trace of race hatred persisted into the postwar era. The existence of strong prejudice and resistance to racial equality on the part of the United States, West Germany's protector, only enhanced the ambivalence Germans experienced as they balanced between rediscovered moral principle and earlier sentiment.

A challenge to the prevailing racism and xenophobia came from an institution fundamentally rooted in European society: the Roman Catholic Church. A liberal trend in the Church also challenged Cold War conformity and world domination by the most powerful nation-states. On May 15, 1961 Pope John XXIII issued an encyclical titled *Mater et Magistra*. Here the pontiff defined the Roman Catholic Church's position on "Christianity and social progress." The encyclical constituted a critical departure from the Church's decades-long inertia regarding social and political issues. "There is a . . . keener interest in world affairs shown by people of average education," the pope observed. "We are witnessing the break-away from colonialism and the attainment of political independence by the peoples of Asia and Africa." Changing times required a reaffirmation of Christian values. "The solidarity which binds all men together as members of a common family makes it impossible for wealthy nations to look with indifference upon the hunger, misery and poverty of other nations whose citizens are unable to enjoy even elementary human rights," the encyclical proclaimed. "Glaring economic and social imbalances" undermined global security.[22]

Pope John XXIII criticized self-interested forms of foreign assistance designed to create dependency and enhance wealthy states' pursuit of "their own plans for world domination." Exploitative aid practices "would in fact be introducing a new form of colonialism—cleverly disguised, no doubt, but actually reflecting that older, outdated type from which many nations have recently emerged." They would "have harmful impact on international relations, and constitute a

menace to world peace." For the Vatican, the "whole raison d'être" of the state
was "the realization of the common good in the temporal order." It identified
this goal with a free market and embraced capitalism, but rejected materialism
in its socialist guise. The Council's purpose was to update the Church in view
of the twentieth century's unprecedented developments. The pontiff sought a
more democratic ecclesiastical body whose incorporation of such changes as the
use of vernacular languages rather than Latin in the mass would strengthen it as
a universal community and ensure its survival into the infinite future. A second
encyclical, *Pacem in Terris*, issued in 1963, gave further backing to proponents of
racial equality, decolonization, and peace. Six years later, Pope John's successor,
Paul VI, issued *Populorum Progressio/The Progress of Peoples* (1967). Paul identified
racism as "a cause of division and hatred within countries whenever individuals and families see the inviolable rights of the human person held in scorn, as
they themselves are unjustly subjected to a regime of discrimination because of
their race or their color."[23] The Vatican's stance enabled a worldwide conversation
about power that formed part of the context in which Europeans viewed emerging social movements in the United States.

THE PEACE MOVEMENT

Attacks on immigrants of color, resistance to decolonization, and racial discrimination formed part of the motif of a Europe having to rapidly adjust to change
in the mid-twentieth century. If reactionary tendencies pulled in one direction, a
desire to defuse racial, ethnic, and international tensions counterbalanced them.
The peace movement served as the common ground from which collaboration and
understanding between European and African American change agents sprang.
An international peace movement emerged from World War II, but it declined
during the Korean War and McCarthy period. African American musical artists Charlie Parker, Marian Anderson, and Pearl Primus numbered among early
supporters of the antinuclear movement, as did sociologist E. Franklin Frazier
and educators Charlotte Hawkins Brown and Benjamin Mays. Peace advocates
were widely discredited as communist dupes until Stalin's death sufficiently eased
East–West tensions so that US activism could resume without substantial risk of
punishment. In 1955, Quakers issued a statement, "Speak Truth to Power," that
reclaimed religious and ethical ground for a movement besmirched by Cold War
politics. The Montgomery bus boycott and subsequent campaigns of nonviolent
direct action lent new credence to the pursuit of peace. Martin Luther King Jr.,
the appointed boycott leader, aligned himself with antinuclear critics well before
his famous speech in which he denounced the war in Vietnam.[24]

    The increasingly terrifying power of nuclear weapons aroused global fears,
especially as post-Sputnik anxieties led to more armament and the growth of
defense establishments around the world. Middle class peace movements emerged
in the United States and Europe, but affluent western citizens were not the only
ones concerned about war.[25] The threat of atomic warfare also troubled African
nations and prompted an important coming together of activists from different countries that joined concerns about peace, civil rights, nonviolence, and

anticolonialism.[26] Most efforts in developed countries during the years of the peace movement's revival focused on northern hemisphere conflicts inherent in the standoff between the West and the eastern bloc. The Hungarian revolt, the Berlin crisis, and the Cuban missile crisis captured the most attention. Few heeded other global theaters where peace had become a vital issue for reasons other than bloc politics. One of these theaters was in Africa. Peace entered the debate in Africa as a by-product of the quest to end colonialism and racism. Strong voices supported nonviolence. Indeed, the South African Defiance Campaign preceded similar religiously influenced protest activity in the US South.[27]

Veteran peace and civil rights activist Bayard Rustin shared the joint commitment to equality and peace. Rustin was the only American on the program at the historic Aldermaston 1958 march in England. Prominent Britons in attendance included the Reverend Michael Scott (of antiapartheid fame), author Doris Lessing, and philosopher Bertrand Russell. British Direct Action Committee official Michael Randle later noted that "Bayard Rustin delivered what many regarded as the most powerful speech of that Good Friday afternoon, linking the struggle against weapons of mass destruction with the struggle of Blacks for their basic rights in America."[28] Throughout the decade, many Africans continued to believe that nonviolent decolonization of the entire continent was both possible and desirable. The historic peace churches, especially influential in Britain and Germany, supported them in this conviction.

The Algerian revolution drew a shadow over this sunny presumption. French zeal in maintaining its principal colony heightened political tensions in Africa. France in 1957 announced a program of nuclear weapons testing in the Sahara that affronted African states and territories. De Gaulle's government created a crisis by arrogantly dismissing African anxieties. News that French and American firms had formed a consortium to explore for Saharan oil and build a pipeline through Algeria indicated that France would give no quarter to Algerian nationalists. Plans also entailed the construction of a modern military–industrial complex.[29] French scientists planned to build a small-scale, portable nuclear weapon whose size would be of little use in a confrontation with powers like the USSR or the United States. Critics inferred that the French intended the bomb to maintain control of weak powers in the decolonizing world, as they were also conducting experiments to study the effects of radiation on Saharan rodents.[30]

Elements in the British peace movement and the Ghanaian government hastily mobilized against French objectives. With the help of the London-based Committee of African Organizations, they coordinated demonstrations at the French embassy in London in late August 1959 and in Trafalgar Square. The focus was anti-imperialist as well as antinuclear. An atomic stronghold in the Sahara, anticolonialists understood, not only facilitated French domination in Algeria, but on the African continent as a whole.[31] Peace advocates had the support of neutralist states at a time when the "Bandung spirit" still prevailed in Afro-Asian chanceries. In Ghana, Nkrumah skillfully exploited the window of opportunity that Cold War tensions had opened. The threat of nuclear war added authority to the neutralist policies that the Ghanaian leader thought appropriate for Africa, and bolstered his ambitions for leadership on the continent and beyond.[32]

Ghanaian finance minister Komla A. Gbedemah, who had once presided over the worldwide pacifist organization, World Federalists, retained as secretary the veteran peace and civil rights worker, expatriate William Sutherland, an African American. Sutherland received permission to mount a protest against French nuclear testing with Accra's full endorsement. Ghana sponsored Sutherland's visits to antiwar events in the United States and Britain to coordinate activities among such organizations as the Committee for Nonviolent Action and the British Direct Action Committee. The Reverend Michael Scott, a highly regarded activist in the fight against apartheid, lent his aid to a program of opposition.[33] The result was the Sahara Protest Team, composed of twenty persons, fourteen of them Africans and six from the United States and Europe. The demonstrators planned to confront French authorities at Reggan, the nuclear facility in the Algerian desert 2,000 miles from Accra. Nationals participated from Ghana, Nigeria, Britain, France, the United States, and what is now Lesotho, whose representative, Jonathan Leabua, thirty-three years later became its president. A. J. Muste from the Fellowship of Reconciliation also joined the effort, flying in to meet the group in northern Ghana. He endorsed a proposition of Gbedemah's: if nuclear testing was safe, then let the French test their bombs in France.[34]

The Sahara Protest Team left Accra on December 5, 1959. They traveled through northern Ghana, pausing to hold rallies. "The plan was to get as close to the test site as possible," Sutherland recalled, "letting folks know about the French plans and preventing the testing through our physical presence." The French stopped the group on the frontier but did not arrest them. The antinuclear team handed out leaflets written in local languages and found a positive reception among the population. French police, recognizing this, then forbade them access to the villages. Some friendly African border patrols allowed them to cross into Upper Volta (now Burkina Faso), but there they were jailed. The next day French authorities had them taken back to Ghana. Bayard Rustin and Sutherland sang "Negro spirituals" at the Upper Volta checkpoint.[35] Rustin proved invaluable in the campaign, helping to unite disarmament with African desires for neutrality, environmental health, and peaceful development.[36]

As the Sahara protesters' activities had received international attention and approval in other African countries, Gbedemah sent them back for another try at the border. This time, with Reverend Scott, they crossed into French colonial territory at night with the aid of "a local guide along a path usually used by smugglers." "We hid in the bush," Sutherland remembered. The next day they took the road to Ouagadougou, hitching a ride in a truck. The driver betrayed them, however, delivering the group to a police station where they were again arrested and returned to Ghana.[37] They made a final attempt on January 17, 1960. The team succeeded in getting 66 miles inside Upper Volta before being turned back. On February 13, French authorities carried out the planned nuclear test despite outrage all over Africa. France exploded a second device at ground level on April 1, 1960. Ghana's ruling Convention Peoples Party (CPP) hosted an April 19 conference attended by representatives of several African states where the mood, as described by a historian of the British peace movement, was "militant and angry."[38] Organizers invited US civil rights leader Ralph Abernathy, pacifist A. J. Muste, and activists from four continents to this Positive Action Conference for Peace and Security in Africa. Advocates of nonviolence and passive resistance held dialogues with such partisans of armed struggle as the Martinican-born psychiatrist Frantz Fanon, who now worked for the Algerian revolutionaries. The crises posed by French bomb testing in the Sahara and the 1960 Sharpeville, South Africa massacre, where police shot and killed dozens of unarmed demonstrators, provided the convocation's larger context.[39]

Still obdurate, Paris authorized the detonation of a third bomb two days after Christmas. The *harmattan* season had begun, when cool Saharan winds blow south into the countries of the Sahel and the forest belt, this time bringing with them unknown quantities of radioactive dust. Africans were livid. While international pressure eventually led France to relocate its nuclear program in French Polynesia, far away from large empowered populations and noteworthy criticism, its dogged contempt for Africans did little to affirm a flagging faith in the efficacy of nonviolence at the turn of the decade.[40]

The Sahara protest took place outside Europe, but brought together a unique combination of people and movements in support of a nuclear-free and decolonized Africa. Sutherland later reminisced: "It was so exciting because we felt that this joining up of the European anti-nuclear forces, the African liberation forces, and the U.S. civil rights movements could help each group feed and reinforce the other."[41] Some of these ties had already been forged. "By the time of the Sahara protest," historian Richard Taylor has written, "there were firm ideological and personal links between American pacifists (and civil rights activists such as Bayard Rustin) and their pacifist counterparts in Britain."[42]

IRELAND AND AFRICAN AMERICA

One of the marchers at Aldermaston was Eamonn McCann, one of several Irish students living in London and absorbing the peace movement ethos who subsequently became active in the civil rights movement in Northern Ireland. Peace served as a bridge to insurgents in Northern Ireland, helping to connect activists to an awareness of struggles in other parts of the world.[43] England had historically stigmatized the Irish as racial inferiors. It thus contributed to an early Irish sensitivity to race and a tendency to make declarations of solidarity with anti-imperialist movements outside Europe. Ireland figured prominently in the global unrest during World War I, when it received rhetorical support from Indian revolutionists and Garveyites, respectively, and when Irish and Indian immigrants living in the United States collaborated on anti-imperialist projects. The Anglo-Irish War led to the 1921 partitioning of Ireland and the creation of a Catholic minority in the dependent territory of Northern Ireland. Once the Irish Free State achieved independence, the Irish Republican Army (IRA) became moribund for decades. Yet Catholics in Northern Ireland under British rule continued to face problems that included voting restrictions, job discrimination, poverty, police brutality, and unequal access to schooling and housing. Since the revolution to create a free Ireland had ostensibly been won, Catholic leaders in the North in the early 1960s applied an analogy that seemed more apt than revolution for the circumstances of the time: that of civil rights. News coverage of civil rights protest in the United States revealed similar modes of discrimination and suggested that campaigns like those taking place in Dixie might work in Northern Ireland.[44]

Unlike most other Europeans, the Catholics in Northern Ireland did not approach the black civil rights movement merely as sympathetic onlookers but rather as an aggrieved minority sharing many of the same disabilities that African Americans did. Ireland had no black American expatriates during that era, but that did not deter Irish activists from adapting (African) American tactics to suit their own needs. "Many of us looked to the civil rights struggles in America for our inspiration," organizer Fionbarra ODorchartaigh recalled. "We compared ourselves to the poor Blacks of the U.S. ghettoes and those suffering under the cruel system of apartheid in racist South Africa. Indeed we viewed ourselves as Ulster's white Negroes—a repressed and forgotten dispossessed white tribe captured within a bigoted partitionist statelet that no Irish elector had cast a vote to create."[45] A youthful, emerging leader, Bernadette Devlin, a Catholic but socialist and nonsectarian in her outlook, told an interviewer that she drew the courage to defy bigotry from religion. She mordantly observed that Christianity, a common faith for all citizens of Northern Ireland in spite of sectarian differences, had become an excuse for Christians to attack one another. Devlin, like civil rights workers in the American South, wanted Christianity to be instead an instrument of reconciliation.[46]

Activists accordingly embarked on a campaign, beginning in 1964, that included litigation and nonviolent demonstrations where picket sign messages compared Catholics' plight to that of black Americans in the Deep South and demanded equal rights. Paul O'Dwyer, a New York City politician of Irish descent, agreed with the comparison, likening the struggle in Northern Ireland to black insurgency in Mississippi. Not all Irish Americans agreed, however. O'Dwyer's remarks contrast with a history of conflict between African Americans and Irish Americans in the United States that began in the nineteenth century and climaxed in the disastrous draft riots of 1863, when Irish mobs attacked blacks in the streets of New York. Discord continued in the twentieth century when Irish-Americans living in Boston violently opposed the racial integration of their neighborhood schools. While the Southern Christian Leadership Conference (SCLC) endorsed the civil rights cause in Northern Ireland, ironically, many Irish American groups that also supported Irish Catholic rights opposed the mission of SCLC and other US civil rights organizations. Calls of "Niggers out of Boston, Brits out of Belfast!" greeted Bernadette Devlin on her 1969 visit to Massachusetts.[47] Civil rights groups in Northern Ireland distanced themselves from the politics of many of their Irish American supporters.

The chance for genuine change through a civil rights strategy in Northern Ireland met resistance from Protestants and from the British government. The banning of public meetings, outlawing of Catholic organizations, and disruption of protests convinced many participants that nonviolent civil disobedience would not work in the face of intransigence from both British officials and Protestant authorities at home, and violent outbreaks that police seemingly could not control. The limited franchise that restricted voting to property holders, and the bias against Catholics in housing effectively restricted their political power. Circumstances were ripe for the reappearance of the IRA.

THE LATE 1960s

This turn to militancy was not unique in the late 1960s on either side of the Atlantic. Radicalism did not erupt suddenly or spontaneously. Every western country has a radical tradition that is constantly in dialogue with conventional consensus politics, even in epochs of ascendant conservatism and comparative prosperity. The United States has plural traditions, with African American forms serving as transnational catalysts. In the sixties and later, "the political militancy of people of color and its centrality within the left and progressive imaginary," in Nikhil Pal Singh's words, suffused the European left's sense of crisis and shaded its interpretation of how to address it.[48]

The peace issue again forged a harmony of interests for European and African American activists and underlay the insurgencies at the turn of the decade. Europe had twice come close to total self-annihilation during the twentieth century, as global wars toppled governments and caused the deaths of millions. The problem of war and a sense of the helplessness of a continent stranded between two superpowers capable of mass destruction heightened sensitivities. Scholars frequently depict the antiwar movement as a campaign of youth, but many Europeans old enough to have lived through World War II endorsed its goals. When African American insurgents arrived in Europe with a message that linked racial justice to peace, they often found receptive audiences. Governments inadvertently aided this process when they failed to resolve critical social and political problems within the scope of what they themselves considered legitimate. In the United States, for example, in spite of the nonviolent movement's achievement of civil rights legislation, black communities remained impoverished and racists learned clever ways to skirt the law. The increasingly brutal and futile Vietnam War absorbed resources needed for national revitalization. In France, De Gaulle's pursuit of preeminence based on military power sacrificed reforms for the benefit of civilian society. In both countries, older strategies to address these problems no longer worked. When European officials succumbed to pressures exerted by US authorities to ban dissidents or repatriate deserters, they incurred further resentment from citizens who decried the domination of a power that advertised itself as a champion of democracy and self-determination while betraying those principles in its international behavior. The door therefore opened for other solutions, specifically, the resurgence of a radicalism that had always lain below the surface of conventional politics.

Malcolm X played a part in the resurgence by substituting a discourse of human rights for one of civil rights. "Civil rights actually keeps the struggle within the domestic confines of America," he explained on a WBAI-FM radio program in 1965. African Americans would thus have to seek remedy at the hands of the very people oppressing them. "Human rights," however, "goes beyond the jurisdiction of this government" and framing the black condition as such would make it possible to seek outside help. "Our problem is not a Negro problem or an American problem, but rather it has become a human problem, a world problem, and it has to be attacked at the world level."[49]

Open condemnation by an African American organization of the United States' military adventures followed when the McComb County, Mississippi chapter of the Mississippi Freedom Democratic Party (MFDP) sharply criticized US foreign policy in a July 28, 1965 newsletter. "No one has a right to ask us to risk our lives and kill other Colored People in Santo Domingo and Vietnam, so that the White American can get richer," the text read. "We will be looked upon as traitors by all the Colored People of the world if the Negro people continue to fight and die without a cause." The state organization, pressured by the Mississippi NAACP and Representative Charles Diggs of Detroit, quickly distanced itself from the McComb statement, but the cat was out of the bag. SNCC in January 1966 issued a statement declaring it had "a right and a responsibility to dissent with the U.S. foreign policy on any issue when it sees fit." The tide turned in 1966 when surveys indicated that the majority of African Americans opposed the Vietnam War, a conflict in which blacks disproportionately served and suffered more than their share of the fatalities.[50]

SNCC charged the federal government with insincerity: it pretended to be concerned with Vietnamese welfare, just as it had falsely claimed sympathy for Dominicans and others. Supporters of the Johnson administration widely rebuked SNCC for its assertions and its temerity in attempting to weigh in on foreign policy matters.[51] SNCC forged ahead, however, creating an International Affairs Commission in 1967 and applying for nongovernmental organization status at the United Nations. James Forman, appointed to direct the Commission, addressed the General Assembly on November 17 in a speech devoted largely to southern Africa. Forman's remarks are significant here because he presented African Americans as a colonized people who were appealing to the world on that basis; and because SNCC had followed Malcolm X's lead in internationalizing the terms of debate.[52]

In subsequent years, SNCC, the Black Panther Party, and other organizations followed the logic laid out by Malcolm and began to practice their own diplomacy. Black organizations, most of them nationalist, felt greater affinities with Africa and Asia, and their most concerted international activity took them to such countries as Algeria, China, and Cuba. They nevertheless cultivated allies in Europe, sending leaders of their respective groups abroad to give speeches and organize chapters in various countries. They encouraged American expatriates to form antiwar groups. In Scandinavia, SNCC helped start an antiwar committee composed of black deserters. The Black Panther Party had support groups in Sweden and Denmark that assisted in fund raising and publicity for imprisoned Panthers in the United States. The Panthers used Denmark as a springboard for contacting black soldiers stationed at military bases in Germany. Eldridge Cleaver's book on US race relations, *Soul on Ice*, was translated into Danish. Students at Denmark's University of Aarhus wanted to present Cleaver with an honorary award, but when the parliament refused him political refugee status, he did not risk coming.[53]

Antiwar activists in Sweden consolidated their efforts in 1967 with the creation of the United National Liberation Front Groups of Sweden (UNLF). This umbrella organization claimed the antinuclear peace movement as parentage. The Swedish government had qualms about the peace movement, but Olof Palme, by early 1968 minister of education, participated in it, much to the consternation of conservatives in Stockholm and Washington, D.C.[54] GIs who defected to Sweden were accorded residence on "humanitarian grounds" and provided with housing and a living allowance. The American Deserters Committee published a broadside that encouraged desertion from the military, instructing those contemplating going AWOL in how to avoid getting caught, and informing them how to find its field offices and liaisons in Scandinavia and other areas. Black soldiers formed their own Afro-American Deserters Committee that combined resistance to racism in US society and in the military with antiwar work.[55]

In May 1970, the United States and South Vietnam invaded Cambodia, dragging an erstwhile neutral country into what then became a larger regional conflict. Members of the Ohio National Guard shot and killed four students on the campus of Kent State University during an antiwar protest. While black students had been killed by police at Orangeburg State College in South Carolina without substantial notice from the mainstream media, the deaths of white students elicited more comment and renewed mobilization by antiwar groups. During the same month, US ambassador Jerome Holland, an African American, was booed when he went to present his credentials to the king of Sweden. According to the *New York Times*, Swedish leftists called him a nigger. Certain Swedes, however, claimed that black Americans present at the ceremony called him a "house nigger." In any case, Holland bore the brunt of opposition to US policy. In a move perhaps designed to parry Cleaver, Holland's book, *Black Opportunity*, an upbeat look at race in America, was translated into Swedish.[56]

Cleaver and Holland's war of books suggests the importance of ideas in the conflicts of the period. African American thought and experience operated on the intellectual level as well as on the plane of political organizing. They influenced the activities of some of Europe's premier scholars. European intellectuals with transnational reputations numbered among those whose writings and political pursuits extended popular interest in peace, anti-imperialism, and African American resistance. These included Jürgen Habermas and Herbert Marcuse in Germany, and Jean Genet and Michel Foucault in France. Habermas later articulated his perception of activists' mindset. They were, he theorized, part of a paradigm shift in which "problems of quality of life, equality, individual self-realization, participation, and human rights" trumped earlier concerns about security and access to wealth.[57] Those sensitized to these new issues sought to preserve the autonomy of both private life and the public sphere from invasive threats by corporate capitalism and totalitarian political orders. Marcuse addressed the sophistication with which late capitalism defused dissent through distributionist practices and thereby rendered classic Marxist formulations about class struggle obsolete. Habermas and Marcuse, both members of the so-called Frankfurt School of Marxist intellectuals, encouraged German students to think critically, but opposed the increasingly militant protests of the late 1960s.[58]

French intellectuals Jean Genet and Michel Foucault showed less reserve. Both plunged into radical politics in ferment all over the West. Genet described the student revolt in France in May 1968 as the erasure of the past: "In May, the France that I have hated so much no longer existed, but rather, during one month, a world suddenly freed from nationalism, a smiling world, of extreme elegance, if you will."[59] As a playwright, Genet was drawn to the Black Panther Party's deployment of style as a political weapon and described the organization lyrically. Genet lived with Party members for three months while in the States during the late summer and fall, writing about black oppression as he observed the 1968 Democratic Party convention in Chicago. The adventurous French writer accompanied the Panthers on speaking tours to universities and opened doors for them in elite circles. He aided Panther support groups in France and spoke in favor of releasing prison intellectual George Jackson and philosophy professor Angela Y. Davis, employing the term "political prisoner," a category that US authorities tended to dismiss. In the United States again in the spring and summer of 1970, Genet gave later anthologized speeches that appeared in the French and US press. An ex-convict himself and gay, Genet came to the United States illegally because American authorities would not issue him a visa. Genet had written five books while in prison in France. His outlaw experiences drew him to George Jackson, also a writer, who like Genet, "honed his intellectual gifts in the carceral world." He wrote the preface to an edition of Jackson's prison letters.[60]

Michel Foucault shared aspects of Genet's outlaw sensibility and his attraction to black rebels. His interest in black insurgency bore directly on his scholarship as a philosopher. He learned about the Black Panther Party and its literature from students he taught in Tunisia in 1968. Forced to leave that country because of his active support for radical students, Foucault returned to France and then traveled to the United States, where he worked at the University of Buffalo. He extended his knowledge of the country in a trip to the Deep South in 1970.

George Jackson, already imprisoned, was on trial with others accused of murdering a guard. Foucault agreed to assist Jean Genet in Jackson's defense. Foucault edited and introduced the French translation of excerpts from Jackson's *Soledad Brother: The Prison Letters of George Jackson*, for which Genet penned the preface. When Jackson's brother Jonathan failed to free him at gunpoint from a California courtroom in August 1970, Jonathan was shot to death, along with the judge and two of the inmates on trial with Jackson. Authorities claimed to have traced ownership of the gun to Angela Davis. Davis fled, and a year later, prison guards killed George Jackson. These events inaugurated a period of major upheavals in American prisons, including, less than a month later, the Attica Rebellion of 1971. Foucault, teaching in upstate New York, an epicenter of the American prison network, visited Attica the following year. The upheavals in the US penal system formed part of the context in which Foucault's *Surveiller et punir: Naissance de la prison/Discipline and Punish: The Birth of the Prison* appeared in print in 1975.[61]

Students, Military, and Mobility

Leading intellectuals were not the only Europeans to visit the United States or to absorb what they encountered there. Exchange students were even more likely to carry influences home or to adopt perspectives based on their travels abroad. British students in the United States with fellowships from the Harkness Foundation had travel money to tour the country. Several came to Montgomery, Alabama in the early sixties, where they visited Clifford and Virginia Durr, a white couple active in the civil rights movement there. Federal agents followed the foreign students who visited the Durrs, but that did not prevent important networking. Through the agency of one, Anthony Lester, Clifford Durr received an invitation to speak in London in 1964. Lester had joined a fledgling organization that investigated human rights abuses: Amnesty International, for which he journeyed to Mississippi in the summer of 1964 to draft a report. Jonathan Steele, another British student who had stayed with the Durrs, participated in a voter registration campaign in Mississippi.[62] Movement influence on Europeans could take place in the United States as well as in Europe. British students were not alone in assessing the American situation and taking an active part in social and political change away from their homes. Three German students who played significant roles in radical politics in the 1960s had come to the United States as exchange students. One of them, Karl-Dietrich Wolff, upon his return to Germany, helped raise funds for Black Panther Bobby Seale's defense. The larger number of German speakers of English as compared to other European countries increased the likelihood that they would be attuned to American conditions.[63]

European student contact with Americans during the height of the Vietnam War again demonstrates the salience of peace as a motivating issue. Vietnam did not only impress European critics as a moral issue; it also revived the possibility of Soviet intervention and thus a conflagration that could bring down the stable order in Europe. Antiwar activity followed that reasoning. Support for soldiers who began deserting the US military in significant numbers by 1967, because clandestine, often eludes the record. American organizations operating in Europe with a network of local collaborators spirited deserters to locations in Scandinavia, France, and elsewhere. Participants in this underground railroad included persons across the center-to-left political spectrum, from Protestant clergy to erstwhile apolitical youth social clubs. Sometimes antiwar efforts reached fantastic extremes, as when a faction of the German student group Sozialistische Deutsche Studentenbund planned a march to a US military base near Berlin where they would "storm the barracks" in coordination with a group of Panther-affiliated soldiers who would stage a simultaneous mutiny. The plot was discovered and called off, however, when US authorities announced that military police would shoot anyone invading the premises. More often resistance took the form of steady and determined opposition to the war, increasingly reflected in proliferating disobedience among US troops.[64]

The armed services of the United States officially desegregated during the Truman era, but racism lingered on as a reflection of both senior brass values and attitudes at large in civilian society. West Germany, where the United States had its largest defense installations in Europe, had been a hotbed of prejudice since the end of the postwar occupation. In addition to the strictly segregated social life available to black soldiers, housing discrimination, and unfairness in military justice, black soldiers were likely to incur the hostility of assorted American Nazis and Klansmen. By the end of 1970, a highly organized black resistance had emerged. The Army initially tried to stop GIs from organizing through heavy-handed repression, but when it allowed them to hold meetings, publish papers, and join dissident organizations, hundreds of ephemeral newspapers, newsletters, and pamphlets urging opposition to war and racism flourished. A mutiny in the Seventh Army caused the cancellation of the trial of fifty-three black soldiers in Darmstadt, West Germany in October 1971. The soldiers saw the problems in the military as complementary to those in civilian life. They protested unequal treatment and lack of opportunities for promotion. Shipboard mutinies took place in the Pacific during the early 1970s as black sailors flatly refused to follow orders and engaged in pitched battles with other sailors and Marines. News of these encounters spread via ship radio and multiplied accordingly.[65]

Military unrest in a time of war led federal authorities to repress the antiwar movement at home and abroad. European governments sometimes cooperated with this initiative for reasons of their own. France deported a number of foreign dissidents for taking part in the events of May 1968, and those remaining had to sign agreements that they would not engage in political activity. At Washington's request, the Ministry of the Interior banned the Paris American Committee to Stop the War, which had worked to find lodgings and work for resisters and deserters. France, shaken by the internal rebellion of its workers and students, and roiled by a run on the franc, yielded to US pressure. German officials refused entry to Black Panther Eldridge Cleaver because he had been indicted for a crime in the United States for which he could be extradited. They curiously extended the ban to his wife, Kathleen Cleaver, who had no charges pending against her. France and Denmark also barred Kathleen Cleaver. Antiwar activists already present in Germany faced efforts to deport them.[66]

GI militancy survived the end of the draft and the winding down of the Vietnam War, but the decline in African American influence on developments in Europe owed something to flaws on the left as well as to government repression. France had never been especially hospitable to the deserters and resisters, who after 1968 decamped to Sweden. French anti-Americanism limited contacts between rebellious students and the GI population in France. Many American soldiers were newcomers to the political consciousness that percolated among many Europeans in their age cohort. According to "Max," identified only by his first name in the reports emanating from the Quaker Centre in Paris, "the [US] Army . . . now concentrates its fire on a weak but essential link: the link between the GI and civilian population." Class and the "cultural/language barrier" separated the largely educated European antiwar population from the working class Americans most likely to be drafted. Even in Germany, where the language barrier was less formidable and well organized antiwar efforts had begun in 1967, it took a while for students to switch their slogan from "Down with GI Murderers" to one of cooperation with soldiers who were increasingly antiwar. As for the soldiers themselves, some expressed trepidation about leftist German students. During the same antiwar march where plans to storm the US military base were foiled, German protesters attempted to seize scaffolding that construction workers had erected to use as podiums from where speakers at a rally could be heard. The workers resisted by burning the demonstrators' picket signs. The result was a free-for-all, pitching students against workers. This scenario echoed similar conflicts between antiwar progressives and blue-collar workers in the United States. The support for the Vietnam War by New York's "hard hats," construction workers who harassed antiwar protesters, demonstrated the inability of the antiwar movement to close the class gap, which constituted one of its most haunting failures.[67]

CONCLUSIONS

This essay will disappoint those seeking a crude cause-and-effect link between European and African American insurgencies, as well as those who assume that the connection did not rise above rhetoric. A complex reality suggests many eddies and byways in the relationship. The search for world peace underlies the gains and losses of an unprecedented period of international coordination across frontiers, nationalities, and classes, and made African American freedom struggles salient to the interests of people in other countries. While conditions in Europe itself ultimately determined how Europeans mounted antiracist and anti-imperialist struggles in their individual states and as members of a continental community, the insights they derived from the African American refusal of racism and imperialism and their activity in support of that stand illustrates how the theme of peace informed social movements throughout the epoch.

NOTES

1. Yohuru R. Williams, "American Exported Black Nationalism: The Student Nonviolent Coordinating Committee, the Black Panther Party, and the Worldwide Freedom Struggle 1967–1972," *Negro History Bulletin* 60 (July–September 1997): 1–13.
2. Manfred Berg, "1968: A Turning Point in American Race Relations?" in *1968: The World Transformed*, ed. Carole Fink, Philipp Gassert, and Detlef Junker (Washington, D.C.: The German Historical Institute and Cambridge University Press, 1998), 400. See also Piero Gleijeses, *Conflicting Missions: Havana, Washington, and Africa, 1959–1976* (Chapel Hill: University of North Carolina Press, 2002), 364, 365.
3. Nancy Prince, *A Narrative of the Life and Travels of Mrs. Nancy Prince, Written by Herself* (Boston, self-published, 1853), 23.
4. James Baldwin, "Stranger in the Village," in *Notes of a Native Son* (Boston: Beacon Press, 1955, 1984), 159, 160–161.
5. Prince, *Narrative*, 22–23; Mary Church Terrell, *A Colored Woman in a White World* (Washington, DC: National Association of Colored Women's Clubs, 1968), 73.
6. W. E. B. Du Bois, *The Autobiography of W. E. B. Du Bois* (New York: International Publishers, 1968), 161–162.
7. David Lionel Smith, "The Black Arts Movement and Its Critics," *American Literary History* 3, no. 1 (Spring 1991): 97–98; Oliver W. Harrington, *Why I Left America and Other Essays* (Jackson: University Press of Mississippi, 1993), 107.

8. On black American expatriates in Europe, see James Campbell, *Paris Interzone: Richard Wright, Lolita, Boris Vian and Others on the Left Bank, 1946–1960* (London: Secker & Warburg, 1994); Harrington, *Why I Left America and Other Essays;* Lloyd Kramer, "James Baldwin in Paris: Exile, Multiculturalism and the Public Intellectual,"*Historical Reflections* 27, no. 1 (2001): 27–47; Ursula Broschke-Davis, *Paris without Regret: James Baldwin, Kenny Clarke, Chester Himes, and Donald Byrd* (Iowa City: University of Iowa Press, 1986); Ernest Dunbar, *The Black Expatriates: A Study of American Negroes in Exile* (New York: E. P. Dutton & Co., 1968).

9. Cary Fraser, "A Requiem for the Cold War: Reviewing the History of International Relations Since 1945,"in *Rethinking the Cold War*, ed. Allen Hunter (Philadelphia: Temple University Press, 1997), 95.

10. Doug McAdam, "Culture and Social Movements," in *New Social Movements*, ed. Enrique Laraña, Hank Johnston, and Joseph R. Gusfield (Philadelphia: Temple University Press, 1994): 43; and Sidney Tarrow, "States and Opportunities: The Political Structuring of Social Movements," in *Comparative Perspective on Social Movements*, ed. Doug McAdam, John D. McCarthy, and Mayer N. Zald (Cambridge, MA: Cambridge University Press, 1996): 53.

11. Dizzy Gillespie with Al Fraser, *To Be, or Not . . . to Bop* (New York: Doubleday & Co., 1979), 287.

12. On the segregationist assault on civil rights "subversives," see Jeff Woods, *Black Struggle, Red Scare: Segregation and Anti-Communism in the South, 1948–1968* (Baton Rouge: Louisiana State University Press, 2004). *Daily Worker*, 8 February 1953, clipping in W. Alpheus Hunton Papers, Organization Series, Correspondence, Box 1, Schomburg Center for Research in Black Culture, New York Public Library; and Martin B. Duberman, *Paul Robeson* (New York: Alfred A. Knopf, 1988).

13. Clayborne Carson, *In Struggle: SNCC and the Black Awakening of the1960s* (Cambridge, MA: Harvard University Press, 1981), 105–107.

14. Gabrielle Hecht, *The Radiance of France: Nuclear Power and National Identity after World War II* (Cambridge, MA: MIT Press, 1998), 208, 209.

15. Jean-Luc Einaudi, *La Bataille de Paris. 17 Octobre 1961* (Paris: Editions du Seuil, 1991), 21, 54, 55, 55n1. 36, 74.

16. James Baldwin, "Equal in Paris," in James Baldwin, *Notes of a Native Son* (Boston: Beacon Press, 1955), 138–158; Stephen Michael Ward, "Ours Too Was a Struggle for a Better World: Activist Intellectuals and the Radical Promise of the Black Power Movement, 1962–1972," PhD diss., University of Texas, Austin, 2002, p. 188.

17. Chris Waters, "'Dark Strangers' in Our Midst: Discourses of Race and Nation in Britain, 1947–1963,"*The Journal of British Studies* 36 (April 1997): 207–238; and D. W. Dean, "Coping with Colonial Immigration, the Cold War and Colonial Policy: The Labour Government and Black Communities in Great Britain 1945–51,"*Immigrants & Minorities* 6, no. 3 (1987): 328.

18. Luther H. Hodges to Canon L. John Collins, 2 January 1959, Committee to Combat Racial Injustice Papers, Box 2, folder, 4, State Historical Society of Wisconsin, Madison.

19. Brian Ward, "A King in Newcastle: Martin Luther King, Jr., and British Race Relations, 1967–1968,"*Georgia Historical Quarterly* 79, no. 3 (1995): 615, 633, 626–628.

20. David Braden Posner, "Afro-America in West German Perspective, 1945–1966," PhD diss., Yale University, 1997, 340, 343, 64, 248–249.

21. Ibid., 341–343, 342n65.

22. *Mater et magistra* online at the Vatican website at http://www.vatican.va/holy_father/john_xxiii/encyclicals/documents/hf_j-xxiii_enc_15051961_mater_en.html. Accessed May 31, 2011.

23. *Populorum Progressio* online at the Vatican website at http://www.vatican.va/holy_father/paul_vi/encyclicals/documents/hf_v_pi_enc_26031967_populorum_en.html. Accessed May 31, 2011.

24. Gerald Horne, *Black and Red: W. E. B. Du Bois and the Afro-American Response to the Cold War* (Albany, NY: SUNY Press, 1986), 127; Mid-Century Conference for Peace, conference call, 28 April 1950, in Mary Church Terrell Papers (Washington, DC: Library of Congress Manuscript Division and Photoduplication Service, 1977), reel 10; Carey McWilliams, *The Education of Carey McWilliams* (New York: Simon & Schuster, 1979), 222; and Thomas J. Noer, "Martin Luther King, Jr., and the Cold War," *Peace & Change* 22 (April 1997): 116.

25. Lawrence S. Wittner, *Rebels against War: The American Peace Movement, 1933–1983* (Philadelphia: Temple University Press, 1984); and Richard Taylor, *Against the Bomb: The British Peace Movement, 1958–1965* (Oxford: Clarendon Press, 1988).

26. "Unanimity and Moderation: The Accra Conference," *Africa Today* 5 (May–June 1958): 11.

27. Plummer, *Rising Wind*, 232, 233; and Noer, "Martin Luther King, Jr.," 116.

28. Jervis Anderson, *Bayard Rustin: Troubles I've Seen* (Berkeley: University of California Press, 1998), 214, 215.

29. "Prospecting in the Sahara US Share in Concession," *Times* (London), January 22, 1959, 8C.

30. "French Explode Third Atomic Bomb Detonator for Hydrogen Type," *Times* (London), December 28, 1960, 8A.

31. Taylor, *Against the Bomb*, 157.

32. W. Scott Thompson, *Ghana's Foreign Policy, 1957–1966* (Princeton, NJ: Princeton University Press, 1969), 111.

33. William Sutherland and Matt Meyer, *Guns and Gandhi in Africa* (Trenton, NJ: Africa World Press, 2000), 36; Irwin M. Wall, *France, the United States, and the Algerian War* (Berkeley: University of California Press, 2001), 138, 161–162; Taylor, *Against the Bomb*, 157–158; and A. J. Muste, "Africa against the Bomb," in *The Essays of A. J. Muste, ed. Nat Hentoff* (New York: Bobbs Merrill, 1967), 399.

34. Sahara Protest Team Fact Sheet, 4 December 1959, Bayard Rustin Papers, reel 1 (Bethesda, MD: University Press of America, 1988); Jean Allman, "Nuclear Imperialism and the Pan-African Struggle for Peace ad Freedom," *Souls* 10 (2:2008), 87, 89; Daniel Levine, *Bayard Rustin and the Civil Rights Movement* (New Brunswick, NJ: Rutgers University Press, 2000), 116–188; Sutherland and Meyer, *Guns and Gandhi*, 37–39; A. J. Muste, "Africa," 397, 398, 403–404; and Protest Team Drive Towards Sahara Attempt to Reach Atom Test Site," *Times* (London), December 7, 1959, 8F.

35. Anderson, *Bayard Rustin*, 219–221.

36. Ibid., 215; John D'Emilio, *Lost Prophet: The Life and Times of Bayard Rustin* (New York: Free Press, 2003), 279–288.

37. Sutherland and Meyer, *Guns and Gandhi*, 39–40.

38. "Second Sahara Atomic Test Weapon of Usable Size Exploded," *Times* (London), April 2, 1960, 6G; S. C. Saxena, "Disarmament: The African Perspective," *Strategic Analysis* 22 (October 1998), online at http://www.idsa-india.org/an-oct8-3.html, accessed May 31, 2011; and Taylor, *Against the Bomb*, 163.

39. Taylor, *Against the Bomb*, 164–166; and B. Marie Perinbaum, *Holy Violence: The Revolutionary Thought of Frantz Fanon* (Washington, DC: Three Continents Press, 1982), 73.

40. Jean-Marc Regnault, "France's Search for Nuclear Test Sites, 1957–1963," *The Journal of Military History* 67, no. 4 (2003): 1240–1241. According to one French militarist, the

Pacific islands had the advantage of being "least exposed to hostile campaigns or worldwide reactions."

41. Sutherland and Meyer, *Guns and Gandhi*, 36–37.

42. Taylor, *Against the Bomb*, 167; and Frances M. Beal and Ty dePass, "The Historical Black
Presence in the Struggle for Peace," *The Black Scholar* (January/February 1986): 2–7.

43. Brian Dooley, *Black and Green: The Fight for Civil Rights in Northern Ireland and Black
America* (London: Pluto Press, 1998), 46; and Richard Rose, "On the Priorities of Citizenship in the Deep South and Northern Ireland," *The Journal of Politics* 38 (May 1976):
247–291.

44. Matthew Pratt Guterl, "The New Race Consciousness: Race, Nation, and Empire in
American Culture, 1910–1925,"*Journal of World History* (Honolulu) 10, no. 2 (Fall
1999): 328; and Naheem Gul Rathore, "Indian Nationalist Agitation in the United
States: A Study of Lala Lajpat Rai and the India Home Rule League of America, 1914–
1920," PhD diss., Columbia University, 1965, 107.

45. Quoted in Gregory M. Maney, "Transnational Mobilization and Civil Rights in Northern Ireland," *Social Problems* 47 (May 2000): 169.

46. John M. Lee, "New M.P. in Ulster: Militant and Almost 22," *New York Times*, April 19,
1969, 10.

47. "O'Dwyer Links Rights Drives In Ulster and Mississippi," *New York Times*, August
21, 1969, 3; Dooley, *Black and Green*, 38–48, 86–92; and Maney, "Transnational
Mobilization,"163–65, 169–170.

48. Locksley Edmondson, "Black America as a Mobilizing Diaspora," in *Modern Diasporas
in International Politics*, ed. Gabriel Sheffer (London and Sydney: Croom Helm, 1986),
164–211; and Nikhil Pal Singh, "Culture/Wars: Recoding Empire in an Age of Democracy," *American Quarterly* 50, no. 3 (1998): 498.

49. Transcript of Malcolm X interview with Harry Ring, WBAI-FM, New York City, 28
January 1965, enclosed in anonymous Special Agent to Special Agent in Charge, New
York, 30 September 1965, Malcolm X FBI File (Wilmington, Delaware, Scholarly
Resources 1995).

50. Beal and dePass, "The Historical Black Presence in the Struggle for Peace,"5.

51. Carson, *In Struggle*, 268–272.

52. The text of Forman's remarks is in "James Forman of SNCC Addresses the United
Nations," *Liberator*, December 1967, 8–10.

53. Robert G. Weisbord, "Scandinavia: A Racial Utopia?"*Journal of Black Studies* 2 (June
1972): 481–484.

54. UNLF, *UNLF—The United NLF Groups of Sweden* (Stockholm: Tryckeri Och Förlags
AB Solidaritet, 1973), pamphlet in Michelle Gilbaud Papers, Wisconsin Historical Society, Madison.

55. American Deserters Committee, "If Your CHOICE Is Political Emmigration
[sic],"mimeographed, Social Action Vertical File, Box 3, folder American Deserters
Committee, Wisconsin Historical Society; Ulf Nilson, "Deserters in Sweden," *Ebony* 23
(August 1968): 120–122; and Barnaby J. Feder, "Deserters in Sweden: An Odd Little
'V.F.W. Post,'" *New York Times*, June 17, 1985, A2.

56. Weisbord, "Scandinavia," 484, 485.

57. Jürgen Habermas, "New Social Movements," *Telos* 49 (1981): 33. See also Herbert Marcuse, *One Dimensional Man: Studies in the Ideology of Advanced Industrial Society* (Boston: Beacon Press, 1964).

58. Nick Thomas, *Protest Movements in 1960s West Germany* (Oxford: Berg, 2003), 76.

59. Pascale Gaitet, *Queens and Revolutionaries* (Cranbury, NJ: Associated University Presses,
2003), 20.

60. Gaitet, *Queens and Revolutionaries*, 106, 157n11. The speeches appear in Jean Genet, *The Declared Enemy: Texts and Interviews* (Stanford, CA: Stanford University Press, 2004). Stephen Barber, *Jean Genet* (London: Reaktion Books, 2004) is a recent biography.

61. Institut Mémoires de l'édition contemporaine (IMEC), Michel Foucault Archive, online at http://www.michel-foucault-archives.org/spip.php?article18, accessed May 31, 2011. Foucault described Attica in *Telos* 19 (Spring 1974): 154–161. See also David Macey, *The Lives of Michel Foucault* (New York: Knopf, 2005).

62. Virginia Foster Durr, *Freedom Writer: Letters from the Civil Rights Years*, ed., Patricia Sullivan (New York: Routledge, 2003), 234, 301, 308–309, 312, 220–221.

63. Doug McAdam and Dieter Rucht, "The Cross-National Diffusion of Movement Ideas," *Annals of the American Academy of Political and Social Science* 528 (July 1993): 70, 71. See also the account of German student experience in Maria Höhn and Martin Klimke, *A Breath of Freedom: The Civil Rights Struggle, African American GIs, and Germany* (New York: Palgrave Macmillan, 2010), 108, 111.

64. Thomas, *Protest Movements*, 159; "Max," "Problems of the GI Resistance in Europe," Gibault Papers, folder 12.

65. Michele Gibault, *La résistance dans l'armée a` l'époque de la guerre du Vietnam* (Paris: Association française d'études américaines, 1976), 86; "Sailors Show How to Fight Back," clipping from anonymous broadside, Gibault Papers, folder 9; Henry P. Leifermann, "The *Constellation* Incident," *New York Times*, February 18, 1973, 301; Earl Caldwell, "Navy's Racial Trouble Persists Despite Long Effort to Dispel It," ibid., 28 May 1973, 5; Curtiss Daniell, "Germany: Trouble Spot for Black GIs," *Ebony* 23 (August 1968): 125–128. Höhn and Klimke, *A Breath of Freedom*, offers the most comprehensive treatment to date of interactions between German citizens and black GIs.

66. "Les Exiles Américains," September 1973, mimeographed report, folder 2; Resistance Inside the Army (RITA), folder 12; Col. David M. Peters to Dr. Georg Burckard, 5 June 1972, folder 5, Gibault Papers.

67. "Max," Report on the GI Movement in Europe; Gibault, *La résistance*, 87; and Thomas, *Protest Movements*, 159.

CHAPTER 7

THE FORMATION OF ASIAN AMERICAN NATIONALISM IN THE AGE OF BLACK POWER, 1966-75

JEFFREY O. G. OGBAR

THE BLACK POWER MOVEMENT HAD A PROFOUND effect on the symbolism, rhetoric, and tactics of radical activism outside of the African American community during the tumultuous late 1960s. Scholars have long credited the civil rights movement for fomenting the emerging movements of women, gays, and others in the late 1960s and early 1970s.[1] Although the black struggle for civil rights undoubtedly affected the growing efforts of other marginalized and oppressed groups in the United States, it was the Black Power movement that had some of the most visible influences on the radical activist struggles of Latinos, Asians, and Native Americans, giving rise to a visible movement of *radical ethnic nationalism.* This nationalism endorses centrally organizing around ethnicity or race, while simultaneously working very closely with other ethnic groups to realize fundamental systemic change and freedoms that transcends race. By 1968, young activists from Asian American communities had been impressed and inspired by the militancy, political analysis, and organization as well as symbolism of black nationalists and Black Power advocates. No organization influenced these burgeoning militants more than the Black Panther Party (BPP).

The BPP experienced precipitous growth in 1968, with over thirty chapters emerging across the country. Thousands of African American militants were willing to embrace the BPP as a vanguard organization to lead the national struggle against oppression, and Asian Americans took notice. Not only black people but other people of color and even poor whites had languished under the domination of white supremacy in the United States. In the late 1960s, the militant call for Black Power also reverberated in the barrios and ghettos throughout the country, engendering such organizations as the Brown Berets, Young Lords, Red Guard, and American Indian Movement.

The creation of the Third World Liberation Front in the San Francisco Bay Area mobilized and inspired thousands of Asian American students, as it had other students of color and many whites. Berkeley's *Asian Student* newspaper provided a history of the Asian student movement and acknowledged the influence that black students brought to the college arena: "Our black brothers and sisters were the first to cry out in protest in the civil rights movement and were the first to make militant radical demands for the transformation of society. Out of this grew the Asian Student Movement."[2]

The first major group of Asians to arrive in the United States was the Chinese. Thousands immigrated to the western states in the mid- to late nineteenth century as free laborers. Although many worked on the expanding railroad system, others mined gold in California or undertook laborious jobs. They were quickly met with anti-Chinese mob violence and rioting throughout the region when white workers complained of job competition with Asians. In 1852, California passed a "foreigners tax" to help exclude Chinese from gold mining. Other anti-Chinese legislation was passed on the local, state, and federal levels, including the Chinese Exclusion Act of 1882, which banned Chinese immigration. Japanese and Filipino immigrants faced similar bouts with racial discrimination and codified policies that severely circumscribed the opportunities of Asians, who were concentrated in the West. The number of Asian immigrants dropped off significantly in the 1920s with nativist laws that limited immigration from Asian countries. Forced into small communities of limited political, social, or economic power, many Asian Americans avoided militant agitation for rights. Some groups even petitioned the courts for legal status as "whites" to avoid the systemic oppression experienced by people of color. They were unsuccessful.[3]

Significant changes had emerged in the political landscape by the late 1960s. Influenced by the cultural and political currents of black nationalism and Black Power, Asian American militants found themselves consciously transforming the public image of their panethnic "nation." Rejecting the stereotype of the timid, obsequious, and quiet Oriental, young Asian American militants affirmed themselves as radical harbingers of progress who were no longer enamored of whiteness. In 1968, the Asian American Political Alliance (AAPA) was formed at the University of California (UC) at Berkeley, for the first time bringing together disparate ethnic groups of Asian students. Richard Aoki, a Japanese American raised in West Oakland, joined the BPP while at Merritt College with Huey P. Newton and Bobby Seale. He later joined the AAPA, after his transfer to UC Berkeley. Aoki, a field marshal for the Panthers, explains that he "went underground to look into the Asian Movement to see if we could develop an Asian version of the BPP." Aoki soon became the spokesperson for the AAPA. The AAPA developed close ties with the BPP and the Red Guard, an Asian American organization modeled after the Panthers.[4] They often cosponsored demonstrations and panels calling for justice for the Panthers and an end to "the pig repression of the Vanguard Party." With some members donning berets and sunglasses, the AAPA organized students around issues related to both university and nonuniversity communities.

As Vicci Wong, a founding member of AAPA notes, "It wasn't just a local thing or just for our little group in college. We identified with the struggles that were going on them. We fought harder because we didn't see it as just our own fight."[5] For Wong and others, their presence on college campuses was simply an opportunity to wage their struggle in the context of the academic domain *and* the larger society. The two—campus and community—were not mutually exclusive.

Students demanded more faculty and students of color as well as an end to the Vietnam War, police brutality, and the hyperexploitation of Asian farmworkers. The Berkeley AAPA worked with a growing number of viable Asian American student leaders in the state, such as Jack Wong, a student activist at UC Santa Barbara. These student activists called for more Asian American representation in college administrations, but also put the politics of prospective Asian American administrators under heavy scrutiny. Asian ancestry was not enough for AAPA support. Wong called the Japanese American acting president of San Francisco State College a "tool of the white power establishment" for resisting demands of the Third World Liberation Front (TWLF). Not satisfied with simply calling President Hayakawa an Uncle Tom, Wong and others also called him an "Uncle Charlie," derived from the fictitious Charlie Chan detective series.[6] It was clear that the younger generation of Asian Americans had made a break with their parents' popular image as tolerant, apologetic, and meek permanent foreigners, unwilling to jeopardize their pursuit of white acceptance by complaining too much. Also, as the derisive term used to ridicule Hayakawa suggests, ethnicity was being subsumed by a larger identity that was determined by the rubric of race. A Japanese American was being called an offensive name that was originally coined for a Chinese person. Declaring a firm alliance with Chicano and black students, the AAPA declared, "We Asian-Americans believe that heretofore we have been relating to white standard of acceptability, and affirm the right of self-definition and self-determination. We Asian-Americans support all non-white liberation movements and believe that all minorities in order to be truly liberated must have complete control over the political, economical and educational institutions within their respective communities."[7]

Dedicated to the mission of strong community ties beyond academia, Berkeley students traveled to Agbayni Village, a poor rural California retirement community for farmworkers, half of whom were Filipino men. These elderly were typically without a family and alone. Students provided development work and petitioned for farmworker rights.[8] In 1973, the Asian Student Union formed a community committee responsible for developing student support for issues in Chinatown, Manilatown, and Japantown.

Often considered less audacious with their radical politics than their white, black, or Latino counterparts, Asian American student activists were visible in the political discourse of the era, particularly on the West Coast. They provided films and sponsored panels on socialism, the Chinese Revolution, and class struggle as well as antiwar activities.[9] The relations between campus militancy and community militancy were as inextricable in Asian American communities as they were in black communities. Activists positioned themselves as purveyors of a new ethnic consciousness and part of a new generation of progressive change.

The number of Asian American radical organizations outside of academia grew considerably as the decade came to a close. The most visible organization was the Red Guard, which emerged from the Bay Area's dynamic political and cultural climate. Founded in 1969, the Guard was named after Mao Tse-Tung's unit of young revolutionaries who burned the property of capitalists and counter-revolutionaries during the Chinese Revolution. The Red Guard saw the Panthers, across the bay, as an example of radical resistance to racial and class oppression. Armed, the Guard openly declared itself a communist organization, a bold move in Chinatown. Fully aware of the intense taboo against radical leftist political activity in the Chinese American community, the Guard initiated a series of projects to meet the basic needs of the people. It was able to prevent the closing of a tuberculosis testing center in Chinatown, exposing the fact that the TB rate in San Francisco's Chinatown was one of the highest in the country. The Guard also worked with the Asian Legal Services and had 1,000 cases of people who resisted the draft, via the Asian American Draft Help Center. The Guard's Breakfast for Children program chiefly fed black children from public housing projects in or around San Francisco's Chinatown. The program was modified to feed poor elderly, which brought many Asian senior citizens to the program.[10]

Although the Guard saw itself as a Chinese American version of the BPP, it was also very well aware that the dynamics of the black and Chinese American communities were different, despite some similarities. Alex Hing, a cofounder of the Guard, who assumed the title Minister of Information (one of several titles that mirrored the titles of the Party), explains, "We tried the model ourselves after the Panthers. When it didn't work, we gave it our own characteristics."[11] To that end, the Guard hoped to serve the people in the same manner as had the Party. But it also had a strong political and cultural affinity to Asia and was particularly concerned about the role of China in global affairs. Moreover, the Guard understood Chinese American anxiety over the tenuous status of Chinese as American citizens. Only in 1965 did the US government lift its over seventy-year immigration restrictions on Chinese. By campaigning for US recognition of Beijing, the Guard demonstrated its political and cultural identification with mainland China. It also invited the repression of the FBI and CIA.

The Red Guard's activities, which included efforts to seat China at the United Nations, were firmly connected to the larger leftist domestic community that proved to be of serious concern for US foreign policy during the Cold War. Increasingly, leftists influenced by the rapidly changing geopolitical landscape, assumed the mantle of radicalism in the contextual framework of anti-imperialism. Anti-imperialism had a profound resonance among radicals who were self-described "Third World People." This term declared their affinity with the struggles of people in Africa, Asia, and Latin America. It also postulated that "internal colonialism" was the mechanism by which people of color were subjugated in the United States. This rhetoric invariably found considerable coverage in the press of both communist and capitalist countries.

International news coverage reported on the plight of black people in the United States to millions worldwide and even influenced the emergence and symbolism of radicals outside of the United States. The urban rebellions, shoot-outs with police, assassinations, and student upheaval were reported in countries that the United States considered friendly as well as in those it considered hostile, causing headaches for the State Department. For communist countries, the social and political unrest were indicative of the inherent contradictions of a capitalist and imperialist society. Following the assassination of Martin Luther King, Jr., in 1968, Mao Tse-Tung led hundreds of thousands of Chinese demonstrators to denounce white supremacy in the United States. Mao was certainly not alone. Fidel Castro, president of Cuba, and other leaders of socialist countries eagerly exploited the news of civil unrest to denounce the United States and its subjugation of black people. The world took notice when Tommie Smith and John Carlos were suspended from 1968 US Olympic activities after their clenched-fist Black Power demonstration on the award stand. The Cuban men's four-hundred-meter relay team announced that in support of Smith and Carlos, it was sending its medals to Stokely Carmichael, who had visited Cuba earlier that year. Athletes from other countries also expressed sympathy with the struggle of black people in the United States.[12]

The militant struggle of black people received more international media attention as the collective efforts of Black Power advocates provided a subtext to the American Cold War dichotomy of "democracy" versus "communism." This was, of course, a false dichotomy that assumed that the United States was prodemocracy, when it was actually procapitalism. As demonstrated in friendly foreign relations with Zaire, Haiti, South Africa, Rhodesia, and scores of other undemocratic states, capitalism was more important than democracy for US foreign policy makers.

For many international observers, the intensification of violent clashes between Black Panthers and the police through 1969 made the Party the rightful revolutionary vanguard of the country's burgeoning Left. The communist countries North Korea and China issued favorable statements regarding the Panthers by 1969. In 1970, the International Section of the BPP, led by Eldridge Cleaver, established an "embassy" in North Korea. David Hilliard, Panther Chief of Staff, requested representation from the Red Guard for the eleven-member trip to North Korea. Alex Hing joined Hilliard and others traveling to North Korea, Vietnam, and Algeria. Although the Guard enjoyed international press and greater visibility in the United States, police harassment led to a steady decline in members.[13]

Like other radical organizations of the era, the Red Guard attracted a youthful membership, peaking with about 200 members before police repression reduced membership to a few dozen. Their uniforms, which included army field jackets and red berets, were instant targets for the police. Red Guard members complained about systematic police harassment, being unable to walk down the street without being put up against the wall, frisked, and asked for identification. Their offices were constantly raided, often without sufficient pretense. In a Cold War climate of fierce anticommunism, the FBI and CIA were eager to undermine the Red Guard and the Panthers for their domestic and international political activism. With joint efforts between federal and local law enforcement agencies, the Red Guard experienced significant challenges from the police and the intelligence community leaving the organization moribund by 1971.[14]

Unlike the Panthers, the Guard avoided the Custer-like defenses of its office during police raids, despite an armed standoff that a member had with police. A March 1969 issue of the Red Guard paper states that four "pigs" arrested Tyrone Won, who was leaving Red Guard headquarters with a disassembled rifle. Later, while released on parole, Won joined a Black Panther who was also fleeing police and escaped to Mexico, where they hijacked a plane for Cuba. In 1971, the remaining members decided to disband the Red Guard. Most joined other Asian American leftist organizations, particularly I Wor Kuen (IWK), a New York–based organization that had become national by the early 1970s.[15]

Founded in 1969, the I Wor Kuen was named after a secret society of Chinese rebels who tried to expel Westerners from China and depose the Ch'ing dynasty beginning in 1895. Called "Boxers" in the West, the I Wor Kuen attacked Westerners and Western influence in China, evoking outrage from the West, which eventually repressed what became known as the Boxer Rebellion. In the United States, the IWK was led by Yu Han and Yu Man, two graduate students from mainland China. The IWK was systematically formed to operate as an extension of the radical ethnic nationalism of the era. It was a Maoist organization that was ideologically modified to adapt to the highly racialized climate of the United States while simultaneously adhering to the class-centered language of Maoism and Marxism. As a former member, Lee Lew-Lee explains, "The IWK was like the Black Panther Party, the Young Lords and the Red Guards." In fact, he continues, "the IWK was patterned after the Red Guards."[16] Like the Red Guard, Chicano Brown Berets, and (most important) the Black Panthers, the IWK hoped to form an essential vanguard in its ethnic community to mobilize its people for a class-based revolution that would destroy racial and class oppression. Synthesizing theories of class struggle from Frantz Fanon, Mao, Lenin, and Marx as well as the ever dynamic Panthers, the IWK considered US Chinatowns internal colonies. Neocolonialism, for the IWK, provided a sound explanation for the system of oppression that exploited Chinese Americans and other people of color in the United States.[17]

While attempting to organize the Asian American community, the IWK, like the Red Guard, was confronted by deep-seated hostility from Chinese Americans who rejected communist China and thought that leftist activities would reflect negatively on the Asian American community at large. Hoping to protect the Asian American community against any police state repression or future attempts to relocate citizens into camps, the IWK maintained a largely marginal voice in Asian American political discourse, despite its growth, which allowed it to work closely with the Red Guard and eventually absorb many of its remaining members. In 1975, it merged with the predominately Chicano August 29th Movement to form the League of Revolutionary Struggle.[18]

The Red Guard, AAPA, and IWK pulled heavily from middle-class, college-educated groups, but a Los Angeles–based organization emerged in 1969 that like the Panthers attracted many "brothers off the block." The Yellow Brotherhood (YB) was formed out of a nexus of political militancy, ethnic pride, and general social pathos. The first radical Asian American organization of young militants in the city, the YB had a membership of former gang members, ex-convicts, and ex-servicemen. Many were Nisei and sansei—second- and third-generation Japanese Americans—who were unnerved by the political reticence that seemed to characterize their communities, particularly in an age when other ethnic groups had galvanized around radical ethnic nationalism. Speaking about their parents, one former YB member states, "They're hypersensitive or hyperapologetic. We [the younger generation] picked up some of that." Another follows, "That is why the Yellow Brotherhood was so controversial. We weren't hyperapologetic." Whereas many Japanese Americans were instructed to resist racism by seeking white approval through cultural assimilation, the YB joined the chorus of black cultural nationalists that vilified assimilation with whites: "We were told to out-white the whites and groups like the YB . . . said 'Fuck the whites. Fuck that shit.'"[19] For Guy Kurose and others, the time had come for radical political organization in the Asian American community. But for Kurose, it was initially an uphill battle that he was not willing to wage.

At age sixteen, Guy Kurose, a Japanese American, joined the Seattle branch of the BPP. Raised in the black community, he naturally gravitated to Black Power with his friends: "I . . . listened to [James Brown singing] 'Say it loud, I'm black and proud.' I wanted to be there too." Unable to fully extricate himself from socially dysfunctional behavior, however, Kurose, like many other Panthers, carried his lumpen life into the party: "I was a renegade Panther. We were what Bobby Seale called 'jakanapes,' kids that had good intentions but were relating strongly to hoodlumism." Deeply involved with the Black Power movement, Kurose was unaware of any community of young Asian revolutionaries, until a visit from Mo Nishida, Victor Shibata, and Warren Furutani from California. His immediate reaction: "I don't need to talk to no Japanese motherfucker who thinks he's white, man." He stayed in the Party until he entered college, where he joined the Asian Student Coalition and carried over the radicalism that he learned in the Party, even fighting police on campus.[20]

Kurose later moved to Los Angeles, where he worked closely with other Asian radicals in leftist groups such as the YB, Joint Communications, and the Asian American Hardcore. Although the YB, like the Panthers, pulled heavily from nonacademics, it also struggled over "jackanape" activities. Los Angeles had a serious gang presence that was also part of the Asian American community. Gangs such as the Ministers, Shokashus, and Constituents became politicized in the late 1960s, as had the Slausons, Gladiators, and Businessmen in the black community. But as Kurose noted, "Gangsters don't give a shit about Red Books."[21] The YB challenged the pervasive notion of Asian meekness, yet simultaneously struggled with self-destructive tendencies. Former members take pride in being the "first ones talking shit and kicking ass" but admit that they were marginalized by the larger Asian American community in ways not experienced by black nationalists in their communities. This alienation did not stop other militant, street-based Asian organizations from developing, however.

The Asian American Hardcore, like the YB, attracted former junkies, gang members, and convicts. Mo Nishida, a former member, explains that the Hardcore grew out of the tumultuous political and cultural climate of the Black Power movement in general and the Black Panthers in particular: "I think that the idea was percolating around because of the notoriety of the Panthers." The Panthers were eager to recruit what they considered the toughest elements of the black community, the lumpen proletariat. For the Panthers, the lumpen composed the vanguard class of the impending revolution: "When the Panthers came forward, the idea of trying to get some of our people back from the other side of capitalism came up, so some of us talked about needing to form a group like that. With the Panthers as a model, we could serve the people."[22] The Hardcore established an office on Twenty-Third and Vermont Avenue and began detoxification programs for drug addicts, as well as a political education class, Christmas programs for the poor, and other programs for the elderly. The group, taking a sartorial cue from the Panthers, as others had, wore fatigues and red berets as part of its uniform. Clearly, the Panthers loomed large for the small band of revolutionaries in Los Angeles.

Members of the Hardcore met with Panthers, including national leaders like Eldridge Cleaver and Bobby Seale. Yet, as Nishida says, "We were small potatoes compared to those guys . . . but we never felt that way." Like many self-described revolutionaries of the period, members of the Hardcore believed that the revolution was imminent, and the Panthers would be its vanguard party: "The Panther Party was the basic acknowledged leadership in the Revolutionary Nationalist Movement. They set the whole stage." But when the FBI unleashed its unprecedented repression, in concert with local police, the Panthers were decimated as no political organization in US history had been: "After the Panthers got wasted by COINTELPRO . . . there was disillusionment about the political line of the Panthers." Nishida explains that despite the Panthers' revolutionary posture, "when they couldn't respond to the killings by the police, it [screwed] everybody's mind up."[23]

After the revolutionary, gun-toting posturing of the Panthers evoked the deadly wrath of the government, many members of the Asian American Hardcore moved into other arenas of political discourse, no longer desirous of following the Party line in toto. The YB and Asian American Hardcore were unique among Asian American radical organizations in one major way: The demographic makeup of their membership was not typically middle class or college educated. As community-based organizations with strong ties to the street, the Brotherhood and Hardcore turned the stereotype of Asian Americans on its ear. Asian-descended young people rejected the term Oriental in the late 1960s and embraced a Pan-Asian term for the first time: Asian American. Many organized around a simple Asian identity, unlike the typically nationality-based organizations prior to the late 1960s, such as the Japanese American Citizens League or the Chinese American Citizens Alliance. Affected by Black Power, they promoted the slogan "Yellow Power" and raised the clenched fist in union with other "Third World People" on college campuses and in streets across the United States. And although they avoided the type of deadly conflict with law enforcement agencies experienced by the Panthers, they offered material and moral support to the Party as well as a scathing critique of the political, social, and economic systems that converged to undermine the Panthers and others like the Party.

The Yellow Power movement and other forms of radical ethnic nationalism were not solely dependent on Black Power for symbolism, political direction, or motivation. In fact, the black and Asian movements necessarily influenced each other in alliances, networks, conferences, and general dialogue. Furthermore, the international dynamics that influenced Black Power similarly informed Latino and Asian struggle in the United States. Mao Tse-Tung was an inspiration to Panthers as well as the Red Guard. Brown Berets and Young Lords had a particular affinity with Che Guevara, who was also an adored icon for the Panthers. The symbiotic relations were extant. Still, the Black Power movement helped form a period of social and cultural transformation that would have substantive effects on the cultural and political landscape of the United States.

The Black Power movement articulated the angst and anger of a generation created by the pervasive and insidious nature of racial subjugation in the United States. In no uncertain terms, it challenged the legitimacy of white supremacy—politically, culturally, and socially. The visibility of Black Power militants could not be ignored. They were featured on television shows, in newspapers, on college campuses, and on the radio. Popular culture paid great attention to the cultural transformation of the United States. In fact, the country was in a process of an upheaval of its long-lasting traditions of racial hierarchy, and no organization caught the media spotlight as did the BPP.

Although the historical backdrop provided different social, cultural, and political exigencies in the various communities, the BPP proved to be a matrix for Asian American radicals. Imbued with a profound sense of duty, obligation, resistance, and idealism, these revolutionaries were inspired, motivated, and significantly influenced by the symbolism, rhetoric, and tactics of the Black Power movement in general and the Black Panthers in particular.

These proponents of radical ethnic nationalism glorified their ethnicity while they eagerly embraced a polysemic nationalist framework that pulled from Fanon, Marx, Lenin and Mao. Too, they were significantly influenced by the political analysis of the BPP and its thesis of revolutionary struggle. But as seen above, Black Power's influence on Asian Americans altered the popular discourse and public discussion of identity and equality in the United States in interesting ways. Outside and inside of the radical leftist ethnic nationalist communities were militants who rebuked whiteness and the implications of whiteness such as status dependent on the subjugation of people of color. In this contextual framework, many militants sought to "humanize" whites by stripping them of any trappings of cultural prestige or supremacy. The cornerstone to this effort was a rejection of integration, though desegregation was welcomed.

Black Power dismissed the notion that black people would have a better quality of life with whites in closer proximity. The Promised Land that black nationalists envisioned was not the integrated world of which King dreamed. It was a black world, for, by and about black people. For radical ethnic nationalists, it was both a world where whiteness was no longer the standard by which all else was judged and a class-free society. Yet, rejecting the traditional class-based rhetoric of the left, the radical ethnic nationalists merged radical interpretations of race and class in their movements. Radical ethnic nationalism revealed the vulnerability of whiteness. Whiteness was not sacrosanct or without flaw. It was corrupt and inextricably bound to the frailties of humanity.

Beyond the cultural and psychological effects that radical ethnic nationalism introduced to the New Left of the late 1960s and early 1970s, the movement was truly a unique phenomenon. There are no major examples of ethnic nationalist struggles that have established alliances as did young radicals of the Black Power era. Asian American radicals merged ethnic nationalist rhetoric with a struggle that emphasized class conflict and interracial coalitions. When the BPP coined the slogan "All power to the people," it was attempting to broaden the call for Black Power by transcending race. According to the Party chairman Bobby Seale, interracial coalitions are powerful examples of the people gaining strength in numbers in their efforts against the "power structure's oppression."[24] Unique among political movements anywhere, this was an example of a radicalism that adapted to the highly racialized climate of the United States while adhering to the fundamental principles of leftist theories that generally criticized nationalism as bourgeois efforts to subvert true radicalism. At the center of this movement was the Black Power movement, providing the earliest examples of cultural nationalism and political organization around ethnic nationalist causes. The BPP served as a paradigm of radical ethnic nationalism and a vanguard party for the revolutionary nationalist movement. The Panthers provided an appeal that was unprecedented in the annals of radical struggle. For young Asian American militants, the Panthers offered a model that was inspirational, encouraging, and also a lesson in success and error.

NOTES

1. A number of studies on the women's liberation and gay liberation movements point to the civil rights movement for inspirations, symbolism, and rhetoric. See Sara M. Evans, *Born for Liberty: A History of Women in America* (New York: Free Press, 1989), pp. 264–274. See also Dudley Clendinen and Adam Nagourney, *Out for Good: The Struggle to Build a Gay Rights Movement in America* (New York: Simon & Schuster Trade, 1999).
2. *The Asian Student* 1, no. 1 (November 1973): p. 13.
3. Ronald Takaki, *Strangers from a Different Shore: A History of Asian Americans* (New York: Penguin Books, 1989), pp. 13–15.
4. "Yellow Power," *Giant Robot*, no. 10 (1998): p. 71; Bobby Seale, *Seize the Time: The Story of the Black Panther Party and Huey P. Newton* (Baltimore: Black Classics Press, 1991), pp. 72–73, 79.
5. "Yellow Power," p. 71.
6. *Hokubei, Manichi*, December 9, 1968, p. 2.
7. Flyer, c. 1969, University of California, Berkeley Social Protest Collection (UCBSPC), Box 18, folder 25, Asian American Political Alliance.
8. Asian Student Union flyer, n.d., UCBSPC, 1964–1696, Box 18, folder 27, Asian Student Union.
9. Ibid.
10. "Yellow Power," pp. 79–80.
11. Ibid., p. 79.
12. "US Women Dedicate Victory to Smith, Carlos," *New York Times*, October 21, 1968, p. 1.
13. "Yellow Power," pp. 79–80.
14. Ibid.

15. Ibid.
16. Ibid., p. 67.
17. Ibid.
18. Ibid., pp. 79–80; Robin D. G. Kelley and Betsy Esch, "Black Like Mao: Red China and Black Revolution," *Souls* 1, no. 4 (Fall 1999): p. 26.
19. "Yellow Power," p. 77.
20. Ibid., p. 76.
21. Ibid., p. 77.
22. Ibid., p. 74.
23. Ibid., p. 75. Although there have been deadly campaigns of repression against Native Americans, slave revolts, and colonial unrest in places like the Philippines, no political organization has experienced deadly conflict with the state apparatus comparable to the Black Panther Party. The Communist Party, the International Workers of the World, and other leftist groups have had violent conflicts with state, local, and federal authorities, but none resulted in a death toll close to the over twenty Panthers killed by police between 1968 and 1970. Moreover, the amount of money spent to disrupt the Panthers was greater than for all organized crime during the late 1960s. The party was the focal point for FBI COINTELPRO activities for at least a three-year period, beginning in 1968. Of the twelve COINTELPRO operations, the file on "Black Extremist Groups" was the second most expensive; the Communist Party USA was the largest. The file "White Hate Groups" ranked fourth with 5,457 pages. The smallest was "Pro Castro" with 59 pages. See http://foia.fbi.gov/redindex.htm (March 27, 2000). For more elaborate discussion of FBI repression of political dissenters, see Brian Glick, *War at Home* (Boston: South End Press, 1989); Ward Churchill and Jim Vander Wall, *Agents of Repression* (Boston: South End Press, 1988); and Nelson Blackstock, *COINTELPRO: The FBI's Secret War on Political Freedom* (New York: Vintage Books, 1976), passim. See also David J. Garrow, *The FBI and Martin Luther King, Jr.* (New York: Penguin Books, 1981), passim.
24. Seale, *Seize the Time*, pp. 210–211.

CHAPTER 8

THE CONGRESS OF AFRICAN PEOPLE

BARAKA, BROTHER MAO, AND THE YEAR OF '74

ROBESON TAJ FRAZIER

As 3,000 black people met in Atlanta, Georgia, on Labor Day weekend in 1970 to found the Congress of African People, both black self-determination and Pan-Africanism were central themes. While the Atlanta Pan-African summit was aimed at black people in the African diaspora, the gathering also embraced other oppressed peoples in the spirit of the Bandung Conference.

—Komozi Woodard, A Nation Within a Nation

KOMOZI WOODARD'S *A NATION WITHIN A NATION* examines the Modern Convention Movement, a 1970s black social movement composed of nationalists, politicians, integrationists, and Marxists who aimed to create a unified black political party; and the organization that spearheaded this movement, the Congress of African People (CAP). Led by its Newark branch and the branch's leader, Amiri Baraka, CAP, in the 1970s, established community-based cultural and political organizations and expanded the scope of black cultural nationalism and community organizing from the local to national.

Although it was founded as a black cultural nationalist party, CAP within its first five years discarded this ideology for Marxist-Leninism-Mao Zedong theory and practice. CAP's transformation into a black Maoist organization displays the ideological heterogeneity of black nationalist politics. It also relays the complexities of the Black Power and Black Consciousness movements.

The author thanks the following people who have either generously reviewed this article or provided advice and assistance in regard to this study of black Maoism: Robert Allen, Charles Henry, Ula Taylor, Gerald Horne, Ramon Grosfoguel, Waldo Martin, Ernie Allen, Patricia A. Patton, Manning Marable, Komozi Woodard, and Robin D.G. Kelley.

One issue left unanswered in Woodard's work is how and for what reasons did CAP alter its ideological stance in late 1974. I, like scholar Peniel Joseph, ask why "Woodard downplayed Baraka's shift to Marxism?"[1] Woodard's passage which introduces this article highlights that CAP's work and ideological relationships with Third World organizations connected CAP to a historic line of anticolonial radicalism that is best symbolized by the Bandung Conference of 1955. With six African nations present—Ethiopia, Liberia, Egypt, Libya, the Sudan, and the Gold Coast[2]—the conference was dominated by twenty-three Asian delegations. Nevertheless, at Bandung China called for "peaceful coexistence," included all Afro-Asia in its conception of a "third force," and tacitly abandoned its alliance to the Soviet Union (the Sino-Soviet alliance would officially come to an end in 1959). These actions drew China deeper into the Asian and African orbits; created a bridgehead between Asia and Africa that stood outside the ideological conflict of the Cold War; and offered China as a possible development model for developing nations. Like many of the African nations present at the conference, future black Maoists found China's proposals generously appealing.

Robin D.G. Kelley and Betsy Esch provide the most valuable overview of black Maoist history in their 1999 renowned article "Black Like Mao." Bill Mullen also supplies useful analysis in his book, Afro-Orientalism, and in a collection of essays he co-edited with jazz musician Fred Ho, *AFRO ASIA*. As these scholars note, organizations such as the Reform Action Movement, the California Communist League, the Youth Organizations for Black Unity (YOBU), the League of Revolutionary Workers, and the African Liberation Support Committee (ALSC) to name a few, prized Mao's bending Marxism to fit the reality and needs of Chinese society. Mao adapted socialism to Chinese tradition, culture, and way of life. He celebrated the peasant masses, as opposed to the revolutionary intellectual vanguard or the working class, as the creators of revolution. Mao also argued that the creativity and creative potential of this population best informed and cultivated a socialist revolution. This creativity carried the revolution into the superstructure—that is, the national culture. Mao moved away from Lenin and Trotsky's theory of "permanent revolution" and offered his own conceptualization of revolution, "the new democratic revolution."[3] Most important, while Lenin, Trotsky, and Stalin designated the Soviet Union as the leader of the world socialist revolution, Mao pointed to the Third World. Mao's "Theory of the Three Worlds" argued that it was up to the world's colonized populations, the Third World, to "combat imperialism, colonialism and hegemonism."[4] Kelley and Esch point out that this conception of global relations "offered black radicals a 'colored,' or Third World, Marxist model that enabled them to challenge a white and Western vision of class struggle."[5]

Additionally, China's developing and altering relationship with Africa played a role in black radicals' support and critique of China. From 1956–1965 and from 1969 onward, Chinese foreign policy emphasized as a high priority the establishment of stronger ties with Africa. Egypt's 1956 opening of the first Chinese embassy in Africa began a period of increased economic and diplomatic relations between China and the emerging independent African nations. Sino-African relations flourished over the course of the next twenty years resulting in

African support for the admission of communist China to the United Nations in 1971. The seating of the Chinese delegation removed Taiwan from the UN and "contributed substantially to the defeat of the long-standing American procedural strategy for keeping Communist China out of the United Nations."[6] China's key African initiatives focused on supporting and training African revolutionary groups, and financing loans for extravagant African infrastructure projects requiring no conditionality relating to fiscal probity or governance. These policies were devised to sway African states away from the influence of the Soviet Union and the United States.

In this work I investigate 1974 as a decisive year in CAP's ideological transition. I do this with two goals. First, my intention is to examine the complexities of black radical politics during the 1970s.[7] Second, I assess how one black organization came to identify with Maoist thought. Twentieth-century black radicals and theorists have not only produced and enacted revolutionary and reformative responses but more importantly have worked to acutely understand them. What is important is not just their "identity formation"—how the ideology, theory, or organization endorsing the ideology/theory played a part in these radicals' developing identity—but also how radicals came to identify with certain political and cultural platforms and how they negotiated this identification thereafter. CAP's ideological transformation in 1974 provides a unique and multifaceted illustration of this and the changing dynamics of black radicalism.

CAP's Founding and Its Role in the Modern Black Convention Movement

The CAP was established in 1970 to organize and engineer the impending Black Power Conference. It developed into a national organization for several reasons, primarily out of the impetus of the declining Black Power movement. The lack of follow-up after each of the previous four annual Black Power Conferences from 1966–1969 motivated black nationalists and radicals to create alternative institutions for America's black communities. CAP was founded on Labor Day Weekend at an Atlanta summit convening black activists and politicians representing a range of political ideologies.[8] With a young Harvard scholar, Hayward Henry, as its first elected chairman, CAP obtained life and vivacity by drawing from a variety of already established black cultural and nationalist organizations and associations. The group to frame CAP's development, future work, and ideology was the Committee for a Unified New Ark (CFUN), led by the former Beatnik poet, playwright, social critic, and then black cultural nationalist, Amiri Baraka.

Baraka, formerly LeRoi Jones, became deeply radicalized in the early 1960s. His July 1960 travel to Cuba with an assembly of black American activists and writers to witness firsthand the developments of the Cuban Revolution was a turning point in his radicalization and in inducing his cultural nationalist stance. Baraka's cultural nationalism was informed and molded by the writings and activism of Fidel Castro, Mohammed Babu, Patrice Lumumba, Robert F. Williams, and Malcolm X. Another influence on Baraka's expanding transnational view and commitment to the black liberation struggle was the African independence movement. The rise to power of black governments in the Sudan in 1956, Ghana in 1957, Nigeria and the Congo in 1960, Sierra Leone in 1961, Algeria in 1962, Kenya in 1963, Zambia in 1964, and Gambia in 1965, to name a few, increased Baraka's faith in achieving black power and black self-determination.

As a leading figure in the Black Arts Movement, Baraka critiqued the cultural imperialism instituted on the black arts and black artists by the American literary and popular cultural establishments. He argued that art is integral to any revolutionary movement and that revolutionary black art could not be created simply for "art's sake." In contrast, revolutionary art is political, didactic, and polemic and should be employed to inform politics and culture. Although Baraka did not yet utilize Maoist theory for creating a methodology for black liberation, during the 1960s he still found high value in Mao's writings on the role of culture and art in politics. For instance, he often referenced Mao's 1942 "Talks at the Yenan Forum on Art and Literature." In the essay, Mao points to the importance of artists in national struggles and their duty to unify motive and effect—that is, ideology and practice. Bill Mullen explains the essay's importance and impact: "There Mao raised two questions regarding national cultural struggles directly relevant to participants in the U.S. Black Arts movement. The first, 'For whom are our art and literature intended?' was fundamental to efforts of Black Arts entrepreneurs like Amiri Baraka in New Jersey and Woodie King in Detroit to develop independent black theater companies for the staging of black authored plays, as well as for publishers like [Dudley] Randall aspiring to black owned publishing ventures. Mao's second question, 'How to serve,' was fundamentally one of aesthetics."[9] After the assassination of Malcolm X, Baraka worked to galvanize Malcolm X's project of modernizing black nationalism by "bridging the old with the new, developing a secular nationalism in tune with the many of the innovations of the civil rights movement."[10] He aimed to cultivate a political culture that embraced the diverging black social and political groups of the period. Only a black united front that aligned the various political organizations and class divisions separating black activists could effectively promote such an outlook. Important to this formation were the grassroots. Baraka envisioned a movement that cross-aligned them and the black political establishment. This force could challenge the white political establishment by rallying the black masses behind a black political party that supported black candidates.

The political and social environment of the mid- to late 1960s was an intense and fiery period in America's urban communities. From 1960–1976, there were 329 major rebellions in 257 cities, 200 of which occurred in 172 cities after the 1968 of Dr. Martin Luther King Jr. Baraka in 1967 moved back to his birthplace of Newark, New Jersey after failing to build a political base in Harlem with the Black Arts Repertory Theater/School (BARTS). Soon after, he was pulled into the violence of the period during the 1967 Newark summer rebellions when he was severely beaten by the Newark police and falsely accused of carrying unregistered weapons. The Newark rebellions prompted Baraka to reposition his line of attack. As an artist and social critic, he was invested in delegitimizing America's interpretation and valuation of the black arts. After the rebellions, it was clear that this same challenge had to be made in the direction of American politics. After Black

Power conferences in Washington, D.C.; Newark; Philadelphia; and Bermuda from 1966 through 1969, what was needed was a black political party.

Baraka attempted to do this on a micro level. In late 1967, he helped establish the United Brothers, an organization that aimed to unify Newark's emerging and different black political and cultural organizations. The United Brothers aligned Baraka with the emerging Newark grassroots movement and with a collective of black electoral aspirants seeking access to Newark's political machine. United Brothers focused their initial efforts on organizing black voter registration and campaigning for the upcoming November 1968 Newark election. They helped establish an umbrella organization, the Committee for a Unified Newark/ New Ark (CFUN), that coordinated political activities among the different local Essex County black organizations. CFUN was composed predominantly of three organizations—Baraka's performing arts group, the Spirit House Movers and Players; United Brothers; and the East Orange–based Black Community Defense and Development (BCD). As CFUN, they mobilized broad and formerly apoliticized sections of Newark including young people and Newark's Puerto Rican community. CFUN's work and organizing led to the 1970 election of Newark's first black mayor, Kenneth Gibson. They also helped elect several other blacks, including Newark's former mayor, Sharpe James, into city council positions.

Riding high on their wave of political success, CFUN along with several national black organizations approved the creation of a national black institution that would foster and cultivate the "growing tensions between the reality of black diversity and calls for African American unity."[11] The institution, the Modern Black Convention Movement, and its leading organization, the CAP, would serve as a bridge for the black freedom movement. They would facilitate working coalitions between its various wings. Many hoped that the congress could alter America's political discourse by establishing a black political party that appealed to the black masses. CAP's Newark branch, formerly CFUN, felt that their model of cadre development could serve as a progressive model for CAP's own cadre development on a national level.[12] Consequently, the Newark CAP came to dominate CAP's national leadership.

CAP's seven work councils focused on politics, education, economics, community organizing, social organizing, communications, and law. As "the programmatic arm" of the congress, they established at least twenty-five branches of CAP in a variety of locations including Newark, Brooklyn, Oberlin, San Diego, Boston, New York City, Philadelphia, Baltimore, Detroit, Chicago, East Orange, New Jersey, and Camden, New Jersey. Komozi Woodard points out that because of the council's hard work, "[t]he Congress of African People galvanized many of the local leaders and organizations into a new generation of men and women who would become national leaders in the Modern Black Convention Movement."[13] Also important to the work councils was their participation in international projects. CAP raised funds for the building of the Tanzania-Zambia railroad and sent boots and other supplies to rebel soldiers in African countries such as Angola.[14]

At their 1972 San Diego convention, CAP elected Baraka as its national chairman. The organization was also made the key organizer of the 1972 National Black Political Convention in Gary, Indiana. The convention would be their site to launch a black national strategy for the looming 1972 presidential election. On March 10, 1972, more than 2,500 delegates attended the convention to debate and discuss issues relating to schools, social welfare, housing, and health care. Their recognition that many local issues were in actuality national issues pushed them to support the idea of an autonomous national black political community. There, the delegates established the National Black Political Assembly, which they emphatically nicknamed the National Black Assembly (NBA). CAP produced a fifty-five-page document, the National Black Agenda, which conceptualized the alternative institutions that were needed in America's different black communities.

Baraka employed cultural nationalism and a variety of political organizations—United Brothers, CFUN, and, CAP—to chart a new political direction for America's black urban communities. However, after the 1972 National Black Political Convention, CAP internally found itself in the midst of an ideological conflict over which theory, nationalism or socialism, was most applicable for black liberation. Baraka had begun studying the works of Amir Cabral, Kwame Nkrumah, and Mao. CAP would soon follow suit. In 1974 they relinquished black nationalism and within a year's time became the Revolutionary Communist League (RCL), a Marxist-Leninist-Mao Zedong (M-L-M) organization.

To accurately conceptualize CAP's ideological transformation, we must return to 1974, CAP's "Year of Ideological Clarity." The dispute that took place in CAP's rank and file during the months of 1974 elucidated a historic and highly controversial debate between nationalists and the left. John Bracey points to the atmosphere of this period:

> What was needed was an ideology and analysis that would offer a coherent theory of the history of Afro-Americans as it related to U.S. history; the relationship of the contemporary struggle of Afro-American to those Africans and other peoples of the Bandung world; the development of a class stratified Black America; and the relevance of Marxist-Leninist views on the revolutionary process to the situation of Black Americans.[15]

CAP from 1973 to 1976 worked as an organization to answer this call for an applicable theory and ideology.

THE CONGRESS OF AFRICAN PEOPLE'S IDEOLOGICAL STANCE1970–1973

To comprehend CAP's developing rejection of nationalism and turn to socialism, it is important to first briefly examine the ideological milieu in which they were dealing. A prominent issue during the five-year period prior to the 1972 National Black Political Convention was the debate over which nationalism—revolutionary or cultural—provided a better model for revolution. Cultural nationalists declared that blacks and whites had separate values, histories, lifestyles, and intellectual traditions. Therefore, America was essentially made up of two countries—one black and one white—and this required black Americans to unify and create a black national community based on a common language and descent. Many cultural nationalists adopted African social, cultural, and religious practices and argued that blacks could not successfully cultivate a political revolution in America without first revolutionizing their minds culturally. Revolutionary nationalists, on the other hand, prioritized armed struggle and political mobilization as more principal than a cultural revolution.

Yet the two sides ideologically were not that distant. While cultural nationalists like Maulana Karenga's US organization did practice self-defense and value armed struggle, revolutionary nationalists like the Black Panther Party for Self Defense (BPPSD) also valued the importance of creating a revolutionary culture among its members and the black community. With regard to several historians' placement of the Panthers and US's nationalist ideologies at opposing ends, Scot Brown asserts, "US's experience with armed struggle invariably challenges a historical view invested in the bifurcation of the two organization's respective approaches to violent resistance."[16] Clayborne Carson agrees: "I believed there was no was necessary conflict between the so-called 'revolutionary nationalism' of the Black Panthers and the cultural nationalism of US. I knew from my conversations with Karenga that he had wanted to become the cultural arm of SNCC and the Panthers."[17] In fact, it was not the ideologies that conflicted, but the two prominent organizations that endorsed them, US and the Black Panther Party (BPP), who found themselves at odds. In July of 1969, US member Claude Hubert-Gaidi murdered BPP leaders Alprentice "Bunchy" Carter and John Huggins during a UCLA Black Student Union meeting. Although they were already critical of US, this provoked the Panthers to perceive US as an enemy of the black revolution. They critiqued US's endorsement of Afrocentricity as a fad and purposeless endeavor.[18] Blacks, they argued, could not simply return to Africa, physically or mentally. African Americans had their own identity and national culture. The Panthers also labeled US's cultural nationalism as "porkchop nationalism," implying that the organization collaborated with the police and the white power structure.

From 1969 onward, this dispute over cultural nationalism versus revolutionary nationalism would continue. Nationalist organizations such as the Republic of New Afrika (RNA) aligned themselves with the Panthers in 1969 and accused Karenga of orchestrating Carter and Huggins' murders. Ultimately, the Black Power Conferences in Bermuda and Philadelphia were conceived as opportunities to amend this disjuncture. It was this environment and Karenga's relationship to the Committee for a Unified Newark/New Ark (CFUN) that also spurred Baraka's aim to create a united front, a political party that aligned nationalists of different positions.

From 1970–1973, CAP was composed of black nationalists representing a range of backgrounds and positions. Calls for "Black Power" among the black masses were slowly declining after black capitalists and President Nixon co-opted the term to imply black capitalism as opposed to black self-empowerment and self-determination. In Black Power's replacement, at least in regards to nationalist rhetoric, was the resurgence of Pan-Africanism, which called for the liberation of all peoples of African descent across the black diaspora. Pan-Africanism was the global expression of black nationalism. It argued that it was Africa that connected the Third World independence movements and the black struggle for national liberation in the United States. However it was soon realized that "Pan-Africanism retained all of the ambiguities and contradictions which Black Power had come to symbolize."[19] Pan-Africanism's inconsistencies and the diversity of CAP's membership consequently compelled CAP's leadership to formulate a more robust praxis and ideology for black liberation.

CAP's outlook was local, national, and international. They believed that black self-determination, self-sufficiency, self-respect, self-defense and control and maintenance of their local communities had both national and global implications. To "develop power bases" locally, they asserted, could "help radically change the balance of power around the world."[20] This developing ideology was influenced by the international scope of Malcolm X and the Organization for Afro-American Unity (OAAU), and by US's doctrine of Kawaida.[21] CAP adopted Karenga's seven principles, Nguzu Saba, to serve as the foundation for their value system and ideology of cultural nationalism.[22] They also subscribed to Ghanaian President Nkrumah's "general Afrikan revolutionary ideology" of nationalism, Pan-Africanism, and ujamma socialism. Baraka argued that ujamma-socialism's diverged from orthodox socialism because it was a socialism based upon the Kiswahili doctrine of ujamma, or cooperative economics. Socialism he argued was an "attitude" and "way of addressing the world," and it was important that CAP's brand of socialist ideology address the world from an African episteme and viewpoint.

CAP's diverse membership compelled it to take an ideological position that attracted both nationalist and socialist communities since from the onset it intended to "set itself up to be a replica . . . of the nation becoming."[23] Yet in practice its committee on ideology discounted socialism and centered itself around a mix of Pan-Africanism and nationalism because, as Baraka argued, "black people, in 1970, ain't going anywhere."[24] Baraka asserted that Marxist-Leninist scientific socialism was useless to CAP's mission. It represented an abstract concept that failed to come to terms with the reality of black life and did not offer the black community a viable plan of action. Baraka labeled Marxist-Leninism a "white boy" ideology that only provided the black masses with "the Identity, Purpose and Direction of the white boy."[25] The parallels between black folks' situation in the United States and that of the emerging socialist countries were few and far between: "The United States is not China nor 19th century Russia, nor even Cuba or Vietnam. It is the most highly industrialized nation ever to exist, a place where the slaves ride Cadillacs and worship their master's image, as God . . . In the Lenin revolution, the masses, the majority, theoretically overthrew the minority, almost overnight. In America the 'minority' i.e., oppressors, are the majority, and think they benefit by oppression."[26]

Baraka also questioned Marxism's status as a scientific understanding of the world[27] and the left's fanatic embrace of China: "We are not the Chinese. Mao raised an army, a State within a State, then separated from the main and waged war on it until it capitulated. (But they were all Chinese!) But even today, the Chinese are just emerging from the almost constantly continuing Cultural Revolution, which seeks to win the minds of the people, so that the overall development of the Chinese nation can continue without being interrupted by externally and internally inspired coups."[28] Ultimately, it was mainly the white Left that troubled Baraka. He therefore argued, "It was more important to make alliances with black civil rights organizations than with the white New Left organizations."[29] To him, black nationalists, socialists, and integrationists had to unify and move away from the black political traditions of the past. It was vital for them to collectively embrace a revolutionized black culture and politics that like black music, was manifested in black folk culture.

Baraka was not against developing alliances with the black left. Of chief interest to him was the consolidation of CAP with black organizations such as the League of the Revolutionary Workers, the BPP, and the Republic of New Africa.[30] Moreover, CAP was faced with this dilemma: "Increasingly, in discussions with the African liberation movements of Angola, Mozambique, Guinea-Bissau, and Zimbabwe, the African radicals asked: if the CAP is truly revolutionary, why is it not socialist?"[31] Post-1972, CAP committed itself to obtaining a comprehensive understanding of Marxist-Leninist theory and its utility when applied to their struggle.

THE TURN: 1974, THE YEAR OF IDEOLOGICAL CLARITY

Robin D.G. Kelley, Betsy Esch, and Komozi Woodard, have briefly examined the leftist turn of the CAP and Amiri Baraka. Kelley and Esch identify several factors. First, they point to the influence and readings of the Communist Labor Party (CLP), the October League, and the ALSC. They also highlight Baraka's significant role in the 1970 Newark mayoral election of Kenneth Gibson. Gibson's betrayal of Newark's black community by increasing police repression and failing to work towards their political interests made more visible the cooptation of black politicians into the power structure and the reality of neocolonialism. Woodard makes this same contention asserting that the rise in racial violence in Newark and Mayor Gibson's undermining of CAP and the Modern Black Convention Movement's legitimacy played a large role in CAP's shift to the left. Woodard maintains that these events, added alongside black elected officials' allegiance to the Democratic Party and withdrawal of support for independent politics, forced CAP to recognize that "internal colonialism, when faced with the challenge of Black Power had changed to neocolonialism."[32] Both Kelley, Esch, and Woodard also reference the ALSC's May 27, 1972 African Liberation Day (ALD) demonstration in Washington, D.C. as a key event in CAP's ideological transformation.

Notwithstanding the multiple events and factors that influenced CAP's ideological transformation between 1973–1976, I contend that three 1974 events were key: a 1974 ALSC conference on racism and imperialism; the resignations of two of CAP's chief members and organizers and the rift that resulted afterward; and CAP's travel to Tanzania for the Sixth Pan Afrikan Congress.

Woodard and Kelley both point to the ALSC's 1972 African Liberation Day demonstration and its thirty thousand protestors who descended on Washington, DC to call for independence of all of Africa as a key moment in CAP's transformation. I include another ALSC event: the 1974 "Conference on Racism and

Imperialism." The conference's eight hundred attendees assembled at Howard University from May 23–24 to debate their respective theoretical positions and ideological differences. As "one of the most important forces for African liberation in African American history,"[33] the ALSC brought together a wealth of black revolutionary nationalists, cultural nationalists, Marxists and separatists. Conference delegates deliberated over new approaches for black liberation and worked to recommit their energy "to organizing new strata within the black community, particularly workers."[34] By the conference's end though, what was clear was the ideological split between nationalists and Marxists—a "two-line struggle . . . between a dominant position asserting that the chief enemy of black people in the U.S. (and Africa) is monopoly capitalism and imperialism, and an opposing line which argued that racism (or European society) is the primary enemy and that capitalism and imperialism are secondary."[35] This split was also transparent in the depths of the ALSC's own leadership.

The YOBU, formally the Student Organization for Black Unity (SOBU), led the Marxist charge. Represented by Owusu Sadaukai, founder of the Malcolm X Liberation University in Greensboro, North Carolina, YOBU promoted the importance of black struggle in the United States and the primacy of mass work in black communities where black workers could take the lead. YOBU had moved from a strict Pan-Africanist perspective to studying Marxism and they linked black revolution to the anti-imperialist and anticapitalist struggles in the Third World. YOBU viewed the ALSC's conference as a site for the "fight for ideological clarity"[36] and used the event to denounce black revolutionary and cultural nationalisms as short-term and narrow methods.

Baraka was very impressed with YOBU's presentation. He publicly agreed with their position, using black Marxist James Boggs's essay "The Awesome Responsibility of Revolutionary Leadership" to suggest that blacks must resolve their oppression in the United States by dealing with the contradictions of the total society, a capitalist society. Baraka asserted to the delegates,

> Most of the old radicals thinking about Lenin in the United States today are still thinking of what he did in Russia and the concepts he evolved to achieve the Russian Revolution. In that sense they have become dogmatists, not recognizing that Lenin was building a party of his time, to change the intolerable conditions in his country, based on the analysis of the specific conditions in that country. Lenin is not relevant to us unless we have done the same for this country and for our time. Marx was writing at a specific stage in Western history . . . if he were living today, he would have advanced his theory . . . for the simple reason that society itself has advanced to another historical stage.[37]

This speech demonstrated that CAP was moving in line with YOBU's Marxist stance. The developing acceptance of Marxist-Leninism by Baraka and other CAP members signaled a "newer level of unity and struggle" between the left and CAP's black cultural nationalism. It also sparked a developing antagonism between black comrades who once shared an ideological position and now found themselves at opposing ends. Manning Marable explains, "The 'Great Debate'

between black independent Marxist-Leninists and the narrow cultural nationalists from 1973–1976 was a kind of replay of the Black Panthers-US battle of
the late 1960s. . . . Cultural nationalists attacked Baraka, Alkalimat, Sadaukai
and others for 'selling out' to the white man."[38] So deep was this "great debate"
that though "a reemergence of the Panther-US conflict [was] exactly what Baraka
[was] attempting to avoid . . . the enmity, distrust and differences between Marxists and Pan-Afrikanists transcend[ed] his attempts to bridge this gap."[39]

This growing divide can be discerned in the 1974 resignations of CAP leaders
Jitsu Weusi and Haki Madhubuti. Weusi—director of The East, a black cultural
organization in Brooklyn, New York, and executive council representative for
CAP's Brooklyn branch—and Madhubuti—director of Chicago's Institute for
Political Education (IPE), editor and publisher of Third World Press, and the
executive council representative for CAP's Chicago chapter—were leading CAP
organizers since the organization's founding. Their resignations in April of 1974
surprised many people and also displayed CAP's altering ideological perspective.

Received in the first week of April, both Weusi and Madhubuti's resignation
letters ended their individual membership from CAP, as well as their respective
organizations' relationship with CAP. Weisu's difficulties with CAP were made
visible on a trip Baraka made to The East earlier that year. At that meeting, members of The East asked Baraka, "Was it the objective of the Chairman to make
all CAP organizations carbon copies of the CFUN? Must all CAP organizations
submit to views held by the Chairman? Does the Chairman see the present state
of leadership within the CAP developing into a personality cult?"[40] The East
and its members were unhappy with Baraka's leadership and the leftist direction to which CAP was heading. Alongside the resignation of Mjenzi Kazana,
CAP's executive council secretary and former finance director, this critical query
of Baraka and CAP policy made Weusi uncertain of his future role and work in
the organization. Weusi argued that he was unable to have ideological discussions
with the Newark cadre of CAP due to The East's continued relationship with
Paul Nakawa, an ex-member of CFUN who was expelled from the US organization. Madhubuti's resignation stemmed from his being told not to question the
purpose of CAP's Kawaidi doctrine and his anger at the constant "bumping of
heads" of the IPE and CAP. He argued that many of IPE's problems resulted
from its change "from community to cadre" after its indoctrination into CAP. As
a result, Madhubuti resigned from CAP and as Midwest Regional Chairman of
the ALSC.

CAP's ideological transition induced Madhubuti and Weusi's resignations.
Baraka would comment on Weusi and indirectly on Madhubuti: "Jitsu Weusi
must . . . see some Marxist conspiracy behind recent writings of CAP which have
quoted Lenin and Marx and Mao."[41] Baraka also labeled the two men "individu-
alist" and "liberalist." He argued that their critique of Marxism as a "white man's
theory" was contradictory in that both Weusi and Madhubuti advocated and
continuously referenced their "emergency survival list," a list of physical health
and recipe books authored by white men. These comments inspired a six month
public commentary by Madhubuti on the merits of Marxist theory. Madubuti
would write, "The root of our difficulty is our tendency to get high off the theory

and not to look at the theoretician. . . . Marx, Guevara, Castro, Lenin, Trotsky . . . are just another set of white boys who are just as racist as Thomas Jefferson, George Washington, Abraham Lincoln."[42] He continued, "What we have here is white world unity superficially divided into the Communist and capitalist camps. Two sides of the same knife. Both systems were set up for the continuation and advancement of white supremacy."[43] Madhubuti referred to black Marxists as the "buffer zone" between the white left and the black community. They used Marxist-Leninism as a "rehashed Euro-American theory" that allowed white communists to "infiltrate and control and destroy black nationalist movements. And they are much more effective with their black Marxist theoreticians."[44] Madhubuti's public resignation and critique of CAP's transforming ideology further solidified the position Baraka would later take at the ALSC conference.

In June of 1974, Baraka and several CAP delegates traveled to Dar es Salaam, Tanzania to attend the Sixth Pan Afrikan Congress (PAC). The 6th PAC, which some labeled "a forum for the ideological showdown between the Pan-African cultural nationalist and the newly emerging Marxist," was organized by a small group of African Americans and Caribbeans who met in the United States and Bermuda in 1971 and 1972.[45] It was attended by fifty-two delegations representing African and Caribbean governments and liberation movements, two hundred-fifty African Americans, and people of African descent from South America, Britain, and the Pacific. Attendees convened to discuss many issues: independence through armed struggle, imperialism, neocolonialism, underdevelopment, education and culture, colonialism that remained in the Caribbean and Africa, and the role of women in the struggle. Nevertheless, they were unable to make any concrete resolutions and failed to set up an organizational structure around which the Congress could function as an institutional base. Still, although the conference was deemed by one journalist to have been hampered by several of its American organizers and attendees's ego-tripping and lack of unified ideology, several observers commented that Maoists Baraka and Owusu Sadaukai emerged from the congress as leaders of the black American delegation.[46] There, they delivered a paper on "Revolutionary Culture and the Future of Pan Afrikan Culture" and held private meetings with the country's political elite.

Furthermore, Tanzanian President Mwalimu Julius Nyerere's socialist approach made a grand impression on a number of the conference's black American attendees, especially Baraka. He departed Tanzania feeling that "the revolutionary line that we are taking and the line we must soon develop must speak very clearly to the need to build socialism."[47] Nyerere, along with Ghanaian President Kwame Nkrumah, was one of the first Africans to embrace Marxist theory as a general guide to government policy. To Nyerere, it was not Russia who served as his model for socialist development, but China. Vijay Prashad relays Tanzania's connection to Chinese Communism:

> The African reaction to Chinese Communism is best captured in President Nyerere's 1965 speech to welcome Chou En-lai to Dar es Salaam. After praising the Long March, Nyerere noted that both China and Africa are on a joint long march, a 'new revolutionary battle—the fight against poverty and economic backwardness.'

But the war was not only economic, because, said Nyerere, Tanzania had to defend against neocolonialism, and carefully take assistance from others, for 'neither our principles, our country, nor our freedom to determine are for sale.'[48]

Nyerere argued that it was integral for Africans and people of African descent to implement revolutionary programs that were scientific and therefore rational. How to put into practice such programs depended on a thorough analysis of the particularities of one's respective national economy and social structure. It was important that they not reproduce other socialist nations' brands of socialism, but that they create socialist blueprints that were unique to the inequalities and oppressions in their own homelands.

Nyerere's pro-China stance was influenced by Tanzania's developing relationship with China. In 1961 Tanganyika, which would merge with Zanzibar in 1965 to establish the United Republic of Tanzania, was one of eleven African states that politically recognized the Chinese Communist government. In 1965, Tanzania signed with China the Sino-Tanzanian treaty of Friendship. With these relations came many incentives. They established in 1967 a Sino-Tanzanian shipping line that exported Tanzanian cotton into China. Also, beginning in 1970, Chinese instructors began training the Tanzanian army, navy, and air force and also assisted in building a naval base in Dar es Salaam and jet airstrip at Ngerengere. In 1964 China expanded its loan program extending $156.40 million in loans, 47.5 percent of which went to Africa. Forty-two million dollars of this aid and economic assistance went to Tanzania.[49] By the 1970s, the majority of China's aid went to Tanzania, Algeria, Ghana, Congo-Brazzaville, and Mali. In 1967 China agreed to finance the Tanzam railway, a project speculated to cost four hundred million dollars. The 1,060-mile railway would connect Zambia's copper belt to Tanzania's ports. Europeans, Americans, and Soviets' refusal to help fund the railway was "interpreted by Africans as a refusal to help land-locked Zambia break away from is economic dependence on Rhodesia, South Africa, and Portugal."[50] China agreed to assist in its building through an interest-free loan requiring repayment over thirty years after an initial five year grace period. By 1971, Tanzania and Zambia had already received $201 million from China for the railway and in 1975 the Tanzam railway was completed.

Through relations with Tanzania, China established an important presence in Africa. This relationship of "Chinese-Tanzanian economic cooperation was a model for the future new economic order in the Third World."[51] "Tanzania considered that it shared a common political experience and a common environmental-situational background with China. Therefore, China's developmental experience was pertinent to Tanzania's development," George Yu explains.[52] The Tanzanian government consequently believed that China's rapid economic development and growth was the perfect model for Tanzanian development. Yu maintains, "The meaning of China's developmental experience lies in the hope it provided, because in general terms the goals were seen as within the reach of most African societies."[53]

Nyerere's endorsement of Chinese Communism had a major impact on African American radicals and nationalists. Baraka followed Nyerere's example and began to reassess the usage of Marxism and Maoist thought. Nyerere's influence on CAP was nothing new. From an early point in the creation of CAP, Nyerere and the Tanzanian African Nationalist Union (TANU), alongside Amil Cabral's African Party for Independence of Guinea and Cape Verde (PAIGC) and Sekou Toure's Democratic Party of Guinea (PDG) in West Africa, served as Baraka's anticolonial African models for cultural nationalism. For example, CAP's archive files contain a 1973 Nyerere speech which posited that the oppressed groups of the Third World had no other option but to follow the principles and framework of socialism because capitalism offered them only a continued existence of sub-servience and dependency.[54] CAP's respect for Nyerere and his political policy was publicly displayed by their including Nyerere's first name in the name of their community center and cafeteria for cooperative eating, "Hekalu Mwalimu."

After returning from Tanzania, Baraka was inspired by Mao Zedong's con-ception of revolution and the decisive role of the peasantry. On July 8, 1974, in his first CAP speech post PAC, Baraka pleaded members and organizers to begin reading and studying Mao's interpretation of Marxist-Leninism. Baraka assigned them to read six of Mao's essays: "On Contradiction," "On Practice," "Combat Liberalism," "Cadres Policy," "Study," and "Party Discipline."[55] And in his closing, he deftly proclaimed CAP's new mission, shouting: "STUDY FOR IDEOLOGICAL CLARITY! GAIN A CLEAR KNOWLEDGE OF SOCIAL-IST THEORY! MOVE TO THE LEFT!"[56]

Many of CAP's critics and opponents were very critical of Baraka's transition from nationalism to Marxist-Leninism-Mao Zedong theory. Nagueyalti War-ren argued that Baraka's support of Marxist theory proved that he was removed from the ghetto and black indigenous ways of life: "Baraka is, after all, a col-lege educated intellectual, turned bohemian, turned cultural nationalist, turned Marxist. True, he writes to the people and perhaps for the people, yet, he is not one of the people, and the people recognize his alienation."[57] In regard to Baraka's understanding of Maoist philosophy, Warren commented, "Dogmatically spout-ing the concepts of Malcolm, Karenga, or Nkrumah was quite different from trying to popularize the ideas of Mao Tse Tung. Many of Baraka's followers felt betrayed and ceased to listen to him."[58] It is difficult to locate an exact number of members who resigned from CAP after the organization's switch. But several CAP documents, among which Baraka's "Second Answer to Houston CAP" is one, do reveal that many of CAP's followers were upset and discouraged with the organization's ideological transformation. Although Baraka's intentions were to increase CAP's level of criticality and to strengthen CAP's ideological stance, some activists felt that CAP's "ideological transformation, among other political developments, hampered both the Black Convention Movement and Baraka's effectiveness as a national black political leader."[59]

By December of 1974, CAP had publicly renounced nationalist ideology. Baraka affirmed that the organization had reached its "highest ideological level" arguing that the nationalist character of the black liberation movement was noth-ing but blacks' reaction to their super-exploitation in America.[60] Despite evolving from a deep historical and sociocultural context, nationalism, Baraka asserted, remained an uncritical perspective because it obtained its currency only from its success during the 1960s. Baraka argued that nationalism was a reaction to the middle class identity of the civil rights movement and was thus the dialectal reaction to white racism. It and black militancy were the antithesis to white supremacy's thesis. Baraka criticized groups such as the Black Panthers for their misapplication of Maoist thought stating that it was their "incorrect and romantic analysis that made the lumpen proletariat, i.e., the pimps, hustlers, those destroyed by capitalism, the leading force of revolutionary action" instead of the black working class.[61] He argued that "nationalism was not enough" and that what was imperative was for black progressives to "show their solidarity and unity with our Puerto Rican brothers and sisters who are struggling against the same system of oppression."[62] When asked about CAP's transition, Baraka responded that CAP's prior cultural nationalist stance was due to its "acceptance of the reactionary aspects of the black-power line that came out of the 1960s . . . the heavy influence of the black Muslim dogma and worldview on nationalism . . . confusing bourgeois nationalism with patriotism and national liberation struggle . . . misunderstanding culture as it applied to blacks in North America."[63]

CAP in 1975 aligned with the Revolutionary Workers League (RWL), formerly the ALSC. The RWL's membership in the Revolutionary Wing, a Marxist umbrella group that brought them together with the Puerto Rican, Asian American, and Mexican American socialist groups, provided CAP with a wealth of other Marxist alliances. By 1976 CAP had changed its name to the Revolutionary Communist League (RCL) reflecting their strict commitment to Maoist theory and practice. In 1978, the RCL merged with the I Wor Kuen and the Chicano August Twenty-Ninth Movement to create the US League for Revolutionary Struggle.[64] Despite China's shift towards capitalism, the league continued to endorse Mao's Theory of Three Worlds and networked with a broad range of Marxists, Trotskyists, and Maoists in both the United States and France. Also, during the 1984 and 1988 presidential elections, they supported Jesse Jackson's primary campaigns.

Maoist thought declined among blacks after 1976 as a result of China's shifting foreign policy. President Richard Nixon's February 1972 visit to China and the signing of the Sino-American joint communiqué signaled that China was realigning itself and its ideology. Also, its emergent relationship with conservative and pro-Western Zairean leader Mobotu Sese Seko in 1973 served as a symbol of China's measured shift to the right. Nonetheless it was China's actions during the 1975 Angolan civil war that troubled and dejected black Maoists. China supported the FNLA (National Front for the Liberation of Angola) and UNITA (National Union for the Total Independence of Angola) rather than the more widely supported party, the MPLA (Popular Movement for the Liberation of Angola). They endorsed the FNLA and UNITA primarily as a reaction to Soviet support for the MPLA. Nevertheless, China's decision had disastrous consequences for Chinese foreign policy.

Support for the FNLA and UNITA aligned China with the racist and apartheid South African government who also backed the FNLA and UNITA. Maoist circles could not believe that China, a nation whose rhetoric was based on notions of a Third World revolution to defeat the imperialist, colonialist, and racist West, would take sides with one of the world's most racist and oppressive governments. China's actions in Angola made it clear to many black Maoists that China's model of development might not suffice in providing them a useful theory of revolution:

> Differences between liberation movements over the issues of race, assimilation and miscegenation, ethnicity, and the roles of the OAU and South Africa were critical in the Lusophone African colonies. The Chinese seldom if ever mentioned these purely African issues and as no analogous controversies had existed in their own revolution, it is questionable whether they in some fundamental sense appreciated the gravity of these questions. The Chinese press, particularly from 1961 to 1973, consistently portrayed the struggles in Angola and Mozambique to be similar to the Chinese Communist Revolution . . . It missed the point that the revolutions in Lusophone Africa were not a simple repetition of the Chinese revolution; Angola and Mozambique had their own distinct features, many of which were entirely foreign to the Chinese revolution.[65]

Thereafter, Maoism was a hard sell to many black nationalists and socialists. After the death of Mao and his chief foreign policy director, Premier Zhou Enlai, in 1976, Chinese domestic and foreign policy was determined by China's new leadership, first Hua Guo-Feng, and then Chairman, Deng Xiaoping. Deng abandoned Mao's class struggle and Third World–centered discourse and focused on modernizing China's industry, agriculture, national defense, science, and technology. To many black Maoists, China, like the Soviet Union before it, was now moving on a revisionist and capitalist path.

Amiri Baraka and the Revolutionary Communist League (RCL) continued to organize and do work in Newark and New York's black communities in the late 1970s and early 1980s. This was done mainly through their publication, *Unity and Struggle*, and theater troupe, the Afrikan Revolutionary Movers. Robin Kelley and Betsy Esch argue that, "[m]ore than any other Maoist or anti-revisionist, Baraka and the RCL epitomized the most conscious and sustained effort to bring the Great Proletarian Cultural Revolution to the inner cities of the United States and to transform it in a manner that spoke to the black working class."[66] An investigation into RCL's and other black Maoist organizations' work and efforts post 1976 would be a useful resource in understanding how black Maoists and black Maoists organizations translated theory into practice on American soil after China's decline as a counter-hegemonic space and revolutionary imaginary for anticolonial internationalism and anti-imperialism. Baraka today no longer defines himself as a Maoist, but continues to often cite Mao as an example for black intellectuals and radicals. In a 1998 interview with Kalamu ya Salaam, a black nationalist writer and journalist who during the 1970s documented the nationalist-socialist debate, Baraka stated, "Going back to Mao Tse-Tung. You ever read the Yenan Forum written in 1941? Mao was trying to build the communist party and one of the things he was talking about was intellectuals. What is the role of the intellectual? What is the role of artists in making social transformation? Now, if anybody needs to know that it's us. That is what Yenan is about."[67]

NOTES

1. Peniel E. Joseph, "Black Power Revisited: A Review of Komozi Woodard's *A Nation within a Nation; Amiri Baraka (LeRoi Jones) and Black Power Politics,*" *The Gaither Reporter* (Houston) 4, no. 4 (April 30, 1999): 3.
2. One could also include Egypt, but during this period Egypt aligned itself with the Arab states. For more information, look to G. H. Jansen's *Afro-Asia and Non-Alignment* (London: Faber and Faber, 1966), p. 23.
3. Mao's two-stage revolutionary process asserted that it was not vital in a Communist revolution to have a stage of bourgeoisie capitalism prior to the emergence of Socialism. Instead, a Nationalist patriotic united front could defeat imperialism spurring a national Democratic revolution that would ultimately develop into a Socialist revolution.
4. Renmin Ribao, "Chairman Mao's Theory on the Differentiation of the Three Worlds Is a Major Contribution to Marxism-Leninism." *Peking Review* 45 (November 4, 1977), 24.
5. Robin D. G. Kelley and Betsy Esch, "Black Like Mao," *Souls* 1, no. 4 (Fall 1999): 8.
6. Mohamed A. El-Khawas, "China's Changing Policies in Africa." *Issue: A Journal of Opinion* 3, no. 1 (Spring 1973): 26–27.
7. Commenting on historical analysis of black politics during the 1970s, Komozi Woodard for instance has suggested that "The division between black nationalist and civil rights advocates must be applied with greater caution during that period; and for historical analysis today, they simply will not do. In other words the lines between forces in the freedom movement of the 1970s were increasingly more complex." See Komozi Woodard, *A Nation within a Nation: Amiri Baraka (LeRoi Jones) and Black Power Politics* (Chapel Hill: University of North Carolina Press, 1999), 203.
8. At CAP's first convention were a wealth of black political figures from a diversity of black political backgrounds and organizations, such as Louis Farrakhan of the Nation of Islam; Betty Shabazz; Owusu Sadaukai of Malcolm X Liberation University; Imari Obadele of the Republic of New Africa; former SNCC worker and freedom fighter Julian Bond of the Georgia legislature; Mayor Richard Hatcher of Gary, Indiana; Mayor Kenneth Gibson from Newark, New Jersey; Rev. Ralph Abernathy of SCLC; Whitney Young Jr. of the National Urban League; and the Rev. Jesse Jackson of People United for Self Help.
9. Bill Mullen, *Afro-Orientalism* (Minneapolis: University of Minnesota Press, 2004), 95.
10. Woodard, *Nation within a Nation*, 60.
11. Ibid., 111.
12. A CFUN file document states, "Local movement of CFUN and evolving national CAP ideology diverges (as practice) at some points. But cadre development of CFUN, we feel would be good model for cadre development of CAP." Found in *The Black Power Movement: Part 1, Amiri Baraka from Black Arts to Black Radicalism* (microform) Editorial advisor Komozi Woodard, project coordinator Randolph H. Boehm (Bethesda, MD: University Publications of America, 2000), reel 2, fiche 580. *Throughout the rest of the paper, this archive will be identified as "TBPM: AB".*
13. Woodard, *Nation within a Nation*, 168.
14. Look to Robin Kelley and Betsy Esch's "Black Like Mao," 6–41; and *Forward: Journal of Marxism-Leninism-Mao Zedong Thought* 3 (January 1980): 29–38.
15. John Bracey Jr., "Marxism and Black Nationalism in the 1960s: The Origins of Revolutionary Black Nationalism," presented at the 72nd Annual Meeting of the Organization of American Historians, New Orleans, Louisiana, 1968, 21.
16. Scot Brown, *Fighting for US* (New York: New York University Press, 2003), 89.
17. See Clayborne Carson's foreword to Brown's *Fighting for US*, vii.
18. For more info on the Black Panther-US conflict, look to Scot Brown's *Fighting for US*.

19. Manning Marable, *Race, Reform and Rebellion* (Jackson: University Press of Mississippi, 1991), 134.

20. Amiri Baraka, "Congress of African People Political Liberation Organizing Manual: Ideological Statement of the Congress of African People," First Annual Meeting of the Congress of African People, September 6, 1970, 3.

21. *Kawaida* means "tradition and reason" in Swahili.

22. The seven principles of Nguzu Saba are black unity, self-determination, collective work and responsibility, cooperative economics, the purpose of nation building, creativity, and faith. They also represent the seven days and principles of Kwanzaa, the weeklong holiday and celebration also established by Ron Maulana Karenga.

23. Amiri Baraka, "The Pan-Afrikan Party and the Black Nation," 6. *TBPM: AB*

24. Ibid., 8.

25. Ibid., 9.

26. Ibid.

27. Baraka asks, "Why should our models for Ujamaa be put forward by Europeans? Why does the term science have to connote Marx and Lenin? How scientific is it, if it yet does not exist, aside from in radical pamphlets and the fantasies of Afro-Americans." in "Black Nationalism: 1972 (Address by Chairman of Congress of African People)," *TBPM: AB*

28. Baraka, "Pan-Afrikan Party," 9.

29. Woodard, *Nation within a Nation*, 111.

30. The League of Revolutionary Black Workers, a Detroit-based coalition of black workers who came from the Ford Revolutionary Union Movement (FRUM) and the Dodge Revolutionary Union Movement (DRUM), was established in 1968. The organization worked "to transcend the Marxist/nationalist, the race/class dichotomy that would plague the succeeding radical organizations in the seventies" and focused primarily on worker's rights by taking an antimanagement and antiunion position. The Republic of New Africa (RNA), a black separatist organization whose agenda was both nationalist and Marxist, called for reparations from the federal government in the form of land acquisition. This territory—South Carolina, Georgia, Alabama, Mississippi, and Louisiana—they asserted would serve as the land for a separate black nation with the RNA as its government in exile. Herb Boyd, "Radicalism and Resistance: The Evolution of Black Radical Thought," *The Black Scholar* 28, no. 1 (Spring 1998): 43.

31. Woodard, *Nation within a Nation*, 171.

32. Ibid., 254.

33. Ibid., 175.

34. Phil Hutchings, "Report on the ALSC National Conference," *The Black Scholar*, July–August 1974, 48.

35. Hutchings, "Report," 48.

36. Ibid., 49.

37. Baraka, "ALSC Conference Speech, May 24, 1974," 30 (*TBPM: AB*, reel 2, fiche 843).

38. Marable, *Race*, 135. Abd-al Hakimu Ibn Alkalimat (Gerald McWhorter), a professor at Fisk University, was one of the founders of the Institute of the Black World who before the 1970s followed a strict black nationalist line. Yet by the early 1970s, Alkalimat switched to Leninism and established a Marxist institute, the People's College, in Nashville, Tennessee.

39. Kalamu Ya Salaam. "African Liberation Day: An Assessment—Tell No Lies, Claim No Easy Victories," *Black World*, October 1974, 18–34.

40. Baraka, "Comments of Chairman on Resignations of Haki Madhubuti and Jitu Weusi (IPE & The East)," *TBPM: AB*, reel 2, fiche 789.

41. Ibid. reel 2, fiche 799.

42. Madhubuti, "Enemy: From the White Left, White Right and In Between," *Black World*, October 1974, 38.

43. Ibid.

44. Ibid., 43.

45. Nagueyalti Warren, "Pan-African Cultural Movements: From Baraka to Karenga." *Journal of Negro History* 75, no. 1–2 (Winter–Spring 1990): 24.

46. Journalist Edith Austin stated, "The Black Americans brought at least ten ideologies with them from the states ranging from socialism, communism, separatism, class vs. color struggles, Garveyism, and you-name-it-ism, but no single position representing a united front on the part of the delegation." Edith Austin, "Reflections of the 6th Pan African Congress," *Sun Reporter*, August 3, 1974, 14.

47. Baraka, "Chairman's Report, Central Council Meeting—July 8, 1974," 2. *TBPM: AB*, reel 2, fiche 702–704.

48. Vijay Prashad, *Everybody Was Kung Fu Fighting* (Boston: Beacon Press, 2001), 143.

49. George T. Yu, "Sino-African Relations: A Survey," *Asian Survey* 5, no. 7 (July 1965): 321–332.

50. Mohamed A. El-Khawas, "China's Changing Policies," 27.

51. George T. Yu, "China's Role in Africa," *Annals of the American Academy of Political and Social Science* 432, Africa in Transition (July 1977): 108.

52. Yu, "China's Role in Africa," 101.

53. Ibid.

54. Mwalimu Julius Nyerere, "The Rational Choice," address delivered at Sudanese Socialist Union Headquarters, Khartoum, January 2, 1973.

55. Baraka, "Chairman's Report," *TBPM: AB*, reel 2, fiche 702–704.

56. Ibid.

57. Warren, "Pan-African," 18.

58. Ibid., 19.

59. Joseph, "Black Power Revisited," 3.

60. Robert Allen explains of the tendencies found in Black Nationalism: "To understand outbursts of nationalism fully, it is necessary to delve into the social fabric of Afro-American life. The foregoing historical sketch strongly suggests that nationalism is an ever present but usually latent tendency, particularly among blacks who find themselves on the lower rungs of the socioeconomic ladder. The members of this class traditionally exhibit a sense of group solidarity because of the open hostility of the surrounding white society." Robert L. Allen, *Black Awakening in Capitalist America: An Analytic History*, (Trenton, NJ: Africa World Press, 1990 [first published 1969]), 115.

61. Baraka, "The Position of the Afrikan People: December, 1974." 8; Baraka, "CAP: Going Through Changes," found in *The Black Power Movement: Part 1, Amiri Baraka from Black Arts to Black Radicalism* (microform) (Editorial advisor Komozi Woodard, project coordinator Randolph H. Boehm, Bethesda, MD: University Publications of America, 2000).

62. Baraka, "Newark, NJ, a Classic Neocolonial Creation," *Monthly Review* 25, no. 8 (January 1975): 23.

63. Sullivan, "Baraka Drops Racism, Shifts to Marx," *New York Times*, December 27, 1974, 35.

64. Prashad, *Everybody*, 136.

65. Steven Jackson, "China's Third World Foreign Policy: The Case of Angola and Mozambique, 1961–93," *The China Quarterly* 142 (June 1995): p. 393.

66. Kelley and Esch, "Black Like Mao," 35.

67. Kalamu Ya Salaam, "Djali Dialogue with Amiri Baraka," *The Black Collegian*, available at http://www.black-black.uk collegian.com/african/baraka-a1299.shtml, February 17, 1998.

PART III

DISRUPTING INTERNAL BOUNDARIES

CHAPTER 9

WAITING TILL THE MIDNIGHT HOUR

RECONCEPTUALIZING THE HEROIC PERIOD OF THE CIVIL RIGHTS MOVEMENT, 1954–65

PENIEL E. JOSEPH

AFTER YEARS OF NEGLECT BY MAINSTREAM AMERICAN academics, the impact of black radicalism[1] on postwar American and world history has begun to be examined in recent social science scholarship.[2] Such historical inquiry requires journeying to the "lower frequencies"[3] and addressing the substantive intellectual, political, and practical questions posed by African American radicals. These intellectual pursuits reflect the resurgence of an increasingly radical black public sphere.[4] Moreover, this new emphasis on the study of black radicalism's shift from a marginal to a central position within a global political arena provides the potential contextual and historical basis for a counterdiscourse to celebratory pronouncements regarding contemporary historical developments. Amid the rather bleak political landscape proffered by contemporary global political developments,[5] the dawn of the twenty-first century has provided a much-needed space to reflect on some of the world-historic events that encapsulated the three decades following World War II. As the progenitor for social and political transformation in the postwar era, the civil rights movement provides a historical context for the confusing contemporary political dialectic that oscillates between the erasure and recovery of a modern black radical tradition.

CONSTRUCTING AN ALTERNATIVE CIVIL RIGHTS NARRATIVE

Although synonymous with the 1954 *Brown* Supreme Court decision, the modern movement for civil rights preceded this court case by over a decade.[6] However, the years between the landmark *Brown* case and the passage of the Voting Rights

Act of 1965 constitute the *heroic period* of the modern struggle for civil rights. During these years, black liberation struggles received national attention through the efforts of a broad-based network of activists, including rank-and-file African Americans, grassroots organizers, and national political mobilizers. Black America's revolt against the legacy of antiblack[7] racism was transmitted to the nation through an increasingly global media apparatus that delivered fantastic images of violent racial confrontation that played out as public theater. In addition to domestic civil rights efforts, international developments in Cuba, Asia, and Africa provided black American radicals with a glimpse of alternative political and world historic realities. As an oppositional social movement challenging the most nightmarish aspects of race and class oppression, the modern struggle for civil rights reached its zenith with the legalistic and legislative victories that marked an end to state-sanctioned apartheid and black electoral disfranchisement. Both popular and historical narratives have conceptualized this era literally and figuratively as the "King years."[8] Undoubtedly, Martin Luther King Jr. is the individual most identified with the movement; the pervasive image of King in contemporary American popular culture is that of an African American minister preaching from the steps of the nation's capital, exhorting the disfranchised in attendance to dream of a truly democratic civil society. Yet this historical and political narrative of the "movement" obscures and effaces as much as it reveals and illuminates. King's subsequent leftward political metamorphosis emerged from the hotbed of radicalism within black politics that existed before the era of Black Power. The absence of civil rights radicals from most chronicles of the movement's heroic years avoids discussion of once-powerful discourses that represent a veritable Pandora's box for the US nation-state. Relocating the black political radicalism that has been chronologically situated during the late 1960s in an earlier political landscape dominated by the Southern movement's struggles against Jim Crow reperiodizes civil rights and Black Power historiography by underscoring the fluidity of two historical time periods too often characterized as mutually exclusive. Moreover, the study of black radical discourses, which traversed a global political expanse problematizing issues of democracy, color, and empire, resituates domestic civil rights struggles within an international arena that witnessed extraordinary events that spanned the world. In the long shadow cast by Cold War political repression, black Americans forged an alternative political philosophy from the ashes of an almost eviscerated black radical public sphere.[9] Comprising college students, ex-communists, military veterans, and an assortment of "organic intellectuals," this collective underground provided the practical and theoretical context for Black Power radicalism. Thus the tendency to ignore black radicalism's impact on the movement's heroic years coupled with the deification of King as a modern-day Moses leading blacks out of an Egyptland of racist denials has rendered invisible whole narratives of civil rights history and attendantly constructed a parochial view of the era that largely ignores the movement's role within international political struggles.

Although the heroic period of the movement has been strategically appropriated by the state to deliver sanitized images that extol the resilience of democratic liberalism, the post–civil rights period of Black Power has fallen victim to what

Nikhil Singh has described as the Panther effect.[10] In his fascinating discussion of the uses and abuses of the Black Panthers by both the conservative Right and the soulless American Left, Singh argues that although the party was popularly utilized as a metaphor for the exigencies of 1960s political radicalism, its incisive and transformative political praxis provides the context for the Panthers's continued haunting of the American intellectual and political imagination today.

The manifold and decontextualized appropriations of the Black Panthers (as well as a variety of 1960s-based radical icons) are part of a larger political and intellectual tendency that marginalizes, silences, and obscures the concrete histories of what the historian Cedric Robinson has referred to as the "black radical tradition."[11] In her remarkable study of the historical roots of radical black intellectualism, Joy James illustrates how the conspicuous absence of black radicals (especially black women) from mainstream civil rights narratives is emblematic of larger conceptual and ideological biases within American historiographies.[12] The erasure and silencing of black radicalism within historical narratives of the civil rights movement has produced a false dichotomy between the heroic period of black liberation struggles and the subsequent Black Power decade. Moreover, the perpetuation of this dichotomy has reduced the rich and multilayered ideological tendencies within African American political discourse to a series of clichés and false binaries that completely ignore the international dimension of black political thought. The catchphrases are all too familiar to even the unfamiliar student of recent American history: "Violence versus Nonviolence," "Martin versus Malcolm," and "Separation versus Integration." From this shortsighted and ideologically informed reading of history, Black Power (and thus black radicalism and issues of force and self-defensive violence) emerged only during the second half of the decade personified by gun-toting militants reciting partially read Marxist slogans.[13]

Locating the roots of late-1960s black radicalism within the internationalism of the black Left of the late 1950s constitutes what I describe as an "alternative narrative"[14] or history that challenges the "silencing"[15] that permeates all sites of historical production. Therefore, the rest of this essay represents a truncated examination of missing parts: an alternative history that challenges the erasure of historical voices, actors, and debates that have been silenced or circumscribed in previous narratives of civil rights and Black Power history. In a limited space, this essay seeks to contribute to the reperiodization of African American liberation struggles in the post–World War II era by illustrating the confluence of radical political activity preceding and contextualizing the Black Power movement. In doing so, scholars and activists take heed of Frantz Fanon's judicious warning of the difficulty inherent in attempting to "state" social and political reality[16] by traversing through muddy historical waters while rejecting a Manichaean historical overview.

ROBERT WILLIAMS AND AFRICAN AMERICAN POLITICAL THOUGHT

In 1959, during the height of what historian Manning Marable has described as a reform period,[17] Robert Williams, head of the Monroe, North Carolina, NAACP (National Association for the Advancement of Colored People), advocated the use of self-defense against white terror in the South. A former autoworker, an army and marine veteran, and an itinerant writer, Williams developed a body of political thought and practice that represented a cogent repudiation of black leadership bound by the strictures of Cold War liberalism.[18] A founding member of the Left-inspired Fair Play for Cuba Committee (FPCC), Williams articulated an internationalist political philosophy that sought to recast black America's struggles in global terms. The case of Robert Williams represents more than just an example of the growing restiveness that many poor and working-class blacks felt toward the mainstream civil rights leadership's middle-class political orientation. Williams's attempt to forge a radical internationalist movement at the peak of the modern black movement reveals both the undercurrents of radical political and intellectual activity within the black public sphere and the expansiveness of the black radical discourses that prefigured and influenced the era of Black Power (1965–75). Williams was an icon of the international Left before Stokely Carmichael, Huey Newton, and Angela Davis and his political philosophy of radical internationalism (an eclectic fusion of black nationalist and Marxist tendencies) would become the benchmark of the new wave of black militancy and radicalism that increasingly conceptualized black liberation struggles in global terms. Drawing inspiration from revolutionary struggles, Williams imagined worlds of color that extended beyond the fictive geographic borders dictated via US foreign policy. Through the periodical he published, *The Crusader*, Williams's political thought both forced and inspired a younger generation of black radicals to expansively reconceptualize black politics in American civil society, explicitly linking national struggles for black citizenship with questions of race, class, and democracy that were taking place in Cuba, Asia, and Africa. With a vision of black liberation that linked events in Bandung, Indonesia, to Birmingham, Alabama, Williams's internationalism provides only a partial example of a small but vibrant black radical public sphere that complicates narratives of civil rights radicalism that begin during the second half of the 1960s.[19] This tendency reflects what historian Charles Payne refers to as the "rough draft of history."[20] In the case of much of civil rights history, this "rough draft" silences and thus renders invisible the profound impact of black radicalism on both black American politics at the height of the Cold War and the subsequent Black Power movement. At least half a decade before the Third World anti-imperialist internationalism that would characterize the utterances of race men such as Malcolm X and Martin Luther King Jr., African American radicals, building on the anti-imperialist legacy of individuals such as W. E. B. Du Bois, Paul Robeson, and C. L. R. James and anticolonial organizations such as the Council of African Affairs,[21] articulated a broad-based vision of American society that went beyond the narrow parameters of mainstream civil rights philosophy. Entering the national discourse on racism, colonialism, and white supremacy through a back door reserved for the disfranchised, black radicals constructed spheres of oppositional activity that overcame inadequate resources, political demonization, and intraracial ideological struggles. Moreover, radical intellectual and political thought during this era critically interrogated and reconstructed the meaning of both "race" and "blackness" in American society through a critical reconceptualization that connected African

American immiseration to the marginalization of people of color globally. In short, at the peak of the civil rights movement's influence in national and international politics and coinciding with the hegemony of black politics bound to the Cold War's ideological sanctions, black radicals reconfigured African American political discourses by linking antiblack racism to structures of domination rooted in histories of colonialism and slavery that undergirded racial state formation during the modernist project. That Williams, as well as other black radicals, would look "outward" for both answers and attention to black America's domestic difficulties was hardly surprising. Despite the exigencies of the Cold War, decolonization efforts in Cuba and Africa as well as the movement for nonaligned nations highlighted the possibility of political transformation unencumbered by the West's emerging vision of geopolitical domination.

CUBA LIBRE!

Although the Cold War precipitated a "winter of discontent" for Robeson and Du Bois in particular and radical politics in general, decolonization efforts in Cuba and Africa as well as the movement for nonaligned nations provided a leitmotif for black radicals operating under the exigencies of the American empire. Against an international and national political backdrop that included revolutionary movements across the Third World and pockets of black political radicalism and militancy in the United States, both an older and newer generation of black activists looked toward the international horizon for a way forward at home. One of the most important sites on this front was Cuba. Located 90 miles off of the coast of Florida, the island illuminated the contours between race and empire both at home and abroad. The Afro-Cuban connection was solidified with a tour sponsored by the Left-inspired FPCC[22] that took a cadre of black writers and activists to Cuba in July 1960. The all-star contingent of characters included the writers Julian Mayfield and Harold Cruse, the avant-garde black poet and future Marxist radical Leroi Jones, and the ubiquitous Williams. This historic trip served to deepen the existing ties between the black left and Cuban revolutionaries. The island's large population of black Cubans and their support of the revolution provided further evidence of the global nature of the civil rights struggle. The idea that both African Americans and Cubans occupied central roles in an increasingly diverse constellation of international movements against imperialism was underscored through mutual cooperation between radicals and the Cuban government. In addition to a special issue titled "Los Negros en U.S.A." featured in the Cuban literary magazine *Limes de Revolution* and FPCC-sponsored rallies in Harlem and elsewhere, the Cuban leader Fidel Castro's legendary weeklong stay at Harlem's Hotel Theresa (and his meeting with Malcolm X) highlighted black-Cuban solidarity amid Cold War anxiety.[23] Williams, by now a global figure owing to the notorious events in Monroe, North Carolina, described his trip to Cuba in the pages of his internationally read *Crusader*. "Yes, I have seen the glorious face of Cuba. Equally as impressive, I have also heard the voice of Cuba. It was the wise and firm voice of great Fidel Castro. I consider it the greatest honor of my life to have heard the greatest humanitarian leader of the age deliver the new sermon on the mount."[24]

Williams was not the only important figure to be inspired by the Cuban Revolution. The poet LeRoi Jones (Amiri Baraka), who would, of course, emerge as one of the leading figures of both the Black Arts and the radical black convention movements, was part of the same group that traveled to Cuba under the auspices of the FPCC. At 25 years old, Jones represented the younger generation of black intellectuals who came of age after the height of Depression-era black internationalism.[25] At the time, Jones was best known as part of an eclectic group of Greenwich Village–based, mostly white writers and poets (including Allen Ginsberg) who eschewed formal political engagement. In the aftermath of his Cuban journey, however, Jones published an important essay titled "Cuba Libre" in the *Evergreen Review* that attempted to exorcise the twin demons of avant-garde cynicism and the American and international political reality that was shaped and contextualized in accordance with the state's morbid vision of national security.[26]

The writer and novelist Julian Mayfield—part of the cadre of New York–based black writers and activists with a rich history of affiliation with radical politics—was equally impressed with events in Cuba. His essay "The Cuban Challenge" was published in the summer 1961 edition of *Freedomways*. Created in 1961 (and an offshoot of Paul Robeson's short-lived *Freedom* magazine) under the editorial leadership of Shirley Graham Du Bois, *Freedomways* quickly positioned itself as a leading radical quarterly of Negro affairs. Mayfield's essay argued that black Harlem's enthusiastic reception of Castro the previous fall was predicated on the mistreatment that the Cuban leader had received upon his visit to the UN Assembly that year.[27] Writing that white Americans "actively or tacitly" propagated antiblack racism, Mayfield contrasted the overt racialism of the United States with the Cuban government's attempts to eliminate racial discrimination.[28] Not only was Mayfield's support for Cuba in sharp contrast to the distilled views of representative race men and women of the era, his advocacy of radical Afro-Cuban political solidarity placed him squarely in a black radical sphere that included Williams, Conrad Lynn, and Dan Watts. Mayfield's internationalism would develop further through meetings with Du Bois and Malcolm X and as a presidential advisor to Kwame Nkrumah during the five years Mayfield resided in Ghana. Upon his return to the United States in 1967, Mayfield would emerge as a leading essayist and critic among the black internationalist Left.

WHERE BLACKNESS IS BRIGHT? AFRICA AND THE POLITICAL IMAGINATION OF THE BLACK LEFT

Although Cuba provided an important site for the black radical political and intellectual imagination, Africa remained the literal and fictive embodiment undergirding the idea of a "global black revolution." The belief that decolonization movements in Africa were intrinsically connected with African American antiracist struggles at home both culturally and politically was manifested in the radical magazine *Liberator*. Founded in 1960 by the architect and writer Watts, *Liberator* provided a forum for "black Atlantic"[29] politics that focused on the international implications of civil rights struggles while not losing sight of local issues. Precipitated by decolonization movements in Africa, the magazine was an outgrowth of the Liberation Committee for Africa that, besides Watts, included the FPCC executive secretary Richard Gibson and the writer John Henrik Clarke. By 1962, the magazine's focus shifted toward domestic issues while it critically interrogated the global implications of American antiracist struggles. During the first half of the 1960s, Watts's *Liberator* offered consistent and radical critiques against the movement, its middle-class orientation, and its principal spokesperson, Martin Luther King Jr. Attacked for his harsh editorials against King,[30] Watts nonetheless established an all-star cast of advisors and contributors to the magazine, including the radical lawyers Len Holt and Conrad Lynn, the Marxist Bill Epton, the legendary *Baltimore Afro-American* journalist William Worthy, Max Stanford, Larry Neal, and Harold Cruse. The impact that the *Liberator* had on black politics cannot be overstated. The magazine offered a discursive site for radicals of various ideological stripes to confront an array of issues. The radicals and militants who served the magazine as writers and editorialists were a group of intellectuals, activists, and community organizers attempting to articulate an alternative political philosophy for black liberation.

AT THE CROSSROADS: THE UNDERGROUND'S MARCH AGAINST WASHINGTON

Nowhere was this alternative political philosophy more evident than in the short-lived Freedom Now Party (FNP). The idea of an all-black political party (one that would play a central role in Black Power convention movement politics) originated among an ideologically disparate group of figures that included William Worthy, Paul Boutelle, the future Black Power theologian Rev. Albert Cleage, Bill Epton, Dan Watts, Harold Cruse, Pernella Wattley, and Patricia Robinson. The fact that party organizers were passing out leaflets for an independent black political party during the 1963 March on Washington underscores the complexities of a time period too often viewed as monolithically quiescent in terms of black radicalism. Boldly asserting that "one hundred years of waiting for Democrats and Republicans to correct our grievances is too long," organizers challenged the participants of the march to join with the fraternity of the oppressed all over the world by casting one million votes for the FNP in 1964.[31] By the 1963 March on Washington, the future of black liberation struggles was, in many ways, at a crossroads. That the march itself took place on August 28, the day after the death of Du Bois in Ghana, infused the event with tragic irony. The march's unequivocal support for American liberalism was a de facto silencing of both Du Bois's anticolonial internationalism and his radical critique of the pervasive inequalities within democratic structures in American society.

Regarded as the most visceral representation of the heroic period's quest for black enfranchisement, the march revealed ideological, class, and gender divisions that belied public pronouncements of unity.[32] Moreover, in many ways, the event represented the (temporary) end of the hegemony of a sphere of reformist Negro activists and political leaders. Although Martin Luther King Jr. would remain forever entrenched as the representative racial spokesperson in the march's aftermath, King presided over a rapidly transforming African American political landscape that he could neither control nor fully comprehend. The dissatisfaction with ineffectual federal enforcement of civil rights that had galvanized cities such as Birmingham, Alabama, during the long and violent summer of 1963 would provide part of the shift in black politics, and the march itself provided a lightning rod for critics. Most radicals agreed with Malcolm X's quip that the demonstration was in fact a "farce" on Washington. The initial suggestions by civil rights militants to shut down the nation's capital with a human blockade were dismissed in favor of what Malcolm X felt was an antiradical feel-good spectacle, one dominated and controlled by the very presidential administration the march was organized in protest against. Malcolm, of course, was far from alone in both his admonishment of the leaders who participated in the march and his attendant analysis of the theoretical flaws of liberal integrationism. The guiding principle undergirding this philosophy was that the elimination of federally regulated racism would allow for blacks to be included in previously all-white institutions in American society. As Mack Jones has observed, "There was . . . an unarticulated but widely shared assumption that . . . the end of state-sanctioned segregation and discrimination would set in motion a train of events that would lead to economic parity between white and black Americans."[33] Infused with a middle-class sensibility that dated back to at least the post-Reconstruction era, black leadership held a vision of African American liberation that was intrinsically shortsighted. In attempting to construct an empowering antiracist black identity, black elites had elevated a colored model of bourgeois humanism, one that fetishized masculinist discourse and aesthetics, patriarchal familial norms, and the notion of a "better class" of Negroes.[34]

REVOLUTIONARY ACTION MOVEMENT (RAM)

The organization that provides perhaps the clearest links between civil rights and Black Power radical internationalism was the Revolutionary Action Movement (RAM). Initially conceived by a group of black student radicals engaged in problematizing Williams's work, RAM soon developed into one of the leading radical internationalist groups of the era. In many ways, RAM members might be described as the theoretical shock troops of the radical black underground. Black students who belonged to a wide range of political organizations—including Students for a Democratic Society, the Congress of Racial Equality, and the Student Nonviolent Coordinating Committee—and members of RAM were influenced by both the radical theories disseminated in magazines such as *The Crusader* and *Liberator* and the political action of individuals such as Williams. A product of the San Francisco Bay Area black nationalism (by way of the East Coast) that arrived in Oakland, California, by 1963, RAM provides an organizational and historical context for the understanding of Black Power internationalism usually identified with the Black Panthers. Led by the lawyer Donald Warden of the Berkeley Afro-American Student Organization, Ernie Allen, and Max Stanford, RAM developed one of the most complex and radical internationalist political philosophies of the era. In its theoretical journal *Soulbook*, RAM covered topics including jazz, poetry, racism, and anticolonialism. Establishing chapters in

California, New York, Chicago, and Philadelphia, RAM attempted no less than the creation of a highly disciplined and committed band of revolutionaries in the organizational tradition of the Nation of Islam. Influenced by the writing of Mao Zedong, RAM was as committed to the creation of revolutionary culture as it was to actual social and political transformation.[35] RAM's efforts to internationalize black liberation struggles provided a practical manifestation of radical political praxis. Although RAM would fade out of the spotlight by the decade's end amid illegal federal harassment and criminalization, the group anticipated the revolutionary zeitgeist that characterized the Black Power era.

CONCLUSION

Described by *Liberator* magazine as the "year of violence," 1963 provides an interesting point of departure for recontextualizing facile and schematic time frames that attempt to "find" Black Power during the second half of the 1960s. Recognition of the fluid and contingent nature of history necessitates a more searing examination of the complex and confusing relationship between the civil rights and Black Power movements. Despite conspicuously lacking the resources for a political base and public recognition similar to that of contemporary civil rights organizations, black radicals during the movement's heroic years provided the concrete political and theoretical framework for the panoply of radical and militant groups and individuals that would predominate in the second half of the 1960s.[36] Building on the discourses and political activities of black underground radicals in places such as Oakland, California; Harlem, New York; and Monroe, North Carolina, black activists situated the struggle for black citizenship in global terms. More than simply aligning themselves with Third World liberation movements, radicals imagined themselves as part of a global assault against white supremacy. The results were both far-reaching and unequivocal. Creatively merging tenets of black nationalism and Marxism, the black public sphere during the late 1960s and early 1970s was dominated by radical internationalists who challenged state power on several fronts. This included efforts to end police brutality spearheaded by the Black Panther Party and the prisoners' rights movement personified by Angela Davis and George Jackson; groundbreaking second-wave black feminist discourses such as Toni Cade's *The Black Woman* and political organizations including the National Black Feminist Organization and the Third World Women's Alliance; the poor people movement led by black women of the National Welfare Rights Organization; community control movements supported by nationalist groups such as the Congress of African Peoples; and the black convention movement that attempted to redefine black politics through the National Black Political Assembly.

Thus even a partial examination of the connections between civil rights and Black Power radicalism defies rigid analyses that ignore radical anti-imperialist discourses that profoundly altered and reshaped both the era's politics and its paradigms. Finally, the efforts by black radicals to situate national antiracist struggles within a larger world of anti-imperialist and anticolonial political thought and practice reveals the resonance and power of a conception of late-1960s black internationalism that has its antecedents in a range of writers, thinkers, and ideological and political traditions.[37] Forged through the crucible of racial domination in American society, black radicals raised vital issues that provide historical context for understanding systems of domination in both post–civil rights America and the newly emerging "postcolonial" global international order.[38]

NOTES

1. By black radicalism, I mean historic efforts to undermine and eliminate racial, gender, and class domination within a capitalist political economy undergirded by an ideology of white supremacy. That being said, a diverse array of thinkers, political activists, and organizations (from socialists to Marxists to black nationalists) have articulated anticapitalist and antiracist political agendas by combining various political philosophies and orientations. Radicals have maintained, however, that the state and its political, economic, and cultural apparatuses must be fundamentally transformed to achieve a truly democratized nation-state. Furthermore, radicals have disputed the effectiveness of liberalism as an undergirding philosophy of American democracy.

2. An admittedly truncated list of recent scholarship that discusses the impact of black radicalism on the larger contours of American and international politics includes Martin Duberman, *Paul Robeson* (New York: Alfred A. Knopf, 1989); Paul Buhle and Paget Henry, eds., *C. L. R. James's Caribbean* (Durham, NC: Duke University Press, 1992); Joy James, *Transcending the Talented Tenth* (New York: Routledge, 1997); Robin D. G. Kelley, *Hammer and Hoe* (Chapel Hill: University of North Carolina Press, 1990) and *Race Rebels* (New York: Free Press, 1994); Penny Von Eschen, *Race against Empire* (Ithaca, NY: Cornell University Press, 1997); Lewis R. Gordon, *Fanon and Crisis of European Man* (New York: Routledge, 1995); Grant Farred, ed., *Rethinking C. L. R. James* (London: Blackwell, 1995); Winston James, *Holding Aloft the Banner of Ethiopia* (London: Verso, 1998); Charles Jones, ed., *The Black Panther Party Reconsidered* (Baltimore: Black Classic Press, 1998); Timothy B. Tyson, *Radio Free Dixie: Robert F. Williams and the Roots of Black Power* (Chapel Hill: University of North Carolina Press, 1999); Komozi Woodard, *A Nation Within a Nation: Amiri Baraka (LeRoi Jones) and Black Power Politics* (Chapel Hill: University of North Carolina Press, 1999); and Rod Bush, *We Are Not What We Seem* (New York: New York University Press, 1999). This is not to ignore the influence of classics such as Cedric Robinson *Black Marxism: The Making of the Black Radical Tradition* (London: Zed Books, 1982) and Mark Naison *Communists in Harlem During the Depression* (Urbana: University of Illinois Press, 1983). My point is simply to underscore the increased institutional receptivity that the intellectual study (not practice) of black radicalism is receiving.

3. I borrow this phrase from Ralph Ellison's imaginative illumination of the uncharted oceans of black existence. See Ralph Ellison, *Invisible Man* (New York: Random House, 1952), 439.

4. The Black Radical Congress (BRC), which convened June 19–21, 1998, at the University of Illinois at Chicago, represents the most recent example of the reemergence of black radicalism. Gathering together an eclectic array of over 1,500 activists, intellectuals, and community organizers of various ideological and political affiliations, the BRC attempted to articulate a radical programmatic political agenda for African American politics in the twenty-first century

5. Clarence Lusane, *Race in the Global Era* (Boston: South End Press, 1997).

6. For a discussion of the early period of the civil rights movement, see Robert Korstad and Nelson Lichtenstein, "Opportunities Found and Lost: Labor, Radicals and the Early

Civil Rights Movement," *Journal of American History* 75, no. 3 (December 1988); Beth Tompkins Bates, "A New Crowd Challenges the Old Guard in the NAACP, 1933–1941," *American Historical Review* 102, no. 2 (April 1997); and Belinda Robnett, *How Long? How Long?: African-American Women in the Struggle for Civil Rights* (New York: Oxford University Press, 1997).

7. My usage of the term "antiblack" racism has been inspired by the work of the philosopher Lewis R. Gordon. See Lewis R. Gordon, *Bad Faith and Anti-Black Racism* (Atlantic Highlands, NJ: Humanities Press, 1995); Gordon, *Fanon*; and Gordon, *Her Majesty's Other Children: Sketches of Racism from a Neocolonial Age* (New York: Rowman & Littlefield, 1997).

8. The best examples of the tendency to utilize King as a prism for historical analysis are Taylor Branch, *Parting the Waters: America in the King Years, 1954–1963* (New York: Simon and Schuster, 1988); David Garrow, *Bearing the Cross: Martin Luther King, Jr. and the Southern Christian Leadership Conference* (New York: Vintage, 1986); and Adam Fairclough, *To Redeem the Soul of America: The Southern Christian Leadership Conference and Martin Luther King, Jr.* (Athens: University of Georgia Press, 1987).

9. Utilizing Jürgen Habermas's notion of a "bourgeois public sphere," the political scientist Michael Dawson has argued for the existence of a "black public sphere" that has existed in certain historical contexts for the advancement and protection of African Americans. See Michael Dawson, "A Black Counterpublic?: Economic Earthquakes, Racial Agenda(s), and Black Politics," in *The Black Public Sphere*, ed. The Black Public Sphere Collective (Chicago: University of Chicago Press, 1995).

10. Nikhil Pal Singh, "The Black Panther and the 'Underdeveloped Country' of the Left," in *The Black Panther Party Reconsidered*, ed. Charles Jones (Baltimore: Black Classic Press, 1998), 62.

11. Robinson, *Black Marxism*.

12. James, *Transcending*, 83.

13. Even sympathetic readings of Black Power radicalism fails to critically interrogate radicals' cogent critiques against capitalism, imperialism, and white supremacy. See, for example, William L. Van DeBurg, *New Day in Babylon* (Chicago: University of Chicago Press, 1992).

14. Utilizing the work of the anthropologist James Scott, the historian Robin D. G. Kelley has argued that "hidden transcripts" represent the undocumented oppositional strategies utilized by oppressed African Americans. See Kelley, *Race Rebels*, 8–9; and James C. Scott, *Domination and the Art of Resistance: Hidden Transcripts* (New Haven, CT: Yale University Press, 1990). My use of the term "alternative narrative," although indebted to Scott and Kelley, is broader in scope than the term "hidden transcript." I suggest that an "alternative narrative" encompasses a veritable litany of "hidden histories"—not just acts of resistance by the oppressed—that *are* documented but have remained marginal within mainstream historical narratives.

15. The work of the historical anthropologist Michel-Rolph Trouillot is instructive here. Trouillot has argued that "silencing" is a constitutive part of the production of history. This is to say that certain actors are privileged over others. In describing this silencing, Trouillot writes, "Silences are inherent in history because any single event enters history with some of its constituting parts missing. Something is always left out while something else is recorded. There is no closure of any event, however one chooses to define the boundaries of an event." For a discussion, see Michel-Rolph Trouillot, *Silencing the Past: Power and the Production of History* (New York: Beacon Press, 1995), 49.

16. Frantz Fanon, *Black Skin, White Masks* (New York: Grove Press, 1967), 137.

17. Manning Marable, *Race, Reform and Rebellion* (Jackson: University of Mississippi Press, 1990).

18. For the best examination of Williams's importance during this era, see Tyson, *Radio Free Dixie*.

19. Van DeBurg, *New Day*.

20. Charles Payne, *I've Got the Light of Freedom: The Organizing Tradition and the Mississippi Freedom Struggle* (Berkeley: University of California Press, 1995), 391–405.

21. See Von Eschen, *Race against Empire*.

22. From almost the beginning of its creation, the FPCC was actively supported by a small but prominent group of black writers. Among the 30 individuals signing the group's initial advertisement in the *New York Times* were Robert Williams, John Henrik Clarke, James Baldwin, Julian Mayfield, and John Oliver Killens. See Van Gosse, *Where the Boys Are: Cuba, Cold War America and the Making of a New Left* (London: Verso, 1993), 9.

23. Ibid., 148–49.

24. Robert Williams, *The Crusader* 2, no. 5 (August 13, 1960), 1–2.

25. This is a point that social critic Harold Cruse, in a highly idiosyncratic yet hugely influential critique, would argue undermined black politics in the post–civil rights period. See Harold Cruse, *Crisis of the Negro Intellectual* (New York: William and Morrow, 1967).

26. Leroi Jones, "Cuba Libre," *Evergreen Review* 4, no. 15 (November–December 1960).

27. Julian Mayfield, "The Cuban Challenge," *Freedomways* (Summer 1961): 185.

28. Ibid., 188.

29. The idea of a "black Atlantic" that is a collective, simultaneously hybridic, black identity forged through the African diaspora is found in the writings of a diverse and historic group of thinkers that includes W. E. B. Du Bois, Frantz Fanon, C. L. R. James, and Eric Williams. The "black Atlantic," then, refers to the dialectical processes that shaped black existence in the modern world. "Blackness" within the "black Atlantic," although embodying a wide array of discrete and collective communities, histories, and political ideologies, has come to represent a both real and imagined counterhegemonic consciousness that stands in opposition against notions of empire undergirded by white supremacy. Two useful, although very different, assessments of Pan-Africanism and the shaping of the "black Atlantic" are Paul Gilroy, *The Black Atlantic, Modernity and Double Consciousness* (Cambridge, MA: Harvard University Press, 1993); and Sid Lemelle and Robin D. G. Kelley, eds., *Imagining Home: Class, Culture and Nationalism in the African Diaspora* (New York: Verso, 1994).

30. Daniel Watts (Spingarn Center, Howard University, Washington, DC).

31. Paul Boutelle (Spingarn Center, Howard University, Washington, DC).

32. For a discussion of these tensions, see Clayborne Carson, *In Struggle* (Cambridge, MA: Harvard University Press, 1981); Paula Giddings, *When and Where I Enter* (New York: William Morrow, 1984); and Robnett, *How Long?*

33. Mack Jones, "The Black Underclass as Systemic Phenomenon," in *Race, Class, and Economic Development*, ed. James Jennings (London: Verso, 1992), 63.

34. Kevin Gaines, *Uplifting the Race: Black Leadership, Politics, and Culture in the Twentieth Century* (Chapel Hill: University of North Carolina Press, 1996).

35. Robin D. G. Kelley and Betsy Esch, "Black Like Mao: Red China and Black Revolution," *Souls* 1, no. 4 (Fall 1999).

36. Gosse, *Where the Boys Are*, 154.

37. James, *Transcending*; Kelley, *Race Rebels*; James, *Holding Aloft*; Von Eschen, *Race against Empire*; Gaines, *Uplifting the Race*.

38. For a remarkable discussion of the confluence of discourses emanating from scholars of civil rights, colonial, and subaltern studies, see Kevin Gaines, "Rethinking Race and Class in African American Struggles for Equality, 1885–1941," *American Historical Review* 102, no. 2 (April 1997).

CHAPTER 10

REVOLUTION IN BABYLON

STOKELY CARMICHAEL AND AMERICA IN THE 1960S

PENIEL E. JOSEPH

INTRODUCTION: IN SEARCH OF AN ICON

STOKELY CARMICHAEL (KWAME TURE) IS ONE OF the most important political leaders of the postwar era yet remains one of the most obscure icons of his generation. A civil rights militant turned Black Power revolutionary, Carmichael's call
for "Black Power" in Greenwood, Mississippi during a late spring heat wave in
1966 sent shockwaves throughout the United States and beyond. Black Power
represents one of the most controversial, enduring, and pivotal stories of the
twentieth century. Individuals and groups that played major and minor roles
in this movement—which range from Malcolm X, William Worthy, Lorraine
Hansberry, the Black Panthers, Lyndon Johnson, black Muslims, the FBI, Sonia
Sanchez, Amiri Baraka, Huey P. Newton, Kathleen Cleaver, Fidel Castro, and the
New Left to name a few—make this period nothing less than a historical epoch
that encompasses the tragic and heroic character of the postwar global era. Spanning continents and crossing oceans, Black Power's reach was global, stretching
from urban projects in Harlem to rural hamlets in Lowndes County, Alabama, to
poor black neighborhoods in West Oakland and out to the revolutionary cities of
Dar Es Salaam, Tanzania, Conakry, Guinea, Algiers, Algeria, and the cosmopolitan internationalism of London, Stockholm, and Paris.[1]

This essay is based on a larger, two-volume, in-progress biography of Stokely Carmichael/Kwame Ture. I
would like to thank Manning Marable, Vanessa Agard-Jones, the *Souls* Editorial Working Group, Femi
Vaughan, Daryl Toler, Larry Hughes, and Catarina A. da Silva for their thoughts and comments on
this essay.

Stokely Carmichael possessed a nuanced appreciation for the everyday struggles of poor African Americans in the rural South through shared experiences in civil rights struggles and personally witnessed the soul-crushing poverty that contoured the lives of too many northern blacks. Travels to Europe, Africa, Latin America, and the Caribbean, which included intimate moments with icons such as Fidel Castro, Ho Chi Minh, and Kwame Nkrumah, allowed Carmichael to imagine the world as a global stage wherein political leaders—no less than black sharecroppers—played pivotal roles in determining the course of history. Carmichael's unusual biography as a Caribbean-born, Bronx-raised, and Howard University–educated activist who traveled down south to register black sharecroppers to vote only to unexpectedly emerge as a mainstream leader, world traveler, and international icon allows for a panoramic view of postwar freedom struggles. Unglamorous everyday people—ranging from men, women, teenagers, schoolchildren, and trade unionists—participated alongside preachers, street speakers, politicians, political leaders, intellectuals, and artists, composing a freedom surge that ranged from gritty Harlem neighborhoods to Detroit's industrial shop floors to Dixie's cradle, Birmingham, Alabama, and out west to Oakland's postwar boom town. Internationally, events in Africa, Latin America, Europe, and the Caribbean turned much of the postwar era into a global age of decolonization where millions staked humanity's future on the spreading of unprecedented freedoms to far corners of the world.

Black Power would scandalize American society, and the national media quickly turned the slogan into a national Rorschach test: One wherein blacks viewed Black Power as righteous and whites interpreted the term to be filled with violent foreboding. Newspapers brooded over Carmichael's words, quickly forming a consensus that judged the slogan to be at best intemperate and, at worst, a blatant call for antiwhite violence and reverse racism.

For the next decade, Black Power would reverberate around the world, galvanizing blacks, outraging whites, and inspiring a cross-section of ethnic and racial minorities. By 1969, a civil rights militant turned Black Power revolutionary, Carmichael abandoned the United States for Conakry, Guinea, and claimed Pan-Africanism as the highest stage of black political radicalism. For the next thirty years, Carmichael remained a diligent political activist, a throwback to the heady years of the 1960s who remained defiant in his belief that a worldwide revolution was still possible if not imminent. Yet Carmichael's iconography obscures as much as it reveals. Carmichael's role as an advocate of radical democracy and a tireless civil rights organizer during the 1960s remains too often buried beneath the celebrity that would engulf him by the summer of 1966.

Carmichael belonged to the small fraternity who literally bled for American democracy during the early 1960s. By Carmichael's own recollection, between June 1961 and June 1966, he was arrested twenty-seven times while participating in civil rights activities. For Carmichael, the decision to endure physical violence, personal discomfort, and economic uncertainty was part of a disciplined commitment to radical democracy in service of racial equality, economic justice, and black community empowerment. As a young student activist at Howard University, Carmichael helped transform American democracy by participating on the front lines of social and political upheavals during the civil rights movement's heroic years.[2] From Cambridge, Maryland to Washington, DC through Mississippi's Delta region to the backwoods of Lowndes County, Alabama, Carmichael helped organize poor, unlettered blacks. Dreams of self-determination bumped headlong into traditions of white supremacy, random violence, and economic retribution. Carmichael's growing realization that political power, rather than legal redress or moral suasion, was the key to racial justice in America would lead him to preach a politics of Black Power that, in his mind, reflected democracy's best face and last hope. By 1966, Carmichael would emerge as a national leader of an insurgent Black Power movement and help inspire the creation of militant groups such as the Black Panthers (where Carmichael would serve as honorary prime minister for a little over one year). An icon to a generation of young people who hailed him as a new Malcolm X, Carmichael would search for common ground with Martin Luther King Jr., experience harassment at the hands of federal authorities, and enjoy the company of international revolutionaries.[3]

Carmichael's political activism during the 1960s provides a unique prism to view issues of race, war, and democracy in the United States at the local, national, and international level. Tall, handsome, and charismatic, Carmichael burst onto the American political scene in 1966 as the leading proponent of Black Power radicalism. A Renaissance man equally comfortable in sharecropper's overalls, business suits, and dashikis, Carmichael projected the passionate temper of a street speaker, the contemplative demeanor of an academic, and the gregariousness of a Baptist preacher, traits that helped turn him into an international icon. The political equivalent of a rock star during the late 1960s, Carmichael's historical significance dimmed over time. In contrast to Malcolm X, Carmichael's political exploits remain both less documented and less revered. The publication of Carmichael's posthumously published autobiography along with the spate of new scholarship that I have elsewhere called "Black Power studies" has ignited a long overdue process of historical investigation and analysis of Carmichael's political thought and activism.[4] Carmichael represents arguably the most important bridge between civil rights and Black Power activism: A grassroots organizer whose unparalleled courage made him at home among sharecroppers in the Mississippi delta and urban militants in Los Angeles and the Bay Area and who was bold enough to trek through Cuba's Sierra Maestra with Fidel Castro and denounce Lyndon Johnson as a warmonger and compassionate enough to share unscripted moments of friendship with Martin Luther King Jr. Ultimately, the controversies and contradictions of Carmichael's political activism complicate narratives of civil rights and Black Power by recovering buried intimacies of the larger postwar freedom struggle.

BLEEDING FOR DEMOCRACY

In June 1961, one month after completing final exams for spring classes at Howard University, Stokely Carmichael flew from Washington, DC, to New Orleans to join an integrated group of freedom riders traveling from Louisiana to Mississippi. He was nineteen years old and he was not alone. Groups of interracial volunteers embarked on an experiment in democracy that spring, placing political principle ahead of personal safety by challenging ancient restrictions that barred blacks and whites from interstate travel. Carmichael arrived in New Orleans at 3 a.m., met by a nervous escort, hopeful that their early morning rendezvous would throw off suspicion of civil rights activity. The sight of strange trees glittered with Spanish moss evoked images of a gothic South teeming with lynch mobs. A large mob outside the New Orleans train station forced Carmichael's fellow freedom riders onto the train for Jackson through a blur of concentrated violence that left them too exhilarated with the relief of survival to dwell on cuts and bruises sustained during the frantic boarding.[5] On June 8, Carmichael and the freedom riders entered a white waiting room in Jackson, Mississippi, and were quickly arrested and, after a short stint in Hinds County jail, sent on a two-hour drive to Mississippi's Parchman Penitentiary. Cattle prods pressed against the naked flesh of prisoners welcomed inmates to Parchman Farm. Ringed by barbed wire fences and defended by shotgun-toting sentries, Parchman's warden added to the tension by evoking the specter of the prison's "bad niggers," including death row inmates with predilections for random violence.[6] Freedom riders in Parchman, which now included Congress of Racial Equality leader James Farmer as well as a yarmulke-wearing young preacher named James Bevel, responded to small and large instances of brutality with prayers, freedom songs, and a hunger strike. Carmichael celebrated his twentieth birthday, June 29, in Parchman Farm, eventually spending more than five weeks in prison before his release on July 19.[7] He would cherish the memory as a rite of passage and preparation for dozens of future arrests.[8]

May Carmichael would spend a tense evening listening to the radio before learning of her son's predicament. Stokely had braced May for his incarceration before heading to Mississippi, gently telling his mother not to worry, that he was "going to jail," and to be "proud," not ashamed. When neighbors asked, "Is that your boy Stokely they've got down there?" she responded as her son had instructed. "Yes, that's my boy and I'm so proud of him I don't know what to do!" Adolph Carmichael frowned upon his son's activism but took Stokely at his word that he would earn a college degree before devoting his life to the movement. Immigrants from Port of Spain, Trinidad, transplanted to the Bronx, May and Adolph Carmichael learned early on to compromise with Stokely, who seemed more willful, mischievous, and political than his two sisters. If May Carmichael identified with her son's independent streak, Adolph retained a stubborn faith in God and hard work. Adolph's hope in the promise of America's immigrant roots contrasted with Stokely's ingrained skepticism. After Adolph's premature death in 1962, Stokely would come to view the American dream as a cruel joke played at the expense of honest men like his father who worked himself to an early grave.[9]

Time in Parchman Farm transformed Stokely Carmichael but in ways that could hardly be expected. Mississippi provided Carmichael a chance to see a landscape teeming with beauty where others saw poverty. The Mississippi delta's wide spaces punctuated by flatlands dotted with decrepit shacks, simple one-story churches, and historic plantations featured an impoverished landscape that most Americans chose to ignore. The region's dense black soil, dark wetlands, and large plantations formed an almost surreal physical environment. Mississippi exposed the young Carmichael to the "pain and joy of struggle" as well as the sometimes melancholy "brotherhood of shared danger within bonds of loyalty."[10]

The delta hid untold potential in the faces of obsidian-eyed sharecroppers who toiled in anonymity, including those whose birth, life, and death would never be officially recorded. These same sharecroppers held the power to alter the course of American history through an individual act of self-determination—the vote— that expressed the collective will of black communities in the South who bore no chains yet still lived in bondage. Black sharecroppers in Mississippi distilled the very meaning of citizenship in their resilient, patient, and courageous folkways, and their example earned Carmichael's undying respect for the inhabitants of the rural delta. Carmichael held more than just admiration for sharecroppers in the Mississippi delta. Stokely Carmichael loved them, developing a lifelong sensitivity to the rhythms, customs, and folkways of rural southern blacks that made him a particularly effective organizer. Older residents viewed him with respect and admiration, and he fiercely guarded their trust in return.[11]

But Carmichael's sensitivity could cut both ways. Carmichael could be temperamental, brash, and arrogant, a know-it-all whose easy smile masked a nervous energy that left him, by the age of twenty-two, with an ulcer. A larger than life personality meant, at times, an outsized ego. The ability to make split-second, life-saving decisions in the field could, in other settings, come off as impetuous, intemperate, and reckless. In the face of dangers seen and unseen, Carmichael—by turns bold and compassionate, belligerent and contemplative—inspired hope and confidence among fellow activists in the field who looked to him as a leader among equals. If Carmichael's aura of uncompromising certitude attracted scores of admirers in the movement that made him a sort of minor celebrity among certified organizers and activists, it would serve as a major repellent once amplified by media projection that cast him as a dangerously charismatic heir to Malcolm X.[12]

Mississippi also housed the grotesque. In 1964, three years after his first trip to the delta, Carmichael served as project director of Mississippi's Second Congressional District during the Student Nonviolent Coordinating Committee (SNCC, pronounced "snick")–led Freedom Summer. That summer Carmichael plotted strategy, coordinated the deployment of resources, and tried to stay alive. SNCC's Sojourner Motor Fleet featured modified cars designed to help civil rights workers outrun local vigilantes, Klansmen, and law enforcement officials; Carmichael's skills behind the wheel earned him the nickname the "Delta Devil."[13]

The next year Carmichael rode the wave of Martin Luther King Jr.'s Selma-based voting rights campaign into clandestine organizing in the rural woods of Lowndes County, Alabama, in the late winter of 1965. Roaming for safe territory on mules and attracting rural people daring enough to talk to civil rights activists (and sometimes brave enough to provide shelter), Carmichael poured all his organizing energies into one of Alabama's most obscure regions.

BLACK POWER

"We are trying to build democracy," Carmichael wrote Lorna D. Smith in 1966, a white SNCC supporter who would remain a steadfast ally. "And we have dedicated our lives to that task." Carmichael's letter discussed SNCC's recent opposition to the Vietnam War, his organizing efforts in Lowndes County, Alabama, and his personal dedication to transforming society. Sacrifice, expressed in the shared willingness of civil rights workers to bleed for democratic principles, continued to animate Carmichael's political activism but the deaths of colleagues—both black and white—made him impatient for enduring justice that transcended legal and legislative boundaries. "Our commitment is to man not to a plot of earth or even our country," wrote Carmichael, confessing appreciative relief for Smith's support in the face of being dismissed by critics as "beatniks or communists." Carmichael resurrected hope in language that found kinship with Martin Luther King Jr.'s notion of political transformation through heroic witnessing against historic miseries: "It is the human contact that we make, while suffering that will make the difference."[14]

Racial demons encountered down south served as Carmichael's point of departure in the new republic, where he expressed measured hope for expanding American democracy, holding up African Americans as a metaphorical battering ram, the prickly conscience of a nation too often content to look the other way as if the abject misery of its black sisters and brothers provided an unacknowledged but much needed safety net. Substituting the painful details of organizing in Alabama with passing references to anonymous martyrs, Carmichael directed his gaze toward an impoverished American political landscape. "The majority view is a lie," wrote Carmichael, "based on the premise of upward mobility which doesn't exist for most Americans." Blunt candor gave way to a roll call of grief, an indictment of Lyndon Johnson's Great Society as "preposterous," and then, finally, a hard earned faith that poor, unlettered sharecroppers represented democracy's best face. Legislative and legalistic racial breakthroughs inspired hope even as they magnified the tragedy of white supremacy's stubborn refusal to regard blacks as fellow citizens. The disenfranchised, declared Carmichael, would "redefine what the Great Society is," imparting meaning that would soar above rhetoric. "I place my own hope for the United States," he wrote, in the ability of black sharecroppers who had shown through quiet determination that "they can articulate and be responsible and hold power."[15]

On May 3, 1966, nine hundred blacks in Lowndes County seemed to justify Carmichael's faith in local people's ability to govern themselves by attending a nominating convention at the First Baptist Church of Hayneville, a half mile from the county courthouse. Carmichael watched with unabashed pride as Lowndes County's African Americans voted to place a black panther on the ballot for the upcoming November election. The black panther inspired black hope and white anxiety and, over time, would come to be seen as a symbol of revolution recognized around the world.[16]

Five days after Lowndes County's convention, Carmichael was elected chairman of SNCC. As chairman, Carmichael sparked immediate controversy by declining to attend a White House civil rights conference and publicly describing integration as "an insidious subterfuge for white supremacy." Carmichael's remarks elicited swift rebuke from Martin Luther King Jr., who regretted SNCC's overt flirtation with black nationalism. King's criticism belied what would become an enduring personal friendship. In fact, shortly after his election, King called Carmichael to offer congratulatory words and advice. Meanwhile, in tense meetings with SNCC staff, Carmichael candidly admitted that he was losing faith in American democracy. Optimistic, now apparently mistaken, assumptions that America "is really a democracy, which just isn't working" had left Carmichael and SNCC reeling, anxious, and unprepared for the naked brutality that met each step toward racial progress.[17]

Carmichael and King's relationship grew that June during an almost three-week civil rights march that forged an enduring personal friendship even as it highlighted political differences. The shooting of James Meredith during his one man "march against fear" attracted major civil rights leaders to Mississippi. Marching side by side, Carmichael and King proved physical and temperamental contrasts. Tall, lanky, and restless, Carmichael laconically told reporters that he held no personal commitment to nonviolence but saw it as little more than a political tactic. The slightly portly, more diminutive King politely disagreed, retaining an outward appearance of self-control honed over a decade in the national spotlight. Behind closed doors, the two men enjoyed an easy familiarity and bantered like old friends. Just thirty-seven, King admired the soon-to-be twenty-five-year-old Carmichael's commitment to struggle, and Carmichael appreciated King's unassuming demeanor and earthy sense of humor. The march allowed Carmichael to see a different, less formal, side of King. "During those sweltering days Dr. King became, to many of us, no longer a symbol or an icon," he remembered, "but a warm, funny, likeable, unpretentious human being who shared many of our values." It also exposed a new side of Stokely Carmichael. "This is the twenty-seventh time that I've been arrested," Carmichael informed a large crowd on the evening of Thursday, June 16, 1966. "I ain't going to jail no more. The only way we gonna stop them white men from whuppin' us is to take over. What we gonna start sayin' now is Black Power!" By the time the Meredith March concluded ten days later, Carmichael, and not King, had become the most talked about figure of America's civil rights movement.[18] Three days after giving a rousing, combative speech in Jackson, Mississippi, that cemented his status as the new spokesman of black militancy, Carmichael celebrated his twenty-fifth birthday.

"THE MAGNIFICENT BARBARIAN"

An Ebony feature story on the heels of the Meredith March opened with an appropriately cinematic scene that described Carmichael in high-speed pursuit of white toughs fresh from screaming racial epithets at a busload of black SNCC workers. Historian Lerone Bennett's profile cast Carmichael as the avatar of a new movement—a handsome, brilliant, cosmopolitan who unnamed SNCC compatriots dubbed "the magnificent barbarian" in homage to his ability to inspire everyday people and alienate powerful figures in equal proportion. Civil rights lawyer Len Holt compared Carmichael to a "statue of a Nubian god," just as Bennett suggested a resemblance to contemporary movie stars Harry Belafonte and Sidney Poitier. Beyond the glamour of Carmichael's good looks and personal charisma lay an intellectual depth and sensitivity at times overshadowed by a brazen confidence and naked candor that, one anonymous civil rights leader admitted, "terrifies me and exalts me at the same time."[19] Invoking self-defense as a personal right beyond political debate, Carmichael offered Black Power as a strategy for self-determination not seen in the black community since Reconstruction. White backlash merely amplified the wisdom in Black Power's rhetorical call to arms by revealing profound inequities carved in centuries-old racial fault lines. Ultimately, Bennett concluded, Black Power would take the lead in society's transformation through the at times unsettling figure of Carmichael, a forward thinking visionary who represented the "most advanced social and democratic interests in America."[20]

Carmichael showcased an uncanny ability to impress the unlettered and elite. In front of a group of Harlem teenagers, Carmichael presented himself as a dashing man about town, donning a fashionable blue suit, Italian boots, and striped tie to deliver a speech that played up the soft remnant of his Trinidadian accent. Before a mature, harder edged crowd in Newark, New Jersey, that included LeRoi Jones (later Amiri Baraka), the black nationalist poet and Black Arts advocate, Carmichael disarmed participants with homespun wisdom packaged in a slightly exaggerated southern drawl—"Is it okay if ah take off mah jacket?" he asked at one point. From Newark, Carmichael traveled to Glen Falls, Vermont, for a leadership institute where he starred as the young sage before an interracial group of middle-aged clergy, seasoned activists, and youthful hippies. Equally effective in all three settings, Carmichael simultaneously channeled a charismatic rage leavened by a playful sense of humor.[21]

In the spring of 1967 Martin Luther King Jr. eclipsed Carmichael's seasoned antiwar rhetoric with a speech that sent shockwaves across the nation. King's April 4 address at New York's Riverside Church lent international stature and moral clarity to antiwar speeches that Carmichael had steadfastly delivered for almost one year. At Riverside, King contrasted Carmichael's bitterness toward the failed promises of American democracy with weary hope. "The world now demands," pleaded King, "a maturity of America that we may not be able to achieve."[22] Although King's words now resound with an authority that has swelled retrospectively, shortly after his Riverside speech, he found himself in the uncomfortable position of "having to fight suggestions at every stop that his Vietnam stance merely echoed the vanguard buzz of Stokely Carmichael."[23] He needn't have worried. King's peace advocacy would be highlighted by historians as a daring rejection of the status quo, just as Carmichael's stridently eloquent antiwar position would, in the long term, be muffled by association with Black Power. More comfortable with Stokely as a youthful saber-rattler than a thoughtful antiwar activist, journalists and future historians would virtually ignore the SNCC chairman's meticulous criticism of American involvement in Vietnam as an example of the larger failure of the nation's democratic experiment.[24]

Carmichael's insouciance struck a chord in *Life* magazine photojournalist Gordon Parks. Parks (an equally adept writer, memoirist, and raconteur) and Carmichael bonded over shared reputations as mavericks. "Stokely gives the impression," Parks impishly observed, that he could "stroll through Dixie in broad daylight using the Confederate flag for a handkerchief."[25] Four months of shadowing Carmichael made Parks appreciate the nuances of a personality that was both outsized and earthy. In Parks's narrative, Carmichael ("complex, sensitive, and angry") popped off the page as a "spokesman not so much of a movement as a mood" that stood in contrast with the presumed passiveness of earlier generations. Parks "marveled" at Carmichael's "ability to adjust in any environment." Tracking Carmichael on university campuses, with hard-core inner-city militants and rural blacks in Alabama, Parks touted the young revolutionary as a new kind of Renaissance man, at ease among sharecroppers, intellectuals, and urban militants.[26] Flashes of humor over childhood reminiscences (the white kids at Bronx Science High School considered Carmichael, a self-proclaimed bad dancer, "their chocolate Fred Astaire") turned to grim recognition of his mother's long days as a maid and his father's premature death due to backbreaking labor. Perceptively, Parks described King's current antiwar stance as following on the heels of Carmichael, whose rage against Vietnam, the draft, and Lyndon Johnson served as a hallmark to his standard stump speech.[27] Carmichael's unshakable antiwar position evoked conflicting feelings in Parks whose son served as a tank gunner in Southeast Asia. Parks wondered which of the two young men's fight was more just. Finding "no immediate answer," Parks concluded that Carmichael's passion for justice gave physical risk a clear political purpose the Vietnam crisis lacked. For "in the face of death, which was so possible for the both of them, I think Stokely would surely be more certain of why he was about to die."[28] Stokely Carmichael had become, for Parks and millions of other black Americans, a surrogate son.

In May 1967, with his tenure as SNCC chairman coming to an end, Carmichael made plans to resume local organizing. "This is sort of my last speaking engagement," he told an audience at a Sunday evening dance that capped off Stokely Carmichael Day in Chicago, "cause after this I got two more to go to, and then I'm going to D.C., and we're going to sure enough take over that city and it's going to be ours, lock, stock, and barrel."[29] Two days later FBI Director J. Edgar Hoover released portions of his printed congressional testimony, taken three months earlier, to the news media. Bombshell allegations charged Carmichael with maintaining contact with communist front groups, and FBI phone lines buzzed with reporters clamoring for more information, only to be informed that Hoover's testimony stood "on its own two feet and we can add nothing." Reporters confronted Carmichael in Grand Rapids, Michigan, fresh from an electrifying antiwar speech at Washington's Lincoln Memorial Congregational Church. Instead of the expected fireworks, Carmichael calmly requested that Hoover prove the charges.[30] Southern University students sat transfixed, the next day, as Carmichael discussed political revolution by way of the radical psychiatrist Frantz Fanon, whose legacy ran past his premature death in 1961 through the publication (and translation) of a blockbuster book *The Wretched of the Earth*.[31]

The timing of Hoover's news release coincided with FBI efforts to exploit "known weaknesses of Carmichael." A search for personal scandal augmented the bureau's efforts, coordinated with the justice department, to build a criminal case against Carmichael (complete with scores of affidavits from informers who attended his speeches) for selective service violations.[32] The FBI judged Carmichael to be a discreet ladies' man who enjoyed the occasional drink, subsisted on income from lectures, and shunned fancy hotels in favor of home-cooked hospitality. A frequent flier who favored no "particular airline," Carmichael exhibited a lack of routine that frustrated agents searching for pressure points found in behavior patterns.[33] Bureau surveillance of Carmichael's private life paralleled frantic reports from Washington civic leaders suggesting that Carmichael's planned residence in the city risked fiscal crisis in the form of cancelled business conventions and higher crime.[34]

But Carmichael's status as a national leader complicated his return to grassroots organizing. Events in California would soon make it impossible. The Oakland-based local activist Huey P. Newton's decision to send an armed convoy of Black Panthers (BPP) to the state capitol in Sacramento on May 2, 1967, triggered bursts of panic and near hysteria that simultaneously burnished the young organization's celebrity while jeopardizing its chances of longevity. Newton's gamble poised the Black Panthers on a high wire between daring improvisation and reckless bravado that mixed threats of brooding violence with the exhilarating spectacle of street corner toughs as political revolutionaries. Like surrealist painters, the Black Panthers imagined a world not yet in existence, but one that they could will into being. Newton's subsequent drafting of Carmichael into the BPP continued a pattern that marked the Panthers as defiant visionaries bold enough to invite Black Power's chief icon and national spokesman to join their modest local group. Newton's mandate conferred the rank of field marshal on Carmichael, with a public commission to "establish revolutionary law, order and justice" over the United States to the Continental Divide.[35] It was a most unlikely reward, conferred in absentia (Carmichael was out of the country at the time of Newton's executive mandate), for Carmichael's ongoing activism in Lowndes County, Alabama, whose panther symbol had been eagerly snapped up by scores of militants, forming its most enduring beachhead in Oakland, California.

There was a whiff of desperation to Newton's order, since Carmichael scarcely needed to lend his name to a group of revolutionaries who could easily be mistaken for misguided, if colorful, black gangsters. An August 1967 *New York Times* exposé resuscitated the waning buzz of the group's Sacramento adventure by publishing "The Call of the Black Panthers" written by *Ramparts'* assistant managing editor Sol Stern. The story was accompanied by a soon-to-be iconic photo of Huey P. Newton. With an open collared white dress shirt peering underneath a black leather jacket, Newton appeared pensive while sitting in flared chair holding a rifle in one hand and a spear in another, contoured by African shields carefully strewn on the floor. The image evoked poetic juxtapositions between the past and present, the modern and the ancient, that suggested forward thinking black revolutionaries required a potent knowledge of history and politics. For Stern, the Panthers's limited impact on the Bay Area's civil rights scene made them less of a political phenomenon than a sociological one.[36] Against the backdrop of national civil disorders in urban cities, the Panthers—with their melodramatic statements, bombastic posture, and dead serious swagger—demanded attention. Stern's profile contained all the ingredients designed to turn the group into a household name. The article lingered over Newton's good looks and smoldering intensity, showcased cofounder Bobby Seale's common touch with everyday people, and documented the Oakland police department's visceral hatred for the Panthers, quoting one anonymous officer's wish that both groups engage in "an old-fashioned shootout." With characteristic brio, the Panthers inflated membership numbers, spoke of mounting a global revolution against American imperialism, and convened sparsely attended rallies where there rage against the police drew more interest from curiosity seekers than new recruits.[37]

THE WORLD STAGE

Stokely Carmichael toured London, his first stop on a five-month international tour, as the Panthers captured local headlines. As critics fumed that he deftly recycled the same anti-American speech into "a first class, round the world airline ticket," international and domestic supporters hailed Carmichael as a global emissary whose political platform spanned nothing less than the entire world.[38] Carmichael's tour coincided with furious FBI investigations attempting to link him to the Communist Party and domestic urban unrest in cities such as Newark and Detroit that, Black Power activists argued, was a mere prelude to a more violent revolution to come. In London to attend the "Dialectics of Liberation" conference that featured well known radical intellectuals, such as Herbert Marcuse, Carmichael dazzled intellectuals and activists alike. Angela Davis, a recent Brandeis University graduate and perhaps Marcuse's most precocious student, found Carmichael to be erudite and insightful. British newspapers described him as a "phenomenon" whose "slogan is Black Power" and whose skin color constituted "his country."[39] Alternately quoting Jean Paul Sartre and Albert Camus, Carmichael mesmerized journalists with stories that mixed personal biography, raw political experience, and intellectual agility into a pungent mix that was both mysterious and revelatory. From working-class neighborhoods of Brixton, Hackney, and Notting Hill, Carmichael recounted how an early infatuation with Western civilization (in Trinidad and the Bronx) curdled with his new found knowledge of the black world's hidden history and the white world's horrific transgressions. Calling Malcolm X his "patron saint," Carmichael announced that urban riots in the United States were actually "rebellions" and predicted that domestic violence was inevitable in a nation birthed in bloodshed.[40] Carmichael dialogued with London's militant Caribbean, African, and white students at Africa House, a headquarters for progressives of all colors. Michael X (nee DeFrietas), a self-styled Black Power activist, fellow Trinidadian, and self-proclaimed Malcolm X disciple, regaled Carmichael with his dark humor.[41] On July 18, 1967, Carmichael delivered a wide-ranging speech that touched upon issues of race, class, and culture at the Dialectics of Liberation Conference. American cities, he proclaimed, would be "populated by peoples of the Third World" unwilling to tolerate cultural degradation and institutional racism.[42] Black urban youth represented the most potentially disruptive force to combat a global system of racial and economic exploitation. Untamed by the forces of racism, the inner city's "youngbloods" composed the "real revolutionary proletariat, ready to fight by any means necessary" for black liberation.[43] Shortly after his visit, British authorities reacted to Carmichael's volatile presence by promptly banning him from ever returning to England.[44] Newark and Detroit burned just as Carmichael arrived in

Cuba, where he held up the island's revolution as a daring experiment in freedom and outraged American officials with forecasts of a domestic race war complete with urban guerrillas. Carmichael's search for an international model for political revolution suitable for black Americans would continue in Africa. After leaving Cuba, and with the US State Department in hot pursuit, Carmichael lunched with Ho Chi Minh in Vietnam, met with guerrilla leaders in Algiers, and arrived in Conakry, Guinea, in time to meet with three of Africa's most respected figures: Sékou Touré, Kwame Nkrumah, and Amilcar Cabral.[45]

Carmichael's meetings in Conakry would prove especially fruitful. In correspondence from Guinea, Carmichael admonished SNCC workers to resist the temptation of petty squabbles and infighting. "Our people are dying in the streets of Detroit, Vietnam, Congo . . . and all over," he wrote, casting the Third World in racial solidarity with black freedom struggles. "I hope my trip and future trips make things HOTTER for you all," Carmichael insisted, since this would separate serious revolutionaries from pretenders. "I wish most of you would wake up and catch up with your people. They are ahead of you."[46]

Guinean president Ahmed Sékou Touré presided over a one party state that advocated a form of African socialism that retained indigenous cultural flourishes appealing to black nationalists. An outspoken and charismatic proponent of Pan-Africanism, Touré impressed Carmichael as a steadfast and unpretentious leader and the two developed a close rapport.[47] Guinea was also the residence of deposed Ghanaian leader Kwame Nkrumah. Ousted in a coup the previous year, Nkrumah was a living legend among Pan-Africanists, a status he retained in spite of his recent political misfortunes. Conakry's coastal surroundings, low rise buildings, and arid climate dotted with mango trees and coconut palms, reminded Carmichael of his native Port of Spain. Nkrumah's scenic coastal villa provided an ironic contrast to the reality of political exile. The Osagyefo (or redeemer of his native land) and Carmichael took an instant liking to each other. In wide-ranging, candid conversations, Nkrumah chafed at Carmichael's impetuous nature while Carmichael came away with renewed Pan-African impulses. Even as he prepared for the next stop on his global tour, Carmichael made plans to return to Africa.

Carmichael's month in Dar es Salaam, Tanzania, which served as the base for competing revolutionary groups with ambitions for sovereignty in far corners of colonial Africa, would prove controversial. Operatives from Europe, Africa, the United States, and other parts of the world trafficked in real and imagined adventures that made Dar es Salaam one of Africa's most dangerous and exotic cities. In Dar, Carmichael recorded taped messages to black youth from Tanzania that stressed the need for pride in black culture and an African identity as the key to a transcendent unity that bound together communities separated by oceans: "First we are African, living in the United States, but first we are Africans." Identification with Africa promised to restore ties that stretched from "South Africa to Nova Scotia" and prepare a generation of blacks scattered across the world to struggle for self-determination no matter the cost.[48]

Carmichael's hope for black unity contrasted with growing political divisions in Africa, whose reach soon spread to Tanzania. Frustrated opposition groups embraced Carmichael as a symbol of free speech even as nervous government officials and United States Information Service agents watched his every move. In picturesque Zanzibar, Carmichael addressed an Afro-Shirazi Youth League rally soaking up spectacular indigenous sights that included clove trees. Carmichael's public criticisms of Africa's jet-setting guerrilla leaders "living in luxurious hotels, mixing with white people" upset rebel leaders who dismissed his charges as the naïve ravings of an amateur. Ripples from Carmichael's outspoken assertiveness swelled into flagrant displays of unsanctioned political activity by campus radicals, the press, and various activists. Carmichael departed Tanzania with painful lessons about African politics, where independence rested on fluid alliances, ancient histories, and indigenous cultures that remained tantalizing incomprehensible to even the most sympathetic outsiders.[49]

A DANGEROUS YEAR

In 1968, Carmichael's presence in Washington, DC, placed him at the center of the growing controversy surrounding Martin Luther King Jr.'s Poor People's Campaign. King's new organizing direction, announced the previous summer in his third book, *Where Do We Go From Here: Chaos or Community?* posited massive civil disobedience as the linchpin behind a national movement for social and economic justice. King's tactics, for different reasons, gave both his supporters and his enemies pause. Southern Christian Leadership Conference's (SCLC) full plans to stage a massive "live in" at the nation's capital struck Black Power militants as foolish, Washington politicians as quixotic, and local authorities as trouble. Journalists alternately described the campaign as a reckless stunt and a last ditch effort that anticipated the demise of nonviolence as a force for social change.[50]

King's determination to organize a mass protest in the nation's capital renewed his combatively friendly relationship with Carmichael forged in the tumult of 1966's Meredith March. Twice during the first week of February, Carmichael and King met to hash over disputes, discuss areas of mutual agreement, and massage political differences. During a closed meeting of two hundred activists at Washington's Church of the Redeemer, King disclosed more detailed plans of the SCLC's upcoming Poor People's Campaign. Carmichael expressed support for the campaign's goals while maintaining SNCC's organizational autonomy. Press reports glossed over the complexity behind these negotiations in favor of characterizing the meeting as part of King's effort to neutralize violent threats posed by Black Power militants.[51]

Behind the scenes, Carmichael assured King that SNCC's intentions were positive. "Stokely, you don't need to tell me that," replied King. "I know you." Privately, King expressed reservations, confiding to advisor Stanley Levison that although Carmichael was now "sweet as pie," he tried to "pull a power play on us in Washington" in a coup thwarted only by a lack of support.[52]

Two days after meeting with King, Carmichael unveiled a more sensitive side at a conference of Methodist ministers in Cincinnati, Ohio. An astonished group of around 250 clergymen patiently listened to a Bible-quoting Carmichael who held up Jesus's dual commitment to saving souls and eradicating poverty as the contemporary challenge facing the ministry. Quoting the book of Acts, Carmichael urged the ministers to "turn the world upside down" in pursuit of social justice and deployed snippets of Jeremiah to relay the message that social upheavals to root out injustice proved consistent with tenets of the Christian faith. Reverend James Lawson, chair of the National Conference of Negro Methodists, informed skeptical reporters that "Stokely has the basic compassion called for in the Christian faith," acknowledging Carmichael's presence as a lightning rod that carried a message that black Methodists nonetheless needed to hear.[53]

On Thursday, April 4, Martin Luther King was shot by sniper fire while standing on the balcony of his room at the Lorraine Hotel in Memphis, Tennessee. King's assassination placed new pressures on Carmichael. Almost four months after returning from his international tour, Carmichael had attempted to return to local organizing in Washington, DC. But efforts to forge a Black United Front with the city's militants and moderates stalled and activists inside of SNCC's Washington Field Office grew resentful over Carmichael's star power. Carmichael's growing alliance with the Black Panthers proved more promising and two public speeches in California in February on behalf of the "Free Huey Movement" left no doubt that he remained the biggest speaking draw among black militants in the nation. Carmichael's private life also attracted intense public scrutiny after he became engaged to South African singer Miriam Makeba. Almost ten years older than Carmichael, Makeba was an international star whose close professional contacts included entertainer Harry Belafonte. Critics charged Carmichael with entering into a marriage of convenience, ignoring the couple's genuine affection toward each other in favor of stories that chronicled Makeba's declining concert schedule after their announced engagement.[54]

As news of King's death spread throughout the city, Carmichael, along with SNCC workers Cleve Sellers and Lester McKinnie, led a group of angry protesters down Washington's U Street corridor of drugstores, supermarkets, and theaters, asking store owners to close. At one point Walter Fauntroy, one of King's advisors, practically dragged Carmichael by the arms pleading with him to stay calm. Small, attentive crowds gathered around transistor radios sifting information from repetitively breathless news stories recounting the details of King's death. As passersby shattered the windows of the Republic Theater, an unlikely diplomat emerged in the form of Carmichael who screamed, "This is not the way!" backed by a chorus of SNCC workers repeatedly chanting "Take it easy, Brothers!" Unable to control the crowd they eventually retreated a few blocks away, back to Carmichael's apartment. Bittersweet memories pulled SNCC activists through the night, with Carmichael leading tearful reminisces of his friendship with King, intense revelations that caught his colleagues off guard.[55]

On September 5, 1968, Carmichael and Miriam Makeba flew to Dakar, Senegal from New York City. Over the next several weeks they made preparations to relocate to Africa and traveled to Conakry, Guinea, where Carmichael met with Kwame Nkrumah for the second time in a year. In conversations with Nkrumah, Carmichael presented the Black Panthers as a group of revolutionaries committed to the deposed leader's triumphant return to Ghana. With the entitlement of a former ruler, Nkrumah preached patience, reminding Carmichael that "without a base we can do nothing."[56]

Three days after Carmichael arrived in Africa, Huey P. Newton was convicted in Oakland, California of manslaughter. Both Newton's conviction and Richard Nixon's narrow presidential election two months later accelerated Carmichael's plans to seek a new political base. Carmichael's marriage to Miriam Makeba and hopes for the future collided with a palpable concern for his own safety. Always the public firebrand, in quieter times Carmichael confessed fear of being assassinated at the hands of the authorities. There were good reasons to be afraid. FBI surveillance of Carmichael had reached comic proportions. After an agent's inquiry into his travel itinerary resulted in a bomb scare following a miscommunication with a Trans World Airlines flight clerk, Carmichael laughed off the incident, unfurling a huge poster of Che Guevara as he traded barbs with reporters, but the harassment exacted a toll.[57]

In November, Carmichael publicly assailed white liberals during a speaking tour in California. At San Jose State he denounced liberals as poseurs interested only in reform and dismissed hippies as misguided and ignorant. At tiny De Anza College, he struck down the question of white participation in Black Power and continued his assault on liberals.[58] Carmichael's speech would be a prelude to his public break from the Panthers. For Carmichael, black unity trumped talk of interracial alliances, a hard lesson learned from his days in SNCC witnessing the deaths of black and white comrades to advance democratic ideals that receded further from view the more they were pursued.

That December, Carmichael continued his plans to move to Guinea.[59] Before leaving he made a series of controversial appearances at southern colleges where he openly discussed revolutionary violence. At North Carolina A & T, Carmichael's address, "A New World to Build," announced that the period of "entertainment" had passed in order to introduce concrete strategies in service of a political revolution. Black people, he declared, suffered through both racial segregation and psychological colonization discussed in Frantz Fanon's riveting treatise, *The Wretched of the Earth*. Fanon's analysis of European colonization's damaging effect on the black psyche had an American equivalent in an unspoken compulsion for white standards of beauty. W. E. B. Du Bois's notion of seeing the world through a veil, the possession of a double consciousness that gifted blacks with prophetic powers yet burdened them with internal conflicts formed the basis of Carmichael's discussion of black self-determination. Pathological behavior in the form of drugs, gangs, and criminal activity were the most visible manifestation of black self-loathing. Denial of African identity and all traces to a continent considered uncivilized left black Americans a people without a history who were ashamed of their own culture. The difference between Negroes and blacks, Carmichael offered, was that the former clung to the antebellum era's notion of the good slave while the latter recognized contemporary symbols of bondage and set out to transform the society that produced slavery. Yet "every Negro was a potential black man" to be patiently converted toward an "undying love" for the community rather than privately ridiculed or publicly attacked.[60]

DREAMS OF AFRICA

In 1969, a reporter for London's *Sunday Times* found Carmichael, a radical elder statesman at age twenty-eight, in Africa and in a playful mood, lounging with his wife Miriam and her fifteen-month-old grandson. Over dinner Carmichael candidly discussed his recent split from the Panthers, decision to relocate to Guinea, and search for new political strategies. If the Panthers represented a political dead end, Carmichael remained unsure of the proper vehicle for the political revolution he still hoped to lead. "I do not know how to begin to cope with the problems" in the United States, he admitted, "so for me to stay there and to pretend that I do is for me to deceive myself and my people." On a hotel balcony in Algiers, Carmichael wistfully contrasted his friendship with the late Martin Luther King Jr. and newfound enmity with exiled Black Panther Minister of Information Eldridge Cleaver. Cleaver's open admiration for Carmichael in early 1967, which had resulted in a flattering essay in *Ramparts* titled "My Father and Stokely Carmichael," had turned sour after Carmichael's resignation from the Panthers. Shortly thereafter ad hominem attacks against Carmichael in the pages of The Black Panther newspaper became common. Political disagreements over strategy and tactics had turned personal, and Cleaver targeted Carmichael in a baffling, highly publicized open letter that variously accused his one-time hero of being antiwhite, a government spy, and a fool.[61] Asked if they could remain friends despite political differences, Carmichael answered, "with Eldridge maybe not," anticipating no end to a torrent of criticism already emanating from the Panthers.

As the conversation shifted to talk of the future Carmichael extolled Nkrumah as Africa's true leader, a statesman bold enough to encourage Pan-Africanism in a continent divided by ethnic and regional differences. The romantic side of Carmichael made it all sound so exciting that the reporter briefly joined the euphoria before stepping back and diplomatically noting that most African leaders did not share Carmichael's enthusiasm for Nkrumah's leadership.[62]

By August, both Carmichael and Cleaver claimed Africa as a political base for far-reaching revolution. From Algeria (soon to be officially recognized by the government as the Black Panther Party's International Section), Cleaver plotted political insurrection in the United States by remote control and welcomed a fashionably eclectic band of exiles from the States that included black militants, hijackers, and other colorful and questionable characters.

From the Congo Republic, Carmichael announced his intention to return Nkrumah to Ghana. "Dr. Nkrumah," he informed reporters in Brazzaville, "was the first man to realize the urgency of forming an organization of African unity." The declaration followed an earlier appearance on British television where Carmichael sketched the international makeup of political struggle and vowed to use Africa as a base for a worldwide revolution.

If Carmichael's activities in Africa made him an icon in world affairs they simultaneously distanced him from the immediacy of domestic Black Power struggles. But in October 1969, he made a comeback of sorts, giving an interview to the black press, and allowing Ethel Minor, a former SNCC news staff director and close advisor, to report on his international travails in *Muhammad Speaks*. Minor defended Carmichael from accusations of abandonment by militants with hidden agendas and openly dismissive white journalists. Real political organizing, Minor suggested, took place away from the glare of rallies and news conferences. Having concluded that he had taken Black Power as far as possible in the United States, Carmichael encountered political worlds at once larger and further removed from his past organizing. Carmichael's new direction revolved around acquiring territory in Africa as a base for a political revolution that would assist black Americans. Carmichael's relatively low profile throughout the year, explained Minor, originated in his quest to do "serious organizing" and culminated in a bombshell alliance with African statesman Nkrumah in an announced quest to return him to Ghana. To this end, Carmichael steadfastly projected a sanitized version of Ghana's recent political history that excluded details of the creeping authoritarianism that helped oust Nkrumah for a morality play that indicted an international cabal of white racists and Uncle Toms.[63]

A REVOLUTIONARY IN SEARCH OF A MOVEMENT

Possessed with secrets imparted from the high priest of Pan-Africanism, Carmichael professed the evangelist's prerogative to spread the word to the uninitiated and would spend the next three decades as perhaps the most robust spokesman of an international Pan-African revolution. The man whose great strength lay in an improvisational creativity that relied more on instinct than ideology, now embraced "Nkrumaism," with the fervor of an acolyte. "I have," he declared, "committed myself to live, to kill, and to die for the return of Dr. Nkrumah to Ghana."[64]

By 1981, Carmichael had changed his name to honor his mentors Kwame Nkrumah (who died in 1972) and Sékou Touré to Kwame Ture, divorced Miriam Makeba, and remarried Marlyatou Barry, a doctor, and had a son the next year, Boubacar "Bocar" Biro.[65] Specks of gray marked the now forty-year-old Ture's hair, and he sported a more notable accent, a combination of francophone West Africa, Trinidad, and the Deep South. Ture snatched moments of domestic tranquility in between frequent tours around the world to raise money and political consciousness. Despite modest success recruiting new members into the All African Peoples' Revolutionary Party, Ture's dreams of mobilizing a political revolution through Pan-Africanism receded against a backdrop of a conservative resurgence in the United States and abroad.

Sékou Touré's death in 1984 triggered domestic upheavals in Guinea that toppled the one party state's ruling faction, the ironically named Democratic Party of Guinea. The coup left Ture in a kind of political limbo and for a while he was detained by the new ruling faction; an ordeal ended only by the timely intervention of old friends including Jesse Jackson and Chicago mayor Harold Washington. Like a soldier fighting on the front line of what many considered a forgotten war, Ture remained "the unrepentant voice of the '60s."[66] In 1992, twenty-five years after its initial publication, Ture wrote a new afterward for *Black Power*, the classic manifesto coauthored with political scientist Charles Hamilton.

An analysis of race in America and around the world since the 1960s intermittently broke through sentences promoting a global Pan-African revolution. *Black Power*, Ture wrote, had been prophetic in many ways, most vitally in its demands for still unimplemented political reforms. Written two months after Los Angeles's massive urban rebellion in April 1992, Ture posited an unbroken legacy of black activism that stretched back to antebellum slavery and crossed oceans into Africa and far away nations. Creative, improvisational measures advocated in 1967 now gave way to "Nkrumahism-Tureism," and the belief that his two deceased mentors possessed secrets capable of changing the world.[67]

A diagnosis of advanced prostate cancer in 1996 would, in Ture's recollection, "bring out the best" in former colleagues and friends who raised funds for medical treatment in the States and abroad. Old friends chipped away at the mask of political certainty in interviews, conversations, and fetes to reclaim fleeting intimacies now buried by Ture's obsession to single-handedly ignite a political revolution. Charlie Cobb, a former SNCC worker and one-time confidant, found that, underneath his old friend's political vigilance lay "the old loose Stokely" full of energy and eager to laugh. More often than not, however, Ture remained inside a cocoon of political certainty, filled with catchy phrases (he routinely answered his phone with "ready for the revolution") and a coterie of loyal admirers.[68]

If Ture lived in a political reality of his own making, it was a world that grew larger as his illness progressed. Frantic efforts for treatment took him to New York hospitals, Cuban clinics, and a holistic healing center in Honduras. Further travels, for sentimental reasons, took him back to Guinea and then on to Ghana, Egypt, and South Africa. There were other trips as well. Perhaps most notable was Ture's return home. On June 12, 1996, Ture made his first public appearance (he had returned clandestinely before this) in Trinidad in three decades. Dressed in an aqua green robe, Ture spoke to two hundred students at the National Heritage Library and implored them to use books as a gateway toward the creation of a more just society.[69]

The race to tie up loose political ends included efforts assisted by former SNCC worker Mike Thelwell to a complete a long overdue autobiography that would be published five years after his death. Old friends and ex-colleagues from SNCC and the Black Panthers called to inquire about Ture's health. The Nation of Islam provided financial assistance for medical treatment and an ad hoc committee of family and advisors provided treatment options in the United States.

Like his friend Martin Luther King Jr., Ture had made a career out of financial chastity. Annual speaking tours provided subsistence but his health crisis left him economically bereft and totally dependent on the goodwill of the black community he affectionately referred to as "my people." Jesse Jackson stopped by Ture's bedside and Louis Farrakhan kept in regular contact from Chicago. A visit by former Black Panther communications secretary Kathleen Cleaver and her two children was followed, coincidentally, by a phone call from Eldridge Cleaver, living his final lonely year in California.

Between 1996 and 1998, Ture spent more time in America than he had over the previous two decades. Ture's illness reunited veterans of the civil rights and Black Power movements in organized tributes to the man whose activism indelibly shaped both eras. On Friday July 5, 1998, Ture departed, for the last time, New York City on route to Guinea. Emaciated, weighing less than one hundred pounds, Ture died in Guinea on November 15 on the west coast of Africa he called home.

CONCLUSION

But Ture's death is not the end of this story. Indeed, far from it. If Martin Luther King Jr. is rightfully considered the avatar of the civil rights movement's heroic period, then Kwame Ture represents, after Malcolm X, the embodiment of the Black Power era. Uncovering the ways in which Ture's legacy ultimately transformed American democracy (even after he long considered America's political system to be hopeless) fundamentally revises narratives of postwar African American history. Moreover, chronicling Ture's political and personal journey allows us to break out of the confines of bottom-up versus top-down history. In both subtle and spectacular ways, Ture's story goes beyond the stark methodological and interpretive lines usually drawn between political and social history. This is to say that Ture's story encompasses both, allowing us intimate, unvarnished portraits of the poor and the powerful; a window into the world of black women organizers who mentored Ture, such as Ella Baker and Gloria Richardson; new insights into the relationship between black and white activists during the 1960s and fresh perspectives of key global powerbrokers—from Martin Luther King Jr. and Lyndon Johnson to Fidel Castro and Kwame Nkrumah—who helped to transform the postwar world.

New scholarship has underscored the need to complicate narratives of both the civil rights and Black Power eras. Yet a search for a synthetic (rather than overarching synthesis) portrait of the postwar era remains tantalizing out of reach. A comprehensive and multifaceted accounting of Kwame Ture and Black Power necessitates a panoramic view that contours the political, social, cultural, and economic spheres that encompass history as it is made rather than written. Ture, perhaps better than any single postwar historical figure, provides a singular bridge that helps to better illuminate and understand the era's regional differences and racial scandals, gender controversies and class struggles, multiracial makeup and challenge to white privilege, and the way in which ordinary people and powerbrokers (sometimes in unison and sometimes at cross purposes) remade America and much of the rest of the world.[70]

From beyond the grave, Ture has managed to burnish his legacy via a posthumously published autobiography, *Ready For Revolution: The Life and Struggles of Stokely Carmichael (Kwame Ture)*. In many ways, this autobiography represents the most important book published to date about Ture. The autobiography's portrait of the young Stokely Carmichael as an incandescent figure during the civil rights era's heroic years goes a long way toward recovering Ture's indelible impact on postwar black freedom struggles. *Ready For Revolution* represents the start of what will be a critical, long, and thoughtful reconsideration of Ture's political activism and contemporary legacy. Ture remained unable or unwilling to delve into precise details of debates, disagreements, and controversies that marked his life. For the historian, appreciating Ture's full complexity will ultimately require nothing less than a rigorously analyzed, meticulously documented, and critically interpretive portrait of the activist: One that will also serve as a comprehensive history of an era.

Through civil rights activism among poor sharecroppers in the Mississippi delta and rural woods of Alabama, Kwame Ture sought to extend America's democratic traditions to black citizens who toiled in anonymity. Democratic breakthroughs collided with heartbreaking failures that assaulted Ture's youthful sense of idealism and turned him toward a pursuit of power that mixed hope, anger, rage, and optimism in a quest for a new America and, over time, a new world. Near the end of his life, American democracy's glaring contradictions seemed to pale in comparison with the crisis of African nation-states that unfolded in the post–Black Power era. But for Ture, opportunities remained hidden beneath each setback and, even at its worst, Africa held untold potential. While such patience struck some as naive, Ture remained confident that his political path had helped shape a better world and to his final breath believed in, indeed remained ready for, revolution.

Ture's activism and influence spanned from Harlem to the Mississippi delta out west to California's Bay Area and the wider worlds of Europe, Africa, Latin America, and the Caribbean. Most often, however, Ture's presence (except for the obligatory recounting of the Meredith March) is either ignored or demonized in the increasingly vast literature on the civil rights movement. The young Stokely Carmichael's pivotal role in reshaping, scandalizing, and transforming American democratic traditions is, inevitably, lost. Ture's own reticence to acknowledge the depth and complexity of his political journey (even in his own autobiography) at times contributed to the lack of serious scholarly interrogation of his extraordinary life. But there were other reasons as well, most notably Ture's unapologetic commitment to a style of black radicalism that made him seem out of touch with the political austerity that followed the heady years of the 1960s. Over four decades after the twenty-five-year-old Stokely Carmichael unleashed words sharp enough to cut through the thick humidity of a Mississippi evening, understanding the political experiences (and recovering the historical context) that led to this momentous declaration, and the events after, will transform our comprehension of not only the civil right and Black Power eras but the larger postwar freedom struggles that inspired and shaped these movements.

NOTES

1. For a comprehensive examination of the movement see Peniel E. Joseph, *Waiting 'Til the Midnight Hour: A Narrative History of Black Power in America* (New York: Henry Holt, 2006). See also Peniel E. Joseph, ed., *The Black Power Movement: Rethinking the Civil Rights-Black Power Era* (New York: Routledge, 2006); Timothy B. Tyson, *Radio Free Dixie: Robert F. Williams and the Roots of Black Power* (Chapel Hill: University of North Carolina Press, 1999); Charles Jones, ed., *The Black Panther Party [Reconsidered]* (Baltimore: Black Classic Press, 1998); Komozi Woodard, *A Nation Within a Nation: Amiri Baraka (LeRoi Jones) & Black Power Politics* (Chapel Hill: University of North Carolina Press, 1999); Matthew Countryman, *Up South: Civil Rights and Black Power*

in Philadelphia (Philadelphia: University of Pennsylvania Press, 2005); William L. Van Deburg, *New Day in Babylon: Black Power and American Culture* (Chicago: University of Chicago Press, 1992); James Edward Smethurst, *The Black Arts Movement: Literary Nationalism in the 1960s and 1970s* (Chapel Hill: University of North Carolina Press, 2005); Curtis J. Austin, *Up Against the Wall: Violence in the Making and Unmaking of the Black Panther Party* (Fayetteville: University of Arkansas Press, 2006); Jama Lazerow and Yohuru Williams, eds., *In Search of the Black Panther Party: New Perspective on a Revolutionary Movement* (Durham: Duke University Press, 2006); Rod Bush, *We Are Not What We Seem: Black Nationalism and Class Struggle in the American Century* (New York: New York University Press, 1999); Manning Marable, *Black American Politics: From the Washington Marches to Jesse Jackson* (London: Verso, 1985); Mike Marqusee, *Redemption Song: Muhammad Ali and the Spirit of the 1960s* (London: Verso, 1999); Nikhil Pal Singh, *Black Is a Country: Race and the Unfinished Struggle for Democracy* (Cambridge: Harvard University Press, 2004); Kathleen Cleaver, and George Katsiaficas, eds., *Liberation, Imagination, and the Black Panther Party* (New York: Routledge, 2001); and Yohuru Williams, *Black Politics/White Power: Civil Rights, Black Power, and the Black Panthers in New Haven* (New York: Brandywine Press, 2000).

2. I use this term to describe the years between 1954's *Brown* Supreme Court decision and the passage of the Voting Rights Act of 1965. This time frame encapsulates the master narrative of civil rights—from the Montgomery Bus Boycott to Emmett Till's lynching; from the Little Rock Crisis to the sit-in movement; and from James Meredith's efforts to enroll at Ole Miss to the March on Washington and the passages of the Civil Rights Act of 1964. Of course a plethora of new scholarship, including my own work, has illustrated the shortcomings of this periodization (some of which is cited in the endnotes of this essay). In a fashion, this period represents America's modern day Iliad, with Martin Luther King Jr. starring as the tragic hero. The cataclysmic events of the period, with its marches, demonstrations, political assassinations, and interracial cast of powerbrokers, lends the era a cinematic flavor that has made for powerful narratives (both media-driven and scholarly) but in the process ossify the movement's contemporary legacy, downplay its ideological diversity, ignore its radicalism, and demonize Black Power as its ruthlessly destructive twin. However, I use the term purposefully to show how historians can transform its meaning by expansively redefining the era's main actors, organizations, geography, and contemporary legacy. See Joseph, *The Midnight Hour* and Joseph, *Black Power Movement.*

3. Joseph, *The Midnight Hour*, 132–204, and Stokely Carmichael with Ekwueme Michael Thelwell, *Ready for Revolution: The Life and Struggles of Stokely Carmichael (Kwame Ture)* (New York: Scribner, 2003).

4. See the special issues I edited on Peniel E. Joseph, ed., "Black Power Studies," *The Black Scholar* 31, no. 3–4 (Fall / Winter 2001) and Joseph, ed., "Black Power Studies," *The Black Scholar* 32, no. 1 (Spring 2002); Joseph, *The Midnight Hour* and Joseph, *Black Power Movement*; and Carmichael with Thelwell, *Ready for Revolution.*

5. Carmichael with Thelwell, *Ready for Revolution*, 192.

6. Taylor Branch, *Parting the Waters: America in the King Years, 1954–1963* (New York: Touchstone, 1988), 483.

7. Carmichael was initially placed in the Hinds County Jail before being moved to Parchman Penitentiary. Carmichael with Thelwell, *Ready for Revolution*, 198–201, 210–11, and FBIKT 100-446080-1166, "Stokely Carmichael: Correlation Summary," February 29, 1968, p. 2.

8. Carmichael with Thelwell, *Ready for Revolution*, 194.

9. Gordon Parks, "Whip of Black Power," *Life*, May 19, 1967, 79; Carmichael with Thelwell, *Ready for Revolution*, 247; and Joseph, *The Midnight Hour*, 124–27.

10. Carmichael with Thelwell, *Ready for Revolution*, 277.

11. For Carmichael's relationship with local people in the South see Clayborne Carson, *In Struggle: SNCC and the Black Awakening of the 1960s* (Cambridge, MA: Harvard University Press, 1981); Charles Payne, *I've Got the Light of Freedom: The Organizing Tradition and the Mississippi Freedom Struggle* (Berkeley: University of California Press, 1995), 335; Carmichael with Thelwell, *Ready for Revolution*; Taylor Branch, *At Canaan's Edge: America in the King Years, 1965–1968* (New York: Simon & Schuster, 2006); and Joseph, *The Midnight Hour*. See also Stokely Carmichael and Charles Hamilton, *Black Power* (New York: Random House, 1967) and Stokely Carmichael, *Stokely Speaks* (New York: Random House, 1971).

12. Joseph, *The Midnight Hour*, 149–61, and Carmichael with Thelwell, *Ready for Revolution*, 520–63.

13. Joseph, *The Midnight Hour*, 124. For black struggles in Mississippi during the civil rights era see Carson, *In Struggle*; Payne, *Light of Freedom*; John Dittmer, *Local People: The Struggle for Civil Rights in Mississippi* (Urbana: University of Illinois Press, 1995); Chana Kai Lee, *For Freedom's Sake: The Life of Fannie Lou Hamer* (Urbana: University of Illinois Press, 1999); Wesley C. Hogan, *Many Minds, One Heart: SNCC's Dream for a New America* (Chapel Hill: University of North Carolina Press, 2007); Taylor Branch, *Parting the Waters, Pillar of Fire: America in the King Years, 1963–1965* (New York: Simon & Schuster, 1998), and Branch, *At Canaan's Edge*; Adam Fairclough, *To Redeem the Soul of America: The Southern Christian Leadership Conference and Martin Luther King Jr.* (Athens: University of Georgia Press, 2001); and David Garrow, *Bearing the Cross: Martin Luther King Jr. and the Southern Christian Leadership Conference* (New York: Harper Perennial, 1999).

14. Stokely Carmichael to Lorna D. Smith, January 15, 1966, pp. 1–4. Stokely Carmichael Lorna D. Smith Papers, Green Library, Stanford University (hereafter cited as SCLDS).

15. Stokely Carmichael, "Who Is Qualified?," *The New Republic*, January 8, 1966, 22.

16. Joseph, *The Midnight Hour*, 130, and Branch, *At Canaan's Edge*, 462–65.

17. Branch, *At Canaan's Edge*, 465.

18. Joseph, *The Midnight Hour*, 132–47, and Carson, *In Struggle*, 209–11.

19. Lerone Bennett Jr., "Stokely Carmichael: Architect of Black Power," July 1966, *Ebony*. SNCC reprint of *Ebony* article, 1.

20. Ibid., 4.

21. Bernard Weinraub, "The Brilliancy of Black," *Esquire*, January 1967, 130, 132–34.

22. Branch, *At Canaan's Edge*, 593.

23. Ibid., 603.

24. King had come out against the war as early as 1965 but was quickly pressured into silence. The SNCC subsequently became one of the war's leading critics and from June 1966–April 1967, Carmichael emerged as the black freedom struggle's most vocal anti-war critic. See Branch, *At Canaan's Edge*, 254–55, 308–9, 591–97, and Joseph, *The Midnight Hour*, 179–83.

25. Parks, "Whip of Black Power," 78.

26. Ibid.

27. Ibid., 78, 80, 82. See also, Joseph, *The Midnight Hour*, and "King Near to Stokely?" *Berkeley Barb*, May 19, 1967.

28. Parks, "Whip of Black Power," 82.

29. FBIKT 100-446080-NR, "Student Nonviolent Coordinating Committee: Stokely Carmichael," May 17, 1967, p. 2. FBIKT 100-446080-197, "Stokely Carmichael," p. 2.

FBIKT 100-446080-230, *Chicago Defender*, May 15, 1967. For Carmichael's plans to resume organizing see Stokely Carmichael to Lorna D. Smith, February 4, 1967, p. 1. SCLDS.

30. FBIKT 100-446080-240, Memorandum, "Stokely Carmichael: Director's Testimony Before House Appropriations Subcommittee February 16, 1967," May 17, 1967, p.1; FBIKT 100-446080-240X, "Proposed Appearance of Stokely Carmichael, Grand Rapids, Michigan, May 17, 1967," p. 1; and FBIKT 100-446080-205, "SNCC: Stokely Carmichael," May 17, 1967, p. 2. Bureau files reported Carmichael asserting that J. Edgar Hoover was in his "dotage and should retire." One angry citizen wrote the FBI director pledging support and alleging that, according to news accounts, Carmichael had referred to the director as "J. Edgar Notetaker." See FBIKT 100-446080-214 Teletype, May 17, 1967, p. 1, and FBIKT 100-446080-215, Correspondence to FBI director, May 18, 1967, p. 1. In Grand Rapids, Cleve Sellers gave a brief speech before Carmichael, discussing his decision to resist the draft. See FBIKT 100-446080-486, "Stokely Carmichael," July 24, 1967, pp. 1–4.

31. FBIKT 100-446080-288, Airtel, "Stokely Carmichael," June 8, 1967, p. 6.

32. FBIKT 100-446080-277, Memorandum, Assistant Attorney General Fred M. Vinson Jr. to Director Hoover, "Stokely Carmichael," June 13, 1967, p. 1; FBIKT 100-446080-454, Airgram, "Stokely Carmichael—Sedition," August 8, 1967, pp. 1–2; FBIKT 100-446080-455, Teletype, "Stokely Carmichael—Sedition," August 8, 1967, pp. 1–4; and FBIKT 100-446080-464, Airmail, From Seattle SAC to Director Hoover, "Stokely Carmichael—Sedition," August 8, 1967, pp. 1–2 (plus eight interviews).

33. FBIKT 100-446080-238, Airtel, Director Hoover to Atlanta SAC, "Stokely Carmichael," May 25, 1967, pp. 1–2.

34. Joseph, *The Midnight Hour*, 182–83.

35. *The Movement*, July 1967. SCLDS.

36. Sol Stern, "The Call Of the Panthers," *New York Times Magazine*, August 6, 1967.

37. Ibid.

38. *Time*, December 15, 1967, 28.

39. FBIKT 100-446080, *The Observer Review*, July 23, 1967.

40. Ibid.

41. Carmichael with Thelwell, *Ready for Revolution*, 573–77.

42. Carmichael, *Stokely Speaks*, 86.

43. Ibid., 88–89.

44. FBIKT 100-446080-521, Foreign Broadcast Information Service, Special Memorandum, "Reportage and Comments on Stokely Carmichael's Activities and Statements Abroad," p. 24.

45. Joseph, *The Midnight Hour*, 191–93; Carmichael with Thelwell, *Ready for Revolution*, 572–82; and Carson, *In Struggle*, 273.

46. Correspondence from Stokely Carmichael to SNCC, undated (probably Fall 1967), Reel 51, frame 14. SNCC Papers.

47. Carmichael with Thelwell, *Ready for Revolution*, 616–18, 622–32; Joseph, *The Midnight Hour*, 195–97; and Carson, *In Struggle*, 276–77.

48. FBIKT 100-446080-1306, "Ndugu Stokely: From Africa," pp. 1–8.

49. FBIKT 100-446080-1038, United States Information Agency, "Stokely Carmichael," January 23, 1968, pp. 1–5; FBIKT 100-446080-1038, "Stokely Carmichael: Talk at Kivukoni College, November 6, 1967," January 23, 1968, pp. 1–8; Carmichael with Thelwell, *Ready for Revolution*, 635–38; and "Stokely Irks African Rebel Leaders," *New York Post*, November 20, 1967.

50. For King and the Poor People's March see Garrow, *Bearing the Cross*; Fairclough, *Soul of America*; Branch, *At Canaan's Edge*; Michael K. Honey, *Going Down Jericho Road: The Memphis Strike, Martin Luther King's Last Campaign* (New York: W. W. Norton, 2007); and Thomas F. Jackson, *From Civil Rights to Human Rights: Martin Luther King, Jr. and the Struggle for Economic Justice* (Philadelphia: University of Pennsylvania Press, 2007).

51. Carmichael with Thelwell, *Ready for Revolution*, 648–50; FBIKT 100446080, "Stokely Carmichael," pp. 77–78; and *Muhammad Speaks*, February 23, 1968, 22.

52. FBIKT 100-446080-NR, "Washington Spring Project: Racial Matters," February 9, 1968, pp. 1–3.

53. Carmichael's trip was unexpected and a surprise to even his closest advisors. FBIKT 100-446080-1173, "Stokely Carmichael," February 26, 1968, pp. 1–12.

54. *London Observer*, March 24, 1968. SCLDS; *Baltimore Afro-American*, May 11, 1968, 21; *Muhammad Speaks*, May 24, 1968, 9; and Carmichael with Thelwell, *Ready for Revolution*, 652–56.

55. Carmichael with Thelwell, *Ready for Revolution*, 656–59.

56. Jules Milne, *Kwame Nkrumah: The Conakry Years: His Life and Letters* (London: Panaf Books, 1990), 261.

57. FBIKT 100-446080-1915, *Rocky Mountain News*, August 22, 1968, p. 70, and Airtel, Denver SAC to FBI Director, August 22, 1968, pp. 1–3.

58. Joseph, *The Midnight Hour*, 240.

59. The State Department had returned his passport months earlier after he agreed to stay out of banned countries, so he could honeymoon overseas. See *San Francisco Chronicle*, July 26, 1968 and *The Oregonian*, August 7, 1968. SCLDS.

60. For these speaking tours and the controversy that they elicited see *Greensboro Daily Times*, December 10, 1968; *Greensboro Record*, January 1, 1969; *Greensboro Record*, January 3, 1969; *San Jose Mercury*, January 3, 1969. SCLDS; and *Baltimore Afro-American*, December 28, 1968.

61. Joseph, *The Midnight Hour*, 246–47.

62. *The Sunday Times* (London), November 3, 1969, 28–29, 31.

63. Ethel Minor, "Black Activist's Activities in Africa," *Muhammad Speaks*, October 10, 1969, 35, 37–38.

64. *The Baltimore Afro-American*, October 14, 1969.

65. Carmichael with Thelwell, *Ready for Revolution*, 712.

66. *New York Times*, April 14, 1996, E9.

67. Kwame Ture and Charles Hamilton, *Black Power: The Politics of Liberation* (New York: Vintage, 1992), 187–99.

68. Charlie Cobb, "Revolution: From Stokely Carmichael to Kwame Ture," *The Black Scholar*, 27, no. 3–4 (Fall 1997), 32–38.

69. Carmichael with Thelwell, *Ready for Revolution*, 764–67.

70. The new scholarship on the postwar freedom era is dense. Important works include Robin D. G. Kelley, *Race Rebels: Culture, Politics, and the Black Working Class* (New York: Free Press, 1994); Robert Self, *American Babylon: Race and the Struggle for Postwar Oakland* (Princeton: Princeton University Press, 2003); Martha Biondi, *To Stand and Fight: The Struggle for Civil Rights in Postwar New York City* (Cambridge, MA: Harvard University Press, 2003); Rhonda Y. Williams, *The Politics of Public Housing: Black Women's Struggle Against Urban Inequality* (New York: Oxford University Press, 2004); Scot Brown, *Fighting For Us: Maulana Karenga, the US Organization, and Black Cultural Nationalism* (New York: New York University Press, 2003); Smethurst, *The Black Arts Movement*; Jeanne Theoharis and Komozi Woodard, eds., *Freedom North: Black Freedom Struggles Outside the South, 1940–1980* (New York: Palgrave Macmillan, 2003);

Sundiata Cha-Jua and Clarence Lang, "Strategies for Black Liberation in the Era of Globalization: Retronouveau Civil Rights, Militant Black Conservatism, and Radicalism," *The Black Scholar* 29 (Fall 1999), 25–47; Williams, *Black Politics*; Jones, *Black Panther Party*; Lazerow and Williams, *In Search*; and Joseph, *The Midnight Hour*. Some key works that specifically address the way in which history is written and the need for scholars to expansively rethink master narratives of the postwar era include Peniel E. Joseph, "Black Liberation Without Apology: Rethinking the Black Power Movement," *The Black Scholar*, 31, no.3–4 (Fall / Winter 2001), 217 and Joseph, "Preface" and "Introduction: Toward a Historiography of the Black Power Movement," in *The Black Power Movement: Rethinking the Civil Rights-Black Power Era* (New York: Routledge, 2006), xi–xii, 1–25. Payne, *Light of Freedom*, 413–41; Jeanne Theoharis, "Black Freedom Studies: Re-Imagining and Redefining the Fundamentals," *History Compass*, 4 (2006), 1–20; and Hogan, *Many Minds*, 1–10, 235–44.

CHAPTER 11

PROTECTION OR PATH TOWARD REVOLUTION?

BLACK POWER AND SELF-DEFENSE

SIMON WENDT

ALTHOUGH THE CURRENT WAVE OF HISTORICAL SCHOLARSHIP on black power has only begun to explore the richness and diversity of this movement, it has already fundamentally altered our understanding of the African American freedom struggle. In popular memory, Black Power continues to be reduced to angry cries for self-defense that fostered violent race riots, betrayed the integrationist and non-violent vision of earlier activism, and ultimately failed to achieve its seemingly unrealistic goals. In reality, as recent studies have shown, what came to be known as Black Power was a multidimensional movement with multilayered ideologies and agendas that accomplished much more than has been acknowledged. Black activists engaged in a wide range of political, cultural, and intellectual activism, which helped reinterpret African American identity and left a significant legacy that continues to shape American society to this day.[1]

While this new scholarship has introduced fresh perspectives and provided important new insights, few scholars have attempted to probe the evolution of self-defense tactics in the civil rights and Black Power eras. If we seek to understand the complexities of Black Power, however, we need to explore the roots and the development of armed resistance. Gaining a deeper understanding of these complexities will help us to answer some of the very same questions that students of Black Power are beginning to formulate. First, researching this aspect of black militancy sheds light on continuities and discontinuities between the post–World War II civil rights struggle and the Black Power movement. Second, focusing on armed resistance helps us to understand the evolution of protest strategies and radical ideologies within the black freedom movement of the 1950s and 1960s. A number of historians have provided tentative answers to these questions. Timothy Tyson, in his pioneering study of black militant Robert F. Williams, has suggested new ways of conceptualizing the links between the pre-1965 southern freedom struggle and the Black Power movement. According to Tyson, Williams's life exemplifies how these seemingly distinct movements "emerged from the same soil, confronted the same predicaments, and reflected the same quest for African-American freedom."[2] In a similar fashion, the scholarship of Emilye Crosby, Lance Hill, Christopher Strain, Akinyele Umoja, and myself has shown that southern activists, the nonviolent rhetoric of Martin Luther King Jr. and other civil rights leaders notwithstanding, used armed self-defense against racist terrorism on a widespread basis.[3] These findings cast doubt on traditional interpretations of Black Power—which regarded it as an abrupt rupture with the nonviolent idealism of Martin Luther King Jr.—and hint at neglected continuities between these two eras.

Yet a closer look at armed resistance in the 1960s also reveals conspicuous discontinuities. In the southern freedom movement, self-defense became a pragmatic necessity, which complemented nonviolent protest and voter registration drives in numerous civil rights campaigns. Consequently, such protective efforts were utilized mainly to help local movements survive in the face of white supremacist terrorism, although they also bolstered the morale of many activists and instilled pride in those who protected the movement by arms. In contrast, armed resistance efforts in the Black Power movement tended to play a more symbolic role. During the Black Power era, African Americans faced legalized state violence, not attacks by individual white terrorists that used extralegal attacks to stop southern civil rights activists. This made it much more difficult to define and combat the enemy. Thus, although radical groups such as the Black Panther Party (BPP) conceptualized self-defense as a revolutionary alternative to nonviolence, it ultimately served primarily as a gendered symbol of defiance and male psychological empowerment. In the case of the BPP, this affirmation of black manhood through self-defense played an important role in gaining publicity and in recruiting new members, but it also put strains on gender relations within the party, impeded their organizing efforts, provoked a wave of government repression, and obscured the party's political message. While some of the roots of black militants' self-defense strategies are to be found in the Deep South, the dynamic reinterpretation of the meaning of armed resistance and revolutionary violence in the Black Power era marks a significant turning point in the struggle for black liberation.[4]

Throughout the 1950s and the first half of the 1960s, the most important benefit of self-defense was that it helped local movements in the Deep South survive when confronted with violent attacks from white supremacy terrorists. As early as 1957, black activists defended themselves against white aggression in Little Rock, Arkansas; Birmingham, Alabama; and Monroe, North Carolina. In the dangerous aftermath of the desegregation crisis at Little Rock's Central High School, Daisy Bates, the local leader of school integration efforts and president of the city's chapter of the National Association for the Advancement of Colored People (NAACP), relied on a "volunteer guard committee" for protection. Since neither federal nor state authorities cared about the safety of Bates, some of her friends and neighbors began to guard her home with shotguns and pistols. On one occasion in 1958, the NAACP activist herself repelled an invader with a volley of gunshots.[5]

In Birmingham, charismatic minister Rev. Fred Shuttlesworth, who was constantly threatened and attacked by white racists for leading the city's freedom movement, accepted similar protection efforts from what came to be known as the Civil Rights Guards. Led by Colonel Stone "Buck" Johnson, one of Shuttlesworth's most loyal followers, the members of this defense group protected the pastor's church and the parsonage. On several occasions, the Civil Rights Guards successfully prevented bomb attacks against the two buildings.[6] The same year that the Birmingham defense group formed, ex-marine and NAACP activist Robert F. Williams organized a protective agency in Monroe, North Carolina. After Klansmen terrorized the black community for demanding the racial integration of the town's swimming pool, Williams and other military veterans established a sophisticated rifle club that guarded the homes of civil rights leaders with pistols, machine guns, and dynamite and, on one occasion, fended off an attack by the Ku Klux Klan.[7]

In the first half of the 1960s, as another wave of racist terrorism swept over the Deep South, more formal and informal black defense groups formed in the region. Most of these organizations were established in 1964, a year when hundreds of nonviolent protests and voter registration campaigns challenged the racial status quo in Alabama, Mississippi, Louisiana, and other southern states. In Tuscaloosa, Alabama, black activists formed a defense organization after police brutally dispersed nonviolent protestors with tear gas. Trying to channel the anger of a number of men who intended to retaliate against the white community into constructive organizing, black war veterans instead proposed the formation of a defense organization that would protect the movement against white aggression and intimidation from the United Klans of America, which was headquartered in Tuscaloosa. Led by Korean War veteran Joseph Mallisham, the group that they organized operated like a military combat unit. A small executive board planned the unit's operations, while ordinary members executed them. Tuscaloosa's defense squad concentrated on protecting the homes of movement leaders, but it also was on call if nonviolent demonstrators were in trouble. One night in July 1964, Mallisham and his comrades rescued several teenage demonstrators from an angry mob at the local movie theater and repelled a Klan attack while chauffeuring the teenagers back to the black neighborhood. Although the nonviolent Tuscaloosa movement won stunning victories in 1964, forcing white authorities to desegregate the city's schools and public accommodations by the end of 1965, the defense group continued to patrol the city's black section for several years.[8]

During the Freedom Summer project of the Student Nonviolent Coordinating Committee (SNCC), which brought hundreds of white volunteers to Mississippi to call attention to the discrimination and racist violence suffered by African Americans in the Magnolia State, a number of local activists used their guns to defend themselves, their communities, and the volunteers they housed in their homes. Assisting voter registration efforts in the all-black community of Milestone, perplexed white student Eugene Nelson wrote home: "The Movement may be non-violent but the people here are by no means so when it comes to protecting their families and property."[9] Indeed, a majority of African Americans who lived in the Milestone area protected their property with guns. Volunteers were required to honk a prearranged signal before approaching black farms. If they failed to do so, black guards were likely to fire at their car.[10] In some towns and cities, informal defense groups protected black churches and the homes of local civil rights leaders and sometimes became enforcers of boycotts against white merchants. In Leake County, for example, black men guarded the newly built community center of the all-black town of Harmony. After a Klan attack on the black community, one volunteer explained in a letter that local blacks had armed themselves because they did "not intend to have all their hard work go up in flames right away."[11] Across Mississippi, similar defense efforts operated in tandem with nonviolent voter registration drives and other civil rights campaigns until 1968.[12]

One of the most famous defense organizations of the southern freedom movement was the Deacons for Defense and Justice, which formed in 1964 in the small mill town of Jonesboro, Louisiana. Armed with rifles and pistols, the Deacons patrolled Jonesboro's black neighborhood day and night to prevent racist attacks. In 1965, black activists formed a Deacons chapter in Bogalusa, Louisiana. The Bogalusa group gained national fame after several shootouts with the Ku Klux Klan. When several carloads of Klansmen shot into the residence of a local civil rights leader at the beginning of April 1965, for example, fifteen armed Deacons welcomed them with volleys of disciplined gunfire. Like the Tuscaloosa group, the Deacons patrolled the black neighborhood, protected the door-to-door canvassing of civil rights volunteers, and provided armed escorts for activists of the Congress of Racial Equality (CORE), which assisted many local movements in Louisiana.[13] Racist attackers who ventured into the black section of town quickly learned that the Deacons took their protection duties seriously. On occasion, white invaders confronted a small army of black men, who suddenly emerged from bushes and dark driveways. Local activist A. Z. Young reminisced about one of those encounters: "They was all smiles. It was 'yes sir' and 'no sir,' and so we let 'em go, and they ain't been back."[14] Most whites stayed away from the black neighborhood once news of the black defense group's patrols had spread. The Deacons, which established several chapters and affiliates in the state, remained an integral part of the civil rights movement in Louisiana at least until 1967.

Although armed protection was primarily a man's job, which many black defenders considered an affirmation of their manhood, women knew how to use guns as well. Southern protective groups consisted primarily of military veterans with a working-class background and did not admit female members, but there were occasions when black women armed themselves to protect civil rights activities. During SNCC's Freedom Summer project, for instance, one volunteer was shocked to find that her host Mrs. Fairly was armed to the teeth. "I met Mrs. Fairly coming down the hall from the front porch carrying a rifle in one hand [and] a pistol in the other," he wrote home in July 1964. "I don't now know what is going on . . . [All she said was] 'You go to sleep; let me fight for you.'"[15] SNCC worker Jo Anne Ooiman Robinson was similarly bewildered when the woman that she stayed with told her about the ax that she hid under her bed. Robinson became even more alarmed when learning that the local activist had slept with a gun under her pillow, which she removed only after nearly shooting a neighbor's son. In April 1965, the wife of Bogalusa activist Robert Hicks, armed with a pistol, saved a CORE worker from a group of Klansmen that had followed him to the Hicks residence. Three months later, a black woman in Ferriday, Louisiana, returned fire when a group of Klansmen shot into her home.[16] While men might have viewed self-defense as a male prerogative, women could and did contribute to the safety of southern black communities during the civil rights struggle of the 1960s.

The protection efforts of these black men and women predated the calls of Black Power militants for self-defense and frequently helped local activists to hang on in an extremely hostile and dangerous environment. As John Salter, a white leader of nonviolent protests in Jackson, Mississippi, in the early 1960s, later reflected, "No one knows what kind of massive racist retaliation would have been directed against grass-roots black people had the black community not had a healthy measure of firearms within it."[17] The fact that the number of white attacks against civil rights activists sharply declined in Monroe, Tuscaloosa, Jonesboro, Bogalusa, and other southern locales once African Americans began to fight back suggests that Klansmen hesitated to attack the black community if their own lives were at risk. For the Black Power movement, such examples of armed resistance were important insofar as they inspired militant organizations such as the Black Panther Party and contributed to the radicalization of the southern freedom struggle. Robert F. Williams and the Deacons for Defense and Justice in particular became minor celebrities among black nationalist circles. Huey Newton and Bobby Seale, the founders of the BPP, later said that the example of Williams and the Deacons had had a great influence on the paramilitary character of their organization.[18] More important, the fact that armed resistance frequently proved very effective in thwarting racist violence triggered numerous disputes among civil rights activists. In growing debates on self-defense within CORE and SNCC between 1963 and 1966, an increasing number of activists came to view armed resistance as a pragmatic necessity. By 1966, the year that Stokely Carmichael introduced the term Black Power to the vocabulary of the black freedom movement, some accepted self-defense as an integral part of the black freedom struggle in the South.

Yet by the time that SNCC and CORE embraced Black Power and self-defense, armed protection became less important in the southern freedom movement. Some pockets of violent white opposition survived, but by 1967, federal and state authorities finally began to take seriously their responsibility to protect civil rights protest. By the late 1960s, groups such as the Deacons for Defense and Justice and Tuscaloosa's protective agency were no longer active. Since the primary reason for their founding had been the security of black communities, their work was simply no longer necessary.[19] Many proponents of Black Power thought otherwise, however, making self-defense a central pillar of a multilayered agenda that included black political and economic power, self-determination, antiracism, and radical internationalism. In many ways, self-defense in the Black Power era represented a revival as well as the continuation of traditions of black militancy that predated the iconographic imagery of the BPP and others.

But any analysis of this revival would be incomplete without taking into account the black nationalist critique of nonviolence and advocacy of self-defense, a strain of Black Power that grew outside the South but might have been even more powerful in shaping the ideas of the new militants. As early as 1961, the New York–based black nationalist journal *Liberator* hailed the "heroic sacrifices" of the nonviolent freedom riders but questioned the efficacy of their tactics. "Unlike them," the editors wrote, "we can feel no love or compassion for either the white hoodlums who attacked them or the white officials who failed to protect them." From the perspective of the *Liberator*, the Freedom Ride only proved the futility of nonviolence.[20] Anecdotal evidence suggests that a number of black militants shared such skepticism primarily because they tended to regard nonviolence as a threat to their manhood. In June 1963, for example, one reader of the *Baltimore Afro-American* insisted, "To those who offer the line that 'nothing is accomplished through violence', they are simply misguided hypocrites attempting to justify cowardice."[21] A black New Yorker similarly concluded in a letter to the same newspaper, "Moses' law was an eye for an eye and a tooth for a tooth. That is the only kind of law real men can respect. Only cowards will hide behind a 'love everybody' teaching."[22] Disputing King and other civil rights activists, these skeptics suggested that nonviolence would only compound the social and political impotence of black men.

In contrast to these condemnations, which received little attention outside the black community, the tirades of Malcolm X against Martin Luther King Jr. were publicized across America, making the black Muslim the most well-known critic of the movement's nonviolent orthodoxy. As the spokesman of Elijah Muhammad's Nation of Islam, Malcolm X preached the sect's gospel of black pride, moral uplift, and economic self-reliance. In addition, he lambasted King's philosophy of nonviolence and insisted on blacks' right to self-defense. "Any Negro who teaches other Negroes to turn the other cheek in the face of attack," he argued in a 1963 television interview, "is disarming the Negro of his God-given right, of his moral right, of his natural right, [and] of his intelligent right to defend himself."[23] From the Muslim minister's perspective, there was no "turn-the-other-cheek revolution." Revolutions, he explained in his famous "Message to the Grassroots," could not be based on loving one's enemy but involved bloodshed, and "modern Uncle Toms" like Martin Luther King Jr. served only as pawns in the white man's scheme to keep African Americans passive and powerless. "Be peaceful, be courteous, obey the law, respect everyone," he told his followers, "but if someone puts his hands on you, send him to the cemetery."[24]

After his split with the Nation of Islam in March 1964, Malcolm X continued to call upon blacks to defend themselves with arms if attacked by white racists. Through his secular Organization of Afro-American Unity (OAAU), whose program encouraged blacks to control their own educational, cultural, economic, and political institutions, he sought to convince African Americans of the need for active armed resistance against white violence.[25] Even before founding the OAAU, Malcolm reiterated his appeal to abandon nonviolence and predicted that the masses of African Americans would soon pick up the gun. The time was ripe, he said, "for the American Negro to fight back in self-defense whenever and wherever he is being unjustly and unlawfully attacked."[26] In particular "in areas where the government seems unable or unwilling to protect our people," blacks ought to organize rifle clubs to safeguard their communities.[27]

Malcolm's militant message—which not only focused on armed resistance but also stressed black pride and Pan-Africanism—had an immense impact on black militants across the United States. In April 1964, the *Liberator* praised Malcolm for "saying out loud what many Americans of African descent have been thinking for years."[28] Echoing this militant gospel a few months later, black nationalist Richard Henry of the Detroit-based Group on Advanced Leadership (GOAL) called for "a quick and widespread formation of rifle clubs by Negroes all across the North" to assist southern Blacks in an imminent guerilla war against white terrorists.[29] A reader of *Ebony* seconded such proposals, arguing in November 1964 that it was "time we stopped turning the other cheek," as Malcolm X had urged blacks to do.[30] The assassination of the militant Muslim only reinforced the power of his message, which became one of the founding documents of the Black Power movement. As William Van Deburg has pointed out, Malcolm X "became a Black Power paradigm—the archetype, reference point, and spiritual adviser in absentia for a generation of Afro-American activists."[31]

The black freedom movement in Cleveland, Ohio, illustrates how Malcolm's tenets translated into militant action even before his violent death. In 1963, a few black Clevelanders began to organize nonviolent demonstrations to protest against de facto school segregation and racial discrimination.[32] The growing disenchantment with nonviolence and the decision of local civil rights leader Lewis Robinson to form a self-defense organization to be prepared for white violence the following year was in large part a consequence of Malcolm's teachings. "[B]eing practical," Robinson later said about the influence of Malcolm on his thinking, "it's impossible for a Black man with his eyes open in America, not to think like Brother Malcolm."[33] In February and March 1964, Robinson and fellow activists repeatedly discussed the black Muslim's teachings, in particular his call to form rifle clubs to protect the black community against racist attacks. In early April 1964, after hearing Malcolm X speak about "The Ballot or the Bullet" in Cleveland, Robinson announced to startled news reporters that he would soon form the Medgar Evers Rifle Club, the name being a tribute to the NAACP leader from Mississippi who was assassinated in 1963.[34]

Unlike southern protective squads, however, the Medgar Evers Rifle Club was primarily a symbol of psychological empowerment, not a physical necessity. Since there were no overt racist threats against civil rights activists (Robinson began to receive threatening phone calls only after he had announced the formation of the defense group), Robinson's rifle club served no protective purpose. Rather it contributed to a new sense of male pride among the group's members. After several weeks of target practice on a farm east of Cleveland, the wives of the black defenders, as Robinson remembered in his autobiography, "showed a new respect for their men and the men, in turn, felt like men, masters of their destinies, protectors of their women and families."[35] In a 1967 interview, the group's leader readily admitted that his organization represented "a psychological way of our educating the Blacks and conditioning them that we're going to have to fight for ourselves."[36] In the end, this affirmation of manhood, coupled with the inspiring teachings of Malcolm X, resolved Robinson and other activists to form a black nationalist cultural center in downtown Cleveland that was intended to promote civic, political, and economic responsibility among underprivileged black youth. Opened in November 1964, the Jomo Freedom Kenyatta House became an important community center and helped reduce juvenile delinquency by offering recreation and cultural events for Cleveland's black teenagers.[37]

The history of the Cleveland movement is instructive because it illustrates some of the differences between self-defense in the southern civil rights struggle and the Black Power movement. The Black Panther Party, for example, similar to the Medgar Evers Rifle Club, utilized self-defense mostly as an effective symbol of defiance. Of course, as Nikhil Pal Singh has pointed out, the Panthers's self-defense efforts were "strategic choices and carefully posed challenges to the so-called legitimate forms of state violence that had become all too regularly used within black communities," and subsequent shootouts had serious consequences for the organization, including numerous incarcerations and deaths of party members.[38] But the BPP's attempts to challenge this tradition of state violence functioned mostly on a symbolic level, namely as a means of gaining publicity, as an affirmation of black manhood, and as tool to recruit new members.

The BPP's well-known armed demonstration at the California State Legislature in Sacramento on May 2, 1967, is perhaps the best example of how such strategic symbolism could gain publicity. Newton and Seale were confident that their widely publicized protest would help them achieve their long-term goal: to establish the BPP as the "vanguard group" of the black revolution. Indeed, within days of the Sacramento protest, blacks from across the nation inundated the organization's Oakland office with requests for permission to start additional chapters.[39]

Within the organization, self-defense also became an important means to affirm black manhood. "The Black woman found it difficult to respect the Black man because he didn't even define himself as a man!" Newton explained in an interview. He was certain that his organization, together with other black militants, had "regained our mind and our manhood."[40] Eldridge Cleaver, the organization's minister of information, similarly pointed out in a 1968 interview that the BPP was "a natural organization" for the young, since it was organized by their peers and provided "very badly needed standards of masculinity."[41] In the early years of the organization, this standard appeared to be defined primarily by guns and the willingness to use them. While similar links between self-defense and black manhood could also be observed in southern defense organizations, such affirmations of manliness remained largely a by-product of the necessity to defend black communities against racist attacks.

Finally, the early fixation on self-defense in the Black Panther Party not only gained the organization publicity and instilled pride in its members but also became one of the reasons why many people joined the group in the first place. Newton and Seale knew that recruiting the unemployed or underemployed "brother off the block" was facilitated by their organization's martial imagery. This seems to have been true not only for the Oakland organization. In the

Philadelphia BPP, for example, as Matthew Countryman has pointed out in his study of the city's black freedom struggle, "it was the party's emphasis on 'the gun' that attracted the vast majority of party members."[42]

As beneficial as this focus on self-defense might have been in creating powerful images of fearless Black men, it was fraught with problems. For one thing, the oft-cited sexism and misogyny that permeated Black Power organizations such as the Black Panther Party was closely linked to notions of masculine self-defense. Of course, gender relations within the party were subject to change, and many female members actively influenced the organization's views on the role of women in the struggle for black liberation. In the 1970s, for example, the number of women in leadership positions increased considerably, although this was primarily due to the leadership vacuum that the imprisonment or exile of male party leaders had created. Still, at least until the late 1960s, the BPP remained a largely male-centered organization that regarded women as readily available sexual objects rather than equal and respected party members. Recent research suggests that this dynamic was not confined to the original Panthers but was replicated in other chapters as well (e.g., Baltimore and Philadelphia).[43] In Ron Karenga's US organization, male members were even more explicit in their adamant opposition to women's equality. Like the Nation of Islam, US required its female members to submit to male leadership and male authority without question, clearly impeding black women's ability to influence the program of US and other black nationalist groups.[44] As Stephen Ward has noted, the Black Power movement's frequent use of the metaphor of manhood "and the male-centered political framework that it represented could be, and too often was, used to silence and discipline the activism of Black women."[45]

It is important to point out, however, that women were far from passive supporters in the Black Power era. Recent studies have demonstrated that black women were often the backbone of community organizing efforts in the urban freedom movements of the late 1960s and early 1970s.[46] More importantly, black feminist organizations such as the Third World Women's Alliance did not simply challenge male-centered interpretations of the black freedom struggle but actively interpreted and shaped Black Power politics and ideology.[47] Some female activists, contesting male Black Power activists' proclaimed protective prerogative, defended themselves against white aggression. In 1967, for example, Baltimore activist Marion Johnson, after moving into one of the city's last white-only public housing complexes, armed herself to protect her children from white supremacists who had burned crosses in the area. The Black Women's United Front, another black feminist organization that was founded in the early 1970s, established defense committees for female black prisoners who had protected themselves against sexual attacks by male prison guards.[48]

In the case of the Panthers, another problem that was closely related to masculine self-defense strategies was the tendency of some activists to overlook the importance of political organizing and social activism. According to Newton's analysis of the early years of the organization, many party members seemed to believe that Mao Zedong's tenet that political power grew out of the barrel of a gun meant that political power was the gun. As he told his followers in 1971, they seemed to ignore that the "culmination of political power" was "the owner-ship and control of land and the institutions thereon so that we can get rid of the gun."[49] Such misunderstandings impeded the effectiveness of the Oakland BPP's organizing efforts within the black community. Focusing on the history of the Panthers in Philadelphia, Countryman similarly concluded that "the gun as a symbol of resurgent manhood" hampered the party's "ability to develop a sustain-able long-term strategy for achieving its goals."[50]

The most harmful consequence of self-defense tactics in the Black Power era was the wave of government repression that black militants' martial posture provoked in the late 1960s and early 1970s. To confront the alleged threat of the BPP and other militant organizations, the Federal Bureau of Investigation used the sophisticated domestic counterintelligence program COINTELPRO.[51] Huey Newton was one among very few militants who admitted that the BPP's self-defense stance became counterproductive once white authorities declared war on the Panthers. In his memoirs, Newton pointed out that the efforts of white authorities to disrupt the activities of his organization had not started until the BPP staged its armed demonstration in Sacramento. Other chapters faced similar problems. Numerous incarcerations and infiltration by police informers weakened the Baltimore chapter considerably. In Philadelphia, police raided the homes of party members and indicted Black Panthers on fabricated charges.[52] By 1969, having become aware of these problems, Huey Newton and Bobby Seale deliberately toned down the militant rhetoric of the party. As early as 1968, they had dropped the term self-defense from the group's original name (Black Panther Party for Self-Defense). But their hope that these measures and a less provocative language would bring an end to police harassment and government repression were ultimately illusory.[53]

The public image of the Panthers, too, changed little, Newton's attempts to use less militant language notwithstanding. In the mind of most Americans, the BPP—and, in fact, the Black Power movement in general—remained inextri-cably linked to guns and violence. The news media continued to focus on the organization's paramilitary character, ignoring the discrimination and abject pov-erty that Newton and Seale wanted to call attention to. It was no accident that the BPP's ten-point platform discussed self-defense after the demand for self-determination, full employment, decent housing, and education for the black community. Yet the American public paid no attention to the efforts of the party to alleviate these dismal conditions, including its free breakfast programs for school children, legal and medical assistance for the poor, and other commu-nity services. Self-defense thus obscured some of the most important messages of Black Power and contributed to the resentment and subsequent misconceptions that burdened the movement in the 1960s and 1970s.

One problem that exacerbated white America's hostility was Black Power mili-tants' tendency to blur the distinctions between self-defense and revolutionary violence. Interestingly, Robert F. Williams was among the first activists to reinter-pret the meaning of self-defense for the black freedom struggle. Williams came out of a tradition of homegrown southern militancy that stressed blacks' right to defend themselves against racist terrorism. Later, however, while living in Cuba and China, he became an ardent advocate of revolutionary violence against the white oppressor. According to Williams, urban guerrilla warfare constituted a form of self-defense. In September 1964, he explained this logic to a journalist of the National Guardian. "[Y]our first step, if you're abused, is to ask people not to abuse you," he said. "Then you defend yourself against that abuse: and then, if necessary, you must be prepared to destroy in order to defend."[54] From this perspective, it was difficult to see any distinction between self-defense and aggressive violence.

Many Black Power organizations, including the BPP, echoed Williams and cited the theories of Frantz Fanon, Mao Zedong, and Che Guevara as additional evidence for their claims that aggressive violence against white authorities was a justified form of armed resistance. For African Americans, as Huey Newton wrote in his memoirs, "the only way to win freedom was to meet force with force. At bottom, this is a form of self-defense. Although that defense might at times take on characteristics of aggression, in the final analysis, the people do not initiate; they simply respond to what has been inflicted upon them."[55] Other revolutionary nationalists, including the Revolutionary Action Movement, the Republic of New Africa, and the Black Liberation Army, followed a similar logic. In contrast to the rationale of southern defense groups such as the Deacons for Defense and Justice, the ultimate goal of the Black Power movement's "self-defense" strategy was not simply the safety of the black community but the creation of a new and just social order that would have to be brought about by revolutionary violence if necessary. Although many activists had abandoned previous plans for armed revolution by 1972, focusing on political organizing instead, this reinterpretation of defensive violence as part of a protracted struggle for black liberation remains one of the lasting legacies of Black Power.[56]

NOTES

1. The most important works include Peniel E. Joseph, *Waiting 'Til the Midnight Hour: A Narrative History of Black Power in America* (New York: Henry Holt, 2006); Peniel E. Joseph, ed., *The Black Power Movement: Rethinking the Civil Rights-Black Power Era* (New York: Routledge, 2006); Matthew J. Countryman, *Up South: Civil Rights and Black Power in Philadelphia* (Philadelphia: University of Pennsylvania Press, 2006); James Edward Smethurst, *The Black Arts Movement: Literary Nationalism in the 1960s and 1970s* (Chapel Hill: University of North Carolina Press, 2005); Jeffrey O. G. Ogbar, *Black Power: Radical Politics and African American Identity* (Baltimore: John Hopkins University Press, 2004); Nikhil Pal Singh, *Black Is a Country: Race and the Unfinished Struggle for Democracy* (Cambridge, MA: Harvard University Press, 2004); Scot Brown, *Fighting for US: Maulena Karenga, the US Organization, and Black Cultural Nationalism* (New York: New York University Press, 2003); Robert O. Self, *American Babylon: Race and the Struggle for Postwar Oakland* (Princeton: Princeton University Press, 2003); Yohuru Williams, *Black Politics/White Power: Civil Rights, Black Power, and the Black Panthers in New Haven* (St. James, NY: Brandywine, 2000); Komozi Woodard, *A Nation Within a Nation: Amiri Baraka (LeRoi Jones) & Black Power Politics* (Chapel Hill: University of North Carolina Press, 1999); Charles E. Jones, ed., *The Black Panther Party [Reconsidered]* (Baltimore: Black Classic, 1998). An earlier study that continues

to provide a good overview but focuses on the cultural dimensions of the movement is William L. Van Deburg, *New Day in Babylon: The Black Power Movement and American Culture, 1965–1975* (Chicago: University of Chicago Press, 1992).

2. Timothy B. Tyson, *Radio Free Dixie: Robert F. Williams and the Roots of Black Power* (Chapel Hill: University of North Carolina Press, 1999), p. 3.

3. Emilye Crosby, "'This Nonviolent Stuff Ain't No Good. It'll Get Ya Killed': Teaching about Self-Defense in the African American Freedom Struggle," in *Teaching the American Civil Rights Movement: Freedom's Bittersweet Song*, eds. Julie Buckner Armstrong, Susan Edwards, Houston Roberson, and Rhonda Williams (New York: Routledge, 2002), pp. 159–73; Crosby, *A Little Taste of Freedom: The Black Freedom Struggle in Claiborne County, Mississippi* (Chapel Hill: University of North Carolina Press, 2005); Lance E. Hill, *The Deacons for Defense: Armed Resistance and the Civil Rights Movement* (Chapel Hill: University of North Carolina Press, 2004); Christopher Strain, *Pure Fire: Armed Self-Defense as Activism in the Civil Rights Era* (Athens: University of Georgia Press, 2005); Akinyele O. Umoja, "The Ballot and the Bullet: A Comparative Analysis of Armed Resistance in the Civil Rights Movement," *Journal of Black Studies* 29, no. 4 (March 1999): pp. 558–78; Akinyele O. Umoja, "'We Will Shoot Back': The Natchez Model and Paramilitary Organization in the Mississippi Freedom Movement," *Journal of Black Studies* 32, no. 3 (January 2002): pp. 271–94; Akinyele O. Umoja, "1964: The Beginning of the End of Nonviolence in the Mississippi Freedom Movement," *Radical History Review* 85 (Winter 2003): pp. 201–26; Simon Wendt, *The Spirit and the Shotgun: Armed Resistance and the Struggle for Civil Rights* (Gainesville: University Press of Florida, 2007); Simon Wendt, "'Urge People Not to Carry Guns': Armed Self-Defense in the Louisiana Civil Rights Movement and the Radicalization of the Congress of Racial Equality," *Louisiana History* 45, no. 3 (Summer 2004): pp. 261–86.

4. For a more detailed discussion of these differences, see Wendt, *The Spirit*.

5. Daisy Bates, *The Long Shadow of Little Rock: A Memoir* (New York: David McKay, 1962), pp. 94, 96, 111, 162; Statement by Mrs. L. C. (Daisy) Bates, Arkansas State President National Association for the Advancement of Colored People, August 13, 1959, box 3, folder 5. Daisy Bates Papers, State Historical Society of Wisconsin (hereafter cited as SHSW); Grif Stockley, *Daisy Bates: Civil Rights Crusader from Arkansas* (Jackson: University Press of Mississippi, 2005), p. 186.

6. Andrew M. Manis, *A Fire You Can't Put Out: The Civil Rights Life of Birmingham's Reverend Fred Shuttlesworth* (Tuscaloosa: University of Alabama Press), pp. 110, 117–18, 169–70; Rev. Fred Shuttlesworth, interview by James Mosby, transcript, September 1968, p. 18. Ralph J. Bunche Oral History Collection, Moorland-Spingarn Research Center, Howard University, Washington, DC (hereafter cited as Bunche Collection).

7. Tyson, *Radio Free Dixie*, pp. 80–89.

8. See Wendt, *The Spirit*, pp. 42–65.

9. Eugene Nelson to Dear Parents, July 3, 1964. Eugene Nelson Papers, SHSW.

10. Griffin McLaurin, interview by Harriet Tanzman, tape recording, March 6, 2000. Civil Rights Documentation Project, L. Zenobia Coleman Library, Tougaloo College, Tougaloo, MS (hereafter cited as Coleman Library); Steven Bingham, "Mississippi Letter." Steven Bingham Papers, SHSW.

11. Nicholas von Hoffman, *Mississippi Notebook* (New York: David White, 1964), pp. 94–95; Ms. Winson Hudson, telephone interview by John Rachal, transcript, August 31, 1995, p. 103. Mississippi Oral History Program, McCain Library and Archives, University of Southern Mississippi, Hattiesburg; Rims Barber, interview by Kim Lacy Rogers and Own Brooks, tape recording, August 30, 1995. Delta Oral History

Project, Coleman Library; Elizabeth Sutherland, ed., *Letters from Mississippi* (New York: McGraw-Hill), 115.

12. See Crosby, *Taste of Freedom*, pp. 167–88; Umoja, "We Will Shoot Back," pp. 271–94; Umoja, "1964," pp. 201–26; Wendt, *The Spirit*, pp. 100–152.

13. For a detailed account and discussion of the Deacons' activities, see Hill, *Deacons for Defense*; Wendt, "Urge People Not to Carry Guns," pp. 261–86; and Wendt, *The Spirit*, pp. 66–99.

14. Quoted in "The Deacons," *Newsweek*, August 2, 1965, p. 28.

15. Quoted in Doug McAdam, *Freedom Summer* (New York: Oxford University Press, 1988), p. 90.

16. "Diary," entry July 14, 1964, box 2, folder 1. Jo Anne Ooiman Robinson Papers, SHSW; Sutherland, *Letters from Mississippi*, p. 45; "Summary of Incidents in Bogalusa, Louisiana, April 7–9," 1965, box 1, folder 6. Southern Regional Office Files (hereafter cited as SRO), SHSW; "4/7/65 Bogalusa, LA," box 7, folder 6. SRO; "Concordia (Ferriday) July 21, 1965," box 4, folder 7. SRO.

17. John R. Salter and Don B. Kates Jr., "The Necessity for Access to Firearms by Dissenters and Minorities Whom Government Is Unwilling or Unable to Protect," in *Restricting Handguns: The Liberal Skeptics Speak Out*, ed., Donald B. Kates Jr. (Croton-on-Hudson, NY: North River, 1979), p. 192.

18. Bobby Seale, *A Lonely Rage: The Autobiography of Bobby Seale* (New York: New York Times Books, 1978), p. 130; Huey P. Newton, *Revolutionary Suicide* (New York: Harcourt Brace Jovanovich, 1973), p. 111.

19. For a more detailed account of this process, see Wendt, *The Spirit*.

20. "Freedom Riders Go Beyond the New Frontier," *Liberator* 1, no. 6 (June 1961): 1–2.

21. Keith Younger, "Violence vs Nonviolence," *Baltimore Afro-American*, June 1, 1963, p. 4.

22. Mr. Revresbo, "Eye for an Eye," *Baltimore Afro-American*, August 24, 1963, p. 4.

23. "Malcolm X Talks with Kenneth B. Clark," in *Malcolm X: The Man and his Time*, ed., John Henrik Clark (New York: Macmillan, 1969), p. 176.

24. "Message to the Grass Roots," in *Malcolm X Speaks: Selected Speeches and Statements*, ed., George Breitman (New York: Pathfinder, 1989), pp. 9, 12.

25. Malcolm X with Alex Haley, *The Autobiography of Malcolm X* (New York: Grove Press, 1965), p. 416. On the OAAU, see William W. Sales Jr., *From Civil Rights to Black Liberation: Malcolm X and the Organization of Afro-American Unity* (Boston: South End Press, 1994).

26. Quoted in M. S. Handler, "Malcolm X Sees Rise in Violence," *New York Times*, March 13, 1964, p. 20.

27. George Todd, "Malcolm X Explains His Rifle Statement," *Amsterdam News*, March 28, 1964, p. 35; Gertrude Samuels, "Feud Within the Black Muslims," *New York Times Magazine*, March 22, 1964, p. 104; William Worthy, "Malcolm X Plans for Rifle Clubs," *Baltimore Afro-American*, March 21, 1964, p. 2.

28. Daniel H. Watts, "Malcolm X: Self-Defense vs. Submission," *Liberator* 4, no. 4 (April 1964): p. 3.

29. Quoted in "Form Rifle Clubs, Militant Detroiter Urges," *Jet*, July 16, 1964, p. 7.

30. Dealia Mathis, letter to the editor, *Ebony*, November 1964, p. 16.

31. Van Deburg, *New Day*, p. 2.

32. On the struggle to integrate the city's schools, see Leonard Nathaniel Moore, "The School Desegregation Crisis of Cleveland, Ohio, 1963–1964: The Catalyst for Black Political Power in a Northern City," *Journal of Urban History* 28, no. 2 (January 2002): pp. 135–57.

33. Lewis Robinson, interview by John Britton, transcript, November 15, 1967, pp. 19–20. Bunche Collection.

34. Lewis G. Robinson, *The Making of a Man: An Autobiography* (Cleveland: Green and Sons, 1970), p. 78; "Negro Rifle Club Leader Expects White Violence," *Cleveland Press*, April 6, 1964, p. A1.
35. Robinson, *The Making*, p. 121.
36. Lewis Robinson, interview by John Britton, transcript, November 15, 1967, p. 8. Bunche Collection.
37. Robinson, *The Making*, p. 122–30.
38. Nikhil Pal Singh, "The Black Panthers and the 'Undeveloped Country' of the Left," in *The Black Panther Party [Reconsidered]*, p. 81.
39. Huey P. Newton, "The Correct Handling of a Revolution: July 20, 1967," in *To Die for the People: The Writings of Huey P. Newton* (New York: Random House, 1972), pp. 15–16; Newton, *Revolutionary Suicide*, p. 122.
40. "Interview with Huey Newton," in *Black Protest Thought in the Twentieth Century*, eds., August Meier, Elliot Rudwick, and Francis L. Brodwick, 2nd ed. (Indianapolis: Bobbs-Merrill, 1971), p. 508.
41. "Playboy Interview: Eldridge Cleaver," *Playboy*, December 1968, p. 92.
42. Bobby Seale, *Seize the Time: The Story of the Black Panther Party and Huey P. Newton* (New York: Vintage, 1970), p. 85; Countryman, *Up South*, p. 287.
43. Ogbar, *Black Power*, pp. 102, 103–6; Erika Doss, "Imaging the Panthers: Representing Black Power and Masculinity, 1960s–1990s," *Prospects* 23 (1998): p. 493; Tracye Matthews, "'No One Ever Asks What a Man's Place in the Revolution Is': The Politics of Gender in the Black Panther Party, 1966–1971," in *The Black Panther Party [Reconsidered]*, ed. Charles E. Jones (Baltimore: Black Classic, 1998), pp. 269, 278; Norbert Finzsch, "'Picking Up the Gun': Die Black Panther Party zwischen gewaltsamer Revolution und sozialer Reform, 1966–1984," *Amerikastudien* 44, no. 2 (1999): p. 239; Rhonda Y. Williams, "Black Women, Urban Politics, and Engendering Black Power," in *The Black Power Movement: Rethinking the Civil Rights-Black Power Era*, ed. Peniel E. Joseph (New York: Routledge, 2006), pp. 89–90; Countryman, *Up South*, pp. 287–88, 293.
44. Andrew Claude Clegg, *An Original Man: The Life and Times of Elijah Muhammad* (New York: St. Martin's, 1997), pp. 101, 122; Brown, *Fighting for US*, p. 56.
45. Stephen Ward, "The Third World Women's Alliance: Black Feminist Radicals and Black Power Politics," in *The Black Power Movement: Rethinking the Civil Rights-Black Power Era*, ed. Peniel E. Joseph (New York: Routledge, 2006), p. 124.
46. For examples of black women's activism in Philadelphia, see Countryman, *Up South*.
47. Stephen Ward, "The Third World Women's Alliance," p. 120. For a similar reinterpretation of the role of black feminism in the Black Power movement, see Kimberly Springer, *Living for the Revolution: Black Feminist Organizations, 1968–1980* (Durham: Duke University Press, 2005); Kimberly Springer, "Black Feminists Respond to Black Power Masculinism," in *The Black Power Movement: Rethinking the Civil Rights-Black Power Era*, ed. Peniel E. Joseph (New York: Routledge, 2006), pp. 105–18; and Joseph, *The Midnight Hour*, pp. 255, 271–72, 294.
48. Williams, "Black Women, Urban Politics, and Engendering Black Power," p. 88; Springer, "Black Feminists Respond to Black Power Masculinism," p. 116.
49. "On the Defection of Eldridge Cleaver from the Black Panther Party and the Defection of the Black Panther Party from the Black Community: April 17, 1971," in *To Die for the People: The Writings of Huey P. Newton* (New York: Random House, 1972), pp. 48–49.
50. Countryman, *Up South*, p. 288.
51. Kenneth O'Reilly, *"Racial Matters": The FBI's Secret File on Black America, 1960–1972* (New York: Free Press, 1989), pp. 293–324; Ward Churchill, "'To Disrupt, Discredit

and Destroy': The FBI's Secret War Against the Black Panther Party," in *Liberation, Imagination, and the Black Panther Party: A New Look at the Panthers and their Legacy*, eds. Kathleen Cleaver and George Katsiaficas (New York: Routledge, 2001), pp. 78–117.

52. Newton, *Revolutionary Suicide*, pp. 149–50; Williams, "Black Women, Urban Politics, and Engendering Black Power," pp. 89–90; Countryman, *Up South*, p. 288.

53. John A. Courtwright, "Rhetoric of the Gun: An Analysis of the Rhetorical Modifications of the Black Panther Party," *Journal of Black Studies* 4, no. 3 (March 1974): pp. 249–67.

54. Quoted in Jane McManus, "An Exile Warns of Race 'Explosion' in the U.S.," *National Guardian*, September 12, 1964, p. 6.

55. Newton, *Revolutionary Suicide*, pp. 111–12.

56. See Joseph, *The Midnight Hour*, pp. 59–60, 269, 275; Van Deburg, *New Day*, pp. 165, 168, 144–49; Akinyele Omowale Umoja, "Repression Breeds Resistance: The Black Liberation Army and the Radical Legacy of the Black Panther Party," in *Liberation, Imagination, and the Black Panther Party: A New Look at the Panthers and their Legacy*, eds. Kathleen Cleaver and George Katsiaficas (New York: Routledge, 2001), pp. 3–19.

CHAPTER 12

THE BLACK BOLSHEVIKS

DETROIT REVOLUTIONARY UNION MOVEMENTS AND SHOP-FLOOR ORGANIZING

ELIZABETH KAI HINTON

IN THE SHADOW OF CIVIL RIGHTS LEGISLATION, as the children of Southern-born parents came of age in Northern cities and assumed new roles in the manufacturing and public service sectors, groups founded upon revolutionary and black nationalist discourses reached extraordinary levels of visibility. Major unions soon confronted workers organized around Black Power's self-determination principle in Chicago's Black Federation of Labor, Newark's United Black Workers, and Black Panther–led caucuses in the East Bay. After the July 1967 Detroit riot, a small group of Wayne State University students organized black autoworkers at Chrysler's Hamtramck Assembly plant, or Dodge Main, as the Dodge Revolutionary Union Movement (DRUM). Founders General Gordon Baker, Luke Tripp, John Watson, Mike Hamlin, and Kenneth Cockrel synthesized the socialist and separatist strains at the core of Black Power ideology to ground DRUM's political platform.[1] The movement they launched remains the most substantive attempt to put revolutionary nationalism, long theorized by black radical intellectuals, into action.

An examination of DRUM during its first year offers a crucial lens on the ways in which major transnational corporations and labor unions responded to Black Power.[2] From rifle clubs to Marxist study groups, DRUM founders participated in a range of political organizations during the 1960s that eventually lead them to theorize, in Watson's words, "How to build a party, a black Bolshevik Party? How to organize black workers, coordinate the activities of black students, how to break away from the old radical organizations?"[3] DRUM held rallies with neighborhood groups; picketed United Auto Workers (UAW) locals and Chrysler headquarters; sanctioned nonunion-sponsored strikes, or "wildcats"; ran candidates in UAW elections; and taught political education classes. After ten months of agitation at Dodge Main, frustrated attempts on the corporate picket line and at the local ballot box convinced Hamlin, Watson, and Cockrel that shop conditions and union alienation did not inevitably result in mass militancy. Even without a committed worker base, however, leaders chose to expand the movement at other Detroit-area plants and formed the League of Revolutionary Black Workers in June 1969. The League operated as an umbrella organization for independent caucuses and other revolutionary union movements (RUMs) scattered mainly throughout the northeastern United States until it disbanded 1973.[4] While the founders created the League as a workers' movement, it quickly evolved into a bureaucratic organization with a newspaper, a host of RUMs, and an internationally distributed film. Instead of supporting and encouraging worker-directed action, the League entrusted founders to make "democratic decisions" in the name of Detroit's black work force.[5]

The first DRUM-authorized wildcat at Dodge Main in July 1968 marked the highest level of direct shop-floor support for the RUM movement in its history. How, then, could DRUM and the League function from 1968 to 1973 as a workers' movement without adequately sustaining an in-plant following?[6] Detroit autoworkers attended DRUM's meetings and educational workshops, but the organization did not recruit the UAW and Chrysler's rank and file on a mass scale.[7] Instead, activists' educational privilege often compromised political ends. Like the constituency they petitioned, the founders grew up in working-class Detroit neighborhoods. But by asking potential members to jeopardize coveted production jobs and to embrace socialist politics, the type of political education and revolutionary action DRUM founders championed isolated them from the workers they sought to organize. As a group of activist-intellectuals and students without a committed base on the shop floor, DRUM could not effectively motivate their prospective vanguard in the face of rapid, organized, and punitive resistance from Chrysler management.[8]

In order to raise funds and awareness, leadership overstated the League's constituency among the rank and file, and the small body of existing literature on RUMs has generally reinforced their claims. When the founders spoke to journalists and fellow activists in the international socialist sphere, they described DRUM as the organic result of the unprecedented entrance of young black workers into Detroit plants during the nascence of Black Power. However necessary for DRUM and the League's survival, this propaganda exaggerated the extent of black workers' commitment to the organization. More than any other consideration of RUMs, Dan Georgakas and Marvin Surkin's *Detroit, I Do Mind Dying: A Study in Urban Revolution* has shaped our understanding of the League as an "effort by working people to gain control of their lives." Published just two years after the organization disbanded, Georgakas and Surkin brought the League into the Black Power pantheon and added a new dimension to Detroit's political history. Yet the authors did not fully evaluate leadership's struggle to build a dedicated base of black industrial employees. While admitting that the RUM movement began with "a small core of black revolutionaries," the authors contended that the movement itself was "led by black workers."[9] Georgakas and Surkin based their account on interviews with Watson, Hamlin, and Cockrel less than a year after they resigned from the League to form the Black Workers Congress in 1971, largely ignoring the questions nonaffiliated workers raised in their testimonies to the authors about recruitment and membership.[10]

Like the Black Panthers, the Student Nonviolent Coordinating Committee, Us, and militant black organizations on hundreds of campuses, we can understand DRUM as a broad-based student movement that unfolded with and through black communities.[11] Civil rights activism encouraged colleges and universities to enroll black students in record numbers over the course of the 1960s. A critical mass of these students both crafted and engaged the rhetoric of Black Power to instantiate a movement that aimed to reconstitute American society. Chrysler's legal injunction after DRUM's first wildcat taught leadership that workers could not risk distributing newsletters, and the demanding nature of organizing and publishing an organ required skills and time workers conceded to the demands of auto production. A dedicated "support cadre" of Detroit high school students woke to leaflet the Dodge Main and Eldon plants at 5:30 every Tuesday morning. Indeed, in these early days of shop-floor mobilization, Baker recognized that "if it had not been for the base of strength that we had from those youth, we could not have done what we done later on."[12] The founders were forced to operate DRUM as a workers' organization disproportionately controlled by students.

If DRUM and the League represent "the most significant expression of black radical thought and activism" and "the most successful social revolutionary experiment" the United States produced in the 1960s, as both Manning Marable and Frederick Jameson have concluded, then a historical treatment that asks why the group's politics could not endure in practice is necessary.[13] The impact of state- and corporate-level repression on the larger Black Power movement as well as the withdrawal of federal funds from social programs and cities may have been ultimately responsible, but the ways in which activists operated on the ground must be considered alongside structural forces. How did the educational resources activists used to inform the politics of the black Left in the late 1960s create internal stratification that prevented DRUM and other Black Power organizations from setting the black radical theory into motion?

While discussions of RUMs tend to begin with the formation of the League and focus on the internal divisions that led to the group's dissolution, a critical vantage on the strategies DRUM founders adopted in their initial efforts suggests how the organization might have compromised its potential power. The founders spent five years studying Marxism and joining other black radical organizations before they decided to organize black autoworkers in Detroit. In order to mobilize this potential vanguard, DRUM relied on high school students and the unemployed to circulate its organ and to fill rallies and strikes. As Chrysler and the UAW strained the founders' ability to interact with the rank and file, DRUM turned to union elections. When DRUM's candidate for local trustee lost the election, the effort to implement a RUM at Eldon Avenue Gear and Axle in early 1969 exposes the leadership's fundamental shortcomings in execution and the types of resistance the movement confronted in the early 1970s. A history of DRUM's organizing tactics during the height of its presence on Detroit's shop floors foreshadows the very issues the founders tackled when they attempted to expand during subsequent years. So goes the old axiom: The seeds of the end to any relationship often reveal themselves at the very beginning.

THEORIZING THE VANGUARD

After the Detroit Police Department and the FBI intercepted General Baker, Luke Tripp, and John Watson's plan to demonstrate in protest of American troops in Vietnam in April 1965, the young members of Uhuru (Swahili for "freedom") retreated from direct action to study politics, history, and theory. Wayne State University student John Watson recruited his classmate Baker—an autoworker at Dodge Main who had recently returned from Cuba, where he met with Fidel Castro, Che Guevara, and Robert F. Williams—and Watson's *Detroit News* loading dock coworker Mike Hamlin. Hamlin's involvement with the Republic of New Africa and the Congress of Racial Equality complemented his appreciation for the class analysis articulated by the Socialist Workers Party and the Communist Party. Watson and Hamlin's *Detroit News* coworker Kenneth Cockrel, who enrolled at Wayne State Law after being discharged from the Air Force, also joined Uhuru discussion sessions.[14] The four budding revolutionaries met in Baker and Watson's house in Paradise Valley, decorated with images of Lenin, Castro, and Malcolm X.[15] Members consumed the histories of the Bolshevik Party and of Nkrumah's Convention People's Party, searching for direction.[16]

Less than a year after Baker and his Uhuru comrades returned from Cuba, members actively prepared for the armed struggle that Williams advocated from his exile in Havana and Malcolm X suggested when he returned to Detroit's King Solomon Baptist Church in April 1964 to deliver "The Ballot or the Bullet" speech. In homage to Malcolm, Baker named his rifle association the Fox and Wolf Hunt Club and went downtown to incorporate the group immediately following the speech.[17] Every Sunday, when twenty Fox and Wolf members gathered far outside the central city to shoot rifles, police monitored their every move. It would take two years of practice before Baker had the opportunity to participate in the kind of insurgency for which he trained Fox and Wolf members. When four police officers began to beat a group of men standing in front of a bar one early evening in August 1966 on Detroit's East Side, black witnesses threw Molotov cocktails and stoned both police and civilian cars.[18] Fearing insufficient force early on could lead to a riot, as in Watts the previous summer, the police called for backup. The Tactical Mobile Unit promptly arrived at the center of the uprising's mile-long zone with sawed-off shotguns and bayonets to run black residents off Kercheval Street.[19] Ten participants faced arraignment for carrying concealed weapons, including Baker and several other Uhuru members.[20] Ignoring the possible effect of rain as a deterrent, the self-congratulatory police department figured they could handle any type of disturbance in Paradise Valley.[21]

On those same streets a year later, the Detroit Police Department and the National Guard encountered a major violent outbreak, interracial and intergenerational in composition, that required President Johnson to deploy federal troops and shook the American auto industry. What Uhuru and many other black Detroiters called "The Great Rebellion" of July 1967, considered the most destructive incident of civil disorder a North American city experienced in the twentieth century, halted the production of all cars in the city for three days. The establishment of martial law prevented residents from access to hospitals or grocery stores, but a badge from Chrysler, Ford, or General Motors could grant an exit from the riot zone. Paradise Valley's unrest posed a new threat to these auto corporations, known as the "Big Three." In response, Detroit's manufacturers engaged in extensive hiring drives. Due to the high concentration of auto production in the city and the overwhelming participation of workers in the rebellion, when the Big Three loosened their employment criteria (waiving oral, written, and physical examinations so that virtually any willing person could work the line), Uhuru identified black Detroiters as the community sector with the greatest potential power in the nation.[22]

The influx of young black workers occupying the most undesirable and dangerous plant positions coincided with Chrysler's increased market share from 10 percent in 1962 to 18 percent in 1968, growth accomplished by running the line in majority-black plants at a near impossible speed.[23] Even with an agreed upon rate established, foremen often moved production from sixty-four units an hour to seventy-six, as practiced at the Ford River Rouge Plant. If line speedup made white workers quit, Uhuru argued, "[black people] are so up-tight for jobs, and there's such a large supply of reserve labor, black labor, cheap labor available . . . [Chrysler] can speed it up on us as much as they want to."[24] Chrysler also ensured that the recruits lacked full rights as UAW members by hiring substantial numbers of black workers and firing them on the eighty-ninth day of a ninety-day probationary period. The UAW, in turn, received three months worth of fees and dues without having to represent the new workers. This process created strikingly high turnovers: forty-six thousand new hires came into Detroit's auto industry in 1968, while management at Ford Rouge, Dodge Main, and Eldon laid off three hundred to six hundred employees a week.[25] Displaying any kind of militancy (such as sporting an afro) justified layoffs. Discharged workers could find a job at another plant with relative ease. Uhuru members assumed that the kind of exploitation to which both the UAW and Chrysler subjected the rank and file would naturally compel workers to revolt.

Employed at Chrysler's Dodge Main plant since 1964, Baker placed himself on the front lines of recruitment for a revolutionary nationalist worker organization. Uhuru's Leninist principles taught that a newspaper should be the first step of any revolutionary organization, and Uhuru members' *Inner City Voice* (ICV) tagged itself "The Voice of Revolution." Editors hoped by incorporating the history of black workers and contemporary political and cultural transformations into articles, the organ could serve as an ideological foundation for radical organizing. To argue for a black dictatorship of the proletariat and workers control, feature stories often discussed dangerous conditions in local plants and the UAW's misrepresentation of black workers.

The *Inner City Voice* helped Baker attract a small following inside Dodge Main's seven-story factory building.[26] In-plant recruits Ron March and Chuck Wooten formed the Dodge steering committee with ICV writers, but the nine members had ideological problems from the outset. The Dodge workers' nationalism clashed with the political orientation of ICV activists. March, seen by ICV editors as a "key person in the plant," had difficulty connecting everyday workplace conditions with the Vietnam intervention and following ICV members when they discussed the theories of Mao and Ernest Allen. Hamlin recounted that it took several months for both Dodge Main employees to arrive at "a sound analysis and with the rest of the group of workers."[27] The committee then resolved to begin organizing at Dodge Main.

By spring 1968, workers no longer tolerated Chrysler's drive to reach new levels of production. On May 2, management soared production from forty-nine to fifty-eight units an hour during the UAW convention in Atlantic City, causing three thousand Dodge Main employees to walk out of the plant.[28] After pickets formed and workers congregated, Chrysler sent photographers and spies to the plant gates. The walkout began in the afternoon, carried into shifts the next morning, and lasted for three days. A small group of white women instigated the strike and white workers also manned the picket lines, but black workers faced discharge, suspension, and time off. A police target since the Fox and Wolf days, Chrysler security successfully ended Baker's career as an autoworker during the wildcat.[29]

Despite Baker's removal from his post on the shop floor, the strike and the walkout helped fuel membership for what leaders chose to call the Dodge Revolutionary Union Movement.[30] The steering committee decided to publish a weekly plant newsletter, *Drum*, and placed three Dodge Main workers on the editorial board.[31] While Hamlin admitted to Georgakas that steering committee members "sometimes" authored *Drum* articles, he contended that "by and large, the [workers] wrote all the material themselves."[32] To protect workers from layoffs, DRUM used ICV's community connections to draw "a reservoir of people from the street" to distribute the paper: nationalists ("who had nothing else to do but sit around [ICV] offices," as Hamlin characterized them), students, and unemployed residents who spent their days on Paradise Valley's corners.[33]

DRUM leaders planned the organization's first wildcat to coincide with the changeover to production of 1969 Dodge models, a period when many workers faced layoffs. Leaders believed that increased production requirements meant that if DRUM shut down the plant on the heels of the scheduled changeover it could deeply rupture Chrysler and impact the US economy accordingly.[34] Because DRUM founders believed, "the entire struggle is wrapped up here in the factories," organizing calculated strikes would both raise the revolutionary consciousness of black Detroiters and disrupt transnational markets.[35] But the leaders' proposed vanguard wielded far less force than UAW officials and plant protection, who received tear gas, nightsticks, and riot helmets from Chrysler management following the May wildcat.[36] Shortly after *Drum* appeared, the organization and its consistent newsletter seemed a "growing serious problem," as a local official wrote to UAW President Walter Reuther.[37]

THE DODGE REBELLION

The punitive barrier Chrysler erected between activists and workers caused DRUM leaders to shift the focus of direct action from corporate exploitation to corruption within the UAW. Local 3's prominence in the auto industry reinforced DRUM's potential in this arena: As the second-largest local in the United States, Local 3, or Dodge 3, counted nearly ten thousand members. Although DRUM leadership believed that plant shutdowns would impact political and economic spheres more substantially than union activity, they grounded the organization's agitation on the goal of wealth redistribution inside the UAW.[38]

Coinciding with *Drum*'s ninth week of circulation, leaders called a rally at Dodge Main to showcase DRUM's new local-oriented platform and advertise the group's first wildcat. DRUM leaders carefully scheduled the rally for July 11 to coincide with the Local 3 executive board meeting. Hamlin and Watson roused three hundred workers to form a picket line and march to the local headquarters. The size of the demonstration pressed the executive board to speak to DRUM's pickets. President Ed Liska and Vice President Charles Brooks (a DRUM-labeled "Tom") defended the union by pointing to the unprecedented amount of jobs Chrysler provided to black workers in 1968 and the UAW's own vulnerability in negotiating with management. Leadership's successful mobilization of black workers sent a message to the union about the growing power of DRUM among its ranks.

After two carloads of pickets arrived at 5:20 the next morning with signs reading "This is for Real, Dodge Rebellion," "No Work for Racism," "No More Toms, No More Tokens," and "Black Working Power," plant security rushed to the Conant Gate scene.[39] Within the hour, ten officers cruised the area while five others managed the crowd. By 7 a.m., approximately two thousand workers stood within a three-block radius. Leaders hoped that carrying hammers and ax handles in self-defense and bringing conga players from a coffee shop they frequented and a "street force" clad in what Chrysler plant protection labeled "Afrocentric dress" would inspire Dodge Main's black work force to join the action.[40] Chrysler operated the plant at one-third capacity as a result of the strike, though the majority of the defectors were not DRUM members.[41] Many workers believed in honoring picket lines and others used the disruption to take much-needed rest. The overall impact of the event nevertheless cost the corporation the loss of nearly two thousand cars.[42] The following morning, when the conga drums started beating in time for the six o'clock shift, plant security immediately notified the Hamtramck police. Standing unmarked cruisers and police cars surrounded Dodge Main to monitor interactions between DRUM members and black employees.[43]

Chrysler quickly responded to the wildcat by restricting the ability of its workers to collectively demonstrate. In June, when management first learned of DRUM's existence, administrators quickly drafted policy stipulating, "If any mass picketing . . . around any gate is observed, with information or signs connecting such people to DRUM, serve as many of the leaders as possible with copies of the Preliminary Injunction."[44] Baker, Tripp, and five other DRUM members received the injunction on the third and final day of the wildcat action. After the Hamtramck police served them, the DRUM members promptly threw the summons on the plant's cement in front of a growing crowd of autoworkers. By seven, with 150 men in front of a plant gate, a white manager pleaded to the pickets on a megaphone to return to the line without serious reprisal. Failure to report, the manager reminded strikers, would constitute violation of contract. Though the workers remained despite management's threat, they disbanded less than an hour later, after thirty Hamtramck police cleared approximately one hundred DRUM sympathizers from Chrysler's property.[45]

For the remainder of July, Chrysler increased surveillance around Dodge Main and moved to incarcerate DRUM leaders.[46] The corporation filed an injunction against Baker, March, Tripp, and Wooten two days after the wildcat, claiming they were "acting, combating and confederating with others to irreparably injure [Chrysler] and its employees." In addition to reducing DRUM's representational demands to a "quota system" and attacking the organization's platform as reverse racist, Chrysler attempted to eliminate mass organization by defining picketing as "the gathering together in groups larger than five persons."[47] To ensure that DRUM would not disrupt production in the future, the injunction threatened to arrest members who picketed or demonstrated within one hundred miles of Chrysler property. DRUM literature or speeches, "designed to incite persons to engage in the now-prohibited act—like encouraging people not to go to work"— faced fines or imprisonment.[48]

The UAW complemented Chrysler's counterattack by appealing to Local 3 members. Shortly after *Drum* reached the rank and file, local officials developed a campaign to squash the organization.[49] The DRUM-led demonstration at the union hall and the Dodge Main wildcat compelled the local executive board to distribute "Common Sense—Or Chaos?" to membership.[50] The memo identified DRUM as an "outside [group] of extremists who want to divide us . . . less interested in helping black workers get better jobs than in sowing the seeds of bitterness, hatred, confusion, and chaos."[51] The letter reminded the local constituency that "our Negro members are too intelligent to permit themselves to be used as pawns," and only the UAW could bargain with Chrysler on behalf of Hamtramck Assembly plant workers.[52] The UAW reduced *Drum* to a set of "extremist hate sheets" and viewed the organ as "a sinister attempt to split the Dodge workers and to make their union ineffective and weak."[53] The local stressed DRUM's outsider status by emphasizing the links between the organization's leaders and ICV writers, who represented "not so much the voice of the Inner City as . . . the voice of a worldwide propaganda network." The executive board stressed the UAW's record on civil rights and warned that shutting down the factory meant "wages lost for nothing." By this logic, the local contended that such actions could never result in improved housing, jobs, or education.[54] Unwilling to contend with DRUM on the basis of its nationalism, the local defended itself on the principle that problems specific to black workers could only be addressed as a united union.

In light of Chrysler and the UAW's counterinitiatives that made demonstrations at Dodge Main impossible, DRUM shifted its revolutionary nationalist leanings to a critique radical in rhetoric but reformist in substance by running candidates in fall UAW elections.[55] With a platform that emphasized racial hierarchies in the UAW, DRUM now called for workers to direct policy decisions.[56] In keeping with the new emphasis on recognition and leadership within the UAW, DRUM also strategized that a series of successful reform efforts would raise black workers consciousness through political engagement.[57] Leaders hoped electing

DRUM members to head the local would gain workers' control for Dodge Main's black majority.[58] DRUM ran cofounder March, one of the only members still employed at Dodge Main, as trustee for the upcoming local election. The March campaign centered on the union's misappropriation of its capital, arguing that the local spent upward of forty thousand dollars a month in loans to the City of Hamtramck to finance service agencies and the salaries of police and firemen for extra security against DRUM.[59] Outraged by the prospect of this supposed transfer, DRUM coined their best-known slogan: "We Finally Got the News of How Our Dues is Being Used."

The city, the corporation, and the union worked together in order to prevent DRUM and March from gaining representational power in the UAW. March had to compete in a runoff against a candidate backed by the union, though he won the majority of votes in the September primary. DRUM knew that retired workers, empowered by the UAW to vote in local elections, could stop March from winning trustee and prepared for defeat in the October runoff.[60] DRUM leadership contended that Hamtramck police destroyed campaign propaganda and issued traffic violations to March supporters throughout the campaign, but on election day, its harassment turned violent. In the alley workers frequented during breaks, officers beat black employees with ax handles; in the union hall, black voters felt mace in their eyes and further physical assaults on their bodies.[61] Unable to galvanize a mass base at Dodge Main, DRUM leaders measured their success by the extent of institutional resistance to the organization's power on the shop floor in order to justify the decision to organize elsewhere.[62]

THE ELDON CRISIS

After Chrysler and the UAW made demonstrating on plant premises impossible, DRUM ran candidates in Dodge Main Local 3 elections, assuming the reformist approach would bring the black vanguard they sought closer to its revolutionary breaking point. As Watson wrote in an editorial two months after the election, leadership resolved that "the union bureaucracy cannot be broken through peaceful, democratic methods . . . thousands of black workers have gained practical experience in a reform movement, they have seen that reform is impossible."[63] DRUM went on to conclude in its initial statement after the election defeat, "[W]e shall strike only when we see fit or when the majority of black workers at Hamtramck Assembly demand that we do so."[64] The questioned remained: who, in fact, directed this struggle?

By October 1968, when it became clear that DRUM's in-plant power could be easily compromised by punitive measures enacted by Chrysler and the UAW, leaders believed the key to the survival of their movement lay in expansion. The founders decided to begin organizing black workers at Dodge Main because of Baker's employment there, but they now identified a special opportunity at Eldon Avenue Gear and Axle. As the only plant in the nation producing housings for Chrysler's cars, to shut down Eldon would be to completely upset Chrysler's productive capacity. Replicating the DRUM formula, leadership decided to call their new organization the Eldon Revolutionary Union Movement (ELRUM) and quickly printed an *Elrum* leaflet styled after their Dodge Main newsletter. Following the previous model, after exactly nine weeks of newsletter distribution, the founders sanctioned a wildcat at Eldon Avenue as ELRUM in January 1969. Hamlin told a radical labor journal, "the workers decided that they wanted to strike," but by assembling black students, intellectuals, and the organization's notorious street force at Eldon Avenue, DRUM leadership literally established their own picket lines.[65]

The ELRUM-led wildcat initially mobilized a greater number of workers than DRUM's strike, but its aftermath proved disastrous. More than 75 percent of the plant participated, owing to Eldon's black majority, but these workers managed to hold out for only one day to Dodge Main's three.[66] Already prepared for counterattack after the young activists demonstrated at Dodge Main roughly five months earlier, management used ELRUM to fire between twenty-two and twenty-six workers seen as militant or undesirable.[67] Four of the discharged had twenty years' seniority; the rest had been on the job for a year or less.[68] None claimed ELRUM membership. The inability to execute the DRUM program at Eldon taught leadership, as Hamlin recognized, "[W]e had a great deal of learning to do in terms of organizing workers."[69] RUMs could not raise a solid base of workers in plant under the legal obstructions Chrysler established, which made the threat of job loss for associating with ELRUM activists immediate.

Baker recruited a cadre of workers to write for *Drum*, but at Eldon, without a single recruit from the shop floor, DRUM members authored the newsletter.[70] In the absence of the rank and file, shop steward Jordan Sims leaked shop-floor exposés to writers. According to Sims, "rather than have [ELRUM] develop issues or items out of their imagination, I would give them credible grievances . . . Then what they would tell in their stories could be based on in-plant conditions."[71] Even if workers hesitated to join ELRUM, they welcomed the organ's reports on race-specific plant dynamics. Sims acknowledged that *Elrum* "was the most popular thing that came out" and a "vehicle to get essential news of what was going on throughout the entire plant."[72] If workers hesitated to join ELRUM, the newsletter magnified issues of union and corporate racism that deeply resonated with them. Eldon employee Carla Cooke remembered, "I wasn't a member of it but I looked forward to reading the paper," adding that the newsletter, "spoke about everyday problems"[73] Despite *Elrum*'s enthusiastic reception, merely talking to an activist from the organization could result in discharge or time off.[74]

The local was well aware of activists' estrangement from Eldon's shop floor and exploited that vulnerability accordingly.[75] Concerned about ELRUM's potential and the "problems" the organization perceivably encouraged within the local, in a note to the director of the UAW's Chrysler department, Assistant Director Art Hughes recognized that "[*Elrum*] is published by non-plant workers distributed by non-plant workers written and printed at Wayne State U."[76] The UAW's perception of activists as "outside agitators" challenged the claims leadership made about method and influence, an assessment that went on to serve as the organizational premise of the League of Revolutionary Black Workers.

The combination of March's electoral loss and the faltered attempt to implement a RUM at Eldon left DRUM founders at tense ideological crossroads, amplified by limited resources. Would RUMs operate as independent black caucuses that would attack management and company racism to improve working conditions, or would they operate as educational vehicles toward structural action? In the wake of the ELRUM wildcat, with Baker pushed underground in Cleveland by the threat of incarceration, the Hamlin-Watson-Cockrel bloc steered RUMs away from shop floors and toward workers' support networks. Planning wildcat strikes at Dodge Main and Eldon led Hamlin to conclude that "no one group of workers in a single plant can win a struggle for control of a plant."[77] DRUM cut their losses to focus on a movement for black workers across the United States rather than engage in the long-term struggle of building a dedicated cadre at Dodge Main.

Hamlin, Watson, and Cockrel wanted to focus on getting resources and "stepping up" political education classes; Baker stressed shop floor and local activity. From the outset, Baker believed a solid base of revolutionaries could be recruited only by the extent of commitment on the shop floor, focusing on everyday plant concerns such as health care, safety, and grievance procedures.[78] Hamlin, Watson, and Cockrel grew increasingly frustrated with Baker and other DRUM members who "tended to practice talism or romanticism toward workers. That is, they would not take a strong or firm position when a worker proposed something that was really stupid, but some things that the workers wanted to do were blatantly wrong."[79] Baker, Simmons, Williams, Tripp, and Wooten maintained that workers themselves should direct and determine the course of struggle, and that activist-intellectuals had no place to judge their actions as right or wrong. Watson, Hamlin, and Cockrel felt reactionary nationalists affiliated with the organization, whether in support cadre or in plant, could impede the coming socialist revolution.

ELRUM explained recruitment discrepancies by claiming that workers were unprepared to engage in, as Hamlin said, "as high a level of struggle as a strike represents."[80] As they had in the wake of Uhuru members' arrest in 1965, the Black Bolsheviks decided to "back away from that to think; to develop a long range perspective and to think about protracted struggle."[81] Convinced that the organization's small-scale operation caused the organizers to falter at Eldon Avenue, Watson, Hamlin, and Cockrel favored a direct action approach that would disrupt the flow of international capital. This leadership faction wanted to pursue the larger goal of recruiting black workers and their respective communities across the United States into revolutionary nationalist struggle more forcefully. If in-plant organizing was deficient, Hamlin and the other leaders "determined that what we had to do, among other things, was to begin organizing in the community."[82] It would be a relatively smooth transition; students and community members always provided a captive audience for DRUM's platform.

Subscribing to the doctrine that consciousness is broadened through struggle, DRUM hoped to provide political influence that would refocus what many activists regarded as the revolutionary potential that lay in the spontaneity of "brothers in the street."[83] Simultaneously, leaders opened up their church-held meetings from only Dodge Main employees to all those "that we feel have the interest of black people at heart and who are capable and in fact feel duty bound to assume this responsibility," as they wrote in an appeal distributed in Paradise Valley.[84] This included white activists, who demonstrated alongside DRUM despite the organization's aversion to organizing the shop floor on an interracial basis like many other nationalist-oriented Black Power groups that worked with white sympathizers.[85]

The history of DRUM exposes the problems that result when students operate as a radical vanguard, urging workers to abandon their union, however flawed, for a vision with no immediate gain. Forty years after DRUM's first wildcat action, Baker reflected, "A student has choices. A worker doesn't. Theoretically [a student] can understand [shop-floor dynamics] as abstractions, but how do you blend it practically with where you're at?"[86] When leaders believed that corporate and union counterinitiatives compromised the ability of DRUM to recruit a black vanguard of Detroit autoworkers, they launched a national organization. The creation of the League of Revolutionary Black Workers in June 1969, to be an umbrella for RUMs in every deindustrializing city, would gather and effectively utilize resources with the ICV as its organ. To acquire resources and systematize the structure, the League needed organizers, facilities, equipment, supplies, technical skills, and assistance. They reasoned bureaucratization would enable the struggle to continue.

BLACK POWER AND THE LEGACY OF REVOLUTIONARY UNIONISM

DRUM founders decided that the "fulfillment of the historic vanguard role of black workers in the Black Liberation Struggle" would be their new year's resolution for 1969.[87] Coming out of 1968, DRUM made history along with radicals and socialist activists around the world. The founders set a long-theorized black radical tradition into action and assisted workers in a series of wildcat strikes that went on to shape UAW and plant dynamics.[88] Without a strong in-plant following after a year of organizing, the old Uhuru intellectuals who now comprised the League's executive board stood on uncertain ground. When RUM-building seemed to reach a standstill at Eldon Avenue, the League equipped itself with a staff and legal apparatus to prepare for the anticipated "do-or-die, toe to toe, head whupping struggle to get these demands met."[89] Consisting of the original Uhuru study group members, the League executive board viewed wildcats at Dodge Main and Eldon as tests of organizational strength that justified further expansion and bureaucratization. For DRUM founders in pursuit of a black vanguard, no action toward the revolution was misguided.

For Chrysler, the practice of speedup and rotation in 1968 gave the company its highest sales numbers and a record increase of its share in the world automotive market, but the corporation's historic victory that year was short lived.[90] As demand for American cars declined while producers in Japan and Germany made inroads during the two year national recession beginning in 1968, the same year DRUM disrupted production at Dodge Main during several wildcats, the Big Three responded by closing plants while increasing automation and outsourcing production of small parts to more modest, nonunionized firms.[91] These actions disproportionately affected low-wage workers, who, as a result of a long history of institutionalized racism, remained predominantly black workers. In the wake of the Great Rebellion, the Big Three ushered black workers into Detroit plants, but as the US auto industry maintained its sluggish economic position through the 1970s, DRUM's ostensible vanguard found themselves vulnerable to widespread layoffs. With the longevity of the industry threatened, the Big Three's survival depended on union concessions and bailouts from the federal government. The dissolution of the League coincided with the 1973 bargaining session between the UAW and Chrysler, which ensured that benefits would not exceed postwar gains.[92] By the close of the decade, the UAW conceded hundreds of millions of dollars in wages and deferred pension plans to Chrysler, along with the surrender of paid holidays.[93]

DRUM's direct action tactics that highlighted working conditions and corporate racism forced the union and the Big Three to come to terms with discriminatory practices. While the process of job rotation and abysmal working conditions persisted and even worsened in some cases as Chrysler demanded overtime to meet its ambitious production objectives, the presence of radical elements inside the plant and the ranks of the UAW forced both institutions to reform labor-relations policy. In line with employment initiatives, the Big Three began endorsing more moderate local leaders to represent workers where black Detroiters edged the majority and promoted select workers to steward and officer positions while removing reportedly racist foremen and replacing them with black hires. Growing numbers of women and black workers rose to supervisory positions inside the shops and black workers participated in skilled trades at unprecedented rates.[94] DRUM also broke down the UAW's ability to control local elections in the early 1970s. Most of the newly elected black moderates opposed DRUM and the League from the outset, but black presidents represented five of Chrysler's plants on Detroit's east side.[95]

Although DRUM's vision of workers' control conflicted directly with the company and union's interests, the Big Three did address DRUM's demand for a liable grievance procedure and improved plant conditions. In the wake of several on-site deaths and daily injuries in the early 1970s, the Big Three and the UAW began to express concern about the physical safety of its ranks by recruiting the Health and Safety Administration to inspect auto plants. The union retained its top-down approach to addressing the humane treatment of its members. As historian Heather Thompson has noted, "[T]he union leadership still did not want to hear what workers themselves thought should be done to correct these problems."[96] As the RUM movement began to lose steam, critique of union and company practices on the shop floor continued to persist. The high turnover rates that resulted from the auto industry's working conditions and hiring practices after the 1967 uprising compromised the ability of the RUM movement to sustain solid membership bases at various area plants. More than three hundred thousand Big Three workers found themselves unemployed by the mid-1970s.

The impact of deindustrialization on black urban Americans placed the beneficiaries of the Great Society and affirmative action, many of whom held college degrees, at the forefront of the legacy of Black Power. By opening up space for representation in the electoral realm and in universities, political and economic institutions fashioned a collective response to progressive and radical demands without disrupting entrenched class and racial hierarchies, even as the civil rights movement helped secure a black middle class. With respect to the DRUM founders, Cockrel and Baker followed a general shift in the black political sphere from participation in direct-action civil disobedience to representation in American politics. After considering a 1973 mayoral bid, Cockrel won a seat on Detroit's city council in 1977, serving for five years before returning to his private law practice. When Hamlin, Watson and Cockrel resigned to form the Black Workers Congress, Baker merged the League of Revolutionary Black Workers with the Communist League (later the Labor Party). In 1976 and 1978, Baker ran as the Communist Labor Party's state representative in the Michigan House.

Other founders remained outside state institutions. Watson and Hamlin kept their revolutionary political commitments removed from the electoral system. Watson traveled to Sweden and Russia to work with socialist groups, and Hamlin continued organizing in black communities across the Midwest. Like other activists who organized black Americans in order to demand that the United States commit to fundamental social, political, and economic changes reflecting the nation's egalitarian ideals, the founders of DRUM helped expand the terrain of acceptable public representation and inspired new models for political action. Today, we feel their legacy in the murals of Black Power icons that decorate cities nationwide, in the sermons of religious clergy, in hip-hop, in the Millions More March, and, as one historian recently suggested, in Barack Obama's presidency.

The guiding ideology of the Black Power movement, framed by Marxism and black socialists, can be grasped most profoundly by the choice DRUM made to organize a black vanguard in Detroit. Yet DRUM was but one of a proliferation of nationalist caucuses and rank-and-file organizations that seized this critical moment in the history of Black Power. These groups, largely absent from the growing body of scholarship on the period, provide powerful insight into the ways that radical conceptions of freedom operate in practice.[97] At the same time, the response to these organizations from sources of entrenched power and privilege offers insights into the limitations of these practices. Given the fact that the RUM movement and the League sought to disrupt corporate power and shift control of major national unions from the boardroom to an increasing number of black workers, the history of DRUM reveals how men like Chrysler President Lynn Townsend and FBI Director J. Edgar Hoover employed similar approaches in their effort to destroy black radical social movements. Although punitive measures at the state and corporate levels severely compromised the social and political potential of both DRUM and the larger movement, we must address the reasons for Black Power's failure to meet its final objectives through closer examination of its organizational tactics. Treatments of DRUM and other Black Power organizations must ask, as Baker, Hamlin, Watson, and Cockrel asked of their revolutionary forbearers: What worked? What didn't? And why? Contending with these questions may allow us to use the history of DRUM and their contemporaries to advance toward the transcendence of institutionalized inequality—the very goal to which these activists dedicated their lives.

NOTES

1. DRUM based revolutionary nationalism on Ernest Mkalimoto Allen's definition. See Ernest Mkalimoto Allen, "Basic Tenets of Revolutionary Nationalism," in *The Black Power Movement*, microfilm, Part 4, Reel 2. Schomburg Center for Research in Black Culture, Harlem, New York (hereafter cited as BPMM).

2. Heather Thompson, *Whose Detroit? Politics, Labor, and Race in a Modern American City* (Ithaca, NY: Cornell University Press, 2004) and David Lewis-Colman, *Race Against Liberalism: Black Workers and the UAW in Detroit* (Urbana: University of Illinois Press, 2008) situate DRUM within the history of black independent caucuses and A. Phillip Randolph's Trade Union Leadership Council. Black power literature tends to focus on the League and the internal divisions contributing to the organization's ultimate dissolution while equivocating on the ways in which DRUM operated on the shop floor. James Geschwender and Judson L. Jeffries *Black Power in the Belly of the Beast* (Urbana: University of Illinois Press, 2006) contextualizes the League's ideology in Black Power but roots the organization in 1930s Detroit labor activism. See also James A. Geschwender, *Class, Race and Worker Insurgency: The League of Revolutionary Black Workers* (Cambridge: Cambridge University Press, 1977).

3. John Watson interview, *Fifth Estate* 1969, reprinted in *To the Point of Production—An Interview with John Watson of the League of Revolutionary Black Workers*, Box 4, Folder 22. Detroit Revolutionary Union Movements Collection, Walter P. Reuther Library of Labor and Urban Affairs, Wayne State University.

4. The League worked with other revolutionary nationalist black worker organizations in New York, Michigan, New Jersey, and Ohio.

5. In "Cognitive Mapping," Frederick Jameson briefly discusses the League to illustrate the consequences of spatial discontinuity on social movements and progressive change generally. According to Jameson, when League members became "jet-setting militants" and "media stars," "nobody stayed home to mind the store." Frederick Jameson, "Cognitive Mapping," in *Marxism and the Interpretation of Culture*, ed. Cary Nelson and Lawrence Grossberg (Urbana: University of Illinois Press, 1988), 352.

6. Dan Georgakas and Marvin Surkin, *Detroit: I Do Mind Dying: A Study in Urban Revolution* (New York: St. Martin's, 1975, 1998). Writing from the perspective of Baker, Wooten, and Tripp, Muhammad Ahmed's essay "The League of Revolutionary Black Workers: A Historical Study" provides a complementary view of the League's 1971 split. See "The League of Revolutionary Black Workers: A Historical Study," Muhammad Ahmed, History is a Weapon, http://www.historyisaweapon.com/defcon1/rbwstudy.html.

7. The single DRUM membership list that appears in the organization's archive includes only ten members outside of the core leadership. See list in Box 1, Folder 5. DRUM Collection, Walter P. Reuther Library of Labor and Urban Affairs, Wayne State University (hereafter cited as DRUM Collection).

8. I use the term "student" here in the broadest sense. Founders instituted a political education requirement for every recruit.

9. Georgakas and Surkin, *Detroit*, 4–5.

10. For example, Georgakas's archive contains numerous examples of contrary opinion among workers that are overlooked in *Detroit: I Do Mind Dying* but are represented here.

11. Literature that emphasizes the connections between students and Black Power includes Martha Biondi, "Student Protests, 'Law and Order,' and the Origins of African American Studies in California," in *Contested Democracy: Freedom, Race, and Power in American History*, eds. Manisha Sinha and Penny Von Eschen (New York: Columbia University Press, 2007); Fabio Rojas, *From Black Power to Black Studies: How a Radical*

Social Movement Became an Academic Discipline (Baltimore: Johns Hopkins University Press, 2007); and Joy Ann Williamson, *Black Power on Campus: The University of Illinois, 1965–75* (Urbana: University of Illinois Press, 2003).

12. General Baker, "Speech to Commemorate the Thirty-Fifth Anniversary of the Detroit Rebellion," March 28, 2003, radio broadcast.

13. Robin D. G. Kelley has also suggested this. See updated edition (1998) of Georgakas and Surkin, *Detroit*; Jameson, "Cognitive Mapping," 352.

14. Peniel E. Joseph, *Waiting 'Til the Midnight Hour: A Narrative History of Black Power in America* (New York: Henry Holt, 2006), 59; Georgakas and Surkin, *Detroit*, 24.

15. Detroit Police Department Interoffice Memorandum, March 16, 1966, vol. 4, reel 2. BPMM. Watson is pictured in front of these iconic images in the League's film *Finally Got the News*.

16. Ibid.

17. General Gordon Baker, in author interview, 16 January 2008.

18. Sidney Fine, *Violence in the Model City: The Cavanaugh Administration, Race Relations, and the Detroit Riot of 1967* (Ann Arbor: University of Michigan Press, 1989), 137; Baker, "Speech to Commemorate."

19. Baker, "Speech to Commemorate"; Fine, *Violence*, 139.

20. "Arraign 10 in Street Disorders," *Detroit News*, August 11, 1966.

21. Baker, "Speech to Commemorate."

22. Ibid.

23. Thomas R. Brooks, "DRUMBeats in Detroit," *Dissent* 17, no. 1 (January 2007): 16–25, 17.

24. Jim Jacobs and David Wellman, "Fight on to Victory: An Interview with Mike Hamlin and Ken Cockrel," in *Our Thing Is DRUM!*; reprinted from *Leviathan* 2, no. 2 (June 1970): 12; Box 1, Folder 6. DRUM Collection, Walter P. Reuther Library of Labor and Urban Affairs, Detroit.

25. Brooks, "DRUMBeats in Detroit," 18.

26. Georgakas interview with Hamlin, Box 1, Folder 19. Dan Georgakas Collection, Walter P. Reuther Library of Labor and Urban Affairs, Wayne State University (hereafter DGC); *Drum* 1, no. 5. See also Charles Denby, "Black Caucuses in the Unions," *New Politics* 7 (1968): 12.

27. Georgakas interview with Hamlin.

28. Muhammad A. Ahmed puts the number at four thousand. See "The League of Revolutionary Black Workers"; "Wildcat STRiKE: Chrysler's Scape Goat," *Drum* 1, no. 1.

29. Chrysler Dodge Main Personnel File, Box 4, Folder 33. DRUM Collection.

30. Wooten "Why I Joined DRUM," Box 4, Folder 12. DGC.

31. DRUM Program, Box 1, Folder 1, DRUM Collection.

32. Georgakas interview with Hamlin.

33. Ibid.

34. Ibid.

35. "Dying in the Streets," *Drum* 1, no. 7.

36. "Prepare for the Worst," *Drum* 1, no. 8.

37. Unsigned letter to Walter Reuther, 2 July 1968, Box 71. Walter P. Reuther Collection, Walter P. Reuther Library of Labor and Urban Affairs, Wayne State University (hereafter cited as WRC).

38. DRUM's demands for power and influence in the economic development of Detroit and aim to create autonomous social institutions were further helped by a base of support in Detroit's radical black clergy. See Angela Dillard, *Faith in the City: Preaching Radical Social Change in Detroit* (Ann Arbor: University of Michigan Press, 2007); *Drum* 1, no. 14; "Local 3 Discrimination," *Drum* 1, no. 3.

39. Daily Activities Log—Plant Protection 12 July 1968, Hamtramck Assembly, Box 4, Folder 31. DRUM Collection. Some of the placards are noted in the Incident Report—Highland Park Plant, 12 July 1968, Box 4, Folder 31. DRUM Collection.

40. Baker, interview; Luke Tripp, "D.R.U.M.—Vanguard of the Black Revolution," *The South End* 27, no. 62 (1969).

41. William Van De Burg, *New Day in Babylon: The Black Power Movement and American Culture, 1965–1975* (Chicago: University of Chicago Press, 1992), 95. The strike is also mentioned in Rod Bush, *We Are Not What We Seem: Black Nationalism and Class Struggle in the American Century* (New York: New York University Press, 1999), 206.

42. Brooks, "DRUMBeats in Detroit," 19.

43. Incident Report—Highland Park Plant, 13 July 1968, Hamtramck Assembly Location (Gate), Box 4, Folder 31. DRUM Collection.

44. "Materials and Information for Use in Relation to D.R.U.M. Picketing," Chrysler Dodge Main Policy on DRUM, Box 4, Folder 31. DRUM Collection.

45. Incident Report, 15 July 1968, Box 4, Folder 31. DRUM Collection.

46. Incident Report—Hamtramck Assembly 19 July 1968, Box 4, Folder 31 DRUM Collection.

47. Ibid.

48. "Chrysler Dodge Main—Injunction Against DRUM members," Box 4, Folder 31. DRUM Collection.

49. Unsigned letter to Walter Reuther, 2 July 1968, Box 71, Folder 4. WRC; Brooks, "DRUMBeats in Detroit," 22.

50. Letter from Solidarity House to all Members of Local 3, 1 August 1968, Box 19, Folder 23. United Auto Workers Chrysler Department Collection, Walter P. Reuther Library of Labor and Urban Affairs, Wayne State University (hereafter cited as UAWCDC).

51. Ibid.

52. Ibid.

53. Letter from Solidarity House to all Members of Local 3, 1 August 1968, Box 19, Folder 23. UAWCDC.

54. Ibid.

55. Black workers represented 63 percent of Local 3 members. *Drum* 1, no. 13.

56. "Local 3 What Are You Doing with My Money???" Box 1, Folder 8. DRUM Collection.

57. Brooks, "DRUMBeats in Detroit," 21.

58. *Drum* 1, no. 13.

59. Ibid.

60. Martin Glaberman, "Survey: Detroit," *International Socialism* 1, no. 36 (April/May 1969).

61. Baker, "Speech to Commemorate."

62. "RON MARCH D.R.U.M. TRUSTEE!," *Drum* 1, no. 15.

63. Watson, *South End*; quoted in Brooks, "DRUMBeats in Detroit," 21.

64. "RON MARCH D.R.U.M. TRUSTEE!," *Drum* 1, no. 15.

65. Jim Jacobs and David Wellman interview with Mike Hamlin, "Fight on to Victory," in *Our Thing Is DRUM!*; reprinted from *Leviathan* 2, no. 2 (June 1970): 12; Box 1, Folder 6. DRUM Collection, Walter P. Reuther Library of Labor and Urban Affairs, Detroit.

66. A Chrysler Corporation memo from 1970 stated that the ELRUM pickets made the company lose 50 percent of workers on the first shift, 70 percent on the second, and 60 percent on the third. Chrysler Corporation Memo to Art Hughes from L. W. Perry, "Chronology of Events since 1969 Contract Eldon Ave. Axle," 19 October 1970, Box 19. United Auto Workers UAW Local 961 Collection, Walter P. Reuther Library of Labor and Urban Affairs, Wayne State University (hereafter cited as UAWL961C).

67. Ibid; Brooks, "DRUMBeats in Detroit," 21. Brooks writes the number at 26; UAW archives have the number at 22.

68. Ibid.

69. Jacobs and Wellman, "Fight on to Victory," 15.

70. The leader of an independent caucus of black workers at Eldon, Sims may have intended to minimize DRUM's appeal within the plant. Yet early issues of *Elrum* seem to confirm his claims. The first edition included a historical account of black workers during slavery, a generalized discussion of conditions at Eldon, and examples of discriminatory representation within the UAW. In contrast to the premier issue of *Drum*, *Elrum* did not reference any specific plant conditions.

71. Georgakas and Surkin interview with Sims, Barksdale, and Cooke, 19 August 1972, Box 3, Folder 18. DGC

72. Ibid.

73. Ibid.

74. Ibid.

75. Ibid.

76. Chrysler Corporation Memo to Art Hughes from L. W. Perry 19 October 1970, "Chronology of Events since 1969 Contract Eldon Ave. Axle," Box 19. UAWL961C.

77. Jacobs and Wellman, "Fight on to Victory," 16.

78. Georgakas and Surkin interview with Sims, Barksdale, and Cooke; Brooks; Brooks, "DRUMBeats in Detroit," 21.

79. Georgakas interview with Hamlin.

80. Jacobs and Wellman, "Fight on to Victory," 18.

81. Ibid., 16.

82. Ibid.

83. "Our Thing Is DRUM!," Box 1, Folder 6. DRUM Collection.

84. Letter to Brothers and Sisters, n.d., Box 1. DRUM Collection.

85. In the fall of 1968, DRUM cosponsored a demonstration with Wayne State chapter of Students for a Democratic Society (SDS) at Chrysler headquarters with a reported 130 pickets in tow. Detroit Police: Interoffice Memorandum October 25 and October 24 1968 vol. 4, reel 2. BPMM; Letter to Walter Reuther from Douglas Fraser, 25 October 1968, Box 54, Folder 4. WRC.

86. Baker, interview.

87. *Drum* 2, no. 1.

88. Manning Marable's introduction to this volume discusses the contours of the black radical tradition and its critical thinkers.

89. Ibid.

90. Chrysler Corporation Annual Report—1968 (January), *America's Corporate Foundation*, 9.

91. Reynolds Farley, Sheldon Danziger, and Harry J. Holzer, *Detroit Divided: Multi-City Study of Urban Inequality* (New York: Russell Sage Foundation, 2000), 9.

92. Thompson, *Whose Detroit?*, 212.

93. Ibid., 214.

94. Jeffries, *Black Power*, 181, 183.

95. Lewis-Colman, *Race Against Liberalism*, 114.

96. Thompson, *Whose Detroit?*, 175.

97. Most recently, David Goldberg and Trevor Griffey, ed., *Black Power at Work: Community Control, Affirmative Action, and the Construction Industry* (Ithaca, NY: ILR Press, 2010) takes up issues of black nationalism in the workplace during the 1970s with respect to the larger goal of community control.

PART IV

STRUGGLING FOR COMMUNITY CONTROL AND AUTONOMY

CHAPTER 13

SEPTIMA CLARK

ORGANIZING FOR POSITIVE FREEDOM

STEPHEN LAZAR

SEPTIMA CLARK'S LIFE AND WORK STANDS AS a remarkable testament to the power of individual empowerment. After Martin Luther King Jr. and Malcolm X, one would be hard-pressed to argue that anyone else did more to build and sustain the structural foundation necessary for the successful battles of the black freedom struggle in the 1960s. While Clark's entire life of eighty-nine years illustrates her commitment to freedom and empowerment for all, it was her work in creating, developing, and overseeing the Citizenship Education Program (CEP) of the Highlander Folk School, and later the Southern Christian Leadership Council (SCLC), that was her greatest and most significant accomplishment. The CEP, which Andrew Young called the basis of the civil rights movement,[1] grew to teach as many as fifty thousand students throughout the South and became the largest program of the SCLC. It enabled a large percentage its students to become registered voters, and perhaps more importantly, literate, while simultaneously developing its teachers into respected grassroots leadership in their home communities, creating a sizeable portion of the local leadership of the civil rights movement. The schools were a humanizing force against the dehumanization of segregation, transforming its students into agents for social justice.

Clark's work with the program falls within the model of black leadership, which Charles Payne identifies as the organizing tradition in *I've Got the Light of Freedom*. This tradition emphasizes the long-term development of leadership and other capabilities by "ordinary men and women."[2] Payne argues that the tradition is best epitomized by the work of Clark and Ella Baker. For Payne, the organizing tradition has "a different sense of what freedom means."[3] By analyzing the Citizenship Education Program and the conflicts Clark had at Myles Horton's Highlander Folk School, where Clark prevailed, and in the Southern Christian Leadership Council, where Clark's arguments fell on deaf ears, I will illuminate Clark's role as an important proponent of the organizing tradition and the positive freedom it desired. Furthermore, by contrasting the success of Clark's arguments at Highlander and the subsequent establishment of the Citizenship Education Program with Clark's inability to change the SCLC's institutional focus on Martin Luther King Jr. and its diminished influence after King's death, I will show the advantage of group-centered leadership to create sustainable structures for social change under the right conditions.

Before analyzing Clark's role, it is necessary to define exactly what the organizing tradition means. In terms of its connection to the black freedom struggle, Ella Baker expressed the main ideas of the tradition most clearly. Baker differentiated between "group-centered leadership" and a "leader-centered group."[4] Within the black freedom struggle, there are numerous examples of the latter, the best being Martin Luther King Jr. and the SCLC. The SCLC revolved around King. This is not to say that King was the SCLC, but he was the group's face and voice. The organization of the SCLC can perhaps best be understood in military terms. King was the general. Individuals such as Ralph Abernathy, James Bevel, Hosea Williams, and Andrew Young served as his lieutenants. Below them were the sergeants—the local leaders of SCLC affiliates, such as Esau Jenkins. The SCLC's tactics consisted primarily of mass direct action protest, voter registration, and appeals to white people's consciousness.

Baker's conception of group-centered leadership, on the other hand, emphasized the development of individuals. Baker believed that "[s]trong people don't need strong leaders."[5] The goal of group-centered leadership is to develop the capabilities of all individuals in a given community so that they may become self-sufficient and not have to rely on outside leaders, or even a sustained protest movement, to be free. Baker saw the need for "the development of people who are interested not in being leaders as much as in developing leadership in others."[6] She attempted to create such a model in the Student Nonviolent Coordinating Committee (SNCC). SNCC did not have a hierarchical arrangement. Rather, it was a coalition of student groups and field workers whose activities were somewhat coordinated by a central organizing committee. SNCC workers typically operated in cells or small groups, working toward a goal in a specific location. After the initial sit-ins, SNCC efforts typically consisted of attempts to organize communities so that they could bring about their own liberation. While SNCC, initially at least, had similar goals to the SCLC, its tactics were very different. Particularly in Mississippi, people such as Bob Moses and Sam Block sought to organize people, rather than lead them. This contrasted with the dominant black political leadership model of what Baker called "leader-centered groups," the model that grew out of the black church. Organizing communities and empowering individuals require a patience, commitment, and confidence that seem to have been more present in female leaders.[7]

Clark's Citizenship Education Program clearly falls within the organizing tradition. The primary goal of the CEP was to teach and develop first class citizens. The rights and responsibilities of the first-class citizen include "the right to vote for the candidate of his choice and the responsibility of exercising that right in each and every election," using voting power effectively to realize citizenship's opportunities, and working together with others to improve one's community.[8]

The concept and rhetoric of first-class citizenship could be found at all levels of the CEP—in teacher training sessions, in Citizenship Schools, and in correspondence between the teachers and program staff. As students began to recognize themselves as first-class citizens, they became more likely to join the ranks of the growing nonviolent army.

The CEP also institutionalized grassroots leadership development. In many ways, it combined the strengths of a national top down organizational structure and the power of local leaders. The CEP built bridges between local leaders in different parts of the South and the national leadership. SCLC Citizenship School teacher training sessions at the Dorchester Center in Liberty County, Georgia, enabled future teachers to interact directly with and be inspired by national leaders such as Septima Clark, Andrew Young, and Martin Luther King Jr. The new Citizenship School teachers left empowered to assume the mantle of leadership in their home communities, where they in turn inspired and developed the leadership capabilities of their students and others in the community.

Many of those directly involved with the CEP's development are well documented within movement literature: Septima Clark, Ella Baker, Andrew Young, Hosea Williams, Fannie Lou Hamer, James Bevel, Diane Nash, Victoria Gray, and Myles Horton. Others, such as Bernice Robinson, Esau Jenkins, Dorothy Cotton, Annell Ponder, and Benjamin Mack, are less well known. The story of the Citizenship Education Program is the story of these people coming together to build what was probably the most effective program of the civil rights movement. Their activities place them within the organizing tradition. For Clark, freedom is a "much bigger than a hamburger," as Ella Baker once said.[9]

The CEP aimed to empower the natural leaders in the community, those Andrew Young called the "PhD minds" with "third grade educations."[10] Through training sessions at Highlander or Dorchester, these people in turn empowered their peers through Citizenship Schools. Just as Baker described, the CEP created a grassroots organizer cadre whose primary responsibility was the development of others. While on the surface the goal of the CEP was to teach literacy for voter registration, the underlying goal was personal and communal liberation. Septima Clark was keenly aware of this when she wrote "Literacy is Liberation."[11] In the context of the Jim Crow South, learning to read and write was both a revolutionary and transformative experience that aimed at liberating individuals from their historical situation.

In the CEP, we begin to see the different kind of freedom assumed by the organizing tradition. For the individuals who built the CEP and SNCC, freedom was not simply freedom from the oppressive regime of Jim Crow and the accompanying white terrorism. This was the freedom for which the SCLC, the National Association for the Advancement of Colored People (NAACP), and the Urban League fought. Rather, people such as Septima Clark and Ella Baker fought to help individuals achieve a freedom—the freedom to write, read, learn, organize, create new institutions, and be the author of one's own life.

The differences in the two conceptions of freedom parallel philosopher Isaiah Berlin's distinction between two kinds of liberty. In his seminal essay, "Two Concepts of Liberty," Berlin differentiates between negative and positive liberty.[12]

He defines the extent of one's negative liberty or freedom as the answer to the question, "What is the area within which the subject—a person or group of persons—is or should be left to do or be what he is able to do or be, without interference by other persons?"[13] The extent of one's positive liberty or freedom is the answer to the question, "What, or who, is the source of control or interference that can determine someone to do, or be, this rather than that?"[14] In other words, negative freedom corresponds to a lack of interference in one's life, and positive freedom corresponds to authorship over one's life.

Both traditions within the black freedom struggle obviously wanted both positive and negative freedom. The differences between the two were on their emphasis and focus. The organizing tradition in general, and the CEP in particular, sought to help individuals become the authors of their own lives. The CEP's goals of literacy education and voter registration both aimed toward this positive freedom. Its liberating pedagogy aimed to give students the necessary skills to achieve the goals *they* desired, and the emphasis on voter registration assumed that once blacks gained the vote they would have a say in the political decisions that affected *their* lives. Voter registration, within the organizing tradition, needs to be understood as a tactic, not a strategy. The SCLC, the NAACP, and the Urban League also encouraged voter registration to various degrees. However, their push for it was coded in terms of achieving political power to achieve certain ends. The CEP's emphasis was not on the achievement of a specific set of goals, but rather on the development of the capabilities of individuals, through which those individuals could change the very conditions of their lives and communities.

The development was a long and tenuous process that Clark led from its infancy. The program's initial gesticulation occurred in conjunction with the Highlander Folk School's efforts to institute a leadership development program. Clark arrived at Highlander prepared to begin the process of affecting social change. She was already an established community leader in Charleston, South Carolina, serving as a public school teacher and a leader in the local NAACP.

In the summer of 1954, Clark brought a group of Charleston area residents to Highlander for a workshop on reforming the United Nations. Included in the group were Clark's niece, Bernice Robinson, a beautician, and Esau Jenkins, a former student of Clark's on Johns Island, South Carolina, and a leader in the black community there.[15] At one point in the workshop, Jenkins was asked his thoughts on the United Nations. He responded that he was not concerned with the United Nations because he had his own problems in his community: the black residents of Johns Islands were largely illiterate and therefore could not register to vote. Johnson had taught a small handful of blacks to read on the bus he drove from Johns Island to Charleston but wanted to develop a way to reach more people. Horton recognized that here was a crisis situation around which he could develop leadership.[16]

Horton had been trying unsuccessfully for a year to develop leadership in Tennessee communities. After Horton and other Highlander staff members spent some time on Johns Island, Horton recognized the possibility of building a successful program. Because people on Johns Island were notoriously skeptical of outsiders, Horton hired Clark to oversee Jenkins's efforts on the island.

Clark soon found herself in conflict with both Horton and Jenkins. Initially, Jenkins did not see the value in involving others in order to develop leadership. At community meetings, he would run everything and control the decision-making process. Over the course of the year, however, Clark successfully convinced Jenkins that developing the capabilities of others was an end in itself. Jenkins began creating committees within the organizations he ran.[17] On the other hand, Horton thought that the program on Johns Island would be about developing the leadership of Jenkins and others in the community.[18] Once leaders had emerged, they could begin registering voters. Clark, however, knew this would not work. She knew that it was necessary to educate people so that they could pass the literacy test to register, but she believed it was even more important to help individuals realize their power as potential voters and citizens. Clark recalled "shouting it out" with Horton until he finally accepted her plan.[19]

The synthesis of Jenkins's new commitment to leadership development and Horton's recognition of the importance of education was the Citizenship Education Program. In 1957, the first Citizenship School, taught by Clark's niece Bernice Robinson, opened on Johns Island. The school aimed to respond to the students' educational needs while simultaneously preparing them to pass the literacy test to register and vote. By June 1961, Highlander had trained 435 people at either the Citizenship School or voter registration workshops at Highlander, and an estimated additional 4,515 off-site. By September 1961, there were Citizenship Schools operated by seven different organizations in 21 counties in Georgia, Tennessee, Alabama, and South Carolina. In 52 classes, 1,476 students attended, 667 of whom successfully registered to vote.[20] Clark's ability to bring both Jenkins and Horton to a point where they saw the need and potential to develop the capabilities of *all* members in a community led to the eventual success of the CEP.

Due to legal problems that eventually led to the temporary shutting down of Highlander, Clark and the CEP transferred to the SCLC in 1961. With the institutional support of the SCLC behind her, Clark built the CEP into a program that taught tens of thousands throughout the South. However, in the SCLC, Clark was forced to deal with a very different institutional culture than the one at Highlander. Not only was the CEP's pedagogy antithetical to the top-down structure of the SCLC, but the perception of the CEP, and education in general, as feminine by the SCLC leadership relegated the program to the background of the SCLC's mass direct-action protest activities. There is little doubt that the inability of King and others to recognize the leadership capabilities and models of Clark, Baker, and others because of their gender greatly diminished both the short- and long-term effectiveness of the SCLC. Although Clark (unlike Baker) did not develop a gendered critique of her time in the SCLC until after her retirement, she frequently came into conflict with the male leadership of the SCLC for their elitism and lack of desire to develop other leaders.

The Rev. Andrew Young initially joined the SCLC with Clark in order to administer the funds for the CEP. Young, who had previously worked among Northern liberal elites in New York after growing up in the South, had to make an adjustment to working with poor blacks.[21] Taylor Branch tells a story about Clark finding Young eating breakfast at Dorchester fresh off a chartered flight, while the trainees who had arrived after an overnight bus ride waited for the session to start without food:

> Clark intercepted him on the way to the pantry. He should not eat unless he shared the food with all the new arrivals, she said patiently, because they had been on a bus all night and were hungry. Young blinked. There was no money for a communal breakfast in the budget, he said, and besides, no one had complained about what was due him as the director. Clark said he must bear in mind that these were people who put sand in Coke bottles just to prove to the folks back home that they had seen the ocean. They would never dream of attending church at Ebenezer, let alone Young's elite congregation, because the worshippers there dressed up too much and were too refined for them, and if the recruits could not feel comfortable doing such simple things, how could they feel worthy to vote against the wishes of the white man? Clark said that the recruits noticed everything. Young's budget priorities and his lack of eagerness to mingle with his recruits spoke as eloquently as his speeches. "If you can pay all that money that the Marshall Field Foundation has sent us to rent a plane, why can't you give them two or three dollars to buy breakfast?" she asked. Failing that, he could share their discomfort.[22]

Clark later similarly critiqued Ralph Abernathy. Branch writes that, in the days following the Birmingham church bombing that killed four girls, Abernathy's jealousy of King reared its head, and he also got in a scuffle with a white man in an elevator because the man did not share his low opinion of the room service. Clark followed Abernathy to his hotel room to tell him "he was a spoiled man, full of unseemly spite, and while she was at it, she also reproached him for his habit of being deliberately late to church services in order to flaunt his mastery over the common people of the congregation."[23] Clark later called Abernathy "'just a spoiled little boy,' who 'never . . . had a chance to grow up and be a real man.'"[24]

Clark's critiques of the elitism of certain elements in the SCLC were symptomatic of her larger critique of the SCLC's emphasis on leader-centered direct-action protest. While working closely with Young on the CEP, Clark was vocally critical of Young's increased focus on protest activities. She also encouraged King to help develop the leadership of others within the organization. Unfortunately, both critiques fell on deaf ears.

After the CEP's first year with the SCLC, Andrew Young became increasingly involved with other SCLC efforts. By the end of 1962, Young took over the SCLC voter registration.[25] In 1963, Young focused his efforts on the SCLC's Birmingham campaign, leaving Clark to do most of the CEP work by herself.[26] Arguing circularly, Young justified spending more time on other SCLC projects because the CEP's success was partly because of the confidence people had in King and the SCLC but also because "the Citizenship Program has laid the groundwork for SCLC's entire program and staff."[27] He also justified it because he thought it a mistake "to assume that education was in itself an answer to the Negroes' problems. Education must be related directly to social change and social action. No foundation grant can do this, rather we must create a climate among the masses of people which demand that the government supplement the education and training of the masses."[28]

Clark was highly critical of Young for the lack of attention he gave to the CEP.[29] In December 1963, Clark wrote to King, giving a state-by-state assessment of the program. With the exception of the program in South Carolina, southeast Georgia, and parts of Mississippi, she saw few results. She attributed this to a lack of supervision and follow-up. As the "only one doing field visitation," Clark also expressed that the other staff working with her in the CEP felt "that the work is not dramatic enough to warrant their time. Direct action is so glamorous and packed with emotion that most young people prefer demonstrations over genuine education . . . It seems as if Citizenship Education is all mine, except when it comes time to pick up the checks." Clark noted that Young was often absent from Dorchester sessions and even when he was there, he was too tired to work with students. Because of his absence, Clark frequently found that reimbursement checks for teachers were sent out months late. Clark was also critical of leaders like Bob Moses and Jim Foreman for coming into places like Greenwood, Mississippi and taking over without involving the people.[30]

The following July, Clark wrote Young directly to criticize him for the lack of attention he gave to the CEP. She wrote that he was not doing the responsibilities his job description (which Young wrote) demanded. Clark was particularly bothered by the "unfair treatment of the people for whom the grant was proposed," noting that in May she found unpaid vouchers for teacher expenses going back to January. She continues, "The people for whom we get the money are those in the most benighted areas and to whom $30 is a great blessing . . . If we fail to do this the great battle for rights is in vain." Clark chastised Young for his desire to give raises to "men with families" while not considering the financial obligations that she and others had to larger family structures.[31]

While Young offered explanations to some of Clark's specific concerns in his response, he also acknowledged that everything she wrote was "quite true." He wrote that the previous year has been "the most confused and complicated year of my life. There were many days when I thought I might be on the verge of cracking up." He emphasizes that his responsibility is "to serve *the people*, not the Foundation or the sponsoring organizations."[32] Clark was unable to influence Young, who left the CEP in 1965 to work with King full time.

Clark was also critical of King throughout her tenure with the SCLC.[33] In 1963, Clark wrote to King emphasizing the need to focus on employment for blacks, not just registration and civil rights.[34] While it is unclear the effect this suggestion had on King, he did move toward placing greater emphasis on economic opportunity after 1965. Clark's strongest critique of King and the SCLC was their inability to develop leadership in others. Clark recalled that when local leaders would ask King to come to their city to lead marches, she would respond, "You're there. You going to ask the leader to come everywhere? Can't you do the leading in these places?" Clark wrote King on at least two occasions to ask him to develop others. In one letter, she asked King not to lead all the marches so that others may take a more prominent role. King read that letter before the staff as if it were a joke.[35]

Clark made a similar argument in a letter to King in 1967. She opened the letter by sharing the thoughts of Esau Jenkins, who by this time not only was developing leaders in his community but also served on the SCLC's executive board. "The men around Dr. King [act] like little children," Clark quotes Jenkins saying. "They must become well-developed creative thinking men and use their creativity to operate in crucial situations or community crises or be able to help with organizing the community so that minute men are at hand when needed." Clark appealed to King on a practical level. She wrote that she saw him as agitated, tired, and stressed, and that he needed someone else to share the burdens of running the SCLC. "You are human," Clark wrote, "you must have time for rest, relaxation and research. You must get someone to share the great responsibilities of a national organizing with you. That person must have the power to act with your support."[36] Unfortunately, King never implemented Clark's suggestions on a large scale. After King's 1968 assassination, the SCLC never again came close to achieving the influence and power it had under King. It is not coincidental that two years later, in 1970, the Citizenship Education Program lost its funding. Septima Clark retired that same year. Despite being well into her seventies, Clark remained active in Charleston as a member of the Old Bethel AME Church, and she became the first black woman elected to the Charleston County Board of Education in the 1980s.

Given the amazing potential of the CEP and the organizing tradition, there is a tendency to bemoan the tradition's decline after 1965. Payne, for one, concludes *I've Got the Light of Freedom* with a lament for the loss of the organizing tradition.[37] He writes, "The Organizing Tradition as a political and intellectual legacy of Black activists has been effectively lost, pushed away from the table by more top-down models."[38] Payne may very well be empirically correct. However, he does not seem to recognize one of the basic characteristics of organizing or group-centered leadership. Whereas in a leader-centered model, the leader is always potentially capable of mobilization on a large scale if she or he has the right personality, the organizing model relies on a very particular set of circumstances under which social change is possible.

In *The Long Haul*, Myles Horton differentiates between what he calls movement and organizational periods.[39] Organizational periods are about building networks and connections between people with similar ideas and goals. These networks can only be built using the strategies and tactics present in the organizing tradition. However, organizational periods are not about causing social change. They are about preparing for the times when social change is possible, which are the periods Horton identifies as movements. During movement periods, the networks built during organizational periods can be put to work to create social change.

Horton worked at Highlander for nearly sixty years. As an institution, Highlander epitomizes the ideals of the organizing tradition or group-centered leadership as well as any institution in the United States. However, in those sixty years, there were only two periods that Horton described as movements—the labor movement in the 1930s and 1940s, and the civil rights movement in the late 1950s and 1960s.[40] The expectation of consistent results from the organizing tradition is unrealistic. However, when the right circumstances exist, institutions built through group-centered leadership can have revolutionary and long lasting effects. Because of the groundwork laid at Highlander in the early 1950s where individuals such as Septima Clark, Bernice Robinson, and Esau Jenkins participated in workshops, Horton had created a network that was ready to take advantage of the growing movement leading to the creation of the Citizenship Education Program.

The genius of Septima Clark was her recognition and development of the power of education not only to enhance the power of their constituents but also to create a community of activists. The philosopher Hannah Arendt wrote,

> Education is the point at which we decide whether we love the world enough to assume responsibility for it and by the same token save it from that ruin which except for renewal, except for the coming of the new and the young, would be inevitable. And education, too, is where we decide whether we love our children enough not to expel them from our world and leave them to their own devices, nor to strike from their hands their chance of undertaking something new, something unforeseen by us, but to prepare them in advance for the task of renewing a common world.[41]

For Arendt, education was the act of welcoming individuals to take part in the public sphere she so valued.[42] Clark harnessed the power of education to empower Citizenship School students to enter a world that was trying to keep them out. She did not have a clear conception in mind of the world the students would create, beyond a commitment to democracy and equality. Clark trusted the students to undertake something new and unforeseen. Through community organizing, she aimed to help students achieve a positive freedom.

ARCHIVES CITED

1912–94. Bernice Robinson Papers, Avery Research Center, Charleston, SC.

1940–90. Field Foundation (FF) Archives, Center for American History, Austin, TX.

Highlander Research and Education Center Records, Wisconsin Historical Society, Madison, WI (cited as HREC).

1929–68. Papers of Martin Luther King Jr., Martin Luther King Center for Social Change, Atlanta, GA (hereafter cited as MLK).

1919–78. Septima P. Clark Papers, Avery Research Center, Charleston, SC (cited as Clark Papers).

1954–70. Southern Christian Leadership Conference Records, Martin Luther King Center for Social Change, Atlanta, GA (cited as SCLC).

NOTES

1. Quoted by Horton in Myles Horton and Paulo Freire, *We Make the Road by Walking: Conversations on Education and Social Change*, eds., Brenda Bell, John Gaventa and John Marshall Peters (Philadelphia: Temple University Press, 1990), 13.
2. Charles M. Payne, *I've Got the Light of Freedom: The Organizing Tradition and the Mississippi Freedom Struggle* (Berkeley: University of California Press, 1995), 3.
3. Ibid.
4. Ella Baker, "Bigger Than a Hamburger," *Southern Patriot* 18 (May 1960): 4.

5. Quoted in Payne, *Got the Light*, 93.

6. Ibid.

7. It is tempting then to argue that the programs modeled on group-centered leadership (or the model of bridge leadership articulated by Belinda Robnett) that were most often initiated by women occurred because either there is something in black women's experiences that predisposes them to such work or that women assumed control of such programs because it was the only leadership avenue open to them. However, to do so belittles the strength of the convictions of women like Clark (and Baker and Hamer). Clark did not build the Citizenship Education Program because it was one of the few avenues of action open to her as a woman (although this is empirically true). Clark developed the Citizenship Schools because she believed them to be the most effective means with which to create a sustainable institution capable of effecting social change. Influenced by Myles Horton, she believed that the only way to liberate the oppressed was to help the oppressed liberate themselves. Clark created her vision; she did not create a compromise.

8. "The Citizenship School," 1963, 24 (13). HREC.

9. Baker, "Bigger Than a Hamburger," 399.

10. Andrew Young, *An Easy Burden: The Civil Rights Movement and the Transformation of America* (New York: HarperCollins Publishers, 1996), 139.

11. Septima P. Clark, "Literacy and Liberation," *Freedomways*, 4, 1 (1964); emphasis added.

12. Isaiah Berlin, "Two Concepts of Liberty," in *Contemporary Political Philosophy: An Anthology*, eds., R. E. Goodwin and P. Pettit (Oxford: Blackwell Publishing, 1997).

13. Ibid.

14. Ibid.

15. Also in attendance was Rosa Parks, who, a few months later, would refuse to give up her seat on a Montgomery bus. Parks would later sight her attendance at this Highlander Workshop as part of her inspiration for her action.

16. John M. Glen, *Highlander, No Ordinary School, 1932–1962* (Lexington, KY: University Press of Kentucky, 1988), 185.

17. Highlander Folk School, Extension Program—Johns Island and Charleston.

18. Glen, "On the Cutting Edge," 528–33; Carl Tjerandsen, *Education for Citizenship: A Foundation's Experience* (Santa Cruz, CA: Emil Schwarzhaupt Foundation, 1980), 153–54.

19. Cynthia Stokes Brown, ed., *Ready from Within: Septima Clark and the Civil Rights Movement* (Navarro Cali: Wild Trees, 1986), 52–54.

20. Tjerandsen, *Education for Citizenship: A Foundation's Experience*, 181–87.

21. Septima Clark, interview with Eugene Walker, 30 July, 1976, 1 (9). Clark Papers.

22. Taylor Branch, *Parting the Waters: America in the King Years, 1954–1963* (New York: Simon and Schuster, 1988), 576–77.

23. Ibid., 899.

24. David J. Garrow, *Bearing the Cross: Martin Luther King, Jr., and the Southern Christian Leadership Conference*, 1st ed. (New York: W. Morrow, 1986), 366.

25. Ibid., 225.

26. Young, *An Easy Burden*, 278.

27. Andrew Young to Wesley Hotchkiss and Truman Douglas, 10 June, 1964, 136 (13). SCLC.

28. Andrew Young, memo to Septima Clark, Dorothy Cotton, and Martin Luther King Jr., re: Citizenship Education Program, 17 December 1963, 29 (1) MLK.

29. Taylor Branch, *Pillar of Fire: America in the King Years, 1963–65* (New York: Simon & Schuster, 1998), 190–91; Garrow, *Bearing the Cross*, 309, 338.

30. Clark's critique of Moses and Foreman begs further analysis, as it runs counter to the most prominent accounts of SNCC's work by Charles Payne and Clay Carson. Septima Clark to Martin Luther King Jr., 12 December 1963, 29 (18). MLK; Clayborne Carson, *In Struggle: SNCC and the Black Awakening of the 1960s* (Cambridge, MA: Harvard University Press, 1981); Payne, *Got the Light.*

31. Septima Clark to Andrew Young, 12 July 1964, 154 (6). SCLC.

32. Andrew Young to Septima Clark, 20 July 1964, 154 (6). SCLC; emphasis in original.

33. Despite the criticisms, Clark adored King. Just to cite one example, in 1964 she wrote King to congratulate him on the Nobel Peace Prize, writing, "I see in the spirit of this recognition the living relatives of Dubois, Richard Wright, and other earlier leaders utter the words, 'God still loves our world, we must continue to follow in His footsteps.' May God's great goodness continue to light your pathway." Septima Clark to Martin Luther King, 15 October 1964, 29(18). MLK.

34. Septima Clark to Martin Luther King, 12 December 1963, 29(18). MLK.

35. Brown, *Ready from Within*, 77–78.

36. Septima Clark to Martin Luther King, 12 June 1967, 29(15). MLK.

37. Payne, *Got the Light*, 363–90.

38. Ibid., 364.

39. Myles Horton, Judith Kohl, and Herbert R. Kohl, *The Long Haul: An Autobiography* (New York: Teachers College Press, 1998), 84.

40. Ibid.

41. Ironically, this passage comes at the end of a chapter slamming the very progressive education techniques, with their roots in the work of John Dewey, that the CEP used. Arendt's critique focused mainly on the lack of scientific data to support the implementation of progressive pedagogies. I would hope that had Arendt been aware of programs such as the CEP, or other accomplishments of progressive education over the past 40 years, that she would have reconsidered her position. Hannah Arendt, *Between Past and Future: Eight Exercises in Political Thought* (New York: Penguin, 1968), 196.

42. See Hannah Arendt, *The Human Condition* (Chicago: University of Chicago Press, 1958).

CHAPTER 14

HARAMBEE NATION

CORE, BLACK POWER, AND COMMUNITY DEVELOPMENT IN CLEVELAND

NISHANI FRAZIER

ROBERT ALLEN'S, *BLACK AWAKENING IN CAPITALIST AMERICA*, shaped the debate on black power and became the defining text on black capitalism during the late 1960s. Allen challenged black capitalism's efficacy as a strategy for community economic empowerment and categorized the concept as a subsidiary of a larger financial system that rewarded the few and subjugated the bulk of the poor and working class into capitalist servitude. Advocates of black capitalism, as well as groups that partnered with capitalist structures (i.e. foundations, corporations, government, etc.) served less the black community and more as mid-level bourgeois elite between the capitalist power structure and its worker class.[1] Organizations that embraced black capitalism as an organizing and funding-raising approach effectively acquiesced to an economic and political system that forced the larger black community into a lower societal stratum.[2] Amid the many denounced groups, the Congress of Racial Equality (CORE) became a target of criticism for its Cleveland Target City Project (TCP)—a "black capitalist" program, which sought, according to Allen, "not an end to oppression, but the transfer of the oppressive apparatus into their own hands."[3]

The "black capitalism" nomenclature ineffectually characterized the CORE philosophy of black power. Contrary to characterizations of CORE by many scholars as bourgeois reformist, CORE's black power philosophy reflected a nuanced and changing multiplicity of voices and approaches. From 1966–1969, CORE strategized two geographically focused programs for political and economic participation and access called Target City Project (TCP).[4] The Target City Projects transitioned CORE from a national directive of community organizing

---

CORE titled its second target city project in Cleveland, Ohio, *Harambee. Harambee* is a Swahili term meaning to build or work in unity.

in Baltimore to aggressive economic and political community development in Cleveland, Ohio.

Cleveland Target City Project manifested from a CORE that was surprisingly progressive, complex, and changing—if only for a short time. Between 1967 and 1968, Ford Foundation funding and the leadership of people like Ruth Turner and Tony Perot from the Cleveland Chapter, and Will Ussery from the San Francisco chapter, pushed CORE toward a black power program of structural and physical development. TCP's political expression was governmental reform, though the Ford Foundation and ultimately CORE paid a heavy price for its reformist intervention. The TCP economic development plan, diverged from formulaic system participation, and exhibited a far more complex and dynamic strategy for mass wealth building. TCP structured a community economic development corporation (CDC) called CORE Enterprises (CORENCO). CORENCO utilized the fiscal policies of Louis Kelso, an economist who advocated ethical capitalism, and aspired to an agenda of broad community wealth share. It was a new frontier, not only as an alternate paradigm for wealth distribution and participation within capitalism, but also as a pragmatic and potentially successful tool of financial rejuvenation for the black community, and by extension, a fiscally strapped CORE.

MOVING TOWARD BLACK POWER

The Congress of Racial Equality formed in the spring of 1942. Early in its formation, CORE concentrated the bulk of its chapter growth in the Midwest and East Coast areas of the United States. After the 1955 Montgomery Bus Boycott, the organization aggressively spread south. By the end of 1961, CORE's successful Freedom Rides project, a protest against discrimination in interstate travel, catapulted the group into the national limelight. The famous Freedom Rides of 1961 fostered a tidal wave of membership growth and expanded the organization's presence in the South, as well as the urban areas of the West, Midwest, and East Coast. Despite CORE's existence in the North, the national office concentrated its efforts on the southern freedom movement, almost to the neglect of its northern chapters. CORE selected Louisiana as the site of its programmatic thrust for voter registration, public accommodation, and cooperative farms. It also aligned with the Student Non-violent Coordinating Committee, the Southern Christian Leadership Conference, and the National Association for the Advancement of Colored People in the 1964 Mississippi Summer Project effort to expand voter registration and operate freedom schools. As the organization achieved its activist potential in the southern arena of the freedom movement, the tide turned away from the South to the one area where CORE was most present but had virtually ignored in terms of its national agenda.[5]

The national spotlight on the freedom movement not only shifted geographical focus from south to north, rural to urban, but so too did the character, structure, and focus of the black freedom movement. In the mid to late 1960s, CORE joined a chorus of voices that called for an end to the structural inequalities that hindered black entrance into all aspects of American society. Freedom activists attacked systems, which not only barred access by law, but hindered ascent from the political and economic lower stratum. The advocates of this form of black empowerment confronted and grappled with the more difficult problems of state surveillance and police brutality, exclusion from the political structure via voting prohibitions and legislative gerrymandering, and an economic system that kept the majority of African Americans locked in poverty as unemployed or low wage earners unable to build wealth. In 1966, these transformations took on greater urgency when Stokely Carmichael articulated it at the March Against Fear in Greenwood, Mississippi in one key phrase, *black power*. But despite black power's southern birth, the public image of these problems, which clearly affected African Americans across the United States, appeared to converge on the problems of America's urban and northern cities in particular.[6]

Simultaneous to black power's emergence, government and private intervention in American poverty intensified, and affected the direction of black power within CORE. Lyndon Johnson pledged in his 1964 State of the Union address to tackle the high poverty rate with a series of government programs, unveiled as the "War on Poverty" government initiative. During the same year the Johnson administration formed the government agency, the Office of Economic Opportunity (OEO), to administer these programs.[7] In tandem with governmental action, wealthy nonprofits like the Ford Foundation encouraged the growth of antipoverty and economic development groups with an infusion of community grants.[8] And though the southern region felt the impact of government and privately funded involvement, the northern and urban areas became central sites for all kinds of experimentations to end poverty, partially because current events demanded it.

The same year OEO started, it met with the first in a series of urban rebellions. Small riots in the cities of New York and Philadelphia illustrated black disenchantment and frustration with the deterioration of America's urban communities. Cities imploded from unemployment, dilapidated housing, declining municipality budgets, and the general downturn in inner-city life. The August 1965 outburst in Watts, a neighborhood outside Los Angeles, signaled the pressing issue of the ghetto more than the previous year's rioting. In six days of revolt, 34 were dead, more than one thousand people injured, and four thousand arrested, Watts both coincided with the more militant, sometimes violent, response to inadequate education, housing, and unemployment, while it also highlighted the need for Johnson's War on Poverty programs, particularly in the black ghettos of America.

When a 1966 uprising rocked Cleveland's Hough community, it was clear something had to be done. Stokely Carmichael could scarcely shout "Black Power" before both the slogan and the riots ignited a fear among America's white citizens that the declining city and the rising call for Black Power harbingered chaos, at minimum and armed revolution at worse. The federal government and foundations were ready for an intervention, but needed partners in the poverty war.

CORE was hardly unaware of the American public's concern over black unrest or the changing dynamics in the black freedom movement. Ruth Turner, a Cleveland CORE chapter leader, captured the mood of the period when she suggested that the 1965 national CORE convention be titled "The Awakening Giant."[9] The convention title not only symbolized a locale change in national CORE's agenda, but it also underlined the key role CORE intended to play in this transition.

The northern chapters' rise in power partially prefigured the 1965 convention slogan, which challenged CORE's legitimacy and effectiveness in the inner city. Chapters from Brooklyn; Baltimore; Washington, DC; San Francisco; and Cleveland asserted themselves more aggressively within the national office of CORE and were at the forefront of this new direction.[10] More willing to embrace the radical and militant elements of the black freedom movement (as exemplified by their early support of people like Malcolm X and the Monroe Defendants), these branches pushed CORE toward black power.[11]

The early 1960s activism of these chapters also forced these groups to struggle with the hidden de facto discrimination that kept black people in place. By 1965, most of these local CORE groups became embroiled in battles against union and employment discrimination, absent city services, poor housing, and neighborhood exclusion. School desegregation fights particularly pressed these chapters toward more assertive tactics of organizing.[12] This proved especially true for the Cleveland chapter, where the death of white minister Bruce Klunder and the recalcitrance of the Cleveland School Board of Education rendered a crushing blow to the morale of the chapter members, and its leader Ruth Turner. The Cleveland school desegregation fight resulted in Cleveland CORE's restructure and an abandonment of direct action for community organizing.[13] Other chapters also experienced these changes.

The power of Turner and other northern chapter leaders within CORE became evident at a meeting of the CORE National Advisory Council (NAC), CORE's advisory board, two days before the 1965 Durham Convention. Turner insisted at that meeting that the fight for integration was dead.[14] In fact, the nature of the freedom movement had changed, and its strategy no longer consisted of desegregation or integration thrusts but issues related to unemployment, inferior housing, displacement or urban renewal, poor schools, and low motivation. CORE had to change or face a reputation that amounted to "exposing civil rights problems but not solving them."[15]

Turner reserved most her criticism for the national office's inability to provide a roadmap that would shepherd local chapters into this new era of activism. Too many CORE chapters unsuccessfully comprehended the nature of community organization or expected instant results. A substantial number of chapters only associated with like-minded organizations, and excluded alliances with disparate black community members and groups. More to the point, many CORE chapters became "unrepresentative of the people they claim to represent."[16]

Worse, low finances precipitated sporadic activism within the chapters and the national office, and thus represented the final lynchpin of CORE's ineffectiveness. Turner learned through personal experience (low funds had at this juncture halted her full time service as Executive Secretary for Cleveland CORE) that CORE chapters could no longer depend on volunteer staff, as such situations left local branches at the mercy of sporadic participation and activity. Each chapter needed paid staff, especially for community organization.[17] However, CORE's deficit crisis realistically prevented programmatic action. CORE's budgetary problems brewed as early as 1964. By 1966, Floyd McKissick took responsibility for an overburdened organizational debt that equaled approximately $350,000.[18] Suggestion of a paid staff for long term community organization went beyond CORE's current cost confinements.

Despite the purported inaptitude of local chapters or the national office's glacial like movement, the 1965 convention diverted CORE from the southern movement. Community organizing became the new directive handed down by national CORE. Though it would be more proper to say that, because of groups like the Cleveland chapter, it was handed up.[19]

CORE now sought to alleviate the hardships of millions of black people caught in poverty and contained in the ghetto by, "harnessing the tremendous economic potential of the ghetto and by developing political movements."[20] Though the 1965 convention finalized CORE's embrace of community organization, the organization also needed to work out a plan for how to "harness" the ghetto potential. Additionally, the difficulty of weak funding and a large budget crisis left open the question of how CORE intended to implement any proposal that detailed a plan for community organization.

BLACK POWER CORE STYLE: CLEVELAND TARGET CITY PROJECT

Local chapters and the national office vetted proposals at the 1965 convention, and initially settled on a blueprint for community centers in three major cities. Each city center explored different avenues of black empowerment. The first was a "large scale political organization aimed at a specific goal (electing a mayor, etc.). The other potential concentrations included a community-owned center, social services project, and an "Alinsky-style" labor organization.[21] Local chapters assisted only when necessary, but otherwise acted separately from the community center.[22] The centers consisted of a small group of trained organizers who solely developed local leadership among poor black people. In addition, the national office planned to organize what it called "flying squads" or staff members who provided brief training for local chapters and these centers.[23] The "flying squads" idea never got off the ground. Or rather, CORE refurbished it as a one-target city project that focused all its energy into a multi-year plan rather than a strategy that required divided resources and mission emphasis. It became national CORE's first national program for black power.

Though CORE formally espoused the call for black power at its 1966 convention, Target City Project was already underway in Baltimore, Maryland. The Baltimore Target City Project (TCP), designated *Breaking the Noose,* in many ways mimicked the activities of the northern chapters and elements of the flying squad concept. Voter registration, community activism, confrontation of white supremacists and police brutality, and job training became cornerstones of *Breaking the Noose* and garnered the project some successes. The Baltimore TCP made forays into the political system by running and supporting candidates, unionized black women into Maryland Freedom Union, and promoted community confidence and activism.[24]

Nonetheless, a number of early issues plagued the first Target City Project. Infighting among the TCP staff, between the Baltimore CORE chapter and the national CORE office, and between the Baltimore Target City Project and the national CORE hindered Baltimore TCP's progress.[25] Although internal battles persisted over much of the project's life, the arrival of Tony Perot, a former Cleveland CORE member who was now CORE's national program director, settled some of the tension.

Perhaps the most vexing issue was low finances. Perot's proposal writing acumen and funding negotiation with the Department of Labor helped increase monetary resources. But, the monies which came in for the job-training component of the Target City program became a particularly prickly issue. Federal funding from the Department of Labor made the Baltimore Target City Project a viable program, but rumblings began almost immediately among CORE's more radical membership regarding the dependence on outside funding. Be that as it may, regardless of unsteady finances and in-house criticism, Baltimore TCP was a vibrant endeavor that advanced CORE's national Black Power agenda. Effectively, it allowed the organization to move forward with a second target city.

CORE considered several cities as the location for the second Target City program, including Newark and Chicago.[26] Perot's powerful reach and influence, among many reasons, affected not only the trajectory of the Baltimore Target City Project but also the choice of Cleveland for the second target city. Joined by Ruth Turner, the two Cleveland CORE members wielded a great deal of power at this juncture of CORE's history. Turner, who was the former executive secretary and public representative of the Cleveland chapter, gained a reputation in the organization as a very influential member of the National Action Council whose support of black power and intellectual prowess led to characterizations of her as a veritable "bogeywoman" of Black Power.[27] During the Target City Project period, Turner served as executive assistant to national director Floyd McKissick, who was preoccupied less with programming and more with solving CORE's debt crisis.[28] Tony Perot, who first earned his reputation as the stalwart leader of the action committee during the Cleveland chapter's tumultuous school desegregation fight, now worked as CORE's national project director, which included among many duties fund raising for the TCPs. Added to that was Cleveland based Arthur Evans, also former leader of the Cleveland CORE advisory board, and now first vice president of NAC.

Outside the presence of Clevelanders in the national CORE office, the selection of Cleveland as the Target City Project also resulted from a fermenting local circumstance. In 1967, black Cleveland resident and politician Carl Stokes made a second bid for mayor. Many of the Cleveland CORE members, including Turner and Perot, disappointedly remembered the failure of the first mayoral run in 1965. Less than a year after Cleveland CORE's school desegregation fight, the chapter entered its first major political fight to overturn the political forces that obstructed school integration. Cleveland CORE's office actually became unofficial campaign space for the 1965 Stokes campaign. When Stokes eventually lost,

Cleveland CORE members bitterly referred to the election as stolen.[29] It was no wonder that national CORE chose Cleveland as the second target city, anchored by a galvanized Cleveland black community on one side and a set of powerful players from the Cleveland CORE chapter on the other.

After CORE received a small grant of $175,000, voter registration obviously materialized as the first TCP initiative. CORE nourished the groundswell of enthusiasm for Stokes's mayoral run, and helped to add close to 20,000 additional black voters to the rolls.[30] Stokes won the position, thus becoming the first African American mayor of a major urban city. Although it was not without the help of a number of organizations engaged in voter registration, CORE topped the list as the prevailing influence.[31] Yet, the success of CORE's new public black power image immediately drew censure from all sides.

Most of the criticism hinged on one particular issue. CORE's second Target City Project was heavily funded by an outside source that gained a dubious reputation as a financial reservoir for Black Power organizations—the Ford Foundation.[32] During the 1960s, the Ford Foundation simultaneously held a position of leftist radicalism in the minds of white conservatives and corporate manipulator in the thinking of radical black activists. Created in 1936, the Ford Foundation's reputation changed over the course of time. In the 1950s, however, white leaders began to view the Ford Foundation as an enemy to the cause. With the entrance of McGeorge Bundy as president of the Ford Foundation in 1966, the Foundation became well known for its "radical" funding decisions.[33] Among those was a grant to Brooklyn CORE, which chapter leader Sonny Carson later came to regret. Other Black Power groups and organizations also received large Ford grants. Additionally, the Foundation strongly supported black-led community development corporations, nonprofit agencies that served the black community.[34]

Bundy's decision to fund these groups, however, raised a great deal of conflict among the foundation's board of directors. Some considered it wasted money in the ghetto, while others believed black leaders, like NAACP head Roy Wilkins and Urban League leader Whitney Young, more reputable. Despite debate among the board, Henry Ford II initially gave tacit approval to Bundy's black power funding enterprise.[35] However, he later resigned from this position, over concern about the kind of groups receiving foundation resources. Henry Ford eventually left the Foundation Board because of irreconcilable differences over Ford's new mission. In his resignation letter, he noted that the Ford Foundation was "a creature of capitalism . . . It is hard to discern recognition of this fact in anything the Foundation does."[36] While the Ford Foundation board continued to look aghast at the staff's decisions, Bundy moved forward with an agenda of ghetto transformation.

As in-house conflict emerged within Ford Foundation regarding funding selection, CORE also faced a similar situation. Foundation funds created a firestorm inside CORE from black radicals wary of "white money". Brooklyn chapter leaders Sonny Carson and Ollie Leeds led the attack against Ford Foundation funding of CORE projects, and maintained that acceptance of the grant amounted to CORE becoming a "tool to blind black people" and a "vehicle for personal fame."[37] Other divisions emerged over the monies given to CORE. Much of it fell into argument categories regarding the use of white funds, the use of white funds to keep CORE afloat, and the use of white funds for programming that essentially sustained the capitalist system. In all cases, the argument centrally hinged on the legitimate fear that white funding sources potentially became mechanisms for controlling CORE and the black community, to the detriment of both.[38]

In spite of the charge that the Ford Foundation simply aimed to usurp black revolutionary transformation, the American white political power structure actually viewed the Stokes victory with great alarm. CORE's relations with Ford led to additional denunciation from a more dangerous direction, the Nixon administration and Congress. Both were horrified by the use of nonprofit funds to facilitate a voter registration drive that influenced political elections, especially one instrumental in the selection of Stokes as mayor. Ford's decision raised the ire of enough government officials that Congress penalized it and all other nonprofit foundations. Not two years after Stokes' election win, Congress passed a punitive law that levied large amounts of taxes against nonprofits. The Ford Foundation and every other nonprofit paid a huge price for the Foundation's perceived intrusion into politics.

Congressman Wilbur Mills, who headed the House Ways and Means Committee, led hearings into non-profit organizations accused of "social engineering". The Ford Foundation was a particular target, but all foundations were scrutinized. Congress passed the Tax Reform Act of 1969, legislation that enforced a 4 percent tax on annual investment income for all foundations. For the foundation, that penalty approximated ten million dollars. Congress also removed tax incentives for creating private foundations and increased rules regarding donations, which effectively acted to hinder and discourage philanthropy. In addition, as a direct response to Cleveland CORE's successful voter registration drive, Congress prohibited all foundations from funding one-time municipal voter registration drives.[39]

The Ford Foundation's leadership, especially McGeorge Bundy, also earned a place on Nixon's infamous "enemies list" of opponents to the Nixon presidency. The Nixon enemy list, exposed in the 1970s, consisted of persons, organizations, and institutions who the administration intended to suppress through prosecution, investigation, IRS probes, and various other means of harassment.[40] The Richard Nixon White House actually investigated the Foundation as a "left-wing" organization. Although the Ford Foundation was anything but "left-wing," the Nixon administration directed Tom Huston, a Nixon aide, to investigate Ford. Tom Huston was no ordinary aid in the Nixon administration. Huston authored the emphasis *Huston Plan*, which authorized illegal surveillance and intelligence collection, as well as searches into the homes of perceived subversives.[41] Huston unreservedly followed Nixon's directive to investigate Ford and noted that "certainly we ought to act in time to keep the Ford Foundation from again financing Carl Stokes' mayoralty campaign in Cleveland." Nixon's response was that he should "follow up hard on this."[42]

Years later, the Ford Foundation annual report painted a rosy perspective on what it called "the troubles of 1969." Ford claimed that it was, "not all that bad," though it took, "greater pains, since 1969, to avoid the appearance of hubris." They also noted that the current regulations and its enforcement had been "consistently fair," and that "the sentiments of the President's men toward organizations like ours had very little effect." This, of course, assumed that a 10 million dollar loss and no participation in voter registration funding could actually be deemed a "little effect."[43]

Although black radicals argued that Ford intervened to the disadvantage of the black community, the reality was the exact opposite. The high numbers of newly registered voters and the Nixon administration's reaction to the election contradicted the notion that black agency was absent or that Ford manipulated CORE. The Stokes campaign movement was already afoot by the black community itself—CORE only purposefully facilitated the outcome. It enabled CORE to argue that the Cleveland Target City Project's first year was a great success, pointing to its position as a key player in the selection of not only Carl Stokes but also his brother Louis Stokes, cofounder of the Congressional Black Caucus, one year later when Cleveland TCP added more registered voters to the rolls.[44] Thus black agency with white funds could, indeed, lead to Black Power—at least black political power—much to the chagrin and annoyance of anti–civil rights forces.

CORE AND COMMUNITY CAPITALISM

For CORE, the next level of black empowerment involved a more difficult issue. National Director, Floyd Mickissick explained that CORE intended "to move politically at first, because it is the first and easiest way . . . and after politics, economic power automatically flows. We are going to work on a total program."[45] It was one thing to place into position an administration more predisposed to assist, or at least not hamper, the black community's development. However, the structures that kept black Clevelanders from economic progress was another face of black inequality. Indeed, the job-training program in Baltimore, though successful, revealed one weakness to the approach of community organizing. Cleveland, as was true of many northern cities such as Detroit and Pittsburgh, had particular problems with low employment opportunities. The city saw a decline of available jobs and a mass exodus and divestment of companies and corporations. In fact, low job availability partially received blamed for the 1966 explosion in Hough that resulted in a six-day riot, which left four dead, thirty injured, and close to three hundred arrested.[46]

Solutions to economic disparity in Cleveland, and in the black community nationally, varied. A veritable hodgepodge of approaches emerged in the latter 1960s both inside and outside of CORE. Within CORE, a number of members viewed business ownership and free market enterprise as a viable solution. In this form of capitalism, workers received the benefit of employment and wages. Businesses would then become the foundation for small black "nation-states" in the ghetto areas of the United States. In effect, those who supported this form of black capitalism, among them Roy Innis leader of the Harlem Chapter, mirrored the current economic system of the owner/laborer relationship but removed the hindering effect of race in the hiring process.[47]

Other CORE members saw the whole capitalist system as an impediment to
black progress. Activists such as Brooklyn CORE leader Sonny Carson argued
that the very essence of capitalism created a class of laborers trapped in place
and beholden to an owner class. It was a corrupt system that meant poor blacks
never achieved freedom. From Carson's perspective, CORE had to take a stand
against capitalism. He argued that "capitalism has to be destroyed if black people
are to be free. We don't want anything to do with the white power structure as it
is now."[48] Some CORE voices, like Ruth Turner, Tony Perot, and Wilfred Ussery, chapter leader of San Francisco CORE, recognized the inherent flaws of the
laissez-faire method of economic empowerment, which left the black masses in a
position of subjugation. In fact, Turner's take on capitalism partially determined
her support for McKissick, whom she pointedly asked to confirm as national
director of CORE his statement of the "need to reevaluate the capitalistic system."[49] However, this group within CORE also surmised that waiting for the
revolution hardly proved any more an option. Pragmatically, there was a need for
a technique that operated within the confines of capitalism, but still propelled
poor and working black people beyond the permanent laborer class.

Cleveland TCP leaders were not the only activists who thought along those
lines. Those who embraced economic development followed along the same
trajectory on the local level. Neighborhood community groups had begun to
ask the same questions. How can the black community achieve economic uplift
while still dealing with capitalism's innate practice of creating hierarchies? Into
this void stepped a number of local organizations whose vision broadened the
conception of capitalism. These ideas of a more open economic system eventually
led to an advocacy of a communal form of capitalism.

Community capitalism became the new theory of black economic uplift.
Community capitalists promoted group ownership of the companies and corporations that operated in the black community. Institutionally, community
capitalism was promoted by the formation of nonprofit entities that took advantage of the funds granted by the government and nonprofit foundations but
managed for-profit endeavors for the whole of the community. These nonprofit
entities became community development corporations (CDCs). CDCs, more
importantly, served as the local partners OEO needed for the distribution of
funds for poverty programming.[50]

In the post-King era of the late 1960s and early 1970s, CDCs cropped up all
across the United States. Facilitated by grants from the Lyndon Johnson's War
on Poverty program, the Office of Economic Opportunity, and foundations
like the Ford Foundation, community development organizations utilized these
contributions to facilitate job training, business ownership, and economic self-
sufficiency. Rochester, Oakland, Newark, and Selma were among the first cities
to experiment with CDCs as an approach to black uplift of the poor. Cleveland,
however, occupied a unique position, as it was both the location of the first OEO
multimillion-dollar funded CDC, Hough Area Development Corporation, and
the site of the last Target City Project cultivated by CORE. Ironically, Hough
Area Development Corporation included a number of CORE members among
its staff. In fact, a couple of the HADC staff members had worked with the

Cleveland TCP, the Cleveland CORE chapter, or the Baltimore TCP. In effect, national CORE lost some of its members to a better funded local organization.

The cornerstone of many CDCs was ownership of neighborhood businesses. Company ownership by CDCs served a number of purposes. It created an enterprise that could employ its job trainees. It redirected business profits toward community programming—an important move for the longevity of any CDC that hoped to avoid being left vulnerable to vagaries of outside "white" funding. Lastly, it facilitated joint ownership of the business with its employees and/or surrounding community. Not all CDC's chose the latter route, but for those who did, it was an important contribution to community capitalism and black economic power. CDCs made the employees more than "cogs" in the capitalist machine, and turned them into bona fide beneficiaries of the system.

The experiments in community capitalism by local CDCs very much reflected CORE's own sensibilities about black economic development. Community development advocates represented a third wing within CORE, and their influence dominated the Cleveland Target City Project, especially its second phase from late fall 1967 through 1968. Under their leadership, CORE faced the reality of America's economic system and Cleveland's financial downturn, but still sought the keys to its access. No job training could rebuild the economic base of a city being deserted by companies, and economic access in the capitalist system had to be more than low-wage employment or sustenance living.

Cleveland TCP held a major conference on black economic development and funded a study of poverty in Cleveland. By the spring of 1968, McKissick announced the initiative's outcome—the development of a plan to tackle poverty in black Cleveland and throughout the United States. McKissick noted that the proposal emerged from CORE's belief that integration no longer served as a central goal for the black community and that the only way to stop poverty in the black community was to "tap this source of wealth to become full partners in the capitalist system."[51] The TCP report on poverty and economic development proved to be much more than a mere study. CORE determined to create a formal community development structure for its economic plan, taking the local CDC movement to a national scale.

The TCP position paper formed the foundation for national CORE's most aggressive and innovative program to date, a national economic and community development corporation called CORE Enterprise Corporation (CORENCO). CORENCO existed as an independently run program and offshoot of the larger Cleveland TCP. CORE created CORENCO as a nonprofit entity geared toward economic research, education and development. Partially facilitated by a second Ford Foundation grant (before the 1969 confrontation with Congress), CORE proposed to transform the black community citywide, and later in multiple cities via CORENCO. CORENCO was the brainchild of now national CORE advisory board chair Wilfred Ussery. The proposal represented Cleveland TCP's intended goal to develop an economically, politically, and socially empowered nation, which it encapsulated in the new Cleveland TCP designation *Harambee*, a Swahili term meaning "to build together."[52]

The CORENCO plan presumed that hindered participation in and stymied ownership access to production created poverty in the black community. In order to eliminate poverty, CORENCO endeavored to facilitate ownership of the economic structures within and produce goods and services for the black community. Though CORE billed CORENCO as a "corporate subsidiary," its membership and staff participants pulled from a variety of persons within the black community. As such, the corporation manifested and morphed from neighborhood to neighborhood as a greater reflection of the surrounding city that it intended to serve.[53]

CORENCO officially opened its doors at 10616 Euclid Avenue in the summer of 1968. Wilfred Ussery came in to personally handle and organize CORENCO. CORENCO measured its success based on the culmination of eight outcomes:

1. Programs of employment and corporate share purchase by new employees
2. Purchase of white-owned small businesses that serviced the black community
3. Identification of new enterprises or selection of companies willing to accept management or franchise purchase by black employees
4. General job training and job placement services
5. Enhancement and preparatory labor training and skill improvement for upper-level management positions
6. Expansion of black small businesses
7. Consumer education
8. And particularly, "engaging in such other activities as may facilitate Black people becoming the legitimate constituents—that is, employees and/or shareholders, and preferably both—of the business community of the Cleveland area."[54]

CORE constructed these outcomes with the assistance of Louis Kelso, a San Francisco lawyer and economist whose ideas about capitalism rested outside the boundaries of common free market economic theories.

Kelso's ideas on capitalism were atypical, but they struck a chord with CORE representatives and provided the foundation from which CORE produced CORENCO's platform. Kelso's idea particularly demonstrated the complexity of CORE's plan.[55] Kelso argued in *The Capitalist Manifesto* and *Two-Factor Theory: The Economics of Reality* that capitalism did not necessarily obviate participation by the average wage earner within the system. Instead, capitalism simply failed to democratize itself for broader participation in wealth building. More to the point, Kelso suggested that his version of capitalism achieved economic justice because it allowed all wage earners to participate in wealth building and ownership while it suppressed the concentration of capital in the hands of the few or what economists call "concentrated ownership distribution." In lay person's terms, no one person could own everything to the detriment of others, particularly laborers.

Kelso founded his economic philosophy on an ideological formula of binary economics. Binary economics basically meant that production emanated from two different sources, capital (land, structure, etc.) and labor (mental and physical).[56] Based on binary economics, Kelso argued that "nations must revamp the traditional strategies of both capitalist and socialist economies. They must eliminate their virtually exclusive dependence on employment, welfare, and traditional growth strategies, and initiate a program to achieve universal capital ownership according to binary economic principles. Only through such an approach can the autonomy that families enjoyed in the preindustrial world be restored in the current industrial era."[57] Kelso further claimed that the current American economic system only allowed those who already had capital to acquire more while it blocked and limited wage earners from attainment of wealth. The current capitalist economy wrongly concentrated its efforts toward unstable and changeable factors like increased employment, tax breaks, and welfare, as opposed to ownership.[58] In other words, ownership was a right of all, not a few.

Kelso's economic plan stipulated the basis for economic justice through three principles: the principle of distribution, the principle of participation, and the principle of limitation. Within these principles, Kelso cited the rules of capitalist exchange and development. First, under the principle of distribution, each person in American society who participated in the generation of wealth received a "distributive share" of the total wealth produced based on the contribution that each person made.[59] Basically, the more you participated/worked the greater your share. Second, through the principle of participation, every person had a right to maintain their livelihood and a basic standard of living through involvement in wealth production. No person can be denied access to the capitalist economy nor receive less than what was required to live. And finally, the principle of limitation argued that no one person, since every person had a right to the means of production, could usurp the second principle and own wealth to such an extent as to exclude others "from the opportunity to earn a viable income."[60] If the American economic system followed these principles, according to Kelso, "it should hardly come as a surprise, therefore, that in a truly capitalist economy, economic freedom and justice will be as widely diffused as the ownership of capital."[61]

Kelso's best-known economic concept became the employee share ownership plan (ESOP). CORENCO incorporated ESOP along with other Kelso economic strategies. In fact, the forty-five page CORENCO proposal all but reiterated Kelso's economic justice strategy in a condensed form.[62] Wilfred Ussery bolstered Kelso's economic theory with his own thoughts, stating that "80% of what makes money in America is owned by 3% of Americans. Negroes . . . are in the white structure of industrial sharecropping, just earning enough to survive, and remain tied to the system."[63]

The CORENCO plan envisioned a community economic development strategy that gave every black person access to income and ownership. Though black revolutionary nationalists considered this notion of black economic development an insufficient endeavor, given the funding source, CORE members who supported the plan were not unaware of how capitalism affected and influenced racial inequality. The CORENCO program had not simply mimicked the current system of capitalism, but attempted to transform its potential impact among Cleveland's lower income wage earners in a positive direction.

CORENCO's outlined goals, for example, allowed minimum-wage earners at a McDonald's restaurant to receive additional management training for possible individual promotion while it also advocated franchise ownership or share purchases for joint wealth building among McDonald's employees—regardless of job level. Most importantly, CORENCO intended to grow beyond otherwise well-known franchises like McDonald's and create a broad range of businesses for economic development and production of manufacturing goods, including: appliances, furniture, food, cars, pharmaceuticals, clothing, and building materials.[64]

The corporation also sought to provide community services in the area of home maintenance and repair, automotive service, medical centers, daycare nurseries, employment services, funeral and memorial societies, group insurance plans, hotels and restaurants, trucking and moving services, and finally, a community development and land holding company to improve structure and land use in the black Cleveland area. Companies that provided these services simultaneously boosted the local economy, while it also served as wealth share companies. As such, manufacturing plants, franchises, or local businesses served as example prototypes for a much larger goal of producing a number of wealth share entities.[65]

Even more, the proposal called for joint relations with financial institutions that assisted independent ownership by the black community. Particular attention was given to banks and credit unions that established associations with African governments. Finally, the proposal called for the operation of media outlets, and argued that "the need for black ownership of a radio and TV station has never been greater than it is now. A black press could combat confusion, rumors, and misinformation. It could also engage in meaningful educational programs to raise the level of living and achievement in the black community."[66]

According to the CORENCO plan, Cleveland would also be the site of an African-styled cultural and business center with a variety of businesses as well as "shops specializing in products imported from African countries" with the intent to "reinforce the black self image as well as provide profitable economic activity." The shopping center, in particular, would hold a travel agency, an entertainment booking agency, a film and communication firm, an export-import distribution center, a restaurant, and other types of commerce that provided jobs and investment possibilities for black Cleveland residents.[67] In addition, any parent franchise corporation could place its plant or company within the black community, if it hired and trained black employees for middle and upper management, and guaranteed technical help and other assistance until the company became self-sufficient. Once the corporation recovered costs and some profit, the parent company would turn over ownership to employees through stock and shares in the company.[68]

CORE intended for the CORENCO plan to overhaul the economic relationship of the black community internally, nationally and internationally. While it halted the outflow of money from the black community for goods and services, it created and boosted economic alliances with African countries and employed technological skills, goods, and resources gleaned from other industrialized foreign countries, with particular attention geared toward Japan.[69]

CORENCO's proposal speculated that an economic relationship with Japan could prove particularly lucrative and would primarily revolve around manufacturing Japanese goods—specifically televisions and automobiles—for sale within the United States.[70]

The complex and comprehensive nature of CORENCO's goals cannot be underestimated. But the revised relationship to community building also meant a partial departure from CORE's idea of community organization, a decision of which CORE leaders were not unaware. Wilfred Ussery contended that CORE was "no longer interested in developing 'community groups and projects' that 'float off on their own thing.' We are talking about things that are tied into CORE and that are controlled by CORE."[71] No doubt much of that attitude stemmed from the existence of groups like the Hough Area Development Corporation (HADC received 1.6 million dollars from OEO the first year and subsequent allotments until 1974), which utilized consciously or unconsciously similar ideas of CORE but received enough monies to make it solvent while CORE limped along in debt.[72] CORE centralized community development through one institution and sought funds that potentially made CORE financially secure, and kept it a viable activist, community-oriented entity.[73]

Though CORENCO's program potentially stood to have a transformative effect on national CORE and on poverty in Cleveland, the company lacked the capital with which to begin to achieve its goals. The second grant of $300,000 sustained Cleveland TCP staff and other activities, but CORENCO needed a third grant from Ford Foundation to aid its first steps.[74] However, the national office received signals that there would be no additional donations. In spite of Ford Foundation's eventual decision not to fund a third TCP, CORE moved forward with promotion of the CORENCO plan.

For help building its new multimillion-dollar nonprofit, CORE turned to political and business leaders of Cleveland. Invited members of the mayor's office, various companies and financial institutions, public officials, and foundations and charities attended a formal press conference and presentation of the CORENCO proposal.[75] CORE next forwarded letters to local business heads, and requested their presence at an economic conference scheduled for October 29, 1968. In the letter, Ussery urged leaders to remember, "'White society is deeply implicated in the ghetto. White institutions created it; white institutions maintain it and white society condones it.' Will you, as one of the responsible business leaders in Cleveland allow this cancerous situation to persist until it engulfs the entire city with its malignant effects?"[76] Ussery also noted that "our intention is not to establish a new welfare burden for present property owners and wage earners, but rather a series of self-sustaining economic institutions whereby black residents can be owners of capital instruments and wage earners."[77]

To that end, national CORE leaders Roy Innis (now national director); Donald Simmons, CORE's economic adviser; Kermit Scott, director of chapter development; and Wilfred Ussery, CORE chairman, met with more than seventy business leaders and requested a pledge toward CORENCO's seed money goal of ten million dollars. The project began in Cleveland but future branches included New York, San Francisco, and Washington, DC[78] The boldness of the CORENCO idea generated heightened interest in CORE's activities, and even got noticed in the *New York Times*, though passing interest was all the meeting produced. No one donated funds, and the intricate and innovative CORENCO model did little to empower the national office or CORENCO itself. CORENCO as a national corporation never got off the ground as hoped.

Ostensibly, CORENCO should have been a program that white business leaders and politicians heavily supported. President Richard Nixon, for example, touted the positive attributes of black capitalism beginning in 1968. In fact, in March 1969, Nixon even established by executive order the Office of Minority Business Enterprise within the Commerce Department. According to Nixon, the concept of black capitalism promoted participation in the economy, investment within the community, "dignity, pride, and self-respect."[79] However, it was not Nixon's intention to be broadly inclusive of the black community when it came to business ownership. The program was built around attracting support (and, more to the point, votes) from the black middle class while also appearing to support some aspects of the Black Power movement. Most importantly, the black capitalism idea became a political tool with which to avoid criticisms of the Nixon administration's anti–civil rights stance while it also portrayed itself as a supporter of black equality.[80]

Additionally, the administration's black capitalism push was further scrutinized by white conservative politicians looking to end any spending related to communities of color that protested over racial inequality. The result was an effort that was often sporadic and haphazard in its approach to supporting black capitalism.[81] It was possible that the CORENCO model never gained federal funds for its program because it simply never connected with Nixon's own sporadic efforts. There was also no doubt that CORE's Cleveland TCP voter registration project dampened prospects for financial backing. Whatever the case, the reason for the CORENCO program's having never moved forward rested partially on the issue of financing, specifically the lack of it.

This was not to say, however, that CORE never turned to other ways of sustaining the CORENCO plan. As a matter of fact, the Cleveland TCP restructured the national CORENCO project as a local model in the form of two small businesses. However, like CORENCO, the TCP was also hampered by disappearing funds. By the time CORE requested an additional grant from the Ford Foundation, three major changes took place that effectively heralded the demise of the Cleveland TCP: congressional hearings and disciplinary action against nonprofit foundations were imminent; internal dynamics at the Ford Foundation had begun to isolate supporters of Black Power organizations; and CORE itself was losing financial and membership ground.

The reduced funds certainly limited CORENCO's possibilities, but CORE's internal fighting took a damaging toll on CORENCO. Unbeknownst to Ford Foundation, national CORE barely maintained the existence of the Cleveland TCP without continuous internal strife, and the waning organizational strength of national CORE. And though the Cleveland TCP started on better economic footing and planning than the Baltimore project, Cleveland TCP suffered more from internal antagonisms—in this case—between national CORE and Cleveland TCP or between Cleveland CORE, TCP staff, and TCP Advisory board members, or just general squabbling among TCP personnel itself.

Between the vociferous power wrangling, declining financial debt which caused many staff members to go unpaid for days or weeks, and the general downfall of CORE, it hardly surprised anyone that some of CORE's national officers began to leave. Ruth Turner left in the summer of 1967 for a couple of reasons—most of them personal. Her father had become terminally ill in the summer of 1967, and she chose to devote more time to his care and to building a family life with her new husband, Tony Perot. After close to a decade devoted to CORE with low or no pay, she left to serve on the Governor's Commission to assess civil rebellions in Newark, New Jersey.[82]

Tony Perot, whose proposal writings and leadership in grant negotiations led to funding for both the Baltimore and Cleveland Target City Projects, was another loss. He resigned May 29, 1968 – a month before Ford Foundation sent its second allotment to national CORE. He intended only to serve in an advisory fashion thereafter. He too, left to pursue married life. Perhaps more compelling, the vying for power within CORE reached its limit for Perot. With the absences of Ruth Turner and Tony Perot, CORE lost two of its leading community organizing and development advocates. On June 19, 1968, Floyd McKissick also grew tired of fighting NAC and the various factions within CORE. Will Ussery was left, as one of the few leading proponents of black community development, to deal with the faction led by Roy Innis. Though a likely candidate for national director, he refused to run against Roy Innis.[83]

Added to that, Sonny Carson and the black revolutionary nationalists believed CORE had failed as a black power organization. Carson and Brooklyn CORE withdrew from CORE in protest at the 1968 convention. Other chapters soon followed, including Philadelphia, Kansas City, Queens, and the Bronx. When delegates refused to elect Innis as national director and chapters walked from the convention, he called a second national CORE meeting in St. Louis in fall 1968. With few chapters present, Innis finally took over CORE. The event damaged CORENCO and CORE irrevocably, as Roy Innis and others who supported a more laissez-faire form of capitalism attained power and effectively became the only leadership left within CORE. Ussery left CORE not much longer after Roy Innis seized power as national director.

Once Ussery departed the organization, the focus also moved from Cleveland to Harlem as the site for Black Power experimentation. Innis turned to a spatial articulation of Black Power via his proposed nation-state black communities. Not only had CORENCO and the Cleveland TCP loss viability, but national CORE soon followed their paths. Innis was ill prepared to obtain funding or write proposals for programs that went beyond Black Power rhetoric of separate nation-states. Staff loss and a lack of fundraising skills left the national office almost assuredly in a downward spiral. Innis and his brand of conservative Black Power effectively determined the rest of CORE's direction.[84]

Cleveland TCP and the community development push was the last Black Power stand of CORE's progressive faction. Both the political and economic elements of Cleveland TCP revealed aspects of an enlightened CORE and the varied nature and potentialities of its black power. The political repercussions in Cleveland stretched for years, but the demand for black economic power reached an impasse. CORENCO's short life illustrated the differing and innovative viewpoints on black economic power, and challenged the notion of a black elite CORE that fed off the people. Though CORE lost its position as a national emblem of community development, this history exposed the intricacies of internal organization dynamics, the complex relations between black power and white money, the dubiety of monolithic corporate control, and the adroit assertion of black agency. Cleveland TCP fell under the weight of infighting and financial decline and reverted to a conservative plan of black capitalism, but the Cleveland Target City Project fundamentally transformed what we knew and what we thought we knew about CORE and black power.

NOTES

1. Robert L Allen, *Black Awakening in Capitalist America: An Analytic History* (Garden City, N.Y.: Doubleday, 1969), 19, 142–57. Accusations of CORE being "bought off" also stemmed from James Forman's book, *The Making of Black Revolutionaries* where he accused McGeorge Bundy of saving CORE to wean it off black power and destroying SNCC. The supposition of "buying off" CORE hinged on too many questionable variables – none of which incorporate the influence of internal dynamics within Ford Foundation, and more importantly, within CORE. Additionally, CORE never received a great deal of money from Ford (compared to other community and national groups) to even consider the notion that it was bought off. More discussion will follow regarding these multi-layered dynamics. James Forman, *The Making of Black Revolutionaries: A Personal Account* (Seattle, WA: University of Washington Press), xvii–xviii

2. For more examples of classic scholarly critiques of black capitalism, see Earl Ofari, *The Myth of Black Capitalism* (New York: Monthly Review Press, 1970); E. Franklin Frazier, "Negro Business: A Social Myth," in *Black Bourgeoisie: The Book That Brought the Shock of Self-Revelation to Middle-Class Blacks* (Glencoe, Illinois: Free Press, 1997): 153–73; Manning Marable, *How Capitalism Underdeveloped Black America: Problems in Race, Political Economy, and Society* (Boston, Mass: South End Press, 1983).

3. Allen, *Black Awakening*, 191.

4. Previous scholarship on black power in CORE tended to pigeonhole the organization's actions as ethnic pluralism, bourgeois reformism, or bourgeois black nationalism. These designations generalized the CORE black power experience, and persistently focused on the role of Roy Innis in CORE's transition to black power to the exclusion of other examples of black power within CORE. This analysis also classified CORE as an elite group as opposed to a community partner. Subsequently, historiography on CORE's black power policy made the organization appear static and without complexity. For examples, see John H Bracey, August Meier and Elliott M Rudwick, *Black Nationalism in America* (Indianapolis: Bobbs-Merrill, 1970), li. Manning Marable, *Race, Reform, and Rebellion: The Second Reconstruction in Black America, 1945-1990* (Jackson: University Press of Mississippi, 1991), 109. William L Van Deburg, *Modern Black nationalism: From Marcus Garvey to Louis Farrakhan* (New York: New York University Press, 1997), 175; August Meier and Elliott M Rudwick, *CORE; A Study in the Civil Rights Movement, 1942-1968* (New York, Oxford University Press, 1973), 409–25.

5. For detailed information on CORE's history and transformation over time, see Meier and Rudwick, *CORE*. For additional sources on CORE in Louisiana and Mississippi during Freedom Summer, see Adam Fairclough, *Race and Democracy: The Civil Rights Struggle in Louisiana, 1915–1972* (Athens: University of Georgia Press, 1999); Doug McAdam, *Freedom Summer* (New York: Oxford University Press, 1990); and Bruce Watson, *Freedom Summer: The Savage Season That Made Mississippi Burn and Made America a Democracy* (New York: Viking, 2010). Relatively few texts examine CORE in the north or west coast. For recent texts see Joan Singler, et al., *Seattle in Black and White: The Congress of Racial Equality and the Fight for Equal Opportunity* (Seattle, W.A.: University of Washington Press, 2011); Brian Purnell, "Drive Awhile For Freedom," in *Groundwork: Local Black Freedom Movements in America*, ed. Komozi Woodard and Jeanne Theoharis (New York, NY: New York University Press, 2005); Patrick Jones, *The Selma of the North: Civil Rights Insurgency in Milwaukee* (Cambridge, MA: Harvard University Press, 2009).

6. Recent scholarship explores the changing nature of black power and its impact on the south, though historically viewed as a northern and urban phenomena. For examples, review Hasan Jeffries, *Bloody Lowndes: Civil Rights and Black Power in Alabama's Black Belt* (New York: New York University Press, 2009); Susan Youngblood Ashmore, *Carry It On: War on Poverty and the Civil Rights Movement in Alabama, 1964–1972* (Athens: University of Georgia Press, 2008); Alton Hornsby, *Black Power in Dixie: A Political History of African Americans in Atlanta* (Gainesville: University Press of Florida, 2009); and Devin Fergus, *Liberalism, Black Power, and the Making of American Politics, 1965–1980* (Athens: University of Georgia Press, 2009).

7. Of particular import to this discussion are the texts that incorporate the history of civil rights with the War on Poverty programs. See Ashmore, *Carry It On*; Robert Bauman, *Race and the War on Poverty: From Watts to East L.A.* (Norman: University of Oklahoma Press, 2008); Robert Bauman, "The Black Panther and Chicano Movements in the Poverty Wars in Los Angeles," *Journal of Urban History* 33:2 (2007): 277–95; Lisa Gayle Hazirjian, "Combating Need: Urban Conflict and the Transformation of War on Poverty and the African American Freedom Struggle in Rocky Mount, NC," *Journal of Urban History* 34:4 (2008): 639–64.

8. Among the various foundations, Ford was particularly known for its grants to community organizations involved in the black freedom movement. It also figures prominently in the history of CORE and among the foundations, which Allen credited for being a negative corporate influence in the black community. See Allen, *Black Awakening*, 121–32; Jerry Gershenhorn, "'Not an Academic Affair': African American Scholars and the Development of African Studies in the United States, 1942–1960," *Journal of African American History* 94:1 (2009): 44–68; Karen Ferguson, "Organizing the Ghetto: The Ford Foundation, CORE, and White Power in the Black Power Era, 1967–1969," *Journal of Urban History* 34:1 (2007): 67–100; Noliwe M. Rooks, *White Money/Black Power: The Surprising History of African American Studies* (Boston: Beacon Press, 2006).

9. Robert Curvin, interview by August Meier, January 19, 1969, August Meier Papers (Box 56, Folder 4), Schomburg Center for Research in Black Culture (hereafter cited as Schomburg), New York, NY.

10. Meier and Rudwick, *CORE*, 194–209.

11. Meier and Rudwick, *CORE*, 202–3. The Monroe Defendants were a group of activists from Monroe, North Carolina who, counter to the movements' philosophical direction of nonviolence, used armed self-defense to protect themselves from an attack against the Klan. Robert Williams and Mae Mallory were among the well-known freedom fighters of this group. See also, Timothy Tyson, *Radio Free Dixie: Robert F. Williams and the Roots of Black Power* (Chapel Hill, NC: University of North Carolina Press, 1999).

12. Meier and Rudwick, *CORE*, 193–94, 246–49. August Meier devotes some discussion to the transformative impact of northern school desegregation fights. In most cases, northern CORE chapters became progressively assertive due to recalcitrance of local politicians and school boards, over which they lacked influence or control. The logical inference led to the belief that seizure of these political spaces were important for stamping out the more subtle forms of discrimination.

13. Cleveland Chapter CORE Action Letter, June 1965. Bonnie Gordon Papers, author's possession. This collection was donated to Western Reserve Historical Society, Cleveland, OH. The materials are housed as accessioned collection, and are not yet officially archived. Meier and Rudwick, *CORE*, 390.

14. Meeting with NAC and Staff, June 29, 1965, Floyd McKissick Papers (Series 3.1.2, Folder 6833), Southern Historical Collection (hereafter SHC) of University of North Carolina at Chapel Hill, Chapel Hill, NC.

15. Ibid.

16. NAC Meeting, December 31, 1965–Jan. 2, 1966, Floyd McKissick Papers (Series 3.1.2, Folder 6964), SHC.

17. Ibid.

18. Meier and Rudwick, *CORE*, 418.

19. Ibid., 330–31.

20. News release, July 7, 1966, Floyd McKissick Papers (Series 3.1.2, Folder 6775a), SHC.

21. Memo Regarding Proposals for Northern Thrust, George Wiley to NAC, no date, Floyd McKissick Papers (Series 3.1.1, 6775a), SHC.

22. Louis C. Goldberg, "CORE in Trouble: A Social History of the Organizational Dilemmas of the Congress of Racial Equality Target City Project in Baltimore, 1965–1967" (PhD diss., Johns Hopkins University, 1970), 115; Minutes of the 23rd annual convention, July 1–5, 1965, Floyd McKissick Papers (Series 3.1.2, Folder 6840) SHC.

23. While national CORE redirected the bulk of its resources to the North, it intended to sustain its southern program via farm cooperatives and aid to black rural residents to foment economic independence, thus implementing community organization activities in the south as well. For a detailed account of CORE's move to community organization, see Meier and Rudwick, *CORE*, 330–57.

24. On CORE and Black Power, see Meier and Rudwick, *CORE*, 402–410, 420. For CORE and Baltimore TCP, see Memo Regarding Proposals for Northern Thrust, George Wiley to NAC; Ruth Turner and Tony Perot, handwritten notes on dissertation rough draft, in author's possession, 2008.

25. Kenneth Durr, *Behind the Backlash: White Working-Class Politics in Baltimore, 1940–1980* (Chapel Hill: University of North Carolina Press, 2003), 130–32; Judith Stein, *Running Steel, Running America: Race, Economic Policy, and the Decline of Liberalism* (Chapel Hill: University of North Carolina Press, 1998), 137–40; Rhonda Williams, "Black Women, Urban Politics, and Engendering Black Power," in *The Black Power Movement: Rethinking the Civil Rights–Black Power Era*, ed. Peniel Joseph (New York: Routledge, 2006), 84–86; Louis C. Goldberg, "CORE in Trouble," 116–23, 184, 339; "CORE Deficit May Close Office," CORE clipping file. Cleveland Press Collection (hereafter cited as CPC), Cleveland State University Archives (hereafter cited as CSU), Cleveland, OH. Ruth Turner and Tony Perot challenge much of Goldberg's account of events at the Baltimore TCP. Ruth Turner and Tony Perot, handwritten notes on dissertation.

26. Allen notes that some of the focus on Cleveland resulted from a secret meeting of civil rights leaders. However, this information in no way incorporated the internal dynamics of CORE. Within CORE, selection of the city was divided over Chicago, Newark, and

Cleveland. In addition, the decision was made over the objections of the NAC, which wanted more cities from which to choose. Allen, *Black Awakening*, 123; NAC Minutes, April 22–April 23, 1967, August Meier/Elliot Rudwick Papers (Box 2, Folder 5), WHS.

27. Turner's reputation led to a high degree of animosity among white leaders of CORE. Turner argued for CORE to have a black leadership, but a support system of committed white members. It was not a position meant to belittle the contribution of whites to CORE. Her attitude stemmed from the belief that the black community had to be the directors of their own movement. For information on Ruth Turner and Black Power, see Belinda Robnett, "African-American Women in the Civil Rights Movement, 1954–1965: Gender, Leadership, and Micromobilization," *American Journal of Sociology* 101, no. 6 (1996): 1661–93. Robnett argues that Turner crafted CORE's Black Power platform. In my interview with Turner, she noted that it was a conglomeration of different ideas among CORE members. For information on Turner and white reaction, see Alan Gartner, interview by August Meier, August Meier Papers (Box 56, Folder 6), Schomburg; Marvin Rich, interview notes by Meier, May 21, 1969, August Meier Papers (Box 56, Folder 6), Schomburg; Wilfred Ussery, interview notes by Meier, August Meier Papers (Box 57, Folder 7), Schomburg; George Wiley, interview notes by Meier, April 25, 1972, August Meier Papers (Box 56, Folder 6), Schomburg; Doris Innis, interview notes by Meier, October 12, 1971, August Meier Papers (Box 56, folder 6).

28. Meier and Rudwick, *CORE*, 411.

29. Cleveland CORE members were among many who questioned the election's outcome. Ruth Turner, interview by author, 2004.

30. Joseph Goulden, *The Money Givers* (New York: Random House, 1971), 26; "New 'Black Program' Is Aim of $175,000 CORE Study," CORE clipping file, CPC; "Defends CORE Grant for Stokes," CORE clipping file, CPC; CORE members were particularly angry at allotted grant amount, particularly given that local organizations like National Catholic Conference for Inter-racial Justice got $200,000 and Negro Industrial Economic Union received $520,000, respectively. Refer to Memo to McGeorge Bundy, no date, Floyd McKissick Papers (Series 3.1.2, Files 6870–6871), SHC.

31. Ferguson argued that CORE was not responsible for Stokes' win as mayor, although other sources counter this argument. Taking Ferguson's argument into account, at the very least, political reaction gave the organization a great public relations boot for its black power work. Karen Ferguson, "'Organizing the Ghetto': The Ford Foundation, CORE, and White Power in the Black Power Era, 1967-1969," Journal of Urban History 34, no. 1 (2007): 67–100. For opposing viewpoints and discussions of the public impact of the Carl Stokes voter registration drive, see Joseph Goulden, *The Money Givers*, 26; Kai Bird, *The Color of Truth: McGeorge Bundy and William Bundy: Brothers in Arms* (New York: Simon and Schuster, 1998), 381; Noliwe Rooks, *White Money, Black Power: The Surprising History of African American Studies and the Crisis in Higher* (Boston: Beacon Press, 2006), 88–89. Noliwe Rooks also discusses Ford's "social engineering" but diverts discussion to the consequences of Ford's actions. This will be discussed in greater detail in Chapter Six. Noliwe Rooks, *White Money, Black Power: The Surprising History of African American Studies and the Crisis in Higher* (Boston: Beacon Press, 2006), 88-89.

32. Most historians assumed—incorrectly—that the Cleveland chapter received the Ford grant. August Meier and Elliot Rudwick also claimed the grant to be the only time a chapter experienced financial stability. However, it was actually an attempt by national CORE to regain fiscal footing. Meier and Rudwick, *CORE*, 420; Allen, *Black Awakening*, 123. For more on Ford and the Cleveland Target City Project see, Ferguson, "Organizing the Ghetto"; Rooks, *White Money*; Bird, *The Color of Truth*;

33. Bird, *Color of Truth*, 20.

34. Ibid., 381–88; Goulden, *The Money Givers*; Homer Wadsworth, "Private Foundations and the Tax Reform Act of 1969," *Law and Contemporary Problems* 39, no. 4 (Autumn 1975): 255.
35. Goulden, *The Money Givers*, 259-260.
36. Bird, *Color of Truth*, 393. For additional information on Henry Ford's mention of Ford Foundation's perceived attack on capitalism see Robert Bradley, *Capitalism at Work: Business, Government, and Energy* (Salem, Mass: M & M Scrivener Press, 2009), 248–49; Peter Frumkin, *Strategic Giving: The Art and Science of Philanthropy* (Chicago, University of Chicago Press,2006), 324.
37. "Rumpus in Hotel Mars Last Session of CORE Parley," July 6, 1968, CORE clipping file, CPC, CSU Archives.
38. Kenneth Marshall, "Log: National Convention in Oakland, California," July 1-July 5, 1967, August Meier/Elliot Rudwick Papers (Box 2, Folder 2), WHS. It is unclear whether Marshall is the actual author of these notes.
39. Wadsworth, "Private Foundations," 255; Bird, *Color of Truth*, 381–82.
40. Bird, *Color of Truth*, 409.
41. Many argue that the plan was the basis for Nixon's illegal break-in into the Watergate Hotel. For more information on the Huston plan, see Joan Hoff, *Nixon Reconsidered* (New York, NY: BasicBooks, 1994), 288-294
42. Bird, *Color of Truth*, 381–82.
43. Ford Foundation, "National Affairs." Ford Foundation Annual Report 1978. (1978), http://www.fordfound.org/ (accessed July 8, 2008), 9.
44. "Ford Grant Aided Stokes, New Book Says," March 16, 1971, CORE clipping file, CPC, CSU; Goulden, *The Money Givers*, 263; "CORE Sets Registration Campaign," September 13, 1968, CORE clipping file, CPC, CSU; "CORE Completes Its Voter Drive with 10,000 total," October 3, 1968, CORE clipping file, CPC, CSU.
45. "We Want Control, Says CORE Director," December 9, 1967, *Cleveland Plain Dealer* article, Urban League Papers (Box 29, Folder 5), Western Reserve Historical Society, Cleveland (hereafter cited as WRHS).
46. Leonard B. Moore, *Carl B. Stokes and the Rise of Black Political Power* (Champaign: University of Illinois Press, 2003), 10, 37, 40–43.
47. Roy Innis presented a report on Harlem CORE's activities around small business investment corporations and black control of schools at the 1967 CORE convention. Robert Allen and many other scholars have suggested that Innis's ideas were the dominant determining character of CORE. Allen, *Black Awakening*, 126, 131–32.
48. Quoted in Meier and Rudwick, *CORE*, 423. Further discussion of Brooklyn CORE can be found in Brian Purnell, "A Movement Grows in Brooklyn: The Brooklyn Chapter of the Congress of Racial Equality (CORE) and the Northern Civil Rights Movement During the Early 1960s" (PhD diss.: New York University, 2006).
49. NAC Minutes closed session, December 31, 1965, August Meier/Elliot Rudwick Papers, (Box 4, Folder 4), WHS.
50. For more information on CDCs and the black community, see Stewart Perry, "Federal Support for CDCs Some of the History and Issues of Community Control," *Review of Black Political Economy* 3, no. 3 (1972): 17–42; William Tabb, "Perspectives on Black Economic Development," *Journal of Economic Issues* 4, no. 4 (1970): 68–81; Frederick D. Sturdivant, "Community Development Corporations: The Problem of Mixed Objectives," *Law and Contemporary Problems* 36, no. 1 (1971): 35–50; Luttrell, "The Effect of the Private Foundation Provisions."
51. Jerry M. Flint, "CORE Bids Business Set Up Plants for Negroes," April 5, 1968, New York Times article, Carl Stokes (hereafter Stokes)Papers (Box 30, Folder 545), WRHS.

Harambee: Cleveland Target City Project, no date, Floyd McKissick Papers (Series 3.1.2, Files 6870-71), SHC.

52. "CORE Unveils $10-Million Plan to Help City Negroes," April 5, 1968, CORE clipping file, CPC, CSU; Jerry M. Flint, "CORE Bids Business Set Up Plants for Negroes".

53. CORENCO Fact Sheet, no date, Stokes Papers (Box 30, Folder 545), WRHS.

54. "Open Application for Funding Grants to CORE Development Corporation," April 4, 1968, Stokes Papers (Box 30, Folder 545), WRHS.

55. "CORE Unveils $10-Million Plan to Help City Negroes," CPC.

56. Robert H. A. Ashford, "The Binary Economics of Louis Kelso: A Democratic Private Property System for Growth and Justice," in *Curing World Poverty: The New Role of Property*, ed. John H. Miller (New Brunswick, NJ: Social Justice Review, 1994), 100. Kelso is not alone in his notion that capitalism can be made ethical. Currently Noreena Hertz, the popular author of *The Debt Threat* and *The Silent Takeover*, has argued for a "co-op capitalism" that creates a joint economic structure that includes businesses, governments, NGOs, and the public. It, too, challenges the supporters of laissez-faire capitalism to move toward a more ethical financial system.

57. Ashford, "The Binary Economics," 100.

58. Ibid., 101; Louis O. Kelso and Mortimer J. Adler, *Capitalist Manifesto* (New York: Random House, 1958), 6.

59. Kelso and Adler, *Capitalist Manifesto*, 54.

60. Ibid., 67–69

61. Ibid., 85–86

62. Though the CORENCO proposal is written by Wilfred Ussery, CORE's national chairman, the structure and wording directly copies Kelso's language in *Capitalist Manifesto*, as well it might, given the fact Kelso directly served as a consultant for this proposal.

63. "Community Role Aired by CORE," no date, CORE clipping file. CPC, CSU.

64. CORENCO Fact Sheet, 31–33.

65. Ibid.

66. Ibid., 34.

67. Ibid., 35.

68. "CORE Bids Business," Stokes Papers.

69. "Businessmen Urged to Aid Black Capitalism in Ghetto," October 30, 1968, CORENCO clipping file, CPC, CSU; CORENCO Fact Sheet.

70. CORENCO Fact Sheet.

71. Minutes of Cleveland Target City Project Review Board Friday, March 22, 1968, McKissick Papers (Series 3.1.2, Folder 6870–71), SHC.

72. For additional information on Hough Area Development Corporation, see Stewart E. Perry, "Black Institutions, Black Separatism, and Ghetto Economic Development," *Human Organization* 31:3 (Fall 1972): 271–79, accessed online May 9, 2011 at Hein Online; Geoffrey Faux, *New Hope for the Inner City, Report of the Twentieth Century Fund Task Force on Community Development Corporation* (New York: Twentieth Century Fund, 1971); Harry Edward Berndt, *New Rulers in the Ghetto: The Community Development Corporation and Urban Poverty* (Westport, Conn.: Greenwood Press, 1977); Stewart Perry, *Communities on the Way: Rebuilding Local Economies in the United States and Canada* (NY: State of NY Press, 1987); Rita Mae Kelly, *Community Control of Economic Development* (New York: Praeger, 1977).

73. "Minutes of Cleveland Target City Project," McKissick Papers.

74. Alma Kauffman, "Inner-City Program Granted $500,000 by Ford Foundation," CORE Clipping File, CPC. The articles notes that CORE received $300,000 of this total

amount. This is the maximum that CORE ever obtained from CORE, though other groups were given more.

75. "Open Application for Funding Grants," Stokes Papers.
76. Ussery to Dear Sir, October 18, 1968, Stokes Papers (Box 30, Folder 545), WRHS.
77. "Businessmen Urged to Aid," CPC.
78. Ibid.
79. Dean Kotlowski, "Black Power—Nixon Style: The Nixon Administration and Minority Business Enterprise," *Business History Review* 72:3 (Autumn 1998): 423.
80. Ibid., 420–21. There was a brief period in which the community ownership concept (referenced in the Nixon Administration as Expanded Ownership) received consideration within the Nixon administration, but most of that was downplayed by conservative elements within the office who held to the free market ideology. For more information consult the White House Central Files of Leonard Garment in the Richard Nixon Papers at the Richard Nixon Library, Yorba Linda, CA.
81. Ibid., 423–25; Robert E. Weems Jr. and Lewis A. Randolph, "The National Response to Richard M. Nixon's Black Capitalism Initiative: The Success of Domestic Détente," *Journal of Black Studies* 32:1 (September 2001): 67.
82. Ruth Turner and Tony Perot, notes on dissertation.
83. Ruth Turner and Tony Perot, notes on dissertation; Will Ussery, interview by author, January 10, 2008.
84. "Form Separate City Innis Tells Negroes," January 9, 1969, CORE clipping file, CPC, CSU Archives; "Community Role Aired by CORE," March 8, 1969, CORE clipping file, CPC, CSU Archives; Meier and Rudwick, *CORE*, 423-425.

CHAPTER 15

"BLACK IS BEAUTIFUL BUT SO IS GREEN":

CAPITALISM, BLACK POWER, AND POLITICS IN FLOYD MCKISSICK'S SOUL CITY

ZACHARY GILLAN

IN THE TUMULTUOUS SUMMER OF 1968, FLOYD McKissick, national director of the Congress of Racial Equality (CORE), announced his retirement from that organization in order to devote his time to the development of the "Black Economy," the growth of which he viewed as "the spearhead of racial equality."[1] Less than a year later, in early 1969, McKissick unveiled his plans for the flagship of his efforts: a new planned community in Warren County, North Carolina. McKissick intended this project, which he named Soul City, to provide a shining example of his ideal of black economic power. In McKissick's vision, this endeavor would help "end the dependency of Black people on the white economy which has so long exploited them" by extending "the Civil Rights struggle beyond job training and equal employment to ownership . . . of the businesses which exist in and of the Black community." African Americans who followed McKissick's lead, in other words, would no longer "be content to eat leftovers in the kitchen," seeking instead "to sit at our own table and carve the financial turkey with all its trimmings."[2] Soul City, as a community expressly planned, built, and led according to black capitalist ideals, would prove the viability of McKissick's thought.

At the time of McKissick's announcement, activists of the "classic" civil rights movement stood at a crossroads, wracked by questions of goals, tactics, and ideology.[3] White allies in the Democratic Party, meanwhile, found themselves alienated on one side by the growth of Black Power and by the Nixonian silent majority on the other. An astute political observer, McKissick recognized the necessity in such a divisive climate of securing support for Soul City from as many groups as possible. For this reason, he carefully couched his appeals in a wide-ranging rhetoric that co-opted ideals from a wide variety of interests, presenting the community as the encapsulation of an African American, middle-class self-help discourse articulated within a capitalist framework. In this manner, McKissick blended an assimilationist "politics of respectability" with the autonomous community-empowering discourse of Black Power in such a way that it appealed to the staunchly procapitalist New Right—linking racial pride with the economic values of the white middle class of the GOP.[4] To that end, McKissick switched his registration to the ascendant Republican Party in 1972, deciding that a pact with the party in charge of the federal budget would be more useful than the civil rights movement's traditional alliance with the Democrats.

As a result of McKissick's desire to appeal to these disparate ideologues, Soul City itself embedded an individualistic capitalist ideal within a centrally planned communitarian utopia.[5] McKissick, in other words, understanding the increasingly hegemonic force of the commodity form within the society of late consumer capitalism, extended an open invitation for the market to colonize his efforts in order to use it to sell his project.[6] McKissick's deeply pragmatic devotion to capitalism presents an example of what we could call "inverted co-optation," an adoption of the rhetoric and tactics of the market for the benefit of a radical political movement. As he explained, black capitalism was not an attempt to "emulate the white man's version of economic power" that had so long victimized African Americans, but an acknowledgement instead that if capitalism "can find a way of accommodating Black People and letting them have real power and effective autonomy, we'll accept power on those terms. If it can't, we'll just have to get power some other way."[7]

Delicately balanced between these strands of thought, McKissick's rhetoric deftly illustrated the interplay between race, class, politics, and economics in the civil rights movement after the end of its "classical" period, an era that still has not received the attention it deserves from historians. As Jacquelyn Dowd Hall has insisted, the era following the 1960s still requires research that "rivals in nuance and complexity what we know about the classical phase." In particular, she insists that "the struggle for economic justice has been erased altogether" from the popular civil rights narrative—a struggle that McKissick and his black capitalism make explicit and central.[8] Further, Soul City stands at the intersection of this call and the rising interest in race and American conservatism, but it has received very little attention in these narratives.[9] To date, the Soul City project has been the subject of only three academic articles, none of which have focused on McKissick's engagement with capitalism and the rightward turn of national politics.[10] Of these, Timothy Minchin's "'A Brand New Shining City': Floyd B. McKissick Sr. and the Struggle to Build Soul City, North Carolina" is the most thorough. Where Minchin focuses on the economics of the actual Soul City development and its relationship with the local press and politics of North Carolina, this article seeks to supplement our understanding of the place of McKissick's ideological project within national developments.[11]

This larger scope, after all, is one on which McKissick himself insisted. Indeed, in order to emphasize Soul City's redemptive qualities for both ideological divisions within the black community and white America's anxieties, McKissick implied that the community would help solve the racial problems of the entire country—throughout both the rural South and the urban ghettos of the North. He intended to accomplish this by luring industry to new communities in the South—modeled after Soul City—which would, in turn, entice those African Americans who had migrated North and thereafter been left behind in the "white flight" epidemic to return to a newly revitalized region. McKissick insisted that though black capitalists would lead the development project and the town itself, Soul City's population would possess a harmonious multiracial character. The construction of Soul City, indeed, would not only empower African Americans and lay the framework for similar ventures for other minorities, but it would also help bring to fruition a capitalist reimagining of the "beloved community" of the civil rights movement. In the long term, McKissick intended for other towns modeled after Soul City to spread throughout the nation. This aspect of McKissick's vision relied implicitly on the monolithic national culture of late capitalist suburbia: What could work in one region of the nation, in this case the Black Belt of the South, could be easily replicated elsewhere.

For all McKissick's rhetorical skill in selling his community, however, Soul City never attracted the industrial base it required to function economically. The federal Department of Housing and Urban Development (HUD) foreclosed on its loans in 1979, withdrawing its support much earlier than McKissick had expected. Both the local press and conservative North Carolina politicians remained consistently hostile to the project, accusing McKissick of everything from financial mismanagement to nepotism to reverse racism. After McKissick's death in 1991, his obituary in the *New York Times* reported that Soul City had proven to be an "economically unviable" project that, by "mid-1979 . . . housed only 135 people, all but 30 of them black, and half of them living in mobile homes." That was an insufficient outcome, in the eyes of the *Times*, and a failure even "in spite of $19 million in Federal aid and $8 million more from state and local sources."[12] McKissick and Soul City, the newspaper implied, deserved to be remembered not for their dreams or meager successes but for their failures. The subtext here is that McKissick's own lifelong narrative remained inextricably linked with the story of Soul City.

Floyd Bixler McKissick was born in Asheville, North Carolina, on March 9, 1922. As he described it, he grew up practicing economic self-sufficiency from a very early age, always managing "to find some source of income from enterprising self-employment," working as "a shoe shine boy, waiter, bus boy, yard man, cleaner and errand boy."[13] After his protocapitalist youth, McKissick interrupted his enrollment at Morehouse University for a stint in the military during World War II. Before leaving for a European tour of duty, McKissick married Evelyn Williams, with whom he would have four children. After he returned from the war and finished his degree, McKissick sued the University of North Carolina for admittance to its law school in Chapel Hill, and he became the first black man to enroll in the program. After graduation, he opened a law office on Main Street in Durham, North Carolina, an area previously exclusive to white-owned businesses. Once established as a lawyer, McKissick represented civil rights activists

facing prosecution for integrating lunch counters, sued to have his own four children admitted to all-white schools, and served as the legal counsel for CORE.[14]
In 1966, he succeeded James Farmer as CORE's national director. Under McKissick's leadership, the organization developed "a six-point program for Black Power
and Self Determination," beginning with "Economic Power" and culminating
with "Mobilization of Black Consumers."[15] Further, as historian Karen Ferguson
has shown, McKissick guided CORE's "Cleveland Target City program" of 1967,
which sought to build "black urban communities' political, economic, and social
power through CORE's 'catalytic presence'" in order to "enable residents to act
for change and help solve their own critical problems."[16] Clearly, McKissick's
emphasis on autonomy for African Americans, economic or otherwise, predated
the founding of Soul City by a number of years. After serving as national director for two years, McKissick resigned in order to focus exclusively on building
economic power for African Americans.

Initially, the drive toward a "Black Economy" took place under the auspices
of Floyd B. McKissick Enterprises, Inc., which worked "to help organize and
finance substantial Black business across the nation," but it found its ultimate
expression in Soul City. As McKissick explained to a newspaper in 1976, the
"real Floyd McKissick never got a chance to step forward during the Civil Rights
Movement," since his activism during those years had "sidetracked his penchant
for commercial enterprises."[17] Just as he had characterized his childhood as one
devoted to the capitalist spirit, McKissick now retroactively cast his entire involvement with the civil rights movement as a distraction from his lifelong love of the
market. Soul City, with its mixture of socioeconomic justice and entrepreneurial
spirit, allowed him to speak simultaneously to both of these impulses. McKissick's
ability to sell himself by means of carefully constructed narratives of this sort
greatly aided his politicking in support of Soul City.

Soul City itself formed a concrete symbol of McKissick's ideals writ large,
a physical and ideological structure to house the communitarian and capitalist
ideas that he had been cultivating throughout his life—at least according to his
public relations materials. Combining the self-reliant community focus of Black
Power—without the hostility to the liberal American political system—with the
free market ideology of the New Right, McKissick and his associates presented
Soul City as either the beginning of an independent black economy or a model
for a newly utopian interracial community, depending on who was listening.
In either vision, the project aimed to correct an impressively wide variety of
socioeconomic problems. Never one for modest goals, McKissick intended Soul
City as the first of many such communities, which would spread throughout the
nation, uplifting African Americans and humanizing—or at least humbling—the
white power structure. In keeping with his larger-than-life persona, McKissick's
expansive vision would not only make right the personal lives of Soul City residents, but it would also refashion the entire American political realm into a more
benevolent edifice.

First, though, he required the help of this political system to get his project off
the ground. Congress passed the New Communities Act in 1968—strengthened
by the Urban Growth and New Communities Development Act of 1970—to

create "a national urban growth policy" that would encourage the "rational, orderly, efficient and economic growth, development and redevelopment" of both rural and urban areas that demonstrated a "special potential for accelerated growth." Such planning would "assure our communities of adequate tax bases, community services, job opportunities, and well-balanced neighborhoods in socially, economically and physically attractive living environments."[18] To aid in this process, HUD would subsidize the new communities by underwriting bonds for their development. While the New Communities Assistance Programs created by this legislation had no explicit link to the question of race in America, Floyd McKissick quickly grasped the ramifications for poor blacks throughout the nation.

McKissick first made his plans for a new community in North Carolina public on January 13, 1969, in a press conference in the office of Orville Freeman, then the US secretary of agriculture.[19] Here, McKissick explained that he had long discussed the application of "New City technology" to the problems of racial minorities and the poor, and had been "among the first to advocate construction of entirely new communities as an alternative to urban ghettos and rural decay." McKissick envisioned his new town, as yet unnamed, as "a totally planned community, utilizing the latest knowledge in the field of city planning to create a harmonious environment and productive working conditions." By locating the community in rural Warren County, McKissick ensured that it would be situated in "the so-called 'Black Belt' of the South," allowing its residents to work toward the "development of black urban technological skills." Warren County's rural character, moreover, would allow the project to pursue the "revitalization of a rural agricultural area to demonstrate that good jobs, quality education and cultural enhancement can be created in decaying rural areas." Last, McKissick insisted that his planned community could be used to inspire similar ventures by impoverished minority groups throughout the nation.[20]

With these lofty aims articulated, McKissick and his associates applied to HUD for the necessary development loans the following year. This began a lengthy series of applications, reviews, and revisions, leading up to a final appeal for a guaranteed loan for ten million dollars in February 1971, which HUD did not approve until June 1972. The final revisions, authored by an "independent consultant" working for the government, increased the amount of the guarantee to fourteen million dollars, and stated that if "Soul City achieved only 2/3 of its goals, the project would be financially and programmatically successful."[21] With the application itself approved, it took the Soul City Company and HUD another two years to work out a feasible project agreement, with the government issuing the first federally backed bonds in March 1974.[22]

By 1975, Warren County had a population of 15,180, of which African Americans constituted about two-thirds. Demographically, it provided an ideal location for the project, which the first issue of the *Soul City Newsletter* identified as "a new community dedicated to providing economic and social opportunities for Black people [and] given to the philosophy that Black people can and should excercise [sic] some control over their own destinies." Not that Soul City would be racially exclusive, the *Newsletter* hastened to add: This was a community "open to *all* people of good will." The community's architects, with the aid of the University of North Carolina's Planning Department, had designed the town as "a self-reliant city [offering] facilities for shopping, recreation, housing, and a sound, diversified economic base."[23] McKissick and his fellow planners intended for the population of Soul City to grow to "some 50,000 people" before the end of the century. The initial thirty-year plan called for 5,287 acres "to create an urban setting in a rural environment to attract a population from both rural and urban areas." In an era when the unemployment rate in Warren County reached upward of 30 percent, the Soul City Company gave "industry first priority in development" as the project could not depend on "an established industrial . . . base."[24] Creating its own employment pool by attracting enough industry, Soul City would provide the ideal location for an example of black capitalism.

McKissick and his associates set up a rather labyrinthine conglomerate of organizations to oversee the Soul City project. Floyd B. McKissick Enterprises, Inc., the company that McKissick had worked through for years to develop black-owned businesses, sponsored the endeavor. The Soul City Company oversaw the development of Soul City itself, while the Soul City Foundation, Inc., bore the responsibility for its "social planning." Soul City's organizational umbrella also contained the Warren Regional Planning Corporation, which aimed to create and sustain minority businesses nearby, and the Soul City Investment Corporation, to raise funds and implement capital projects. HealthCo, Inc., as its name suggests, would offer health care not only to future residents of Soul City but to those in Warren and Vance Counties as well. The Soul City Sanitary District, the first local government body voted into office, provided public services and had the power to "levy taxes and issue bonds to support those utilities." Finally, the planners established the nonprofit Soul City Utilities Company to build a sewage system and treatment facility.[25] This arrangement, while seemingly cumbersome, was necessary because of Soul City's isolated location and the absence of any previously existing infrastructure.

Soul City's planned and controlled environment revolved around well-demarcated zones of activity within the town, maintaining a connection with nature even while developing the industry necessary for the community to thrive. Planners allotted Soul City's land use as 30 percent housing, "18 per cent for industry, 5 per cent for commercial development, 11 per cent for institutional use (including education), and 28 per cent for community parks and natural open spaces." After the end of thirty years of development, planners envisioned a city comprising eight villages, each housing approximately six thousand residents. Housing within these villages would be a mix of detached single-family homes, apartments, and townhouses, all grouped near community activity centers. An industrial park in the north, accessible to the "major transportation corridors" of the region, would be its "major employment center." At the center of the town would sit the "Soul City Plaza . . . designed as a major regional shopping, office, government, and entertainment complex." Each of these villages would include an elementary school, augmented by an educational park, located on the southern end of the main road, offering schooling from junior high all the way to university courses.[26]

In addition to roads and pedestrian walkways, a "Bikepath system" would connect the "major activity points" within Soul City. Furthermore, around 1,500 of Soul City's 5,000 acres were initially reserved for "recreational and open space use." Fully 900 of these acres, "characterized by heavy tree cover and stream valleys and 120 acres of man-made lakes," would be set aside as "permanent natural forest and wildlife areas," while the rest would be devoted to a municipal park system.[27] This provided one of the benefits of Soul City's isolated location, as the proximity of a metropolitan center would have greatly complicated the creation of a park and the community's proximity to nature. McKissick relied on Soul City's isolated location to emphasize its distance, both physically and conceptually, from the overcrowded spaces and lack of opportunity of the nation's urban poor. Soul City's isolated location made it unique among the fourteen new towns created under the Urban Growth and New Communities Act of 1968: It was the only one not developed as a satellite to a previously extant city.[28]

Along with its freestanding location, Soul City stood alone among the New Communities of the 1970s because of its black leadership. As McKissick often reminded his audiences, he oversaw "the largest and most innovative project ever undertaken by a minority-owned developer" at the time.[29] By combining a quest for economic justice with a devotion to the capitalist free market, Soul City offered the perfect way to co-opt the "white economic system" for the betterment of African Americans. As McKissick remarked in 1978, "[b]lack is beautiful but so is green and if blacks are going to develop green power, they have got to become part of the economic free market system. We are not going to develop economic power from the outside in. We are going to get economic power by moving inside the economic system and earning our piece of the action." Soul City, therefore, represented nothing less than "an opportunity for all aspects of the free enterprise system to prove its worth—to prove it internally to all persons who believe in that system by example. Soul City is an example of what our forefathers meant America to be."[30] Previous civil rights leaders had often pointed to the contradictions between American racial politics and the founding ideals of the American dream, but McKissick turned this tactic into a much more aggressive stratagem. By linking Soul City with both racial equality and the free market, McKissick positioned his project as not merely a good business plan but also a downright patriotic proposition. In this, he relied heavily on the traditional utopian narrative of the United States—what W. E. B. Du Bois called the "American Assumption," that any individual, no matter her or his economic standing, could, by means of thrift and hard work, join the upper classes of the economic elite.[31]

This assumption lay at the heart of McKissick's black capitalism, which revolved around a form of "sweat equity," whereby a family's labor would be applied toward their stake in the community.[32] Community, in Soul City, would benefit from capitalist business interests, but even the poorest residents would simultaneously gain from the communal structure of the project, as their standard of living steadily improved through their residence and participation in the market. Soul City, then, represented a co-optation of the trend of "spatial restructuring by race," the newly dominant form of segregation created by the white urban diaspora and the monopolization of skill, jobs, and capital in white suburban enclaves.[33] McKissick designed Soul City, in contrast, to grasp such geographic mobility and spatial restructuring on behalf of African Americans. Unfortunately, as with the majority of McKissick's goals, Soul City's sweat equity never got off the ground, and his projected dream of widespread homeownership never materialized.

Despite the claims of detractors to the contrary, McKissick and Soul City proponents stood on the side of democracy and the American way, not with Black Power revolutionaries. Furthermore, Soul City stood for "the basic aspirations of black Americans who believe in constitutional government and who seek to be involved in promoting the free enterprise system by lawful means. These are the people that should be supported rather than those who seek to overthrow the government."[34] By the Nixon era, as historian Dan Carter has observed, "fears of blackness and fears of disorder" formed the "warp and woof of the social agenda," with many white Americans connecting "blackness and criminality, blackness and poverty, blackness and cultural degradation."[35] Thus the ever astute McKissick subverted his opponents' rhetoric: Rather than the dominant political discourse, wherein nods to "law and order" signified white America's fear of African Americans and Black Power, McKissick pointed to Soul City's "lawful" nature as a new alternative to the problem of race.

McKissick and the Black Power ideologues, then, offered differing utopian alternatives to the current dystopia of the African American urban "underclass." McKissick, as usual, demonstrated his adept understanding of shifting political winds by emphasizing what he knew had become a matter of great concern to the Nixon administration. Daniel Patrick Moynihan, a Nixon adviser on urban affairs, wrote to the president in 1970 that this class "terrorizes and plunders the stable elements of the Negro community—trapped by white prejudice in the slums, and forced to live cheek by jowl with a murderous slum population." Moynihan's solution, then, was to transform the urban lower class "into a stable working class population," after which the "cultural revolution" of middle-class African Americans would become "an exciting and constructive development."[36] If groups like the Black Panthers called this "internal colonization," McKissick sprung at the opportunity to offer Soul City to men like Moynihan: An ideal utopian fix of good politics and good business, a homegrown multiracial American alternative to more radical solutions.

In addition to presenting his community as the black capitalist American alternative to black nationalism, McKissick co-opted the dominant narrative of American suburbanization by emphasizing Soul City's potential attraction for migrants—both those looking to escape the problems of the urban North and those fleeing the rural South. As the first *Soul City Newsletter* put it, "Soul City also hopes to find new solutions to the problems of overcrowded cities and the frustrations of the ghetto by stemming the out-migration of young people to the existing urban/industrial areas—and, hopefully, encourage some who have left to return."[37] To McKissick and his associates, a reinvigorated black presence in the South represented the best way to fight the blight caused by "white flight" away from urban centers. Rather than attempt to fight a losing battle to revitalize the urban centers of the North, Soul City would create a new black economy in the traditional southern Black Belt—and provide a model for elsewhere. Even before taking white suburbanization into account, McKissick observed that "[w]e are losing people and these people are untrained when they go to the city and there is no place for them, so, if we are really talking about solving the problems of the cities and trying to solve the problems of the minorities who go to the cities and fight the problems of race, then you have to start at the roots of the problems."[38] White flight further compounded such problems by ravaging the urban tax base. By attracting a large industrial base, Soul City would help shift the majority of the rural black Southern population from an agriculturally based work force to one more strongly oriented toward industry.

Even the region's traditional reliance on agriculture, in large part responsible for its economically disastrous state, could become a positive attribute in McKissick's rhetoric. In 1974, McKissick wrote a letter to John Lamb, president of the Minneapolis Marketing Corporation, in which he insisted, the "'New South' has certain basic advantages which other regions do not presently have" to attract industrial development. His list included an "adequate supply of labor . . . manpower programs to assist in training . . . [and] lower wages since the unions have not found it feasible to conduct their activities here." In other words, the lack of industrial development in the past, combined with the "right to work" laws of the Southern states, left the potential proletariat in the South unprepared to bargain wisely for it now, and the work force remained desperate enough to refuse union interference. Choosing Soul City as a location for industrial development, McKissick insisted, would equal "good, sound economics."[39] Even while working toward an avowedly middle-class community, McKissick recognized the necessity of industry to community development. His union bashing supported his goal of leading Southern African Americans out of the ranks of the working poor and into the middle class. There, they would require the guiding hand not of unions, but of the free market.

By presenting Soul City as the answer to both individualized and class-based issues confronting the nation at the close of the 1960s, McKissick tapped into much the same sentiment as did Richard Nixon in his 1968 bid for the presidency. Popular notions of the "dystopia" of the inner city—commonly if not entirely accurately understood to be African American—involved some of the same confusion between individual and community as did Soul City itself.[40] As historian Michael B. Katz has noted, poverty and the underclass in the United States has long involved a debate about "the extent to which individuals are responsible for their own poverty" in terms of "the balance between individual agency and structural forces."[41] Nixon's silent majority, of course, sided firmly with the former view, as befitted the forces of conservatism, with their unyielding emphasis on the individual. To them, the underclass consisted of individuals who had made their choices to reject law and order and exist parasitically within the American system. Floyd McKissick understood the issues differently, but attempted to use the political power of the New Right to fix that same system while aiding the members of the "underclass."[42]

The latter half of the twentieth century, indeed, represented a sea change in the spatial structure of poverty in the United States. Historian Thomas J. Sugrue suggests that the combination of declining industry, suburbanization, and racism in the years after World War II created "a new form of concentrated poverty, largely restricted to deteriorating inner center cities, which has replaced the episodic and spatially diffuse poverty" of the past.[43] Soul City, then, represented a novel solution to a new form of an old problem. From the dystopia of the day-to-day existence of poor urban African Americans living within a racist system, McKissick forged Soul City as both utopian means *and* end. In terms of spatial separation and isolation, utopian suburbia and dystopian downtowns provided distorted mirror images of one another, much as Soul City simultaneously mirrored the American focus on individualism and the radical insistence on communitarianism.[44]

By co-opting elements of the disparate ideologies of the civil rights movement, Black Power, and the capitalist free market, McKissick fashioned an ideal image of Soul City to appeal to a large variety of social groups and potential backers. He set the stage by latching onto the popular disillusionment with the 1960s, proclaiming that the passé spirit of that decade, full of protest and revolution, had to give way to a more utilitarian ideal in the 1970s. In this manner, he appealed not only to African Americans seeking a new direction for the civil rights movement but also to Black Power advocates, the silent majority of Nixon followers, and social pragmatists. The *Kansas City Times*, reporting on a speech McKissick gave at a 1975 "Black Leadership Conference," quoted him as saying, "[i]n the 1960s blacks and other minorities demonstrated for principles. . . . But the 1970s are a time for economic battles . . . Somehow or another we've always been told there's something wrong with money. There ain't nothing wrong with money." Rather than offending the mainstream through protests, McKissick suggested, "Blacks and other minorities must now learn how to use the system—a system that revolves around politics and economics."[45] The system, he insinuated, simply *owed* those African Americans who relied on the lawful American dream rather than rebellion to better their place in life—and what better way to reward them than to help finance Soul City?

This realist message of the interconnectivity of politics and economics resonated throughout McKissick's thought, and proved one of the few ideas that he consistently expressed no matter what the composition of his audience. Likewise, where the mainstream media emphasized the animosity between the civil rights movement and Black Power, McKissick situated Soul City firmly at the intersection of these two tendencies—especially in the association of both movements with Afro-Christianity and the black church. Often, McKissick introduced this idea in his lectures with a biblical passage he claimed whites had "taken to heart" but that blacks had overlooked: "A feast is made for laughter, and wine maketh merry, but money answereth all things."[46] Similarly, in a speech entitled "God's Economic Plan," McKissick insisted that "God was the first industrial developer. God created men of all colors from the start to share as trustees of God. We must continue to carry out God's purpose to use God's land for the benefit of all his people. God's economic plan depends on our being trustees through God's plan."[47] In 1978, McKissick also noted that black Americans "have our ethnic heritage as given us by God with noble assistance from our parents. But politically, we are American first, which fact is not fully understood by all of our majority businessmen."[48] McKissick relied on Christianity, like the free market, to define his middle-class African American dream. In doing so, he fused capitalist individualism with the Christian communitarianism of the civil rights movement, capturing the utopianism of both. At the same time, he tapped into the growing political involvement of white evangelical Christians with the New Right, further tangling his political rhetoric and alliances.

Even while using his own participation in the civil rights movement for legitimation, McKissick criticized both its goals of the 1960s and its long-term effects, more closely aligning his personal sympathies with Black Power. As he wrote in his 1969 book *Three-Fifths of a Man*, the emphasis had to shift "from the more glamorous tactic of nonviolent, direct-action demonstrations to the more tedious, solid tactic of community organizing. Black people . . . instinctively knew that Black Power was not racist but necessary, not anti-white but pro-Black."[49] The chief problem with the old civil rights leaders, in McKissick's view, lay in their exclusive focus on black integration into white society: "Integration is a valid concept, but it should not continue to be interpreted as blacks seeking to get into white schools, churches, businesses, etc. There must be a recognition that what blacks have created is just as good for whites . . . Integration should never mean an absorption of a culture." Following in the Black Power tradition, McKissick followed this critique with a call for self-reliance. The recognition of African American worthiness, he continued, "should place a greater responsibility on blacks which we are willing to accept."[50] In McKissick's worldview, "[e]conomic power is the first prerequisite for political power. Unless the Black man attains economic independence, any 'political independence' will be an illusion. White intimidation and control, especially in the ghettos and the rural South, will continue as long as the Blacks are economically dependent."[51]

Soul City, of course, occupied the vital center of McKissick's plans to correct the misguidance of both the civil rights and Black Power movements. In "The Economics of Being Black," a 1978 lecture he delivered to the senior management of the Standard Oil Company of Indiana, Soul City became "the catalytic force for focusing those issues which confront minority businessmen in the American society."[52] But the community itself had more potential benefits. "Soul City represents an initiative on behalf of black people to help the nation as a whole solve its problems . . . For it is Soul City and it may be *only* Soul City," McKissick pointedly proclaimed, "that provides an interface or a consolidation of all major social issues now confronting the American society." This seemingly all-inclusive list included "economics, housing, education, underemployment, unemployment, equal rights, civil rights, energy, transportation, poverty, prisons, drugs, paroles, welfare, justice, [and] overpopulation in our cities." For McKissick and other black capitalists, he reminded the managers, shared with them not only the goals of "making the free enterprise system workable in a free society" and "making profits" but also a "common political interest" in utilizing capitalism for the good of all Americans regardless of race.[53]

Indeed, McKissick's associate Louis Kelso, an economist, insisted that Soul City would epitomize a "radical capitalism" wherein "a man's equity or stake in the community will depend on his labor, in other words, will be created by his labor."[54] In contrast, Elizabeth Tornquist, of *The North Carolina Anvil*, pointed out that McKissick himself intended to make a profit from the initial capital he had invested in land for Soul City, and that "his whole idea of developing black businesses depends on making enough profit from every venture to have money to invest in others."[55] This certainly involved capitalism, but its radicalism, in Tornquist's view, remained doubtful. On the face of it, her assessment, while mostly accurate, proved a bit unfair to McKissick: If he had eschewed a capitalist slant altogether, it seems unlikely that the federal government would have supported his endeavors. As always, the nuances of McKissick's message depended on his audience, and so here he couched the project in the rhetoric of individualism and the free market rather than communitarian development. Even with Soul City firmly ensconced within a capitalist narrative, McKissick had to shift from the Democratic to the Republican Party in order to garner the necessary support from the federal government. Ironically, this also compromised somewhat his emphasis on self-reliance.

McKissick officially switched his political affiliation in 1972. He steadfastly maintained the decision represented simply the final application of a political pragmatism that he had been espousing for the black community for years. Others accused him of selling out in order to attach himself to the rising star of the Nixon administration. Civil rights activist and Georgia State Representative Julian Bond, for example, delivered a 1972 diatribe against black "political prostitutes" who had joined the "fascist forces" supporting Nixon, "the wizard of the wiretap, the architect of law and order, the former Attorney General."[56] McKissick, in reply, stressed the importance of the two-party system, insisting that "the problems in this country would never be solved as long as black people belonged to and supported only one party."[57] Three years later, McKissick still faced the same attacks, although their focus had shifted away from the specifics of the Nixon campaign. To the accusation that Soul City had been a "political pay-off," McKissick insisted that he could "only say that if this were the case, we would not have languished so long in the HUD pipeline."[58] While the benefits were not immediate, the practical utility of McKissick's shift is apparent: In the three years between the public inception of the Soul City project and McKissick's shift to the Republican Party, the federal government provided $250,000 in grants. In his first three years as a member of the GOP, that amount grew to more than $19 million.[59] A Soul City promotional book, published in 1975, claimed, "McKissick's move from the Democratic to the Republican Party in 1972 certainly opened doors for him [but as] McKissick himself has said, however, 'What matters is what you do when you get in the door.'"[60]

For years, McKissick had told anyone willing to listen that African Americans would be wise to shift their political allegiances, although he always carefully crafted his message to please his various audiences. To blacks and liberal whites, he preached not that they should embrace the ideals of the Republican Party so much as utilize the two-party system "to bring fresh ideas and perspectives to the other major political party in this country."[61] To Republicans and the public at large during his campaigning for Nixon, McKissick stressed the GOP's reliance on private enterprise and capitalism rather than the welfare state. As he wrote in an editorial in 1972, "Black Americans who believe in jobs rather than welfare, who want a piece of the action, not a piece of the dole, [should] get behind the New Majority of the President of the United States, Richard Nixon."[62]

This contrast between private enterprise and "the dole" played a highly significant role in McKissick's thought and in the development of Soul City. By attacking the Democratic Party and welfare state subsidies, McKissick focused attention toward his insistence on local communitarianism and self-reliance. The welfare state and the Democratic Party, which McKissick often conflated in his speeches after 1972, prevented African Americans from participating fully in the free-market American system by encouraging them to depend on outside sources of support, rather than their own initiative. Americans, in McKissick's assessment, "play God at times, by use of the Congress and over-legislation, and are moving towards killing initiative and incentives to do. This is wrong. I believe that one who works long and hard should be paid in direct proportion to his output." Lest this be considered too close an appeal to socialism, McKissick linked his call to the disappointingly unrealistic dream of the founders: "All men are born equal on the day they are born. They do not remain equal in this society."[63] Here again, McKissick linked "radical capitalism" and sweat equity with the drive to improve the lives of African Americans—as individuals.

The central goal of helping African Americans also proved a major factor in McKissick's relationship with the Congressional Black Caucus (CBC). McKissick, of course, did not allow his newfound commitment to the Republican Party to forestall his communication with the almost exclusively Democratic CBC. This relationship, moreover, provides another excellent example of McKissick's ability to ply his audiences with the rhetoric most appropriate to their interests. While McKissick stressed Black Power in the vein of Stokely Carmichael to his everyday black audiences and economic self-interest and profit margins to his industrial contacts, his communications with the CBC reveal an intensely pragmatic concern with the everyday problems of African American life. Accordingly, this correspondence also contains some of his most explicit references to the multiracial nature of Soul City. For example, in a July 9, 1974, letter to Representative William Clay of Missouri, McKissick described Soul City as an "interracial project that has brought together skills of blacks, whites, and Indians working together under black leadership for the development of one of America's most economically deprived areas."[64] This in spite of a "widespread mistrust of government, the belief that nothing can be accomplished and the belief that polarization of the races is something we must live with." Soul City, in McKissick's plea to the CBC for support, offered nothing less than "a continuation of the integration struggle on the economic frontier—a barrier yet to be penetrated."[65] In this, McKissick's rhetoric reflected the growing importance of economic justice in the last days of the classic civil rights movement, channeled most clearly into the Poor People's Campaign (PPC) of 1968, which called for an expansion of public housing and a guaranteed annual income. McKissick's focus on the dichotomy between racial and economic polarization followed the rhetoric of that movement, focusing on a multiracial coalition of the poor. As historian Robert T. Chase has written, the PPC failed, in large part, because its economic emphasis repulsed white middle-class liberals, who had formerly backed racial progress on moral grounds.[66] McKissick, then, aimed to correct this misstep by emphasizing the creation of wealth through self-help, rather than its redistribution—an answer that could appeal to both racial liberals and fiscal conservatives.

After the initial flurry of activity and despite Floyd McKissick's political acumen, Soul City quickly floundered. The reasons for its failure were as varied and convoluted as the ideas the project was predicated upon. They can, however, largely be traced to McKissick's centrist political posturing, which opened him to attacks from both Right and Left. As the *Soul City Sounder* pointed out, Soul City's racial makeup "prompted many conservative publishers to write heated editorials on the evils of Black Separatism and its threats to our society." Simultaneously, Soul City faced an attack from "the more militant component of the black community who is [*sic*] appalled at the fact that we have white men living and working at Soul City."[67] Additionally, the project suffered consistent opposition from the North Carolina press, a lack of industrial development, and an overly optimistic belief on the part of the planners of the community's ability to attract new residents.

Due in large part to McKissick's own conflicting messages, the majority of the public believed Soul City a black-only development. This greatly hurt the project's reputation among the very Republicans that McKissick had spent so much energy courting. From the outset, the name "Soul City" suggested Black Power and separatism to white conservatives, and perhaps even to white moderates. McKissick and his compatriots continually stressed the multiracial layout of the town, but the distasteful resonance of the word "Soul" with Black Power to the likes of US Senator Jesse Helms lingered. To the editor of *The Soul City Sounder*, on the other hand, "the name Soul City is not indicative of race. *Soul*, in this case, is a state of being. We are striving to create an environment of love, prosperity, and brotherhood exclusive of racial strife and economic prejudice."[68] This argument sounds less than convincing given the close association of the word "Soul" as a textual identifier with the "Black Power" movement, and, knowing many of McKissick's convictions, one can only assume that the association was intentional. What is surprising, then, is that such a masterful politician would select such a divisive title for the crowning project of his life's work.

For the most part, despite some of his insinuations made during presentations selling Soul City to black audiences, McKissick insisted on Soul City's projected multiracial nature. Most important, in his view, was the demonstration of capable black leadership of such a project, not the exclusion of other races from the final product. In *Present at the Creation*, a souvenir book available at Soul City's groundbreaking, McKissick rather angrily insisted that "[i]t's not going to come out an all-black thing and never was an all-black thing and never was intended to be an all-black thing. Among job applications, you'll find that we have a tremendous number of white persons who apply for jobs here, who want to work here, who want to move here period."[69] Indeed, whites comprised 40 percent of the initial job applicants at Soul City, and fifteen of the community's ninety-five residents in 1977.[70]

Despite the mounting opposition, it seems likely that McKissick could have maneuvered Soul City to success were it not for an ongoing lack of industrial development and the early foreclosure of its HUD loans. By going ahead with the groundbreaking before obtaining a solid commitment from a large industrial employer, McKissick gambled and lost. Warren County, while perhaps an ideal location for McKissick's dream due to its racial and economic status, remained an unlikely spot for industrial development for many of those same reasons. Similarly, Soul City was poorly located in terms of its appeal to middle-class African Americans. This demographic, which should have supplied some of the strongest supporters of such a suburban-style development, remained nonetheless unlikely to return to an economically depressed area of the South, particularly one lacking an employment infrastructure to support them. This sealed Soul City's fate. McKissick, while adept at co-opting various ideologies to crib support for the project as a utopian community, could not build the practical structures for bridging the gap between his vision and reality.

These problems were not lost on HUD. In announcing the foreclosure of Soul City's loans, William J. White, general manager of HUD's New Community Development Corporation, explained, "We just don't consider the project economically viable. It's not a question of mismanagement. The area itself just didn't work out. There was not enough of a market to draw from."[71] As *The New York Times* pointed out in its coverage of the foreclosure, the original development plans for Soul City called for "a community of 1,824 people and 930 industrial jobs by the end of 1978." As of June 29, 1979, though, "only 135 people, all but 30 of them black, live in the town, half in mobile homes" while the "large modern office building [Soultech I] has only one tenant, a company making duffel bags for the United States Army."[72] McKissick's request for an additional four million dollars in guaranteed assistance from HUD, the *Times* continued, prompted the decision to foreclose. Clearly, the *Times* and HUD agreed, McKissick's dream had been a noble but impossible goal.

In response, McKissick and his supporters lambasted the idea that HUD could accurately judge such a thirty-year plan after only six years of activity. Supporters had funneled massive amounts of money into Soul City by that point: more than $19 million from the federal government and $8 million from local sources.[73] Jesse Helms's legislative assistant, Ralph Hill, for example, insisted that Helms's opposition to the project "was not a personal vendetta, but a matter of fiscal responsibility—they were spending $26 million to put up 33 homes."[74] McKissick and his allies retorted that these funds had gone "to surrounding communities for the building of roads, water, sewerage and electrical system, recreational and health facilities that provide direct benefits for more than 82,000 people in the region."[75] John Harris, a white resident of Warren County whose construction firm had been employed by Soul City, agreed: "I would like to see anybody do all these things cheaper or better than we have in Soul City. Ninety percent of your cost is always in preparing the area for homes and industry and that's what we've done."[76] Even opponents recognized the integral relationship between McKissick and his town. William White, the HUD manager who made

the decision to pull the plug, insisted that his decision had been "very, very difficult. The man put his life into it."[77]

What remains truly impressive about McKissick's dedication to this project is
the skill with which he sold it to other people. By linking civil rights and capitalism, religion and business, and even communitarianism and individualism,
McKissick tied Soul City to the goals of a variety of audiences. In doing so, he
oversold his ability to deliver. Nevertheless, he drew attention to the fundamental
links between race and class in American society and helped illustrate the continuing need for social and economic justice even after the so-called end of the
civil rights movement. In this fashion, he placed Soul City at the forefront of
the ongoing struggle, if only for a small number of people. As Soul City resident
Johnie Johnson, "a widow, former domestic, factory worker and civil rights activist," told *The New York Times* when it announced the foreclosure: "Lord knows,
I thought I was through marching, that the struggle was over for me and that I
could get a little peace. Now I guess we'll just have to start marching on H.U.D.,
and get back into political organizing."[78]

By presenting Soul City as an idealized location of African American assimilation into the capitalist landscape of the nation, McKissick demonstrated an
intuitive understanding of his historical moment. By playing to the contradictions
of late capitalism—between individualism and communitarianism, suburban
and urban landscapes, utopia and dystopia—McKissick worked to improve
the lives of the American dispossessed. Even through its failure, the narrative
image of Soul City stands as testament to the power of these tropes in modern
American history—and its remarkable invisibility in mainstream memories of the
civil rights movement and Black Power only makes this power that much more
poignant. In McKissick's combination of economics and politics, we can find a
unique window into the state of the movement for civil rights in the era after
much of the white nation considered it to be completed. Soul City's absence in
the broader story, indeed, marks the Right's presence. Despite his efforts to utilize
conservatism and capitalism on behalf of African Americans in order to "carve
the financial turkey with all its trimmings," the complexity of McKissick and his
vision do not fit easily within the narrative of "good" versus "evil" on which the
Right depends to sell its version of history.

NOTES

1. Soul City Company, "Soul City: A Fresh Start," undated, box 10, folder 146. Soul City
   Papers, Chapin F. Stuart Jr. Planning Library, University of North Carolina at Chapel
   Hill (hereafter cited as Soul City Papers).
2. "Floyd B. McKissick Announces a New Program for Economic Development," press
   release, 3 October 1968, box 343, folder 7472. Floyd B. McKissick Papers #4930,
   Southern Historical Collection, Wilson Library, University of North Carolina at Chapel
   Hill (hereafter cited as McKissick Papers).
3. By "classic" civil rights movement, I mean what Jacquelyn Dowd Hall, relying on
   Bayard Rustin, described as the "dominant narrative" of the movement that runs from
   the *Brown v. Board of Education* decision of 1954 through the Civil Rights Act of 1964

and the Voting Rights Act of 1965 and of which Martin Luther King Jr. is the "defining figure." Jacquelyn Dowd Hall, "The Long Civil Rights Movement and the Political Uses of the Past," *Journal of American History* 91, no. 4 (March 2005): 1234.

4. For more on the New Right, see Kevin Kruse, *White Flight: Atlanta and the Making of Modern Conservatism* (Princeton: Princeton University Press, 2007); Matthew Lassiter, *The Silent Majority: Suburban Politics in the Sunbelt South* (Princeton: Princeton University Press, 2006); Joseph Crespino, *In Search of Another Country: Mississippi and the Conservative Counterrevolution* (Princeton: Princeton University Press, 2007); Kim Phillips-Fein, *Invisible Hands: The Businessmen's Crusade Against the New Deal* (New York: Norton, 2009); Dan T. Carter, *From George Wallace to Newt Gingrich: Race in the Conservative Counterrevolution, 1963–1994* (Baton Rouge: Louisiana State University Press, 1999) and *The Politics of Rage: George Wallace, the Origins of the New Conservatism, and the Transformation of American Politics* (Baton Rouge: Louisiana State University Press, 2000); Donald T. Critchlow, *Phyllis Schlafly and Grassroots Conservatism: A Woman's Crusade* (Princeton: Princeton University Press, 2005); Kevin Mattson, *Rebels All! A Short History of the Conservative Mind in Postwar America* (New Brunswick, NJ: Rutgers University Press, 2008); Bruce J. Schulman and Julian Zelizer, eds., *Rightward Bound: Making America Conservative in the 1970s* (Cambridge, MA: Harvard University Press, 2008).

5. For more on the utopian impulse, see Russell Jacoby, *Picture Imperfect: Utopian Thought for an Anti-Utopian Age* (New York: Columbia University Press, 2005). For the role of utopia in the civil rights movement, see Francis Shor, "Utopian Aspirations in the Black Freedom Movement: SNCC and the Struggle for Civil Rights, 1960–1965," *Utopian Studies* 15, no. 2 (2004): 173–89.

6. See Fredric Jameson, *Postmodernism, or, the Cultural Logic of Late Capitalism* (Durham, NC: Duke University Press, 2003); David Harvey, *The Condition of Postmodernity: An Enquiry Into the Origins of Cultural Change* (Cambridge, MA: Blackwell, 1990).

7. "Speech by Floyd B. McKissick: Rhode Island Urban Coalition," 15 May 1969, box 336, folder 7447. McKissick Papers.

8. Hall, "The Long Civil Rights Movement," 1254, 1258. For other historiographical examinations of the civil rights movement, see Charles M. Payne, "The Social Construction of History," in *I've Got the Light of Freedom: The Organizing Tradition and the Mississippi Freedom Struggle* (Berkeley: University of California Press, 1995), 413–43; Charles W. Eagles, "Toward New Histories of the Civil Rights Era," *Journal of Southern History* 66, no. 4 (November 2000): 815–48; Peniel E. Joseph, "Rethinking the Black Power Era," *Journal of Southern History* 75, no. 3 (August 2009): 707–16. For a more critical engagement with the idea of the "long civil rights movement," see Sundiata Keita Cha-Jua and Clarence Lang, "The 'Long Movement' as Vampire: Temporal and Spatial Fallacies in Recent Black Freedom Studies," *Journal of African American History* 92, no. 2 (Spring 2007): 265–88. For more on the civil rights movement after the end of its "classical" phase, see Manning Marable, *Race, Reform and Rebellion: The Second Reconstruction and Beyond in Black America, 1945–2006* (Mississippi: University Press of Mississippi, 2007); Timothy Minchin, *From Rights to Economics: The Ongoing Struggle for Black Equality in the U.S. South* (Gainesville: University Press of Florida, 2007).

9. McKissick himself, to the best of my knowledge, has never received any scholarly biographical treatment. Some of his specific activities have garnered some attention, however; for more on his activism in Durham, see Christina Greene, *Our Separate Ways: Women and the Black Freedom Movement in Durham, North Carolina* (Chapel Hill: University of North Carolina Press, 2005). For his tenure in the Congress of Racial Equality, see August Meier and Elliott Rudwick, *CORE: A Study in the Civil Rights Movement,*

1942–1968 (New York: Oxford University Press, 1973), and William L. Van Deburg, *New Day in Babylon: The Black Power Movement and American Culture, 1965–1975* (Chicago: University of Chicago Press, 1992), 133–35.

10. Christopher Strain, "Soul City, North Carolina: Black Power, Utopia, and the African American Dream," *Journal of African American History* 89, no. 1 (Winter 2004): 57–74; Roger Biles, "The Rise and Fall of Soul City: Planning, Politics, and Race in Recent America," *Journal of Planning History* 4, no. 1 (February 2005): 52–72; Timothy J. Minchin, "'A Brand New Shining City': Floyd B. McKissick Sr. and the Struggle to Build Soul City, North Carolina," *North Carolina Historical Review* 82, no. 2 (April 2005): 125–55. See also Van Deburg, *New Day*, 135–37.

11. In addition to these thematic differences, I also rely in this essay on the heretofore unavailable Soul City Papers collected at the Chapin F. Stuart Jr. Planning Library at the University of North Carolina at Chapel Hill.

12. Glenn Fowler, "Floyd McKissick, Civil Rights Maverick, Dies at 69," *New York Times*, April 20, 1991.

13. "Biographical Notes on Floyd B. McKissick." October 3, 1968, box 341, folder 7537. McKissick Papers.

14. For more on the integration of the McKissick children into Durham public schools, see Greene, *Our Separate Ways*, 73–75, 84, 95–96.

15. "Biographical Notes on Floyd B. McKissick."

16. Karen Ferguson, "Organizing the Ghetto: The Ford Foundation, CORE, and White Power in the Black Power Era, 1967–1969," *Journal of Urban History* 34, no. 1 (November 2007): 76.

17. Industrial Management Association of Greater Pensacola, "Floyd McKissick—January Program Speaker," *Pensacola Helmsman*, January 1976, box 343, folder 7494. McKissick Papers.

18. "Statement by Floyd McKissick, Sr." Press Conference 20 March 1975, box 343, folder 7479. McKissick Papers.

19. The Soul City Foundation, *Soul City: History of A Free Standing New Community* (Charlotte, NC: The Soul City Foundation, 1975), 3.

20. Von Blaine, McKissick & Associates, Inc. "McKissick Enterprises to Build New Town" 13 January 1969, folder 141. Soul City Papers.

21. Soul City Foundation, *Soul City*, 4.

22. Ibid., 5.

23. Warren Regional Planning Corporation, *Soul City Newsletter*, March 1971, box 10, folder 142. Soul City Papers.

24. "Basic Fact Sheet on Soul City, North Carolina," Promotional Material for Press Conference March 30, 1975, box 10, folder 143. Soul City Papers.

25. Ibid.; Vance County is to the immediate west of Warren.

26. "Basic Fact Sheet."

27. Ibid.

28. Soul City Foundation, *Soul City*, 2.

29. "Basic Fact Sheet."

30. Floyd McKissick, "The Economics of Being Black," address to Standard Oil Company of Indiana Senior Management Meeting, 23 June 1978, box 343, folder 7481b. McKissick Papers.

31. W. E. B. Du Bois, *Black Reconstruction* (New York: Harcourt, Brace and Company, 1935), 182–83.

32. Elizabeth Tornquist, "Black Capitalism and Soul City, North Carolina," *The North Carolina Anvil*, 9 April 1969, box 10, folder 129. Soul City Papers.

33. Thomas J. Sugrue, "The Structures of Urban Poverty: The Reorganization of Space and Work in Three Periods of American History," in *The "Underclass" Debate: Views From History*, ed. Michael Katz (Princeton: Princeton University Press, 1992), 100.

34. McKissick, "The Economics of Being Black."

35. Carter, *From George Wallace*, 42.

36. Daniel Patrick Moynihan, "What Has Been Pulling Us Apart?" in *The New American Revolution*, ed. Roderick Aya and Norman Miller (New York: Free Press, 1971), 11.

37. *Soul City Newsletter*, March 1971. Soul City Papers.

38. Soul City Corporation, "Present at the Creation," Souvenir Book, 9 November 1973, box 10, folder 145. Soul City Papers.

39. McKissick to John Lamb, President Minneapolis Marketing Corporation, 9 May 1974, box 1, folder 20. McKissick Papers.

40. For a discussion of this image of the "urban dystopia" as a "bourgeois construction," see Guy Baeten, "Hypochondriac Geographies of the City and the New Urban Dystopia: Coming to Terms with the 'Other' City," *City* 6, no. 1 (2002): 103–15.

41. Michael B. Katz, ed., "The Urban 'Underclass' as a Metaphor of Social Transformation," in *The "Underclass" Debate* (Princeton: Princeton University Press, 1992), 5.

42. As Katz also notes, this is a problematic term, revolving around stigmatization and not actually defining a "class" as such. See Katz, *The "Underclass" Debate*, 16–23.

43. Sugrue, "The Structures of Urban Poverty," 116.

44. See Katz, *The "Underclass" Debate*, 18.

45. John Dvorak, "Money: Rx for Blacks," *Kansas City Times*, 23 August 1975, box 341, folder 7548. McKissick Papers.

46. Eccles. 10:19; "McKissick Calls Money Blacks' Path to Equality," *Minneapolis Tribune*, 11 November 1975, box 341, folder 7537. McKissick Papers.

47. Floyd McKissick, "God's Economic Plan," draft, undated, box 343, folder 7488. McKissick Papers.

48. McKissick, "The Economics of Being Black."

49. Floyd McKissick, *Three Fifths of a Man* (New York: Macmillan, 1969), 140–41.

50. McKissick, "The Economics of Being Black."

51. McKissick, *Three Fifths*, 42–43.

52. McKissick, "The Economics of Being Black."

53. Ibid.

54. Tornquist, "Black Capitalism and Soul City, North Carolina."

55. Ibid.

56. Paul Delaney, "Blacks for Nixon Sharply Rebuked," *New York Times*, 3 August 1972.

57. James T. Wooten, "McKissick Calls on Blacks to Join Two-Party Politics," *New York Times*, 10 August 1972.

58. "Statement by Floyd McKissick, Sr." Press Conference 20 March 1975, box 343, folder 7479. McKissick Papers.

59. "McKissick Calls Money Blacks' Path to Equality," *Minneapolis Tribune*, 11 November 1975, box 341, folder 7537. McKissick Papers.

60. Soul City Foundation, *Soul City*, 5.

61. "Statement by Floyd McKissick, Sr." Press Conference 20 March 1975, box 343, folder 7479. McKissick Papers.

62. Floyd McKissick, "McKissick for Nixon," *Cincinnati Herald*, 23 September 1972, box 341, folder 7551. McKissick Papers.

63. McKissick, "The Economics of Being Black."

64. McKissick to William Clay, 9 July 1974, box 342, folder 7556. McKissick Papers.

65. Ibid.

66. Robert T. Chase, "Class Resurrection: The Poor People's Campaign of 1968 and Resurrection City," *Essays in History* 40 (1998).

67. Janice Crump, "What's in Our Name," *The Soul City Sounder*, March 1976, box 10, folder 142. Soul City Papers.

68. Ibid.

69. Soul City Corporation, "Present at the Creation."

70. Wayne King, "Soul City, N.C., is Moving from Dream Stage to Reality," *New York Times*, 4 January 1974.

71. A. O. Sulzberger, "H.U.D. to Foreclose on Soul City, Troubled 'New Town' in Carolina," *New York Times*, 29 June 1979.

72. Ibid.

73. Thomas Johnson, "Blacks in Carolina Battle to Save Soul City," *New York Times*, 3 July 1979.

74. Ibid.

75. Sulzberger, "H.U.D. to Foreclose."

76. Johnson, "Blacks in Carolina Battle."

77. Sulzberger, "H.U.D. to Foreclose."

78. Johnson, "Blacks in Carolina Battle."

CHAPTER 16

INTEGRATION, BLACK NATIONALISM, AND RADICAL DEMOCRATIC TRANSFORMATION IN AFRICAN AMERICAN PHILOSOPHIES OF EDUCATION, 1965–74

RUSSELL RICKFORD

The greatest Negro revolution is that mothers are now determined that their children are to get an education.
—Inner City Parents Council (Detroit), 1967

RECENT FREEDOM STUDIES HAVE PORTRAYED CIVIL RIGHTS and Black Power as equally significant and interrelated stages of struggle. This view, central to the "long civil rights movement" outlook, helped correct an earlier tendency to artificially segment black protest outlooks and strategies. Overemphasis on continuity, however, may obscure the extent to which the "new black nationalism"—the renaissance that provided Black Power's intellectual and cultural impetuses—represented genuine political innovation.[1] One solution to this interpretive dilemma lies in our willingness to transcend distorted readings of the role of black nationalism in African American life.[2] We must resist the myth of nationalism as the creed of the disaffected fringe while rejecting the fantasy of nationalism as subterranean religion. When we accept integrationism and nationalism as more dualistic than dichotomous, acknowledging that neither is more intrinsic to African American realities than the other, and recognizing the powerful currents of consciousness that flow from creative tension between the two, we will better understand black political culture and the evolution of black insurgency.[3]

Such insight demands candid assessment of the breadth of the nationalist revival that swept African American communities after the mid-1960s. Though rising militancy and shifting tactics cannot be attributed to black nationalism alone, legions of rank-and-file black Americans appropriated nationalist discourse while rethinking the nature of citizenship and freedom. Black Power in its broadest conception[4] represented a groundswell of ideas and activities designed to infuse blackness with radical possibility. Black insistence on self-definition, self-determination, and self-defense reflected strong elements of alienation—from the platitudes of liberal democracy, the conscience of white America, and the goodwill of the federal government. The richness of African American intellectual and cultural production also signaled a measure of optimism, an audacious belief that, armed with an array of new or revamped theories and approaches, black people could exercise genuine power within the United States and on the world stage. Far more than a retreat to narrow identity politics, Black Power unleashed a surge of creative energy that emboldened African Americans, enlarging the political repertoires of even those who eschewed its separatist or revolutionary implications.

As we guard against viewing Black Power as a politics of despair, we must also avoid portraying the movement as static or ideologically homogeneous, or as the property of elite theorists who bestowed fully formed ideas upon the people. Black Power heralded a popular awakening. Black nationalism's rebirth as a dominant idiom of black expression compelled the African American masses to confront its myriad principles and themes. Nonideologues and nonelites theorized, improvised, and amended Black Power concepts at the grassroots, writing an assertive new chapter of struggle in their homes, neighborhoods, workplaces, and schools. An expansive view of Black Power must unearth the movement's democratic character, demonstrating how aspects of nationalist thought proved relevant to the everyday strivings of African Americans and thus garnered wide support in black communities.

The complexity of black ambitions offers one explanation. In the Black Power era, as in earlier periods, African Americans faced the task of fulfilling the promise of human universalism (redeeming the American democratic creed) while reinventing the politics of racial difference (affirming a positive black particularity). They did so in a time of sharply rising expectations and evolving demands, as shifts in the nation's political economy, the deepening isolation of black communities, and ideological growth inspired the reworking of ongoing efforts to achieve racial justice. The 1960s complicated the African American condition of "double-consciousness," fostering a sense of dual citizenship that affirmed the values of black distinctiveness and solidarity while redefining black attempts to participate fully in American life.[5]

That dynamic profoundly shaped African American educational thought. The arena of education demonstrates how attempts to reform deteriorating institutions and social services in black communities creatively drew on Black Power ideas. Such campaigns included demands for integration, an objective that even in Black Power's heyday remained vital to the pursuit of privileges reserved for white children. African American educational struggles revealed the influence of a pragmatic black nationalism that sometimes complemented integrationist efforts, proving pliant and strategic rather than static, dogmatic, or defeatist. Many African Americans acknowledged the need to refine or transcend the elusive goal of integration, undertaking a search for alternatives that reflected powerful impulses of self-affirmation within black life.

This essay surveys the educational perspectives of black parents and other working-class and middle-class theorists, highlighting moments of ideological transition and stressing the rich political adaptation and inventiveness that the new nationalism helped enable. The notion of pragmatic nationalism as an enduring feature of black political consciousness helps explain why local African American struggles that pursued school integration in the 1950s and early 1960s (whatever their specific tactical and ideological configurations) after the mid-1960s embraced black autonomy and the rhetoric of cultural distinctiveness, a change sometimes described as a wholesale move to separatism.[6] In truth, popular philosophies of black education displayed a complexity too often obscured by more doctrinaire or exclusive varieties of contemporary African American politics and protest.

The quest for emancipatory black education reflected deep awareness of the political nature of schools and the social implications of their twin functions: imparting skills and transmitting cultural norms. Determined to gain for their children meaningful access to middle-class prosperity, black parents launched interventions in the realm of culture; only by cultivating notions of black nationality could they fully satisfy the egalitarian claims of American citizenship. The mingling of integrationist and nationalist currents in black educational efforts generated a third discursive course that sought to enlarge the potential for democratic participation and cultural pluralism in America.[7] Black philosophies of education envisaged a reallocation of resources and power that promised to end the cultural, economic, and political colonization of black communities while empowering *all* children. Thus, in the years after 1954 and *Brown v. Board*, African Americans transformed a landmark but constricted Supreme Court ruling—a Cold War-era decision unable to ensure swift material or political redistribution—into a radically democratic, deeply pluralistic vision of social change.

WE WANT WHAT WE HAVE

Black parents tested new expressions of educational thought in countless forums during the late 1960s, including one stormy San Francisco school board meeting in early 1969. The event featured discussion of a school busing plan designed to relieve "de facto" segregation in the district, whose black pupils constituted 22 percent of the student population. Many of the more than one thousand residents who packed an auditorium to attend the meeting fiercely opposed "forced busing." During the public discussion that evening, white women representing Mothers Support Neighborhood Schools (MSNS), a local group, denounced busing as a threat to the "family unit," prompting cheers from the mostly white crowd.[8]

As the middle-class MSNS leaders spoke, the audience's large minority of black residents remained mostly silent. MSNS and other groups (including Americans

Against Communism, Crime and Corruption) that had staged an antibusing rally prior to the meeting insisted that they opposed not Negroes themselves, but coerced integration and the endangerment of tight-knit, local "neighborhood schools." The assurance hardly eased the resentment of the black throngs at the forum. Ironically, the speaker who many of *these* attendees supported also opposed the integration plan. Inez Andry, an African American who followed the MSNS leaders in addressing the board, provoked a raucous ovation—and pleased white and black onlookers alike—by declaring, "*We* don't believe in busing, either!"

Andry, in her late thirties or early forties, stressed that she represented "a great portion"—though hardly all—of the parents of local black schoolchildren. Despite the disclaimer, black residents assembled that evening greeted her comments enthusiastically, demonstrating that they, too, could claim the politics of neighborhood pride, and thus, implicitly, the sanctity of culturally or racially homogeneous schools. Black aversion to busing stemmed from different motives than those that had galvanized MSNS and other conservative groups across the country, Andry explained. She declared,

> We don't want to go to no other neighborhood. But we want education—the kind *we* need in our neighborhood. We don't [just] want to see books—we want to see *all* kinds of books. Black books. We want to be recognized. We don't want integration—we'll get that. We want education. And integration will not educate our black children. Black books, more black principals, some more black people on the school board—a black woman up there, too. You said you want it integrated, well let's have it down the middle.[9]

Andry's remarks reflected the repudiation of racial assimilation that galvanized contemporary African American politics. The woman's tone conveyed the new militancy, and she punctuated her demands with the threat of insurrection. "You want to keep your pretty little San Francisco pretty?" she said, alluding to the uprisings that had beset American cities. "Well you have to come with it, because I want to live here and nobody is running me out." Yet Andry's message hardly constituted an outright rejection of integration. Indeed, her casual assertion that "we'll get" racially mixed schools suggested desegregation's decline as a dominant index of black freedom as well as its lingering status as a symbol of black progress.[10]

Not a formal leader of a specific movement, Andry nevertheless exemplified the double consciousness that defined African American educational reform. During her remarks to the school board, she dismissed as "a game of craps" the efforts of San Francisco authorities to ensure racial justice. She then acknowledged the colloquial flavor of the remark, explaining, "I don't know how to speak like these other ladies [the antibusing MSNS representatives that had preceded her at the microphone] because I didn't have that kind of education." She hastened to add that she didn't *want* her children to receive "that kind" of education—one that was sterile, bourgeois, and white. "We want the kind that we can use to better our condition," Andry insisted. "We don't want to be taught how the white people live, how they speak. We want to be educated. We want what we have."

This last sentence captured the rich irony of Andry's perspective. On one hand, the woman rejected the white, middle-class standards by which educational authorities and other experts had scorned the culture of black children and their families. Education meant self-discovery—not mimicry of whiteness. On the other hand, she articulated a conventional vision of success and social mobility—the wish to "better our condition" that had inspired African American faith in education since Reconstruction.

Andry expressed frustration with the pace and aims of liberal reform, revealing her distrust of white officialdom. Alienation, however, did not preclude petitioning authorities for redress—albeit forcefully, and with the option of rebellion in one's back pocket. Finally, Andry advanced the kind of citizenship claim that had long propelled the civil rights movement. "They don't tell us our tax dollars are smaller because we are black!" she proclaimed.[11]

THERE WILL BE NO MORE RESIGNATION

Andry's sensibilities reveal the complexities and possibilities that black nationalism represented in the late 1960s. Her outlook suggests why *Brown*, which unleashed a reservoir of political energy, seemed increasingly frail to those impatient with the pace and failed promises of racial reform. African Americans rediscovered nationalist impulses as they struggled to redesign American democracy. While the principle of full citizenship remained paramount, freedom campaigns saw renewed emphasis on schooling as a means of instilling black identity.

Concern for arming black children with a sense of racial integrity represented a longstanding priority. African Americans had combated discrimination in education throughout the twentieth century, rarely limiting their energies to strict integration and sometimes downplaying the value of desegregation as the path to a sound education.[12] Scholars who note the primacy and militancy that black integrationist efforts assumed in the early to mid-1960s acknowledge that the approach never constituted an end in itself. Indeed, the syncretic outlook George Frederickson called "nationalistic integrationism" achieved considerable salience in postwar black America. As Martha Biondi argues, efforts to blend the seemingly clashing philosophies "resonated with deeply rooted, and often interlocking, African American struggles for political sovereignty, cultural nationalism and civil rights."[13]

Far from supplanting an integrationist consensus in black life, the resurrection of nationalism provided a resilient lexicon of struggle that African Americans deployed in the cause of educational justice, an objective that proved confoundingly elusive. The 1960s unleashed the full force of black anger upon American education and its mockery of the aspirations of minorities. Black parents surveyed the squalor of public schooling for their children—an outrage that had intensified in the postwar years—and levied scathing critiques. Detroit's Inner City Parents Council in 1967 accused the local schools of preparing black youngsters only for welfare rolls or the front lines of Vietnam.[14] By 1974, with the national outlook only slightly less grim, the Black Social Workers of Louisville,

Kentucky, denounced two American penal systems specially designed, in their view, for African Americans—one controlled by correctional departments, the other by boards of education.[15]

The late 1960s revived the rhetoric of "educational genocide," a charge that black radicals had leveled in the early 1950s.[16] Now African Americans of various political strains adopted the cry. Militant New York City integrationist Milton A. Galamison maintained that "the only healthy exercise for the black community is warfare against the educational system." Observers in Boston identified the cause of educational justice as the main "ferment of change" within the African American enclave of Roxbury. "Blacks are directing rage at school with the same intensity as that formerly reserved for bus stations in dusty southern towns," author Price Cobbs declared. "The startling and frightening realization has come that they are both the same."[17]

African Americans had nurtured faith in nineteenth-century reformer Horace Mann's romance of education as the "great equalizer . . . the balance wheel of the social machinery." Dedication to this ideal continued to breed desperation after World War II, as great waves of black migrants swept into northern and western cities, filling neighborhoods and schools that white families fled and municipal authorities neglected. African American critics counseled against messianic hope in public schooling, citing the institution's feeble record of ensuring social mobility for lower classes. "It is not the education of black men that will assure their effective liberation," black leftist Doxey A. Wilkerson said in 1969. "[I]t is the liberation of black men that will assure their effective education."[18]

Yet the theme of education as liberation endured. Indeed, black nationalist logic cloaked the principle in mystical heritage. "This . . . ideal which has caused such pain . . . stems from our African heritage of the love of knowledge manifested in our temple-building in Thebes, our invention of writing in Memphis, and our education institution building in Timbuktu," Howard University School of Education dean Nancy Levi Arnez proclaimed in an Urban League tract. Al Vann of New York's Afro-American Teacher's Association likewise invoked "the empires of ancient West Africa" to explain black America's old and sometimes frantic obsession with schooling.[19]

Less fancifully, Black Panther theorist Eldridge Cleaver explained that black parents had come to envision schools as the principal tool for passing to the next generation "the means for waging the struggle." Schools had long offered African Americans a target for protest and a base for social organizing. Their political value surged amid the transition to Black Power, as African Americans pondered anew the relationship between identity, citizenship and freedom. Many black intellectuals, workers and students now saw schools as "the final battlefield of the colonized," with no less at stake than the future of the oppressed.[20]

This perspective reflected changes in the freedom struggle's terrain. The collapsing New Deal coalition, the unraveling Great Society, industrial attrition, and deteriorating central cities meant declining fortunes for black urbanites in the late 1960s and 1970s. However, even as policies of "benign neglect" replaced "maximum feasible participation" of the poor, African Americans embraced the creed of self-determination, buoyed by the rise of black consciousness, the emergence of African and Caribbean nations, the ascent of black elected officials, and the growth of a black professional class still linked—materially and in some ways psychologically—to the fate of the ghetto.[21]

The years between the crescendo of legislative civil rights (1964–68) and the political disarray of the mid-1970s witnessed fierce battles over open housing, welfare rights, and labor. However, education alone constituted the main front of two essential black campaigns: the struggles for self-definition and for home rule over urban space. These crusades, rooted in acceptance of permanently black central cities, signaled the realization of African Americans that they must make the ghetto a genuine home. They also embodied the rising ambitions that a Harlem mother described in 1968, "A revolutionary change has taken place in the minds of black parents. There will be no more resignation and accommodation to the status quo as a way of life for them . . . They may not know all the facts about their history, but since Lumumba, Nkrumah and others, they know they have a history. They have roots."[22]

LET THE COMMUNITY RUN THE SCHOOL

Black America's creative marriage of integrationism and nationalism—and some of its most ingenious visions of social transformation—crystallized in the cause of community control of schools. We need not rehash the familiar details of community control's inaugural struggle, which unfolded in New York City in the late 1960s and remains associated with the conflict between the local teacher's union and black and Latino residents of Brooklyn's Ocean Hill-Brownsville. It is necessary only to discredit the thesis that the nationalist themes that surfaced during the crisis reflected the influence of black separatists whose racial chauvinism spurred white backlash.[23] In truth, nationalist strategies grew organically from the history of black educational activism in New York[24] and complicated rather than displaced integrationist outlooks.

The community control wars began in Harlem, where public schools stood as stark symbols of oppression.[25] As early as 1958, when the city announced plans to build a new school in the neighborhood to relieve overcrowding at two junior high schools, local parents expressed cautious hope. In 1965, with construction under way, the board of education designated the facility an "intermediate school," a new model designed to ease racial concentration by operating in fringe areas and drawing students from both white and minority neighborhoods.

Though New York school officials had pledged to reverse de facto segregation in the district, Harlem parents had ample cause to doubt that authorities would integrate the planned school, IS 201. Neither the civil disobedience of Harlem mothers in the 1950s nor citywide boycotts against school segregation in the early to mid-1960s had relieved the educational plight of black and Latino New Yorkers.[26] Many Harlemites remained devoted to integration as a means of winning essential resources that remained concentrated in white schools. Harlem parents had petitioned the board of education for integrated education from the moment they learned of plans for IS 201, convinced that only the presence of white children would guarantee adequate funding, modern facilities, innovative academic programs, and experienced personnel. Never content to lobby solely for integration, they also pressed for a solid curriculum of the three Rs.

The proposed site for the school—near the elevated railroad tracks in a gritty section of East Harlem—seemed to vindicate those who dismissed the board of education's promises. In early 1966, the board revealed the sort of "integration" that would prevail at the school: 50 percent black and 50 percent Puerto Rican. Outraged parents from both groups denounced the maneuver and resolved to resist the opening of IS 201 as a "segregated ghetto school."[27] Local parents and antipoverty workers continued weighing options, unwilling to fully withdraw demands for integration. By that spring they shifted their hopes to another strategy: local self-government.

"Either they bring white children in to integrate IS 201 or let the community run the school," the president of Harlem's Parent Teacher Association alliance declared at a meeting between neighborhood residents and school officials.[28] Some observers interpreted the call by Harlem activists for the creation of a neighborhood council with powers to select administrators and set policy as a retreat from the goal of integration. In truth, while insisting upon a measure of local governance, parents continued to push for new zoning patterns to help desegregate IS 201, refusing to relinquish what many saw as intertwined though hardly synonymous demands for integrated and quality education.[29]

The parents and their antipoverty allies demanded a detailed program to raise academic standards as well as an integrated staff of competent teachers. They also sought a black or Puerto Rican principal of their choosing, convinced that the presence of such a figure would help boost their children's self-esteem and racial pride, qualities they deemed crucial to successful learning. It now seemed obvious that IS 201's student body would remain as solidly black and Puerto Rican as any other Harlem school and that "quality education, segregated-style" had become the rallying cry of a growing portion of the community.[30]

Harlem's tactical swivel from integration to "home rule" presaged the rise of the city's community control struggle. To understand the ideological complexity that accompanied this transition, one must recognize the ways in which African American educational philosophies continued to combine elements of integrationism and nationalism. The Harlem struggle embodied this dialectic. As activism escalated around the fate of IS 201 in 1965, parents saw the fight for "QUALITY integrated education" (original emphasis) as a quest for academic excellence, one that might secure the means to prepare neighborhood children to compete for specialized jobs in the age of automation. No mere attempt to commingle black and white bodies, the campaign sought access to modern pedagogical techniques. That August, for example, the Harlem Parents Committee (HPC), an integrationist group formed in 1963, helped organize a workshop for local families in which a middle school teacher used "simple household articles" to demonstrate "the new math."[31]

HPC and other local reformers dismissed one-dimensional integration schemes that neglected the priorities of educational excellence and equity. Neighborhood protests against the district's offers of "open enrollment" and "free transfers," programs widely seen in the community as palliatives for educational apartheid, rejected these measures as placing "unjust burden solely upon Negro parents and children." Harlem's pursuit of "other-way" integration—the transfer of white students into black neighborhood schools—itself reflected a vision of desegregation as a process of mutual sacrifice and benefit.[32]

Yet HPC could not ignore the community's resurgent nationalism. The group acknowledged in 1965 that years of thwarted integration efforts had reinforced the belief "that it is both desirable and possible to achieve academic excellence within the segregated schools, either as an end in itself or as preparation for eventual integration." HPC therefore vowed to measure progress toward "upgrading the segregated schools," even as integration battles continued.[33] Nor did the organization reject militant efforts on behalf of black sovereignty. Its August 1965 newsletter endorsed a biography by a Kenyan revolutionary that chronicled the guerilla campaign against British rule, a rebellion widely described in the West as terrorist savagery. By contrast, the HPC reviewer expressed appreciation for "the 'other side' of the 'Mau Mau' story."[34]

By 1966 this independent spirit, along with mounting frustration over the "status crow"[35] of local education, inspired Harlem families and activists to diversify demands. Even moderates prioritized reforms that would leave largely unchanged the racial composition of neighborhood schools. Faith in the American creed persisted; amid the sobering expansion of technocracy, many Harlem parents merely redoubled efforts to grant local students opportunities for social mobility, demanding that the schools equip them "to compete with all other children on an equal basis."[36] Neighborhood reformers petitioned anew for typewriters, a full music program, and racially diverse faculty; curricular upgrades and some concept of integration still anchored their agenda. However, HPC also rushed to defend the emerging Black Power concept, identifying "white power, NOT black power" as the inexorable source of black servitude. Special emphasis now rested on the demand for a Negro principal, reflecting growing faith in the buoying effects "a new image" of black authority might have on local schoolchildren.[37]

Embracing such concerns, HPC announced plans in 1966 for a community-wide campaign to record African American folklore and transmit this "valuable store of culture" to area youngsters. The following year, a cartoon in the group's newsletter illustrated the view of black cultural pride as an essential complement to other ingredients of sound education.[38] Black nationalist–oriented organizations like New York's Afro-American Teachers' Association (ATA) espoused similar ideals, celebrating possibilities for black affirmation in interracial settings. The group convened a May 1967 conference whose prescriptions for black schools included traditional remedies (smaller classes) and cultural nationalist reforms (Swahili lessons). While calling for more minority teachers and administrators, ATA recommended the hiring of black and Latino parent assistants who might "orientate [sic] teachers with the neighborhood and the style of living of its inhabitants," a proposal that defended the coherence of black working-class life while accepting the presence of white teachers in its midst.[39]

Mainstream media tended to overlook such convergence of black perspectives, depicting "integrationist" and "separatist" forces as hostile sects.[40] Harlem activists chafed at journalism's reduction of what they recognized as a "terribly complex" struggle for dignity through the schools. By 1968 periodicals like *Newsweek* reported that the cry for school integration had all but subsided in most large cities. The irony of such pronouncements stung black city dwellers who in many cases had sustained the multiracial ideals that obstructionist officials and fleeing white families scorned. "I don't want segregation," IS 201 parent leader David Spencer declared in 1966, "but if I have it, I want it on my own terms."[41]

As late as 1969, E. Babbette Edwards, a parent member of Harlem's community board, reaffirmed the view of neighborhood involvement in school governance as "a significant step toward integration," even as she rejected as offensive and unreliable the prospect of further desegregation schemes engineered by white authorities. "Our priority is black community control," she acknowledged. Spencer and Edwards embodied the pragmatism of a position that groups like the Inner City Parents Council of Detroit endorsed. African Americans, the organization asserted in 1967, had resolved that "the separation which the white man has forced upon them shall now be used for their advancement rather than their exploitation."[42]

Despite the pervasiveness of such sentiments in black communities, pundits continued to misread the educational revolts in Harlem and Ocean Hill-Brownsville. In their estimation, Black Power represented "a side issue"; the radical rhetoric suffusing the protests flowed chiefly from "revolutionaries without a following."[43] Members of the Student Nonviolent Coordinating Committee (SNCC), Congress of Racial Equality (CORE—in its radical New York iterations), and the early Black Panther cadre of Harlem (a formation that slightly preceded the Oakland-based party) had indeed "attached themselves to the silent fringes of the community," in the graceful phrase of local activists. The view of these elements as outsiders, however, struck indigenous parents as absurd. "They are known to all of us," an HPC leader said, recognizing the role such parties played in channeling genuine grievances.[44]

More to the point, the agendas of the militants often proved largely indistinguishable from those of the aroused rank and file. In late 1966, for example, Harlem's incipient Black Panthers organized demonstrations around a series of already-popular demands: African and African American history; black principals; and the renaming of public schools to "reflect the history and achievement of OUR PEOPLE" (original emphasis). At least one magazine contributor grasped the significance of these nodes of black consensus, acknowledging in 1969 the blurring line between community control as a route to school reform and as "the basis for a new social contract."[45]

The distinction may have proven immaterial. Truly organized radicalism never captured the masses; African American parents in New York and elsewhere continued to act upon specific quarrels with the school system (e.g., racist academic tracking and disciplinary procedures) and the thrust of black opinion remained wary of separatism. "This has nothing to do with all-black schools," Margaret Wright, a creator of the Los Angeles Community Black Board of Education, said in 1968. "We don't care whether [teachers] are black, white or yellow, just as long as they respect the values of the community."[46]

However, one radical critique—the colonial theory of black America—*did* penetrate black educational thought. Intellectuals who took the concept literally rarely achieved great influence, as Republic of New Africa devotees must have recognized as they organized a 1969 plebiscite on the matter of formal political sovereignty for Ocean-Hill Brownsville. But as an analogy for African American suffering, the notion that black communities constituted domestic colonies of white America captivated urbanites engaged in school struggles. An official from a Harlem antipoverty group lectured on the idea in 1967. Two years later, IS 201 administrator Charles Wilson polished the rhetorical turn. "Ocean Hill-Brownsville is like Kenya," he said. "We are like another part of West Africa. We have all been excluded from the seats of power."[47]

The colonial thesis strengthened the rationale for community control. Local self-government seemed a viable solution for the brutality of police, the contempt of welfare agents, and the offenses of absentee landlords and ghetto merchants. A wide segment of black Americans embraced this outlook. Its logic seized avowed integrationists like Galamison, who imagined block captains mobilizing against the startling density of liquor stores in Bedford-Stuyvesant. The neighborhood's wine peddlers, rent gougers, and "ethnomaniacal school teachers," he noted, all hailed from distant territories. The 1966 newsletter of an East Harlem Protestant parish decried exploitation "by overseers who commute into the neighborhood by day, wreak havoc with the lives of the black people, and withdraw by night with big paychecks."[48]

Community control as a crusade for greater dominion over urban institutions energized black nuns who applied the concept to Catholic schools in African American neighborhoods; workaday parents who saw a path from rent slavery to home ownership; and politicians like Adam Clayton Powell Jr. who leveraged the broad appeal of self-rule. The community control groundswell reinforced the perception that the vanguard of black opinion had abandoned integration. Powell, whose professional survival rested upon a discerning comprehension of Harlem politics, shrewdly resisted this notion. "You say I talk like a segregationist," he declared in 1970. "No! I have given up on the idea of a black man and a Puerto Rican man getting a decent education, a decent life on the basis of integration only."

African American educational thought remained diverse. Mel King of Boston's New Urban League observed in 1970 that the sheer variety of Roxbury school reform efforts (afterschool programs, busing initiatives, and independent schools of sundry ideologies) confounded the search for a common outlook. Acknowledging similar challenges, organizers of a 1969 African Americans Concerned About Education conference in Baltimore rejected the pursuit of philosophical accord and embarked upon a more prudent hunt for "operational unity."

Yet one detected growing consensus on the question of political autonomy.[49] Like African American culture more broadly, educational struggles reflected the determination of black urbanites to claim their patch of earth, an adaptation of a theme that had shaped black consciousness since emancipation. Raw necessity, along with the flowering 1960s awareness that made "black" a badge of pride and "Negro" an epithet, deepened this desire to transform African American reservations. "To us, a ghetto is not a bad place to live because its residents are all Negro or because most of them are poor," a founder of the Newark Community School said in 1967, shortly after that city's epic riot. "What makes a ghetto despicable—and what keeps it that way—is that the people in it have no control over the decisions that affect their lives."[50]

The quest for control never rendered integration obsolete; it merely cast the approach among a wider field of demands. The fight to redeem black space broadened the vision of dignified citizenship that also propelled integration battles. Barred from the full benefits of the welfare state, wartime spending, unionization, and machine politics, African Americans had inherited obsolescing central cities increasingly starved of public and private capital.[51] Amid the growing crisis of civic decay, community control became an attempt to enlarge the public sector and deliver social services, developing the ghetto and its people.

This required a revolution in the function of the school. By 1968, Harlem reformers—including veterans of community action who had comprehended and helped to deepen the social democratic implications of the War on Poverty—envisioned not mere sites of formal instruction, but centers for organizing mutual aid committees, credit unions, consumer cooperatives, and daycare programs. Supporters of IS 201 created a twenty-point agenda for genuine control that included complete medical services and free breakfast and lunch for all children. They demanded full employment for neighborhood residents, adult education classes, and drug rehabilitation programs.

The local board now governing IS 201 published a 250-page manual designed to prepare Harlemites to battle job discrimination, earn a high school diploma, and otherwise resist degradation. Community control advocates in Harlem and Central Brooklyn discussed plans to deposit payroll funds in local banks, employ ghetto residents as teacher aides and library assistants, and hire black and Puerto Rican contractors to repair and maintain neighborhood schools. These and other efforts revealed a determination to convert alienating urban bureaucracies into bulwarks of community enterprise. Local parents and organizers now regarded schools as arenas for confronting powerlessness, despair and "those larger issues which impinge so critically on the lives of school children in the ghetto."[52]

THAT WE LOSE NOT OUR IDENTITY

In the growth of the community control struggle, one glimpsed signs of black America's complex relationship to the idea of integration. From the start, Harlem parents had recognized the need to wrest from hostile forces the power to define racial reform. HPC in 1965 had taken pains to differentiate between "desegregation" and "integration." In the group's estimation, New York's central board of education had misused the latter term in vain promises to produce multiracial classrooms. If and when accomplished, racial admixture would constitute only a cessation of segregation. True *integration*, HPC insisted, connoted "the ongoing social process that can begin only after desegregation is accomplished, and should not be confused with the physical shifting of children."[53]

Historian Oscar Handlin drew a similar distinction in 1966. Far from a prescription for the mere dispersal of minorities, he argued, the "open society" vision of integration entailed a "leveling of all barriers to association other than those based on ability, taste and personal preference." At least one Harlem parent felt compelled to refine the critique. For activist David Spencer of the IS 201 Planning Board, "integration" meant that white America could not rob the black child of resources without also depriving his white peer. "But you say *integration* to the mother and father of the white kid, and they only think that my kid is going to move in next door and marry their daughter," he said in 1968. "So now I'm going to fight to see that my kids get an education, and if they do, then integration will take care of itself."[54]

Spencer's perspective implied a rethinking of not only "integration" but also "segregation." This reevaluation had proven central to the emergence of New York's community control movement. The shift to demands for local school governance gained momentum during a 1966 meeting of Harlem parents in which black Columbia University social worker Preston Wilcox called for community control. While cautioning against resignation from the integrationist cause, Wilcox urged a reappraisal of its terms. "If one believes that a segregated white school can be a good school, then one must believe that a segregated Negro and Puerto Rican school, like IS 201, can also be a good school," he declared. "We must be concerned with those who are left behind and who will be left behind even if the best conceivable school desegregation program should be implemented."[55]

Rejecting the stigma attached to all-black schools represented a longstanding black nationalist impulse.[56] Malcolm X had embodied this position, assailing the double standard by which all-white schools escaped designation as "segregated," a condition he equated not with blackness but with control "by someone from the outside." New York's Afro-American Teachers Association echoed this logic. "A school is not segregated because it is all black," the group declared in 1967. "A school is segregated when it is controlled by outsiders whose only interest is exploitation."[57]

If some African Americans eschewed such reasoning, many nevertheless recognized the widening gulf between black understandings of integration and those of most white Americans. While many black parents imagined school integration as a proportionate exchange of ideas and culture, even liberal white authorities generally envisioned a set of reforms that would gently infuse white environments with dark faces. Black ambivalence toward integration thus rested partly upon the question of control; forces remote from black communities typically orchestrated efforts to relieve racial isolation. "The same whites who yesterday fiercely resisted school desegregation today effectively determine its tone and pace," *Ebony* magazine noted in 1971.[58] The dearth of black input in implementation ensured that the routine inconveniences of the process fell chiefly upon African Americans, a reality that HPC had lamented as early as 1965. Piecemeal transfer programs placed on the black child "the burden of correcting the evil from which he has suffered," the organization complained that year.

The injustice of African American children rising early to venture into often-hostile white neighborhoods continued to alienate black America. "Negro parents

in the South never speak of sending their children to the 'integrated school,'"
psychologist Alvin Poussaint remarked in 1966. "They say, 'My child is going to
the *white* school.' No white children are ever 'integrated' into Negro schools since
integration is only a one-way street that Negroes travel to a white institution."
Boston activist Mel King observed in 1972 that African Americans perceived
one-way integration as perpetuating the very offense they most wished to end—
"the one-sided view of who's valuable in this society."[59]

Black Americans also found odious other assumptions of liberal integrationism. The *Brown* decision had affirmed a central component of the NAACP's
legal strategy by holding that separation from nonblack children generates in
African American pupils an indelible feeling of inferiority. Subsequent government reports, including *Racial Isolation in the Public Schools*, a 1967 study,
reinforced the premise that academic and psychological harm befalls black children consigned to "segregated" (all-black) schools. Floyd McKissick of CORE
deciphered the affront underlying such theories: "Mix Negroes with Negroes and
you get stupidity."[60]

Such offensive implications exacerbated injuries endured during assaults on
segregation. These included the emotional and occasionally physical bruises
African American children suffered amid expeditions onto white campuses. The
decimation (through demotion and dismissal) of black teachers and administrators that accompanied integration-related mergers and closings of Southern
schools further darkened the prospect of desegregation. For many African Americans, black people's capacity to maintain social and cultural integrity in integrated
contexts posed equally sobering questions. A 1968 cartoon in an Ocean Hill–
Brownsville community newspaper tweaked this concern. The strip depicted a
black man seated at a table in an upscale restaurant. "No bean 'n' rice, no turnip
greens 'n' hog jowl, no kinda soul food!" the diner quipped. "You call this inter-
gration? I calls it starvation!"[61]

The treatment was facetious but the anxiety proved quite real. African Americans had long contemplated the intangible costs of desegregation. In 1955, for
example, a member of the Oklahoma Association of Negro Teachers had warned
comrades about the hidden dangers of the "inevitable transition" to an integrated
world, and had counseled vigilance to ensure that in the process "we lose not
our identity as a capable and ingenious race nor lose a single phase of our cultural heritage." Black ambivalence deepened in the early 1970s as white hysteria
over school desegregation enveloped northern communities. "Black people were
struggling so hard to be passengers on a train, they did not stop to ask, 'Say, baby,
where is this train going?'" scholar-activist Bill Strickland remarked in 1970.[62]

In the end, neither the moral shortcomings of the white mainstream nor the
threat of black cultural erosion extinguished African American faith in the promise of integration. For some black critics, reforming the "dual system" of education
came to mean replacing white administration of black and white schools (singular
control) with a system that guaranteed African American authority over separate
black facilities (dual control). However, many black neighborhoods saw concur-
rent and even complementary integration and community control campaigns,

as African Americans claimed the right to self-determination and to unfettered access to the bounty of American prosperity.[63]

Integrationist sentiment contained elements of resignation. "If we can't get quality education without integration, then integration it will be," a black postal worker declared at a 1971 Pittsburgh school board meeting. While lamenting the prospective demise of traditions (including a popular homecoming football game) that had defined a local black high school, an African American electronics salesman in Richmond, Virginia, embraced a 1972 desegregation proposal that would dissolve the school as an exclusively black entity. "We will never get to the bottom of integration" unless the process received an honest trial nationwide, he explained. For him the alternative—"all the whites move out in the county and don't want to help pay the costs of the city"—seemed inauspicious.[64]

However, African Americans also exhibited optimism that modes of integration that honored black culture and autonomy—in short, *equitable* integration—remained possible. This conviction, fueled in part by earlier civil rights gains, proved capable of overcoming deep black misgivings about the less than salutary consequences of racially mixed schools. Indeed, visions of just integration helped reconcile seemingly competing impulses toward black autonomy and full inclusion.

W. Hazaiah Williams, black director of Berkeley, California's, board of education, stressed the complexity of this reconciliation, a feature of black political consciousness whose significance many historians later overlooked. Speaking before the US Senate Committee on Equal Educational Opportunity in 1971, Williams acknowledged that the process of school desegregation in Berkeley had unveiled the spectrum of African American opinion. Participants in the internal debate included those who clung to definitions of integration based on classical Liberal formulas (a position Williams associated with the NAACP), and those who championed the cause of independent black schools.

Black Berkeley had reached tenuous consensus, Williams testified, partly by affirming methods of integration that rejected "simple arithmetic arrangements" while preserving a sense of racial mutuality, political inclusion and respect. "We have always been subjected to white definitions of what is quality education," Williams explained. "We will be presumptuous enough to suggest that quality education that deals with our definitions might well be quality education for white children also."[65]

SWINGING OUR OWN PARADES

Rising confidence about the potential for black self-assertion and the promise of full citizenship drove efforts to redefine integration. This spirit of reassessment deepened existing hostility toward powerful social theories of cultural deprivation. School reforms and antipoverty programs had long prescribed compensation for purported deficiencies in the homes and neighborhoods of "disadvantaged" black students. The deprivation thesis eclipsed crudely racist explanations for the academic failure of minorities, and provided an alternative to ongoing assertions of black genetic inferiority.[66]

Yet African Americans increasingly rejected underlying assumptions of devi-
ance, dismissing the notion that cultural weaknesses caused their children's
academic distress. Parent members of IS 201's personnel committee disdained
teacher applicants who, having never visited a black or Puerto Rican home, cited
the dearth of books in such households as a source of the achievement gap. As one
irate Harlem mother exclaimed during the community control struggle, "I don't
want to be told that my daughter can't learn because she comes from a fatherless
home or because she had corn flakes for breakfast instead of eggs."[67]

Black poor and working-class parents and their defenders in the African
American professional ranks grew to resent the condescension of "experts" who
presumed to diagnose black pathology. By failing to challenge the normative values of public schools or acknowledge the colonial status of black communities,
ambitious studies of racial disparities, including the 1966 Coleman Report on
educational inequality, only inflamed black suspicion of liberal posturing. "Ho
hum! Another study!" HPC declared in 1966. The following year the group
protested the proliferation of reports chronicling "the breakdown that every day
becomes distressingly more obvious to ordinary parents of school children who
simply use the senses [with which] they were born."[68]

The rebuke of white interpretive authority signaled two trends in black
thought: an inversion of the gospel of deprivation ("we need a program for culturally deprived white people to show you what a slum is," one black teenager
told interviewers from the US Commission on Civil Rights) and the pursuit of
educational relevance. The idea that African American school experiences must
complement the realities of black life drew upon countless precedents, from
historian Carter G. Woodson's demand that formal instruction equip Negroes
"to face the ordeal before them," to Nation of Islam leader Elijah Muhammad's
insistence that the education of black Americans benefit their people rather than
replenish the "store house" of the oppressor. Such principles gained currency in
the 1960s as black America undertook new struggles for cultural and political
self-government.[69]

Campaigns for relevance reflected utilitarian concerns. Harlem's community
control proponents demanded that the revamped IS 201 curriculum explore
questions of unemployment, malnutrition, and poor housing. A black high
school student from a large, eastern city displayed similar priorities in 1970 when
he complained to the US Commission on Civil Rights about the absurdity of his
having to study Alexander Hamilton in school. "They don't teach you how not
to be exploited by credit companies or how to get together and maybe form a
co-op," he lamented.[70]

Augmenting coverage of African American history and culture in the classroom marked another major objective of the search for relevance. The sense that
public education, mythic "melting pot" of cultures, actually functioned as "a
WASP rubber stamp" bolstered support for black studies.[71] Longstanding efforts
to "integrate" Dick and Jane readers and to purge curricula of Little Black Sambo
yielded to more aggressive battles for the provision of Swahili courses and the
right to fly black liberation flags on campus. If such demands divided black people along generational and ideological lines, they also reflected the widespread

conviction that, far more than the African American child, public education required remediation to ensure black success. "And you wonder why they don't want to sit up in school," a black, Omaha, Nebraska, barber told the 1968 Kerner Commission after testifying that racist curricula "whipped the spirit" from black children.[72]

This philosophical shift captured the essence of relevance. More than an exaltation of Negro contributions, the doctrine conveyed a desire to seize from paternalistic outsiders what Stokely Carmichael called the "dictatorship of definition." Psychological passage from the stigma of cultural deprivation to the politics of "educational genocide" required nothing less than a reconstruction of black consciousness. Asserting interpretive control of the African American experience seemed a crucial step in reordering power relations and completing the theoretical revolution one Harlem activist described as a transition "from melting pot to share the pot."[73]

Achieving relevance thus required an assault on the cultural standards that marked black Americans as unfit for full participation in the American dream. Black intellectuals defended the distinctiveness and coherence of black dialect and "learning styles," seeking pedagogy that might harness rather than suppress these abilities.[74] Meanwhile, grassroots visions of social reallocation drove many black parents and activists to rethink the nature and meaning of educational expertise.

The People's Board of Education, a self-conceived group of antipoverty workers and activists that emerged from New York's community control struggle, exemplified this reevaluation. The body, whose existence itself challenged the moral and professional legitimacy of the official school board, argued in 1967 that poor parents in Ocean Hill-Brownsville possessed deep knowledge of the strengths and weaknesses of local schools and thus deserved a central role in the district's reform efforts. "These are the 'inside' experts who should be given a real say in policy-making and administration," the organization declared. Later assertions of the qualifications of indigenous black residents to evaluate and govern schools in their own neighborhoods proved more adamant. "No need for a white man to come and supervise or inspect us" through accreditation procedures, an organizer of a private black preschool on Chicago's South Side proclaimed in 1969.[75]

Such sentiments hardly constituted an outright rejection of professional prerogatives. Despite their suspicions of professionals who drew their livelihood from the ghetto, Harlem parents had long petitioned for more experienced, certified, full-time teachers. However, respect for formal expertise also threatened to reinforce traditions of deference, erecting another obstacle to African American involvement in the formulation and delivery of education.

Attempts by the black poor and working class to transcend the mysticism shrouding school professions thus represented an assault on both the external bureaucracies and corrosive inner doubts that thwarted their dreams for the future. "When I started teaching, the black community had the feeling that the schools were not theirs," recalled Al Vann, head of New York's black teacher's union.[76] Yet a sense of possession of local institutions, however empowering, hardly guaranteed academic success or social mobility. Study-fatigued and determined to resist their children's subjection to further insults or guinea-pigging, many black parents remained desperate to secure a place for their progeny in the technological revolution enveloping the larger society.

Here lay the ultimate meaning of relevance—the search for a new social contract enshrined in schools that honored and preserved black identity while instilling skills rewarded in the marketplace. This vision may have inspired four Bay Area mothers to demand in 1968 that the Cupertino, California, board of education eliminate textbook references to African "savagery," place volumes of the Negro Heritage Library encyclopedia in each district school, and pursue "proper remedial measures" to boost the academic performance of African American pupils. Detroit's Inner City Parents Workshop displayed a similar outlook, cautioning that the black cultural enrichment for which it campaigned should never come "at the expense of academic studies."[77]

If academic excellence remained paramount, true cultural fluency required mastery of Anglo and Afro styles. Speaking before a national black education conference in 1968, New York City author and schoolteacher Edwina Chavers Johnson appealed for more creative, black-themed lessons, hoping to ensure that African Americans "will be swinging our own parades down the avenue" rather than find themselves relegated to applauding the pageants of others. Johnson then suggested synthesis rather than separation: kindergarteners singing "Kumbaya" as well as "Mary Had a Little Lamb" and secondary students interpreting Baraka's *We Are Beautiful People* as well as Tennyson's *Charge of the Light Brigade*. In a similar vein, black teachers, parents, and students planning a community controlled school in Chicago's inner city imagined concerts offering Beethoven and B. B. King, ballet and "the bugaboo."[78]

African American cultural heritage thus held both distinct and universal meaning. The relevance doctrine epitomized the reformist character of Negro revolt; even the militant black parent tended to embrace the ethic of schooling as a process of individual achievement in preparation for future job competition. However, insofar as it entailed a defense of the tantalizing concept of "black values," relevance also constituted a repudiation of Nathan Glazer and Daniel Moynihan's 1965 claim that "the Negro is only an American and nothing else."

Black people had once clung to such principles as defense against damning assertions of racial difference. In 1963 Gertrude Elise Ayer, for many years New York City's only African American principal, bristled at a Harlem superintendent's suggestion that "chasms of language, cultural patterns and values" separate the white, middle-class teacher from the black child. In response, Ayer offered a classic defense of the Negro as moral exemplar, arguing that Harlem parents cherished the quintessential American values of personal dignity, opportunity for advancement, and legal equality.[79]

By contrast, freedom struggles in the late 1960s engaged the proposition that black people possessed a distinct, more humanistic and therefore superior code of ethics that should balance or replace the "white," bureaucratic values strangling public schools in the ghetto. Though he denied rejecting "middle-class values" per se, Harlem activist Preston Wilcox in 1968 condemned the bourgeois orientation of public education for imposing on the slum child an ethic of materialism and an overformal, wooden cultural style.[80]

Black parents remained reluctant to endorse the active cultivation of separate black values, whatever dimensions of truth lay in such critiques. While they expected education to assist in developing a positive black consciousness, they never relinquished the demand that schools arm their children with tools of mainstream success. They might have condemned the rehabilitative view of integration as a process of "majority values" displacing "minority values."[81] However, forced to choose a viable strategy for advancement in a racist society, they gravitated toward pragmatic solutions. Thus the largely poor and working-class organizers of Boston's Roxbury Community School concluded in 1967 that schools in the ghetto "must bridge between what [the child's] society expects of him, and what the middle-class world demands of him."[82]

WE ARE NOT PLAYING

This vision of educational purpose found its philosophical moorings in the concept of "black survival." More a popular motto than a specific political ideal, the phrase proved capable of expressing diverse African American aspirations for social deliverance. The language of survival suggested the crisis of education for the oppressed. Should schools prepare African Americans for absorption into the American mainstream (survival as assimilation) or equip them to resist dominant cultural values while working to change the entire social system (survival as counterhegemonic struggle)? Union leader Al Vann likely had the latter aim in mind when he stressed the survival principle during a 1972 meeting of black teachers in an Ocean Hill–Brownsville school:

> In the Yeshiva schools the teachers teach the Jewish kids what they need to know to survive in this world. This is a black school. It's made up of black and Puerto Rican kids. If you see any white kids here, you show them to me because there ain't any. This is a black school for black kids and you've got to teach them what they need to know to survive.[83]

Vann saw this premise as incontrovertible, and many African Americans might have agreed. Yet as we have learned, black parents viewed their children's survival as inseparable from the accumulation of skills necessary for material success. "Our children must be taught to compete . . . whether they like it or not," one Roxbury-area mother declared in a 1973 parent evaluation of a local alternative school. "We are not playing games with them!"[84] At the same time, many African Americans now regarded black pride and self-awareness as essential not only to skill acquisition but also to full enjoyment of citizenship rights in a pluralistic society. Social mobility and democratic participation could never merely mean assimilation.

Survival also suggested preservation of those contested attributes or "values" that constituted black distinctiveness. Attendees of a 1969 black and Puerto Rican political convention in Newark, New Jersey, embraced this definition, endorsing curricular reforms designed to foster respect for African heritage and the Spanish language, a strategy "to insure Black and Puerto Rican survival." A similar philosophy drove contemporary Native Americans to form "survival schools" combining teaching of basic skills with attempts to revive indigenous traditions and culture.[85]

Ultimately, survival encompassed elements of both cultural conservation and social transformation. High-quality education would enable black children to effectively navigate a racist society, achieving middle-class status while remaining psychologically unscathed—a feat that required recourse to African American ingenuity and cultural traditions. Survival also demanded ongoing political engagement; relevant education would arm youngsters with the practical tools and social awareness necessary to advance protracted struggles for dignity and equality. As Gunnar Myrdal observed as early as 1944, African Americans valued the democratic implications of standardized teaching and universal curricula, but desired an education specially designed "to make Negroes better prepared to fight for their rights."[86]

Yet even the capacious theme of survival failed to contain the full scope of black ambitions. African American parents dreamed of social, cultural, and material prosperity for their children. They themselves had survived—they wanted the next generation to thrive. Black philosophies of education in the late 1960s remained imbued with visions of a truly open, democratic society, not colorblind so much as genuinely multicultural, in which African American youngsters could embrace the affirming qualities of black identity while realizing the promise of unhindered social participation.

If such a cosmopolitan, free society seemed unlikely in the near future, black parents resolved to see that their children at least had a chance to enter the prosperous mainstream without being denatured in the process. To claim his or her rightful place, the black child needed savvy, confidence, and the multiple proficiencies that an expansive education might provide. The same Roxbury mother who in 1973 stressed academic mastery ("we are not playing games!") also asserted that "blacks must be exposed to all facets of life, and all kinds of education."[87] Exposure would foster cultural dexterity—the ability to maneuver gracefully in multiple contexts. The National Association of Afro-American Educators endorsed such agility in a 1968 resolution urging teachers to help black children master "the language of the marketplace" while honoring the soulfulness of street dialect. "Nurturing and respecting our own language and effectively manipulating the other, we will become a truly bilingual people," the organization proclaimed.

In other words, education should neither cloister the African American child in parochial blackness nor subject her or him to a "long séance in whiteness." Rather, it should make him or her over—not in the arid image of white respectability, but according to the broad vistas of democratic possibility. Regenerative schooling promised to satisfy the desire of black parents to control the socialization of their children, an aspiration few hesitated to convey. "This is our community . . . this is our community . . . and we don't own anything in it!" a Harlem mother exclaimed in 1969. "Not even our own children."[88]

The escalation of black struggle and its preoccupation with cultural resistance underscored the acculturating function of education. Depending on what is taught them and by whom, Harlem's Black Panther Party declared in late 1966, black children "will mature *either* to become instruments of the white power structure used to keep our people politically unaware and vulnerable, or to become proud black men and women with love and concern for their own kind."[89] For African American radicals enamored of the anticolonial theories of Frantz Fanon and other Third World revolutionaries, education signified the imperative to create "the new man." Invocation of this ideal—sometimes cast as a black nationalist quest to engender "the African personality"—signaled an ideological commitment to restoring positive cultural traits seen as traditionally African or essentially racial while cultivating oppositional consciousness based on a deep critique of the social, economic, and political structures of the United States.[90]

Many African American parents adopted a more complex view of how education should mold their children. If they heeded Fanon's famous plea to "set afoot a new man," their manifest philosophies of education demonstrated a desire to produce the *whole* man—or woman. Black poet and writer Eugene Perkins captured aspects of this perspective in 1974 when he argued that black alternative schools must devote themselves to "the making of a new black child; one free from identity conflict, self-persecution, and a feeling of hopelessness."[91]

A fuller expression of the richness of African American educational ambitions came in 1970, when community control advocates in Dayton, Ohio, asked scores of urban black parents, teachers, and students what constituted an ideal African American pupil. The resulting portrait reflected the intricate blend of black nationalism, integrationism, and social transformation that characterized African American life and politics.

The "new black student," respondents suggested, appreciates his heritage; values the worth of African Americans in his community; feels a sense of personal dignity and a duty to generate positive change in black America; embraces the history and culture of oppressed groups; exhibits a special awareness of the American social and economic system; knows how to negotiate that system, with "specific strategies for dealing with unyielding exclusions and oppressions"; possesses outstanding academic and other skills necessary for smooth entry into college or meaningful employment; and displays "the kind of psychic strength which will allow him to survive in the face of forces which will attempt to destroy him because he has become a free man who is trying to free other men."[92]

THE STORY HAS YET TO BE TOLD

This composite profile represented not merely local ideals, but the dreams of many African American parents nationwide. Examining such perspectives is essential; one finds few more poignant expressions of the spirit of a people than that people's wishes for their children. In declaring such ambitions, individuals and groups also reveal who they imagine themselves to be and what they hope to become. The multidimensionality of black Dayton's "new black student" seems emblematic of the complex identity and political consciousness that during the 1960s broadened the search for redemptive black education.

The themes of self-government, equitable integration, relevance, survival, and cultural rebirth in African American philosophies of education suggest a vision of schools as sites of entry into the democratic order and as mechanisms for rendering that order more hospitable to black folk and others on the margins. Besides providing a staging ground for encounters with majoritarian values, education served as contested territory on which struggles over the meaning of blackness and citizenship unfolded. Despite their great promise, many such battles produced bleak outcomes—a blend of defeats and pyrrhic victories. Black campaigns for educational justice faltered in the 1970s and 1980s amid overlapping crises of economic retrenchment, cultural dismay, and political reaction. The counterrevolution of corporate capital, the escalating violence of the police state, and a host of other economic, political, and social setbacks helped drain the radical ingenuity that had fueled African American educational thought.[93]

Of course, that dynamic energy never merely dissipated. Black visions of emancipatory education reawakened in crusades for "multiculturalism," Afrocentric academies and other strategies for reform, many of which incorporated black nationalist ideals. Though some of these newer initiatives reflected black nationalism's rightward drift, a trend evident in certain African American campaigns for tuition vouchers and charter schools, education remained a central theater for the articulation of nationalist sentiments, especially as such outlooks enjoyed a resurgence in the 1990s.[94]

The strategic interlacing of nationalism and integrationism that most visibly influenced African American political thought between the mid-1960s and mid-1970s continued to represent a wide spectrum of black aspirations. Indeed, the enduring appeal of pragmatic nationalism and the principle of self-determination helped inspire a reunion of New York's community control activists in 1995—three decades after Harlem parents had ignited the struggle for local autonomy. Sponsors of the Brooklyn event declared on promotional flyers that despite the copious scholarship chronicling the black educational activism of the late 1960s, "most of the community's side of the story has yet to be told."[95] Recovering a portion of that story means revisiting the philosophies of black parents, students, teachers, workers, and others who wielded new nationalist ideas with a commitment to creative adaptation that has long driven African American politics.

Future efforts to fulfill the promise of racial justice and democracy through the troubled medium of education must reckon with these grassroots theorists and their notions of black dignity and American citizenship. Attempts to comprehend the evolution of black protest must confront the intellectual complexity and moral depth of their ideals. As scholars continue to free themselves from the impulse to dismiss or vindicate black nationalism, they will depict African American political culture in the late 1960s and early 1970s as replete with all the hope, dynamism, and contestation that distinguished earlier phases of black activism. Their work will finally demonstrate that the broad politics of the Black Power era represented not cultural constriction but a process of political growth and innovation—one that confounds facile accounts of continuity or change within the freedom struggle.

NOTES

1. See Jacqueline Dowd Hall, "The Long Civil Rights Movement and the Political Uses of the Past," *Journal of American History* 91 (2005): 1233–63. Numerous studies linking the Black Power and civil rights movements exist. For example, see Timothy B. Tyson, *Radio Free Dixie: Robert F. Williams and the Roots of Black Power* (Chapel Hill: University of North Carolina Press, 1999); Robert O. Self, *American Babylon: Race and the Struggle for Postwar Oakland* (Princeton: Princeton University Press, 2003); Jeanne Theoharis and Komozi Woodard, eds., *Freedom North: Black Freedom Struggles Outside the South, 1940–1980* (New York: Palgrave Macmillan, 2003); Matthew J. Country-man, *Up South: Civil Rights and Black Power in Philadelphia* (Philadelphia: University of Pennsylvania Press, 2006). For a caution against the tendency to exaggerate historical continuity and thus to conflate civil rights and Black Power, see Sundiata Cha-Jua and Clarence Lang, "The 'Long Movement' as Vampire: Temporal and Spatial Fallacies in Recent Black Freedom Studies," *Journal of African American History* 92 (2007): 265–88.
2. See, for example, Theodore Draper's linking of black nationalism and alienation in Theodore Draper, *The Rediscovery of Black Nationalism* (New York: Viking, 1971).
3. This essay reinforces the outlook of black historian Lerone Bennett Jr., who noted in 1970 that the fabled integration-separation binary failed to "enclose all of our options" or "exhaust the possibilities of our situation." See Lerone Bennett Jr., "Liberation: Integration or Separation Dilemma is Called False Choice by Advocates of Transformation," *Ebony*, August 1970, 36.
4. Note that the term's useful and confounding ambiguity assured diverse interpretations within and beyond black America.
5. The rebirth of black nationalism intensified this phenomenon, which anthropologist Charles A. Valentine saw as reflecting the "biculturation" of African Americans who simultaneously learn and practice "mainstream" and black cultural forms. See Charles Valentine, "Deficit Difference and Bicultural Models of Afro-American Behavior," *Harvard Educational Review* 44 (May 1971): 173. Cal State San Jose professor Thomasyne Lightfoote Wilson eloquently articulated this duality in 1972, declaring, "What we seek is a kind of sovereignty of Afro-American *being* within a social system that preserves the selfhood of all peoples." See Wilson, "Notes Toward a Process of Afro-American Education," *Harvard Educational Review* 42 (August 1972): 376.
6. For a more balanced treatment of the transition from integrationism to black nationalism, see Dionne Danns, *Something Better for Our Children: Black Organizing in the Chicago Public Schools, 1963–1971* (New York: Routledge, 2003).
7. For a broader discussion of "transformation" as a third political path beyond the traditional African American strategic alternatives of integration and separation or black nationalism, see chapters 17 and 18 of Manning Marable, *Beyond Black and White: Transforming African-American Politics* (New York: Verso, 1995). Lerone Bennett also heralded transformative politics, observing that the assertion of a simplistic integrationist-separatist binary "ignores the infinite gradations between integration and separation and the fact that there is a third choice, pluralism, and beyond that a fourth, transformation." See Bennett, "Liberation: Integration or Separation Dilemma is Called False Choice," 38. Kevin Gaines elegantly acknowledged the vision of democratic transformation within

black nationalist assertions of the right to full participation, identifying "the expansiveness of blackness as the grounds for national belonging, for international identification, and ultimately for a radical democratic political articulation universal in its applicability." See Kevin Gaines, *African Americans in Ghana: Black Expatriates and the Civil Rights Era* (Chapel Hill: University of North Carolina Press, 2006), 205.

8. Daryl Lembke, "Long Battle Seen Over S. F. School Integration," *New York Times,* March 17, 1969, 3. My account of the school board meeting is based on "Eyewitness Exclusive: The School Bus Issue," a 1969 television news report by KPIX, San Francisco. See the video reel in the University of Georgia Libraries Archive.

9. Lembke, "Long Battle Seen Over S. F. School Integration."

10. Ibid.

11. Ibid.

12. See in general Jack Dougherty, *More Than One Struggle: The Evolution of Black School Reform in Milwaukee* (Chapel Hill: University of North Carolina Press, 2004). For another study highlighting the political complexity of black school struggles, see Clarence Taylor, *Knocking at Our Own Door: Milton A. Galamison and the Struggle to Integrate New York City Schools* (Lanham, MD: Lexington Books, 2001).

13. David N. Plank and Marcia Turner, "Changing Patterns in Black School Politics: Atlanta, 1872–973," *American Journal of Education* 95 (August 1987): 584–608; George M. Frederickson, *Black Liberation: A Comparative History of Black Ideologies in the United States and South Africa* (New York: Oxford University Press, 1995), 26; Martha Biondi, *To Stand and Fight: The Struggle for Civil Rights in Postwar New York City* (Cambridge, MA: Harvard University Press, 2003), 5. Theodore Draper also noted what he called the "peculiar symbiosis" of integrationism and black nationalism in black political philosophies. See Theodore Draper, "The Fantasy of Black Nationalism," *Commentary* 48 (September 1969): 29.

14. Inner City Parents Council, "Detroit Schools—A Blueprint for change," *Liberator* 7 (September 1967): 8.

15. "Thought Stimulator #423: Schools as Prisons," Box 23. Preston Wilcox Papers, Schomburg Center (hereafter cited as Wilcox Papers).

16. For an early example of this concept, see William L. Patterson, ed., *We Charge Genocide: The Historic Petition to the United Nations for Relief from a Crime of the United States Government Against the Negro People* (New York: Civil Rights Congress, 1951); also see "We Charge Genocide," *Harlem News*, March 1970, 1–11. For later invocations of the "educational genocide" concept, see the Harlem Parents Committee's newsletter *Views* (November 1967), Box 52, Folder 17. United Federation of Teachers Collection, Tamiment Library & Robert F. Wagner Labor Archives, NYU (hereafter cited as UFT); also see Preston Wilcox, "The Kids Will Decide—And More Power to Them," *Ebony*, August 1970, 134.

17. Milton A. Galamison, untitled transcript, Box 13, Folder 84. Milton A. Galamison Papers, Schomburg Center (hereafter cited as Galamison Papers); "Ferment of change" quote from page 275 of Ruth M. Batson, *The Black Educational Movement in Boston: A Sequence of Historical Events (1638–1975)*, manuscript, Box 1. Ruth M. Batson Papers, Schlesinger Library, Radcliffe Institute; Price Cobbs, "The Black Revolution and Education," *NASSP Bulletin*, May 1969, 15.

18. Mann quoted in Clarence J. Karier, ed., *The Individual, Society, and Education: A History of American Educational Ideas* (Champaign, IL: Illini Books, 1986), 61; Horace Mann Bond, *The Education of the Negro in the American Social Order* (New York: Octagon Books, 1966), 12–13; Doxey A. Wilkerson, "The Ghetto School Struggles in Historical Perspective," *Science and Society* 33 (1969): 146.

19. Nancy Levi Arnez, "The Struggle for Equality of Educational Opportunity," pamphlet, 1975. National Urban League, Schomburg Center; Albert Vann, "The State of Education for Black People—1973," *New York Amsterdam News*, September 1, 1975.

20. Eldridge Cleaver, "Education and Revolution," *The Black Scholar*, November 1969, 47; Vincent Harding, "Fighting the 'Mainstream' Seen for 'Black Decade,'" *New York Times*, January 12, 1970.

21. For a description of important developments in this changing political economy, see Manning Marable, *Race, Reform and Rebellion: The Second Reconstruction and Beyond in Black America, 1945–2006* (New York: Macmillan, 1984).

22. Maude White Katz, "End Racism in Education: A Concerned Parent Speaks," *Freedomways* 8 (1969): 347.

23. See, in general, Maurice R. Berube and Marilyn Gittell, eds., *Confrontation at Ocean Hill-Brownsville* (New York: Praeger, 1969); also see description of Ocean Hill-Brownville struggle in Diane Ravitch, *The Great School Wars: A History of New York Public Schools* (Baltimore: Johns Hopkins University Press, 1974).

24. See, for example, Jennifer de Forest, "The 1958 Harlem School Boycott: Parental Activism and the Struggle for Educational Equity in New York City," *Urban Review* 40 (2008): 21–41.

25. For an account of the bleak performance of Harlem schools, see HARYOU, *Youth in the Ghetto: A Study of the Consequences of Powerlessness and a Blueprint for Change* (New York: HARYOU, 1964).

26. See, for example, Adina Back, "Exposing the Whole Segregation Myth," in *Freedom North: Black Freedom Struggles Outside the South, 1940–1980, eds.* Jeanne Theoharis and Komozi Woodard (New York: Palgrave Macmillan, 2003), 65–92.

27. Jason Epstein, "The Politics of School Decentralization," *New York Review of Books* 10 (June 6, 1968); "A Summary of the Controversy at IS 201," *IRCD Bulletin*, Winter 1966–67, 1–2; New York Civil Liberties Union, "The Burden of Blame: A Report on the Ocean Hill-Brownsville School Controversy," *Urban Education* 4 (April 1964): 9; Herbert Kohl, "Integrate With Whom?" *Interplay*, June–July 1968, 27.

28. Gene Currivan, "Board Sets Talks in School Dispute," *New York Times*, September 11, 1966, 79.

29. Marlene Nadle, "Ghetto Fight: Quality, Segregated Education," *Village Voice*, September 29, 1966, 11.

30. Andrew Kopkind, "Down the Down Staircase: Parents, Teachers, and Public Authorities," *New Republic*, October 22, 1966, 12; "Quality Integrated Education" had served as the previous mantra. See "Decentralization: A Game of Chance," *Views*, August 1965, Box 13, Folder 27. Ella Baker Papers, Schomburg Center (hereafter cited as Ella Baker Papers).

31. "Important to Parents," *Views*, August 1965 and "Seminar in 'New Math' for Parents," *Views*, August 1965, Box 13, Folder 27. Ella Baker Papers. Urban blacks may have proven especially sensitive to the perils of automation since the mechanization of agricultural labor had helped force many of them out of the rural South in the first place.

32. "Decentralization: A Game of Chance."

33. Harlem Parents Committee, "The Education of Minority Group Children in the New York City Public Schools," manuscript, 1965, Box 1, Folder 28. James Weldon Johnson Community Center Papers, Schomburg Center.

34. See *Views*, August 1965.

35. A pun playing on "Jim Crow," the Southern system of segregation. Harlem Parents Committee, "The Education of Minority Group Children."

36. Helen Testamark of Parents Council District Number Four, quoted in "A Slice of IS 201 History, April 1966," Box 24, Folder 1. Wilcox Papers.

37. Dorothy S. Jones, "The Issues at IS 201: A View from the Parent's Committee," *Integrated Education* 4 (October–November 1966): 23; "Here We Stand," *Views*, July 1966, Box 13, Folder 25. Ella Baker Papers; "Spotlight on Schools," *Views*, July 1966, Box 13, Folder 25. Ella Baker Papers; Community activists alternately demanded a "Negro" and "Negro or Puerto Rican" principal.

38. "Harlem Parents Committee Freedom School Summer Program," *Views*, July 1966, Box 13, Folder 25. Ella Baker Papers; "Key Bricks for a Sound Education" *Views*, November 1967, Box 52, Folder 17. UFT.

39. "Negro Teachers' Association Conference," *Integrated Education* 4 (August–September 1967): 35–37. Also see "Resolutions: Negro Teachers' Association's Conference, Saturday, May 28, 1967," pamphlet, Box 24, Folder 8. UFT.

40. See, for example, Christopher Jencks, "Private Schools for Black Children," *New York Times Magazine*, November 3, 1968.

41. Jones, "The Issues at IS 201," 20; "Who Should Run the Schools?" *Newsweek*, October 28, 1968, 84; Spencer quoted in Jeremy Larner, "IS 201: Disaster in the Schools," *Dissent* 14 (January–February 1967): 29.

42. Lillian S. Calhoun, "New York: Schools and Power—Whose?," *Integrated Education* 7 (January–February 1969): 33; Inner City Parents Council, "Detroit Schools—A Blueprint for Change," 11.

43. Thomas K. Minter, "Intermediate School 201, Manhattan: Center of Controversy: A Case Study," pamphlet, Box 52, Folder 17. UFT; "The Talk of the Town: Notes and Comment," *New Yorker*, October 26, 1968.

44. Untitled timeline, n.d., Box 14, Folder 96. Galamison Papers; Jones, "The Issues at IS 201," 25.

45. George M. Miller, letter, August 20, 1966, Box 1, Folder 8. Black Panther Party Harlem Branch Papers, Schomburg Center; David K. Cohen, "The Price of Community Control," *Commentary* 48 (July 1969): 29.

46. "Who Should Run the Schools?," *Newsweek*, October 28, 1968.

47. "Ocean Hill Target for Black Militants," *New York Amsterdam News*, March 22, 1969; Jeremy Larner, "IS 201: Disaster in the Schools," *Dissent* 14 (January–February 1967): 33, 39; Calhoun, "New York: Schools and Power—Whose?," 25.

48. Milton A. Galamison, "Bedford Stuyvesant: The Land of Superlatives," unpublished manuscript, n.d., Box 13, Folder 84. Galamison Papers; "big paychecks" quote from Larner, "IS 201: Disaster in the Schools," 38.

49. Alexander M. Bickel, "Desegregation: Where Do We Go From Here?" *The New Republic*, February 7, 1970; Powell quote in "Action Stimulator #24: Adam Clayton Powell and Community Control," flyer, March 20, 1970, Box 25, Folder 9. Wilcox Papers. At a March 1970 meeting of black educators in Boston, Mel King of the New Urban League noted the difficulty of identifying a "community-wide black educational philosophy." See "Black Education Conference, 1970," pamphlet, Box 56. Freedom House, Inc. Records, Schomburg Center; "Frontline: Baltimore," *Foresight* 1 (August 1969). UFT. Chester Davis, a fellow at the Institute of the Black World in Atlanta, observed in 1970 that "significant constellations of black people are emerging in the fight for community control and the development of community schools." See Chester Davis, "Black Pre-College Education: Notes on an agenda for the 70's," transcript, July 1970, Box 13, Folder 44. Ella Baker Papers.

50. Eric Mann, "The Newark Community School," *Liberation*, August 1967, 26.

51. For a local study of some of these historical forces, see Self, *American Babylon*.

52. Preston R. Wilcox, "The Community-Centered School," in *Radical School Reform*, ed. Beatrice and Ronald Gross (New York: Simon & Schuster, 1969), 129; Preston Wilcox, "The Kids Will Decide—And More Power to Them," *Ebony*, August 1970, 136; "Black and Puerto Rican City-Wide High School Council Demands," flyer, n.d., Box 52, Folder 7. UFT; "Action Stimulator #32: A Twenty Point Program for Real School Community Control" (reprint of "Position Paper: The Future of the Arthur A. Schomburg, IS 201 Complex Demonstration Project, April, 1970"), flyer, Box 24, Folder 2. Wilcox Papers; Martin Buskin, "What Else is New at Ocean Hill?," *Newsday*, November 3, 1968, 6W; "Tentative Plan—Parents Community Council, JHS 271, Ocean Hill-Brownsville," flyer, May 20, 1968 and "Position Paper—The Parent-Community Council," flyer, n.d., Box 55, Folder 16. UFT; Calhoun, "New York: Schools and Power—Whose?," 27; "The Rape of the Ocean Hill-Brownsville Community," flyer, September 25, 1968, Box 52, Folder 20. UFT; Kenneth W. Haskins, "A Black Perspective on Community Control," *Inequality in Education* 15 (November 1973): 32. Forecasting this rich vision of schools as bastions of community autonomy, W. E. B. Du Bois wrote in 1935, "instead of our schools being simply separate schools, forced on us by grim necessity, they can become centers of a new and beautiful effort at human education." See Du Bois, "Does the Negro Need Separate Schools?" *Journal of Negro Education* 4 (July 1935): 334–35.

53. Harlem Parents Committee, "The Education of Minority Group Children"; this formulation echoed a principle underscored in a leaflet circulated by integrationist forces prior to the massive New York City school boycott of February 1964. The handout cast desegregation as "only the necessary first step," after which "the Board of Education must be ready with schools, texts, attitudes and firm Board policy in order to create a meaningful integrated educational experience." See "Questions and Answers on New York's Schools," in *Black Protest*, ed. Joanne Grant (New York: Fawcett Premier, 1968), 410.

54. Oscar Handlin, "The Goals of Integration," *Daedalus* 95 (Winter 1966): 268–86; David Spencer, "A Harlem Parent Speaks," *Foresight*, November 1968, 21–22.

55. Preston Wilcox, "The Controversy over IS 201," *The Urban Review* 1 (July 1966): 13.

56. W. E. B. Du Bois had displayed this impulse. See Du Bois, "Does the Negro Need Separate Schools?"

57. Malcolm X quoted in Kimberlé Crenshaw, Neil Gotanda, and Garry Peller, eds., *Critical Race Theory: The Key Writings That Formed the Movement* (New York: New Press, 1995), 128; "African-American Teachers Association Demands Self-Control, Self-Determination, and Self-Defense for Schools in the Black Community," flyer, September 1967, Box 24, Folder 8. UFT.

58. Alex Poinsett, "The Dixie Schools Charade," *Ebony*, August 1972, 145.

59. Harlem Parents Committee, "The Education of Minority Group Children"; Alvin F. Poussaint, "The Negro American: His Self-Image and Integration," *Journal of the National Medical Association* 58 (November, 1966): 421; Mel King, "Thoughts on Busing: 1972, not 1954," manuscript, March 1972, Box 25, Folder 10. Wilcox Papers.

60. The *Brown* decision asserted that separating black children from their peers on the basis of race "generates a feeling of inferiority as to their status in the community that may affect their hearts and minds in a way unlikely to be undone." Quoted in Earle H. West, ed., *The Black American and Education* (Columbus, Ohio: Merrill, 1972), 196; See *Racial Isolation in the Public Schools* (Washington, DC: US Government Printing Office, 1967); Floyd McKissick, "A Communication: Is Integration Necessary?" *New Republic*, December 3, 1966.

61. For an account of the hemorrhage of black teachers occasioned by desegregation, see Adam Fairclough, "The Costs of Brown: Black Teachers and School Integration,"

Journal of American History 91 (June 2004): 43–55; "'Jist Funin'" (cartoon), *Community Advocate* (Ocean Hill-Brownsville), n.d., Box 53, Folder 2. UFT.

62. "Problems of Integration," in *The Black American and Education*, ed. Earle H. West (Columbus, Ohio: Merrill, 1972), 198. Esteemed black studies scholar St. Clair Drake later emphasized the desire to preserve black culture and identity that often accompanied integrationist sentiment. He noted in 1963, "As the processes of integration in the United States proceed at an accelerated pace, many Negroes may find themselves wishing to cling to certain aspects of Negro life in America which seem to them rich, familiar, and warm, despite the fact that they will, at the same time, demand all of their civil rights." See St. Clair Drake, "Hide My Face? An Essay on Pan-Africanism and Negritude," in *Soon One Morning: New Writings by American Negroes*, ed. Herbert Hill (New York: Alfred A. Knopf, 1963); Bill Strickland, "Black Studies and the Struggle for Black Education," manuscript, May 1970, Box 37, Folder 23. John Henrik Clarke Papers, Schomburg Center.

63. For a local examination of the complexity of ambitions within black educational struggles, see chapter 6 of Countryman, *Up South*. Countryman also stresses the pervasiveness, pragmatism and flexibility of black nationalist outlooks within black educational philosophies. He writes, "More than the black nationalist critique of integration, it was black students and parents' experiential knowledge of the limited impact of school desegregation that transformed the black nationalist approach to education reform from a marginal demand into a dominant political issue within the city. By combining the demand for black studies courses with the call for community control of the public schools in black neighborhoods, BPUM activists were able to shift the focus of black educational advocacy in the city from school desegregation to efforts to raise the quality of schooling in predominantly black schools." See Countryman, *Up South*, 256.

64. Michael K. Drapkin, "An Elusive Goal: Pittsburgh's Try Shows that School Integration in North Will Be Hard," *Wall Street Journal*, June 28, 1971; Ken Ringle and Paul G. Edwards, "Richmond's New School Merger Spawns a New Melting Pot," *Washington Post*, June 17, 1972.

65. *Equal Educational Opportunity: Hearings Before the Select Committee on Equal Educational Opportunity of the United States Senate: Part 9A—San Francisco and Berkeley, CA* (Washington, DC: US Government Printing Office, 1971), 3985.

66. For an example of the cultural deprivation thesis in education, which liberal as well as conservative policymakers and professionals embraced, see Benjamin S. Bloom, Allison Davis, and Robert Hess, eds., *Compensatory Education for Cultural Deprivation* (Austin, TX: Holt, Rinehart and Winston, 1965); for an example of the resurgence of racist theories of genetic intellectual inferiority, see Arthur Jensen, "How Much Can We Boost IQ and Scholastic Achievement?" *Harvard Educational Review* 33 (February 1969): 1–123.

67. Calhoun, "New York," 18; Ravitch, *Great School Wars*, 299.

68. "Ho Hum! Another Study," *Views* July 1966, Box 13, Folder 25. Ella Baker Papers; "Times Change—'Pros' Don't," *Views*, November 1967, p. 7, Box 52, Folder 17. UFT.

69. *What Students Perceive: A Report of the U.S. Commission on Civil Rights* (Washington, DC: US Government Printing Office, 1970), 80; see preface by Carter G. Woodson, *The Mis-Education of the Negro* (New York: Associated Publishers, 1933); Elijah Muhammad, *Message to the Blackman in America* (Phoenix, AZ: Secretarius MEMPs Publications, 1973), 39; and numerous other examples of this sentiment exist. For example, novelist Charles S. Johnson observed in 1938 that, "The education of the Negro youth might begin as several writers . . . seem to favor: namely, with the familiar and the real in their own lives rather than what is familiar and real only in the experiences of others." See Charles S. Johnson, *The Negro College Graduate* (Beloit, KS: McGrath, 1969).

70. "Action Stimulator #32."

71. Preston Wilcox, "Integration or Separation in Education: K-12," manuscript, Box 5. Wilcox Papers (also see Preston Wilcox, "Integration or Separatism in Education: K-12,") in *Integration and Separatism in Education*, ed. Peter L. Clark (Syracuse, NY: Syracuse University Press, 1970), 28.

72. For a description of the evolution from agitating for "integrated" textbooks to championing black studies, see St. Clair Drake, "Black Studies: Toward an Intellectual Framework," transcript of lecture, September 23, 1969, Box 27, Folder 19. St. Clair Drake Papers, Schomburg Center; "Educators Support Liberation Flag-Flying," *New York Amsterdam News*, January 8, 1972; Ernest W. Chambers, "We Have Marched, We Have Cried, We Have Prayed," *Ebony*, April 1968, 29–32.

73. Preston Wilcox, "Black Power and Public Education," manuscript, n.d., Box 4. Wilcox Papers; Stokely Carmichael "Toward Black Liberation" in *Black and White American Culture: An Anthology from the Massachusetts Review*, ed. Jules Chametzky and Sidney Kaplan (Amherst: University of Massachusetts Press, 1969), 76.

74. See, for example, George O. Cureton, "Using a Black Learning Style," *Reading Teacher* 31 (1978): 751–56.

75. New York City Peoples Board of Education, press release, January 3, 1967, Box 55, Folder 14. UFT; Norm Freelain, "Black Teacher Establishes: Unique School for the Exceptional Child," *Muhammad Speaks*, January 3, 1969, 38.

76. See Al Vann interview in Carlos E. Russell, *Project Demonstrating Excellence: Perspectives on Power: A Black Community Looks at Itself (Profiles in Political Acumen)*, manuscript, n.d., Box 6. Robert Beecher Papers, Schomburg Center. This was not a new sentiment. In 1941, for example, black novelist Richard Wright asserted that, "Deep down we distrust the schools that the Lords of the Land build for us and we do not really feel that they are ours." Richard Wright, *12 Million Black Voices* (New York: Thunder's Mouth Press, 2002 [1941]), 64; similarly, David Tyack noted in 1969 that African Americans "saw themselves as subjects rather than as citizens of the educational system." See David Tyack, "Growing Up Black: Perspectives on the History of Education in Northern Ghettoes," *History of Education Quarterly* 9 (1969): 290. Preston Wilcox noted that through their participation in the community control of schools struggle, black parents in New York City "moved from the status of a psychological tenant to that of responsible landlord within the school setting." See Preston Wilcox, "Organization and Finances of Public Schools: A Black Response to a Black Assessment," pamphlet, n.d., Box 5. Wilcox Papers.

77. Yvonne Givens, Dorothy Hicks, Wilms Hopper, Carolyn Lewis, "Proposal to Cupertino Board of Education," in *Proposals for Black Studies Programs for Various Types of Educational Institutions* (East Palo Alto, CA: Black Liberation Publishers, 1969), 11, Wisconsin Historical Society Pamphlet Collection; Albert B. Cleage Jr., "Inner City Parents' Program for Quality Education in Detroit Inner City Schools," *Integrated Education* 5 (August–September 1967): 44.

78. Edwina Chavers Johnson, "Commemorative dates in the School Calendar," *Foresight*, February 1969, p. 15–16, Box 52, Folder 23. UFT; "Prepared Statement of Barbara A. Sizemore," in *Equal Educational Opportunity: Hearings Before the Select Committee on Equal Educational Opportunity of the United States Senate, Ninety-Second Congress, First Session on Equal Educational Opportunity. Part 13—Quality and Control of Urban Schools. Hearings Held Washington, DC, July 27–29, and August 5, 1971* (Washington, DC: US Government Printing Office, 1971), 19. In 1970 NAACP Director Roy Wilkins offered a more cautious version of the principle Johnson had articulated. Circulating a multicultural curriculum titled "American Majorities and Minorities" for use in schools, Wilkins

316 RUSSELL RICKFORD

noted somewhat defensively that the syllabus, "is not an effort to replace white history with black history, to substitute George Washington Carver for George Washington" ("Statement of Roy Wilkins, NAACP Executive Director," press release, September 21, 1970, Box 46, Folder 6. Ewart Guinier Papers, Schomburg Center.)

79. Nathan Glazer and Daniel Patrick Moynihan, *Beyond the Melting Pot: The Negroes, Puerto Ricans, Jews, Italians and Irish of New York* (Cambridge, MA: Harvard University Press, 1963), 53; Gertrude Elise Ayer, "Notes on My Native Sons—Education in Harlem," *Freedomways* 3 (Summer 1963): 376–77.

80. Jim Leeson interview with Preston Wilcox, manuscript, May 1968, p. 13. Ralph Bunche Civil Rights Documentation Project, Moorland-Spingarn Research Center, Howard University. For a fascinating discussion of the principle of "black values" in African American educational philosophies, see Jerald E. Podair, "'White' Values, 'Black' Values: The Ocean Hill-Brownsville Controversy and New York City Culture, 1965–1975," *Radical History Review*, Spring 1994, 36–59.

81. An Ohio principal demonstrated this view of integration in 1971, describing school desegregation as involving a "basic problem" of "majority values displacing minority values . . . over a period of time, without losing individual identity." See "Chocolate Faces in Vanilla Places," *Rap of Dayton*, June 1971, 20; in *Equal Educational Opportunity, Part 13*, 210.

82. See "Prospectus for the Roxbury Community School, Inc.," position paper, 1967, Box 4, Folder 38. James P. Breeden Papers, Rauner Special Collections Library, Dartmouth College.

83. February 17, 1972 letter, Box 24, Folder 9. UFT.

84. See Jean Murrell Parent Evaluation Report in Appendix of "Report to the Federation of Boston Community Schools, Inc. on Self-Evaluation, 1973," manuscript, Box 24. Wilcox Papers.

85. Connie Woodruff, "Blacks, Puerto Ricans Show How It's Done; Pick Slate," *New York Amsterdam News*, November 22, 1969; for a brief discussion of Native American "survival schools," see Jorge Noriega, "American Indian Education in the United States: Indoctrination for Subordination to Colonialism," in *The State of Native America: Genocide, Colonization, and Resistance*, ed. M. Annette Jaimes (Boston: South End Press, 1992).

86. Gunnar Myrdal, *An American Dilemma: The Negro Problem and Modern Democracy*, vol. 2 (New Brunswick, NJ: Transaction Publishers, 2009 [1944]), 901.

87. Jean Murrell Parent Evaluation Report.

88. David B. Kent, ed., *Proceedings of the First National Association of Afro-American Educators Conference held June 6, 7, 8, 1968 in Chicago, Illinois* (NAAAE, 1968), 32. "Séance in whiteness" quote from Jack L. Daniel and Curtis E. Porter, "Black Paper for Black Studies," *New Pittsburgh Courier*, July 19, 1969, 13; Miriam Wasserman, "The IS 201 Story," *Urban Review* 3 (June 1969): 4.

89. Original emphasis. George M. Miller, letter, August 20, 1966, Box 1, Folder 8. Black Panther Party Harlem Branch Papers.

90. See, for example, Frank J. Satterwhite, *Planning an Independent Black Educational Institution* (New York: AFRAM Associates, 1971), 14. Like other invocations of this ideal, Satterwhite's emphasis upon inculcating "an African Personality embodied in a New African Man" as an educational goal did not entail a total rejection of the American mainstream political and economic systems. For a discussion of the nuances of "the African Personality," see Walter Rodney, "Education in Africa and Contemporary Tanzania," in *Education and the Black Struggle: Notes from the Colonized World*, ed. Institute of the Black World (Cambridge, MA: Harvard Educational Review, 1974), 83–84. For Rodney, the African personality reflected precolonial Africa's mores and values, especially its peoples' awareness of essential ties to kin, land, and ancestors.

91. See Frantz Fanon, *The Wretched of the Earth* (New York: Grove Press, 1963), 316; Eugene Perkins, "The Need for a Pan-Africanist Alternative to the Street Institution," *Black Books Bulletin* 2 (Winter 1974): 10.

92. "Community School Council: Philosophy and Framework for Urban Educational Change," pamphlet, May 1970, Dayton, Ohio, in *Equal Educational Opportunity,Part 13*, 228–29.

93. For example, the community control movement in New York City produced a "decentralization" law that many activists and parents saw as a nominal, "clerical" change—a symbol of "neocolonialism"—that failed to meaningfully involve black and Latino parents in the fashioning and delivery of high-quality education. See Sheila Rule, "Locally Run Schools Disappoint Minority Educators and Parents," *New York Times*, June 27, 1980; for a broader discussion of the outcome of New York's community control struggle, see Daniel H. Perlstein, *Justice, Justice: School Politics and the Eclipse of Liberalism* (New York: Peter Lang, 2004); for a general discussion of the waning of radical black political organizing during the decline and aftermath of the Black Power movement, see Manning Marable, "Black Nationalism in the 1970s: Through the Prism of Race and Class," *Socialist Review* 50–51 (March–June 1980): 57–108.

94. See, for example, the concluding chapter of Daugherty, *More Than One Struggle*; for an example of the nexus of conservatism and black nationalist models of education, note that Ronald Reagan's efforts to privatize education through "school choice" voucher programs drew support from black and African-themed community schools. See Susan Walton, "Local Independent Schools Offer Minorities 'Educational Option,'" *Education Week*, November 16, 1983.

95. "Community Control Revisited—28 Years Later," flyer, October 28, 1995, Box 25, Folder 10. Wilcox Papers.

ABOUT THE CONTRIBUTORS

Zaheer Ali. Under the direction of the Manning Marable, Zaheer Ali served as one of the project managers and a senior researcher of the Malcolm X Project at Columbia University, a multi-year research initiative on the life and legacy of Malcolm X. As project manager, he was associate editor of an online annotated multimedia version of *The Autobiography of Malcolm X* (2004), and later contributed as a lead researcher for Marable's comprehensive biography *Malcolm X: A Life of Reinvention* (2011). He is currently a doctoral student in history at Columbia University, where he is focusing his research on twentieth-century African American history and religion. His dissertation examines the history of the Nation of Islam's Temple/Mosque No. 7 in Harlem, New York, from 1954–1964, during the time of Malcolm X's ministry.

Nishani Frazier, assistant professor in the Department of History at Miami University, received her doctorate from Columbia University in 2008. Prior to teaching at Miami University, Frazier held positions as associate curator of African American history at the Western Reserve Historical Society, assistant to the director of the Martin Luther King Jr. Archives at the Martin Luther King Center for Nonviolent Social Change, and personal assistant to Dr. John Hope Franklin, during his tenure as chair of the Presidential Advisory Board on "One America" under President Bill Clinton. Dr. Frazier's research interests include the post–World War II black freedom movement, oral history, and Black Power in Guyana. She is author of the forthcoming articles "To Die For the People: Prophecy and Death in the Rhetoric of Martin Luther King, Malcolm X, and Fred Hampton" in *Homegoings, Crossings, and Passings: Life and Death in the African Diaspora* and "Black Power and Golden Arches: McDonald's Corporation, Operation Black Unity, Hough Area Development Corporation, and the Push for Black Economic Empowerment" in *The Business of Black Power*. Her current manuscript in progress, *Haramabee Nation: Cleveland, CORE and Rise of Black Power*, examines the philosophical evolution of the Congress of Racial Equality (CORE) toward Black Power with particular attention given to influence of the Cleveland chapter on the national CORE's Black Power policy.

Robeson Taj Frazier is an assistant professor of communication in the Annenberg School for Communication and Journalism at the University of Southern California. His research and teaching examine race, cross cultural exchange and traffic, social movements, and popular culture. Frazier traces how articulations and representations of race and gender travel globally through performance, media, art, athletics, diplomacy, and activism. He has had work published in *African Americans in Global Affairs* (2010), as well as in *The Journal of African American History, Souls: A Critical Journal of Black Politics, Culture and Society, The San Francisco Chronicle,* and *The Black Arts Quarterly.*

Zachary J. Gillan holds an MA in history from North Carolina State University. His research interests revolve around the relationship between late capitalism and social movements in the United States. He resides in Raleigh, North Carolina.

John A. Kirk is chair and George W. Donaghey Professor of History at the University of Arkansas, Little Rock. He has published a number of books, articles, and essays on the civil rights movement in Arkansas, the South, and the United States. His books include *Redefining the Color Line: Black Activism in Little Rock, Arkansas, 1940–1970* (2002), which won the Arkansas Historical Association's 2003 J. G. Ragsdale Book Award; *Martin Luther King, Jr.* (Pearson Longman, 2005); *Martin Luther King, Jr. and the Civil Rights Movement: Controversies and Debates* (Palgrave Macmillan, 2007), which he edited; *Beyond Little Rock: The Origins and Legacies of the Central High Crisis* (University of Arkansas Press, 2007); *An Epitaph for Little Rock: A Fiftieth Anniversary Retrospective on the Central High Crisis* (University of Arkansas Press, 2008), which he edited; and a coedited volume with Jennifer Jensen Wallach, *Arsnick: The Student Nonviolent Coordinating Committee in Arkansas, 1962–1967* (University of Arkansas Press, 2011).

Elizabeth Kai Hinton is a doctoral candidate in history at Columbia University. Her research interests include the politics of crime control, urban policy, and violence in the late twentieth century. Hinton is completing, "From Social Welfare to Social Control: Federal War in American Cities, 1968–1988," for which she received a dissertation fellowship from the Ford Foundation.

Peniel E. Joseph is professor of history at Tufts University and author of the award-winning *Waiting 'Til the Midnight Hour: A Narrative History of Black Power in America* and *Dark Days, Bright Nights: From Black Power to Barack Obama*; he is also the editor of *The Black Power Movement: Rethinking the Civil Rights-Black Power Eras and Neighborhood Rebels: Black Power at the Local Level.* He is a frequent national commentator on issues of race, democracy, and civil rights who has appeared on CNN, MSNBC, and NPR. During the 2008 presidential election, he provided historical analysis for the *PBS NewsHour* with Jim Lehrer. Professor Joseph's essays have has appeared in *The New York Times, The Washington Post,* the *Chronicle Review,* the *Journal of American History,* the *American Historical Review,* the *Black Scholar,* and *Book Forum.* The recipient of fellowships from Harvard University's Charles Warren Center, the Woodrow Wilson International Center for Scholars, and the Ford Foundation, he has been recognized as a Top Young Historian by History News Network, an Emerging Scholar by *DIVERSE: Issues in Higher Education,* and an Emerging Leader by *Ebony* Magazine. He is currently working on a biography of Black Power icon Stokely Carmichael (Kwame Ture).

Stephen Lazar is a National Board Certified high school social studies and English teacher who works in New York City public schools. He earned his BA in political philosophy and religious studies at Brown University where he completed the Undergraduate Teacher Education Program. Lazar received his MA degree in African American studies at Columbia University. He writes about education at http://blog.stephenlazar.com.

Donna Murch is associate director of history at Rutgers University. She is the author of *Living for the City: Migration, Education, and the Rise of the Black Panther Party in Oakland, California* (2010), as well as a number of academic journal articles. She is currently codirector of the Rutgers Center for Historical Analysis and director of the Black Atlantic Lecture Series. Professor Murch is researching the postwar history of the Bronx and completing a new book on youth culture and underground economy.

Jeffrey O. G. Ogbar was raised in Los Angeles, California, and graduated with honors and received his BA in history from Morehouse College. He earned his MA (1993) and PhD (1997) in US history with a minor in African studies from Indiana University. Since 1997, he has taught at the University of Connecticut where he is professor of history and an associate dean for the Humanities in the College of Liberal Arts and Sciences. Dr. Ogbar's current research focuses on black nationalism and hip-hop. Though he has lectured on various topics of hip-hop, he has addressed groups in five continents and the Caribbean and has published articles on subjects as varied as the hip-hop generation, the Black Power movement, African American Catholics, and civil rights struggles. Dr. Ogbar has received several awards and honors including membership in the Phi Beta Kappa international honor society. He was awarded a research fellowship at Harvard University's W. E. B. Du Bois Institute for African and African American Research, where he completed his book manuscript, *Black Power: Radical Politics and African American Identity* (The Johns Hopkins University Press, 2004), a winner of an "Outstanding Academic Title" from *Choice Magazine* (2005). Ogbar was a scholar-in-residence at the Schomburg Center for Research in Black Culture in New York City while working on his second book manuscript, which is on hip-hop. He was a visiting fellow at the University of Miami's Africana Studies program, where he continued work on his book, *Hip-Hop Revolution: The Culture and Politics of Rap* (University Press of Kansas, 2007), which is the winner of the W. E. B. Du Bois Book Prize from the North East Black Studies Alliance (2008). Ogbar is also editor of *The Civil Rights Movement* (Houghton Mifflin, 2003). His most recent book, *The Harlem Renaissance Revisited: Politics, Arts and Letters*, an edited volume, was published in 2010 by the Johns Hopkins University Press. In January 2005, *Black Issues in Higher Education* (currently *Diverse Issues in Higher Education*) identified him as one of ten national "Stand Out Scholars" in its annual special issue on rising stars in academia. In 2007, he was featured as one of six national "Movers and Shakers Under 40" by *Trumpet* newsmagazine and also inducted into the Connecticut Academy of Arts and

Sciences learned society. Before being named associate dean, he served six years as director of the Institute for African American Studies at UConn.

Brenda Gayle Plummer received her PhD in history from Cornell University. She is currently employed at the University of Wisconsin–Madison in the departments of history and Afro-American studies. Dr. Plummer is the author of *Haiti and the Great Powers, 1902–1915* (Baton Rouge: Louisiana State University Press, 1988); *Haiti and the United States* (Athens, GA: University of Georgia Press, 1992); and *Rising Wind: Black Americans and U. S. Foreign Affairs, 1935–1960* (Chapel Hill: University of North Carolina Press, 1996). *Rising Wind* was cowinner of the American Historical Association's 1997 Wesley-Logan Prize and winner of the Society of Historians of American Foreign Relations's Myrna Bernath Prize. Plummer edited the collection *Window on Freedom: Race, Civil Rights, and Foreign Affairs, 1945–1988* (2003). Plummer has won research grants from the Social Science Research Council and the National Endowment for the Humanities, among other sources. She served on the Historical Advisory Committee of the U. S. Department of State, which consults with the State Department on historical declassification issues, from 2001 to 2005. Plummer taught at historically black Fisk University, the University of California at Santa Barbara, and the University of Minnesota before coming to the University of Wisconsin–Madison. Her major research interests are the history of US foreign relations, race in international affairs, African American history, and Caribbean history.

Russell Rickford is an assistant professor of history at Dartmouth College, where he teaches courses on black politics, social movements, labor, and recent US history. He specializes in African American political culture after World War II, the black radical tradition in the United States, the Black Power movement, and the history of education. He is currently working on a book about education, black nationalism, and independent black institutions during the 1960s and 1970s. Dr. Rickford is the editor of *Manning Marable: Beyond Boundaries* and the author of *Betty Shabazz: Surviving Malcolm X*, a biography of Malcolm X's late widow. He also coauthored *Spoken Soul: The Story of Black English* along with his father, Stanford University linguist John Rickford. Rickford holds a PhD in history and an MA in African American studies, both from Columbia University.

Lisa Yvette Waller is director of the High School at the Dalton School in New York City and has been a member of the history department in that division since 1995. *The Pressures of the People* grew out of research that provided the foundation for her dissertation, "Holding Back the Dawn: Milton A. Galamison and the Fight for School Integration in New York City, a Northern Civil Rights Struggle, 1948–1968." She remains interested in the historical connections between democratic ideals, educational reform, and social justice. Committed to connecting her research interests to educational praxis, she conceived of the Parkhurst Program, a twenty-first-century, student-centered, cross-disciplinary, project-based collaborative composed of Dalton students and faculty. In response to this work, Dalton has recently been awarded an Edward E. Ford Foundation grant that will contribute to the implementation of the Parkhurst Program beginning in 2012. She is also an invited member of the President's Advisory Council of Oberlin College and of the New York Association of Independent Schools Professional Development Committee.

Rebeccah Welch received a BA in English from Williams College and a PhD in history from New York University. She has served as a research fellow at Boston University and Harvard University and has written about the history of New York City in the academic and popular press. A longtime resident of Brooklyn, Welch currently works in the nonprofit sector on community and economic development issues.

Simon Wendt is assistant professor of American studies at the University of Frankfurt, Germany. His research interests are African American history, the history of racism, gender history, and the history of heroism. Wendt is the author of *The Spirit and the Shotgun: Armed Resistance and the Struggle for Civil Rights* (Gainesville: University Press of Florida, 2007) and coeditor of *Racism in the Modern World: Historical Perspectives on Transfer and Adaptation* (New York: Berghahn Books, 2011). He is currently working on the first full-scale history of the Daughters of the American Revolution.

INDEX